NEW CREATION IN PAUL'S LETTERS AND THOUGHT

As a biblical motif, "new creation" resonates throughout the pages of the Jewish and Christian Scriptures, and occupies a central place in the apostle Paul's vision of the Christian life. Yet the biblical and extra-biblical occurrences of this theme vary widely in meaning, referring to either a new cosmos, a new community, or a new individual. Beginning with the Old Testament and working through the important texts of Second Temple Judaism, Moyer V. Hubbard focuses on how the motif functions in the argument, strategy, and literary structure of these documents, highlighting its role as the solution to the perceived plight. He then explores in detail which senses of the term Paul intends in Galatians 6.15 and 2 Corinthians 5.17, concluding that "new creation" in Paul's letters describes the Spirit-wrought newness of the person in Christ, and is fundamentally anthropological in orientation.

MOYER V. HUBBARD is Associate Professor of New Testament Language and Literature at Talbot School of Theology, Biola University. He has published in the *Journal for the Study of the Pseudepigrapha, Journal for the Study of the New Testament*, and *Eerdmans Bible Dictionary*.

SOCIETY FOR NEW TESTAMENT STUDIES

MONOGRAPH SERIES

General Editor: Richard Bauckham

119

NEW CREATION IN PAUL'S LETTERS AND THOUGHT

New Creation in Paul's Letters and Thought

MOYER V. HUBBARD

Biola University, California

CAMBRIDGE
UNIVERSITY PRESS

PUBLISHED BY THE PRESS SYNDICATE OF THE UNIVERSITY OF CAMBRIDGE
The Pitt Building, Trumpington Street, Cambridge, United Kingdom

CAMBRIDGE UNIVERSITY PRESS
The Edinburgh Building, Cambridge CB2 2RU, UK
40 West 20th Street, New York, NY 10011-4211, USA
477 Williamstown Road, Port Melbourne, VIC 3207, Australia
Ruiz de Alarcón 13, 28014 Madrid, Spain
Dock House, The Waterfront, Cape Town 8001, South Africa

http://www.cambridge.org

First published 2002

Printed in the United Kingdom at the University Press, Cambridge

Typeface Times 10/12 pt.   *System* LATEX 2ε   [TB]

A catalogue record for this book is available from the British Library

Library of Congress cataloguing in publication data

Hubbard, Moyer V.
New creation in Paul's letters and thought / Moyer V. Hubbard.
    p.   cm. – (Society for New Testament Studies monograph series; 119)
Includes bibliographical references and indexes.
ISBN 0 521 81485 5 (hardback)
1. Man (Theology) – Biblical teaching.   2. Creation – Biblical teaching.
3. Bible. N.T. Epistles of Paul – Theology.   4. Bible. O.T. – Theology.   I. Title.
II. Monograph series (Society for New Testament Studies); 119.
BS2655.M3 H83   2002
227'.064 – dc21   2001052872

ISBN 0 521 81485 5 hardback

For Heidi

Τὸ δὲ πνεῦμα ζῳοποιεῖ

2 Corinthians 3.6

CONTENTS

PART III
THE OLD AND THE NEW: NEW CREATION IN THE
CONTEXT OF PAUL'S LETTERS

ACKNOWLEDGMENTS

This monograph began as a doctoral thesis accepted by the University of Oxford in 1998. A doctoral program is never undertaken alone, and thanks are due to many for their help and encouragement in the completion of this task. Generous financial assistance was provided by the Evangelical Covenant Church, the Committee of Vice-Chancellors and Principals of the Universities of the United Kingdom, the Oxford University Faculty of Theology, and the Spalding Charitable Trust.

More than the usual word of thanks is owed to my supervisor, the Revd. Robert Morgan. His perceptive balance of guidance, criticism, and encouragement allowed my research to flourish, and kept me from traveling too far down the many blind alleys of New Testament scholarship. He made himself available academically and personally, which may be the most important attribute in a supervisor. Professor Christopher Rowland provided invaluable input throughout the course of my study, and his contribution to the shape and focus of the final product is no doubt greater than he realizes. Especially important during my years in Oxford were the graduate seminars which he organized and moderated. His gracious manner and intellectual rigor exemplify the best in Christian scholarship.

Our time in England was immeasurably enriched by friendships forged through the shared experience of doctoral research. Among them, Tony and Jayne Cummins, Bruce and Carolyn Hindmarsh, and Norm and Anne Klassen (and families) were vital. The support of others was equally crucial during these years, including Patrick Cain, Revd. Tom and Hazle Houston, and Dr. Mike and Shirley Dobson.

It is an honor to have my work included in this series, and I extend my sincerest thanks to Professor Richard Bauckham and the expert editorial staff at Cambridge University Press. My research assistants, and friends, Zeke Pipher, Steve Earle, and Joanne Jung, spent many tedious hours reformatting and editing. Their conscientious labor was as encouraging as it was helpful. My colleagues at Talbot School of Theology, Mike Wilkins and Clint Arnold in particular, offered crucial support during the final phase of my doctoral research, and our Dean, Dennis Dirks, generously provided release time for preparing this manuscript for publication. To have your friends as your colleagues is a treasure indeed.

Most importantly, however, I am grateful to my family. To my mother, who taught me to dream big, and to my father, who taught me to love an adventure, I offer my heartfelt thanks. Likewise, my father-in-law and mother-in-law, Revd. John and Miriam Notehelfer, supported and encouraged us at every turn. Without their joyful assistance, the dream of doctoral work would have never materialized. My two sons, Scott and Jeffrey, kept me sane during the long months of research and writing. They are a daily reminder of what is truly important in life, and our evening ritual of playing, reading, and so on, are among my fondest memories of Oxford.

No word of thanks can adequately express my gratitude to and affection for my wife, Heidi. Her encouragement, patience, and joyful perseverance sustained me throughout my research. She has been my partner and co-laborer in this project, and it is to her, with all my love and admiration, that this book is dedicated.

ABBREVIATIONS

Most abbreviations follow S. Schwertner, *Internationales Abkürzungs-verzeichnis für Theologie und Grenzgebiete* (Berlin: Walter de Gruyter, 1976). Others are as follows:

ANRW   H. Temporini and W. Haase (eds.), *Aufstieg und Niedergang der römischen Welt*, many volumes (Berlin: Walter de Gruyter).

BAGD   W. Bauer, W. F. Arndt, F. W. Gingrich, and F. W. Danker, *A Greek–English Lexicon of the New Testament and Other Early Christian Literature*. Chicago: University of Chicago Press, 1979.

BDB   F. Brown, S. R. Driver, and C. A. Briggs, *Hebrew and English Lexicon of the Old Testament*. Oxford: Clarendon Press, 1951.

BDF   F. Blass, A. Debrunner, and R. W. Funk, *A Greek Grammar of the New Testament*. Chicago: University of Chicago Press, 1961.

LCL   Loeb Classical Library, Harvard University Press.

OTP   James H. Charlesworth, *The Old Testament Pseudepigrapha*, 2 volumes. New York: Doubleday, 1983 and 1985.

1

INTRODUCTION

The current debate

The biblical story, from beginning to end, can rightly be described as an epic of *new creation*. As its prologue opens with Elohim's creation of heaven and earth, so its epilogue closes with the dramatic appearance of the new heaven and the new earth – a place where sorrow and death are no more, and where the dwelling place of God is with his people. *Creatio originalis* gives way to *creatio nova* as the one seated upon the throne announces, "Behold, I make all things new!" (Rev. 21.5). But this grand inclusio, while hopeful in its preface and jubilant in its finale, brackets a history of *tohu wabohu*. As early as Genesis 3 the battle lines are firmly fixed. The creature has shunned the creator, the creation groans in bondage to decay (Gen. 3.17–18; Rom. 8.19–22), and posterity is left with a legacy of despair: "O Adam," laments Ezra, "what have you done? For though it was you who sinned, the fall was not yours alone" (4 Ezra 7.117; cf. Rom. 5.12–21). But before we let *Heilsgeschichte* degenerate into *Angstgeschichte,* it is worth recalling that the biblical story is a drama of *redemption.* And while the plot is not without its twists and turns, it does reach a fitting and moving climax in the passion narratives.

The motif of "new creation," however, is not confined to the opening and closing chapters of the Christian Scriptures. The prophets, the psalmists, the evangelists, and so on, all exhibit a robust faith in the creative activity of God, and this faith was not focused solely on the remote past or the distant future. The prayer of the penitent sinner that God would "create a pure heart, and grant a new spirit" (Ps. 51.10), as well as the bold declaration of the prophet that Yahweh was, even now, "making something new" (Isa. 43.18), reflect a deep-seated belief in the continuing new-creative work of God, and form part of the vibrant, if variegated, biblical witness to *new creation.*[1]

[1] Cf. Ps. 104.29–30; Matt. 19.28; John 3.1–8; Acts 3.21; Rom. 6.4; 2 Cor. 4.16; Eph. 2.15; 4.23–24; Titus 3.5; 2 Pet. 3.13.

The scope of this present study, however, is far more modest than this sweeping summary of Scripture and salvation-history might suggest. The primary focus of this monograph is the motif of "new creation" as it is found in Paul's letters, specifically the meaning of καινὴ κτίσις in 2 Corinthians 5.17 and Galatians 6.15. This short, two-word expression admits of several interpretations, and I will simplify and synthesize these under the headings Creature, Creation, and Community.

New creature

Any historical survey of Paul's new-creation motif would have to grant pride of place to the anthropological interpretation "If anyone is in Christ, that person is a new creation." This reading finds support in Clement of Alexandria, Tertullian, Jerome, Augustine, and many others.[2] The comments on these passages from the Greek fathers, as collected by Karl Staab,[3] show no deviation from this pattern, and here Paul's terse phraseology is regularly expanded to make this reading more apparent. Compare, for instance, the illuminating emendations of Severian (fourth–fifth century) and Oecumenius (sixth century):[4]

2 Corinthians 5.17	Severian
εἴ τις ἐν Χριστῷ,	εἴ τις ἐν Χρισῷ ζῇ καὶ βαπτίζεται
καινὴ κτίσις	οὗτος καινή ἐστι κτίσις

Galatians 6.15	Oecumenius
οὔτε γὰρ περιτομή τί ἐστιν	πάντες γὰρ οἵ τε ἐμπερίτομοι
οὔτε ἀκροβυστία	καὶ ἀκρόβυστοι πιστεύοντες
ἀλλὰ καινὴ κτίσις	καινὴ κτίσις γεγόναμεν

The commentaries of Calvin and Luther, along with Luther's translation of the Bible, perpetuated an anthropological reading of καινὴ κτίσις, which was the standard interpretation of the great German theologies and monographs of the nineteenth and early twentieth centuries.[5] Reference to

---

[2] Clement of Alexandria, *Stromata* 3.8; 5.5; Tertullian, *On Modesty* 6; *Against Marcion* 4.1.6; 4.11.9; 5.4.3; 5.12.6; Jerome, *To Oceanus*; Augustine, *On the Baptism of Infants* 1.44; *Reply to Faustus* 11.1; 19.10; *Grace and Free Will* 20; *Sermons* 26.12; 212.1. But cf. Tertullian, *On Fasting* 14.2; Clement, *To the Greeks* 11; *The Rich Man's Salvation* 12.

[3] Staab (1933).

[4] See also Didymus of Alexandria on 2 Corinthians 5.17 in Staab (1933: 29).

[5] E.g., B. Weiss (1882: 463–64; first edition, 1868), Pfleiderer (1877: 207–8; first edition, 1873), Gunkel (1979: 104, 110–11; first edition, 1888), Deissmann (1892: 108), Holtzmann (1911: 66, 165, 225, 305; first edition, 1897), Bousset (1970: 241; first edition 1910), Schlatter (1922: 327; first edition, 1910), Schweitzer (1931: 15–17, 119; first edition, 1930).

a specific Jewish background to this idea was rarely made by these authors, though Adolf von Harnack is an important exception. In a study entitled "Die Terminologie der Wiedergeburt und verwandter Erlebnisse in der ältesten Kirche" (1918), von Harnack treated καινὴ κτίσις with other renewal terminology (παλιγγενεσία, ἀναγεννάω, etc.), and suggested that Paul was using a traditional rabbinic motif unfamiliar to his readers. According to von Harnack, while the rabbinic notion of a "new creature" referred only to the new situation of the proselyte,[6] this subtlety was lost on the Corinthians and Galatians, who understood Paul literally: in Christ they had been newly created.[7]

Von Harnack's contribution is important for at least two reasons. First, while others had made the connection with the rabbinic material before him,[8] von Harnack made it crucial for the interpretation of Paul's terminology. This shifted the discussion away from the related soteriological symbolism of Paul's letters, which had dominated the analyses of, for example, Pfleiderer, B. Weiss, and Holtzmann, and placed all the emphasis on understanding the Jewish context of Paul's thought. Second, von Harnack's admirable attempt to take Paul *seriously* without taking him *literally* brought out the larger theological dilemma implicit in Paul's language. Von Harnack's forensic interpretation of Paul's new-creation motif stood in stark contrast to the ontological interpretation of his contemporaries, and labored to preserve Paul's indicative–imperative dialectic, which the alternative view threatened to undermine. It has the disadvantage, however, of tacitly acknowledging that if Paul had intended what von Harnack believes he did, one would never know it from what the apostle wrote.

The anthropological interpretation of Paul's new-creation motif was certainly the dominant view of commentaries and monographs through the post-World War II era, and many of its supporters will be mentioned in the following pages. The seeds of its demise, however, were sown by von Harnack himself. In anchoring this motif so firmly in the (then) prevailing consensus regarding the socio-religious context of the pre-Christian Paul, von Harnack's interpretation was destined to be only as convincing as the Jewish background he assumed. As the one has fallen, so has the other, as the quest for the historical Paul moved steadily forward.

---

[6] The rabbinic material is collected by Strack and Billerbeck (1924–26) and treated in conjunction with the "new birth" imagery of John 3.3 (vol. II, 421–23; cf. vol. III, 519) and painstakingly analyzed by Sjöberg (1950).

[7] Von Harnack, (1918: 106–8).

[8] Most notably J. B. Lightfoot in his commentary on Galatians, first published in 1865.

New creation

In 1935 R. H. Strachan's commentary on 2 Corinthians appeared, and his interpretation of 2 Corinthians 5.17 would prove to be a harbinger of the exegesis of subsequent generations. Making reference to Paul's "apocalyptic thinking, which represents Jewish cosmology," Strachan argues that Paul adopts "the language of current Jewish thinking," and so defines ἐν Χριστῷ in 2 Corinthians 5.17 as "being in a 'new world,' a 'new creation.'"[9] Applying this to both 2 Corinthians 5.17 and Galatians 6.15, Strachan defines καινὴ κτίσις soterio-cosmologically as the advent of the new age: "There is a new creation whenever a man comes to be in Christ."[10]

The rise of the "apocalyptic Paul," however, is inevitably associated with Ernst Käsemann, who endeavored to demonstrate that apocalyptic was truly "die Mutter der christlichen Theologie." In his comments on Romans 4.16–17, Käsemann describes justification as "the restitution of creation," which he takes to be "the decisive motif of Paul's soteriology,"[11] and it is through Käsemannian lenses that many interpret Paul today. To be sure, the (soterio-)anthropological interpretation of Paul's new-creation motif was only gradually dislodged from its position of preeminence, and still has important proponents,[12] yet the clear trend of recent monographs and commentaries is toward a soterio-cosmological interpretation of καινὴ κτίσις,[13] and this is largely the triumph of one historical background over another.

New community

Ernst Käsemann's exegetical agenda was, to some extent, a response to the theological program of his teacher, Rudolf Bultmann, and Paul's new-creation motif has often been caught in the cross-fire of this great debate.[14] Regrettable though it may be, John Reumann is probably correct in noting that translating καινὴ κτίσις as "new creature" versus "new creation," "is precisely a point at issue in interpreting Paul."[15] Yet Käsemann's cosmological horizon is not the only interpretive option for those wishing to

---

[9] Strachan (1935: 113–14).
[10] Strachan's translation of 2 Corinthians 5.17 (1935: 113).
[11] Käsemann (1980: 123).   [12] E.g., Thrall (1994), Witherington (1995, 1998).
[13] See the doctoral dissertations of Aymer, and Hoover; the commentaries of Barnett, Cousar, Dunn, Furnish, R. P. Martin, and Martyn; the recent *New Testament Theology* of Caird (1994: 161); and the literature cited in chapters 10 and 11.
[14] Cf. H.-J. Kraus (1964), Reumann (1973: 8–15), Mell (1989: 2–7), G. Schneider (1992: 368–70).
[15] Reumann (1973: 14).

avoid an alleged anthropological narrowing of Paul's gospel. An increased awareness of corporate themes in Paul's letters has given rise to the view that καινὴ κτίσις in Galatians 6.15 expresses a "Gemeindewirklichkeit," and that Paul's new-creation motif speaks of a new community.[16] While this recent position trails far behind the other two in number of supporters, it has found an important advocate in Wolfgang Kraus.[17] Kraus argues that Paul derived this theme from Isaiah 66.18–23, where cosmos and community are seamlessly joined in the eschatological vision of the prophet: " 'As the new heavens and the new earth that I make [will] endure before me,' declares the LORD, 'so will your name and descendants endure' " (Isa. 66.22).

While far from comprehensive, this introductory survey outlines in broad strokes the contours of the current debate. The critical consensus today regards early Jewish apocalyptic as the theological matrix from which Paul derived his new-creation motif, and some have gone so far as to designate καινὴ κτίσις a *terminus technicus* of apocalyptically oriented Judaism.[18] Moreover, this *traditionsgeschichtliche* background is assumed by almost every recent discussion of this motif, even by proponents of an anthropological interpretation, who argue that Paul has radically modified its original cosmological dimensions.[19] The resulting soterio-cosmological reading of καινὴ κτίσις understands this phrase as a pregnant allusion to the advent of the new age, and it is this position that will be critically appraised in the following pages.

Method and sources

While there is still room for argument concerning the precise meaning of Paul's elusive καινὴ κτίσις, all would agree that the correct approach to the problem is via the well-trodden path of the history-of-traditions methodology. The governing assumption of this school of thought is that every idea has its prehistory, and the key to understanding significant ideas is to discern and trace their historical development. In this scenario, knowing the Jewish context of the pre-Christian Paul is absolutely critical, in that this alone provides the definitive point of reference for understanding the apostle's subsequent thought and terminology.

While not questioning the basic soundness of this approach, when applied to Paul's new-creation motif it has almost always resulted in

---

[16] Citing W. Kraus (1996: 251). Similarly Klaiber (1982: 97–101).

[17] W. Kraus (1996: esp. 247–52).

[18] So Stuhlmacher (1967: 1), Mell (1989: 254) and now Adams (2000: 227).

[19] E.g., Baumgarten (1975), Aune (1993: 32–33).

a circular exegesis, in which the key to this idea is discovered, not surprisingly, in the prevailing consensus regarding the socio-religious background of the apostle. Paul's new-creation motif has been explained with reference to Hellenistic mystery religions,[20] rabbinic literature,[21] Qumran,[22] and apocalyptic,[23] and if none of these fully persuade, Peter Stuhlmacher's article on the subject offers a magisterial compromise: "Wir müssen Paulus aus einer zwischen apokalyptisch-essenischer und hellenistisch-jüdischer Denkweise vermittelnden Zwischenposition her-aus zu begreifen suchen."[24]

The history-of-traditions approach to καινὴ κτίσις reaches its apex in the work of Ulrich Mell, who discerns (divines?) numerous specific lines of development of this motif from (so-called) Deutero-Isaiah into the literature of Second Temple Judaism. More comment will be offered on Mell's contribution at the close of this study; its strengths and weaknesses are succinctly expressed in Jerome Murphy-O'Connor's review:

> It is a classical German doctorate thesis, predictable in method, complicated in argument, and one- sided in documentation. Over half the book (257 pages) is devoted to a detailed examination of every known mention of new creation from Deutero-Isaiah to the tannaitic rabbis and the hellenistic synagogues of the Diaspora. This is done with exemplary care and in itself is a most use-ful compilation. Its irrelevance to the elucidation of Galatians 6.15 and 2 Corinthians 5.17 is underlined by the meagerness of M[ell]'s conclusions.[25]

Murphy-O'Connor's criticism may be overstated, but it does highlight the pitfalls of the methodology Mell has chosen: it forces the exegete to concentrate on secondary sources, leaving much of the primary source material (Paul's letters) untouched. Yet for all Mell's apparent comprehensiveness, it is nonetheless stunning that he focuses solely on the Isaianic oracles in his examination of new creation in the Jewish Scriptures, while also ignoring the anthropological new-creation texts of, for example, *Jubilees* and *1 Enoch*. This prejudicial selectivity not only *affects* Mell's conclusions, it was probably the *function* of

---

[20] Reitzenstein (1910: 192–99), H. A. A. Kennedy (1913: 220). While not stated explic-itly, this derivation is implied in the writings of Bousset, Pfleiderer, and others of the history of religions school.

[21] In addition to numerous commentaries, see Strack and Billerbeck (1926: 519), W. D. Davies (1955: 119–23), Schwantes (1963: 26–31), Reumann (1973: 96–97).

[22] Kuhn (1966: 120–23), Stuhlmacher (1967: 8–10); cf. Sekki (1989: 221–23).

[23] E.g., Furnish (1984), Martyn (1985), Barclay (1988), Mell (1989), etc.

[24] Stuhlmacher (1967: 20).   [25] Murphy-O'Connor (1991b: 150).

these (predetermined?) conclusions, and further illustrates the *de facto* circularity of this approach.

The following analysis will proceed on the assumption that the primary context for explicating Paul's new-creation motif is the letters of the apostle Paul.[26] While there is no need to replicate the wide-ranging *traditionsgeschichtliche* analyses of Mell and his predecessor Gerhard Schneider,[27] there is a pressing need to improve on their approach to this important Jewish background material. Rather than offering a superficial examination of isolated texts, this study will select two important works of Second Temple Judaism and attempt to understand the motif of new creation as it functions in the argument, strategy, and literary structure of these books. Rather than positing complex and imaginative lines of development which are neither verifiable nor falsifiable, my goal is simply to compare Paul's new-creation motif with two of his Second Temple counterparts. This cannot be done by examining brief extracts of these works, but through understanding the work as a whole and relating new creation to the dominant themes of the work in question.[28]

After surveying the motif of new creation in Jewish Scriptures, I will focus attention on the book of *Jubilees* and the book of *Joseph and Aseneth*.[29] Representing both Palestinian and Diaspora Judaism, the former is the work most often used to explicate Paul's new-creation motif, while the latter is the work least often used. Because I will be critically interacting with the conventional wisdom regarding the connection between Paul's new-creation motif and that of apocalyptic Judaism, it is important that I examine the strongest possible link in the proposed history-of-traditions chain. Of the apocalyptic works usually cited in reference to 2 Corinthians 5.17 and Galatians 6.15, *Jubilees* lies in closest chronological proximity to Paul, and is the only work where the precise phrase "new creation" occurs *twice*. While *Joseph and Aseneth* is not often noted in the commentaries on 2 Corinthians 5.17 and Galatians 6.15,[30] its

[26] Although the argument of this monograph could be supported by considering the evidence of Ephesians and Colossians, my conclusions will be based only on the undisputed letters of Paul.

[27] G. Schneider (1959).

[28] The error of Taylor (1958), Rey (1966), and Gloer (1996) must also be avoided, who all but ignore the relevant Jewish background material.

[29] Material from Qumran and the Rabbis could be marshaled in support of the following argument, though I will have to leave these to one side in order to evaluate adequately the dominant "apocalyptic" view of contemporary scholarship. The difficulties inherent in using rabbinic texts to illustrate NT material are widely accepted, and the "dunklen Stellen" from Qumran (Baumgarten's term [1975: 165]) are fraught with interpretive and textual problems.

[30] But see Furnish (1984) and Thrall (1994).

elaborate description of Aseneth's re-creation contains striking parallels to prominent themes in Paul's letters, and deserves more than the passing reference it occasionally receives.

Following this analysis of select Jewish material (part I), I will then try to understand "new creation" in the contours of Paul's thought (part II) and the context of his letters (part III). In keeping with my methodological critique of previous work on this subject, the bulk of the study will be devoted to an in-depth examination of "new creation" in the letters of Paul.

PART I

New creation: central Jewish texts

As indicated in the introductory comments, the interpretation of Paul's new-creation motif has been intimately connected with the Jewish context of the pre-Christian Paul, and this is a more than reasonable starting-point. The primary concern here is to determine what (if any) Jewish antecedents might have exerted a formative influence on the apostle's conception of new creation. I have already provided a rationale for the selection of primary sources to be examined in part I, and more comment on this subject will be offered at the beginning of each section. While an adequate treatment of this theme requires a full analysis of a very select group of extra-biblical texts, close attention to the footnotes will reveal a broadly researched argument, with ample corroboration from the literature of the period.

Following a survey of this theme in the prophetic literature of the Hebrew Bible (chapter 2), I will look closely at the book of *Jubilees* (chapter 3) and *Joseph and Aseneth* (chapter 4). These sources provide evidence for a variety of applications of new-creation imagery in the literature and thought-world of first-century BC/AD Judaism, and each of these uses may be regarded as potentially influential on Paul the apostle. While it would be wrong to limit Paul to only these interpretive options, effectively disallowing his own creative intellect, it would be equally imprudent to examine Paul's letters in a historical vacuum. Original thinkers occasionally part company with their contemporaries, yet sometimes the better part of originality is a fresh reformulation of primitive faith.

2

NEW CREATION IN THE JEWISH
SCRIPTURES: AN OVERVIEW

Creation and redemption belong together, as the obverse and
reverse of the same theological coin.

Bernhard Anderson, *From Creation to New Creation*

By all accounts, the motif of new creation as encountered in the literature
of Second Temple Judaism had its ultimate origin in the eschatological hopes of the later prophets.[1] Whether mediated through subsequent
developments of this idea or not, Paul's own application of this motif is
commonly linked to these prophets, principally the so-called trito-Isaiah,[2]
so any analysis of new creation in Paul must begin here. In the following
pages I offer only a survey of this Old Testament theme, outlining the
main contours of this idea as it is found in Isaiah, Jeremiah, and Ezekiel.
Nothing controversial will be argued in this section, and the focus therefore will be on the primary source material. Unlike the following sections,
interaction with secondary literature will be kept to a minimum.

Yet while the analysis here must be brief and to the point, I do not mean
to give the impression that this material is unimportant for understanding
the motif of new creation in Paul. As noted above, contemporary scholarship traces the Pauline application of this idea to the Isaianic oracles
concerning the new heavens and the new earth, and this connection is
considered crucial to the interpretation of καινὴ κτίσις in Paul's letters.
But contemporary scholarship seems unaware that there is more than one
new-creation motif in the later prophets, and apart from excluding the
witness of Jeremiah, Ezekiel, and Isaiah 40–55, any adequate survey of

---

[1] E.g., G. Schneider (1959), Black (1976: 3–21), Hoover (1979), Aymer (1983), Mell
(1989).
[2] E.g., Stuhlmacher (1967: 10–13), Baumgarten (1975: 164), Furnish (1984: 315), Beale
(1989: 552–55), W. Kraus (1996: 247). In light of so much recent interest in reading the book
of Isaiah as a literary unity, the designations "deutero-" and "trito-" Isaiah will be avoided.
On this see Watts' two-volume commentary (1985, 1987), Brueggemann (1986: 89–107),
Clements (1988: 117–29).

this theme will have to reckon with more than one possible Old Testament background.[3]

Most of this material will be familiar, and my concern to evaluate these writings from the vantage point of Paul means that I can bracket out certain critical issues relating to the authenticity and collection of these prophetic traditions. Assuming nothing more than that these writings were known and read by Paul, I will discuss them in their canonical order, beginning with Isaiah 40–55.

Isaiah 40–55: a new exodus

See, the former things have taken place, and new things I declare; before they spring into being I announce them to you. (Isa. 42.9)

Forget the former things; do not dwell on the past. See, I am doing a new thing! Now it springs up; do you not perceive it? I am making a way in the desert and streams in the wasteland.
(43.18–19)

I foretold the former things long ago, my mouth announced them and I made them known . . . From now on I will tell you of new things, of hidden things unknown to you.   (48.3–6)

One of the distinguishing features of the prophetic oracles of Isaiah 40–55 is their rich and evocative use of the couplet "former things/new things." This language surfaces in numerous contexts with a variety of meanings,[4] and the fact that Paul himself alludes to this idea in explication of his new-creation statement in 2 Corinthians 5.17 underscores the importance of this material for this study. Because the "former things/new things" of Isaiah 40–55 are intimately connected with the dominant themes of these chapters – "exodus," "creation," and "redemption" – the ensuing analysis will approach this motif through these categories.

Creation and redemption

Isaiah 40–55 contains the highest concentration of creation language in the entire Bible.[5] The principal verbs of the Genesis account are sprinkled

---

[3] Correctly, G. Schneider (1959).

[4] In addition to the texts cited above, see 41.22–27; 43.9; 44.6–8; 45.11, 21; 46.9–10; 48.12–16; 51.9.

[5] For lexical statistics and a detailed discussion of the terminology see Stuhlmueller (1970: 209–29), B. Anderson (1987: 124–31).

generously throughout this material (ברא, 16x; יצר, 14x; עשׂה, 27x), and combine with other images depicting God's victory over the primordial chaos to form a powerful witness to the protological interests of the writer. Equally abundant is redemption terminology (גאל, 23x; ישׁע, 31x), and the interconnectedness of this language – a regular topic of discussion in the secondary literature – has been aptly designated *Creative Redemption in Deutero-Isaiah* by Carroll Stuhlmueller.[6] Yahweh's (simultaneous) role as Creator, Redeemer, and Savior can be illustrated through scores of passages, and justifies Newsome's observation that "creation and salvation (re-creation) are inextricably tied to one another by the Second Isaiah."[7] A short sampling of texts should suffice:

> This is what God the LORD says – *the one who created* (בורא) the heavens and stretched them out, who spread out the earth and all that comes out of it, who gives breath to its people, and life to those who walk on it: "I, the LORD, *have called you* (קראתיך) in righteousness; I will take hold of your hand." (Isa. 42.5–6)

> But now, this is what the LORD says – *the one who created you* (בוראך), O Jacob, *the one who formed you* (יצרך), O Israel: "Fear not, for I *have redeemed you* (גאלתיך); *I have called you* (קראתי) by name; you are mine." (43.1)

> This is what the LORD says – *your Redeemer* (גאלך), *who formed you* (יצרך) in the womb: "I am the LORD, *who has made all things* (עשׂה כל), who alone stretched out the heavens, who spread out the earth by myself." (44.24)

> Listen to me, O house of Jacob, all you who remain of the house of Israel, you whom I have upheld since you were conceived, and have carried since your birth. Even to your old age and gray hairs I am he, I am he who will sustain you. I have made (עשׂיתי) and I will carry; I will sustain and *I will save* (אמלט). (46.3–4)

> Awake, awake! Clothe yourself with strength, O arm of the LORD; awake, as in days gone by, as in generations of old. Was

---

[6] This is the title of Stuhlmueller's important study (1970). See also Muilenburg (1956: 400–2), von Rad (1958: 138–47), B. Anderson (1987: 119–31), and the lengthy bibliography in Watts (1987: 93–4).

[7] Newsome (1984: 149). Similar comments proliferate: "In Deutero-Isaiah, 'to create' and 'to redeem' (גאל) can be used as entirely synonymous" (von Rad [1965: 241]); "[In Isaiah 40–66] God's activity in creation and redemption are one" (Westermann [1969: 129]); "In Second Isaiah's prophecy, Creation is a broad conception which includes all God's saving actions" (Anderson [1987: 123]).

it not you who cut Rahab to pieces, who pierced that monster through? Was it not you who dried up the sea, the waters of the great deep, who made a road in the depths of the sea so that *the redeemed* (נאלים) might cross over? The ransomed of the LORD will return. They will enter Zion with singing.   (51.9–11)

Von Rad, whose thesis is expanded by Reumann, and meticulously demonstrated by Stuhlmueller, speaks of the "soteriologische Verständnis des Schöpfungswerkes" in Isaiah 40–55, in that creation language is employed in the service of "das Hauptthema," the proclamation of salvation. In von Rad's view, creation imagery "ist die großartige Folie, von der sich die Heilsworte um so mächtiger und vertrauenswürdiger abheben."[8] According to Reumann, "Deutero-Isaiah presents us with the most massive use of creation language in the whole Bible. But the primary purpose of it all is to get across a message of redemption . . . a new redemptive act."[9] One new redemptive act in particular is emphasized in these oracles, an act of redemption that Soggin has referred to as the *creatio ex nihilo* of God's people: the impending return from exile.[10]

New creation and second exodus

The great vision of Isaiah 40–55 concerns the expectation of an imminent release from captivity and a return to the land of Palestine. Already alluded to in texts cited above (51.9–10), the analogy repeatedly offered by the author is that of the exodus from Egypt.[11] As Anderson has argued, "for Second Isaiah the time of Israel's creation was the time of the Exodus. When he thinks of Yahweh as the creator of Israel he calls to mind the events of *Heilsgeschichte*, especially the great miracle of the sea."[12] The paradigmatic function of the exodus narrative is admirably illustrated by 43.15–21, described by Kiesow in his study of this theme as the "Kernstelle" of the exodus motif in Isaiah 40–55.[13] This passage offers the closest parallel to Paul's allusion in 2 Corinthians 5.17:[14]

---

[8] Von Rad (1958: 139–42). See also Stuhlmueller (1970), Reumann (1973: 60–78).

[9] Reumann (1973: 78). Note the opening comments of Stuhlmueller's comprehensive analysis: "One, therefore, cannot write in an extensive and authentic way about 'creation' in [Deutero-Isaiah] unless 'creation' be presented as it is found there, an aspect or characteristic subordinate to the work of redemption" (1970: 3).

[10] Citing Soggin (1989: 372).

[11] See 41.17–20; 42.5–9; 43.1–3, 14–21; 50.1–2; 51.9–11; 52.7–12.

[12] B. Anderson (1987: 127). Similarly Westermann (1969: 127), Stuhlmueller (1970: 69).

[13] Citing Kiesow (1979: 190). So too C. R. North (1957: 116).

[14] Both Nestle–Aland[27] and UBS[4] refer the reader to Isa. 43.18 in their marginal annotations at 2 Corinthians 5.17.

I am the LORD, your Holy One, Israel's Creator, your King. This is what the LORD says – he who made a way through the sea, a path through the mighty waters, who drew out the chariots and horses, the army and reinforcements together, and they lay there, never to rise again, extinguished, snuffed out like a wick: "Forget the former things; do not dwell on the past. See, I am doing a new thing! Now it springs up; do you not perceive it? I am making a way in the desert and streams in the wasteland. The wild animals honor me, the jackals and the owls, because I provide water in the desert and streams in the wasteland, to give drink to my people, my chosen, the people I formed for myself that they may proclaim my praise."

In contrasting the former exodus with a new exodus, the author is also implicitly announcing "a new 'creation' of Yahweh's people."[15] God's new act of redemption (the new exodus), is described in terms of the re-creation of his people and, again, Bernhard Anderson states the issue well: "Second Isaiah understands the 'New Exodus of salvation' to be a new creation, comparable to the event of the creation of Israel in the first Exodus ... The New Exodus will be the climax of Yahweh's work and, in a profound sense, something never heard of before."[16]

Having outlined the primary theological context of the "former things/new things" of Isaiah 40–55, it is now possible to look specifically at this important theme.

The "former" and the "new"

As noted earlier, the couplet "former things/new things" occurs in a variety of contexts throughout Isaiah 40–55, and is open to more than one application by the author.[17] Most often, the "former things," or "things of old," have in view the entirety of redemptive history, with no special emphasis placed on any single event (41.21–29; 43.9; 44.6–8; 45.20–21; 46.9–11). In these passages, the "former/old things" stand in antithesis to "the things to come," a phrase which has an equally general point of reference.[18]

[15] Stuhlmueller (1970: 167).

[16] B. Anderson (1987: 129). So too D. M. Russell (1996: 65–66).

[17] The terminology is varied, but the most frequently used words are ראשׁות, "first/former things" (41.22; 42.9; 43.9, 18; 46.9; 48.30) and חדשׁות, "new things" (42.9; 43.19 [חדשׁה]; 48.6). The corresponding language in the Septuagint is τὰ πρῶτα/πρότερα (43.18; 48.3; 46.9), τὰ ἀρχαῖα (43.19), various verbal constructions with ἀπ' ἀρχῆς (42.9; 43.9; 45.21), and (τὰ) καινά (42.9; 43.19; 48.6).

[18] See Volz (1932: 25, 40), Watts (1987: 120), Barstad (1989: 94), W. J. Webb (1993: 121–25).

These "saving acts of God," as McKenzie calls them,[19] epitomized Israel's past and formed the basis of the prophet's hope for the future.

Occasionally however, this language does have a specific event in view, and where this is so, the "new thing[s]" refer to Israel's impending exodus from Babylon (42.9; 43.15–21; 48.3–16). This was particularly evident in 43.15–21, cited above, where Yahweh promises a new act of redemption so wonderful that Israel could simply "forget" the exodus of old (43.18). Westermann is certainly right to insist that this exhortation constitutes no disparagement of Israel's formative experience in the wilderness,[20] yet the language is deliberately provocative, and is meant to focus all attention on the new act of deliverance to come. Standing in antithesis to the generative event in Israel's history, the exodus from Egypt, it is no exaggeration to say with Stuhlmueller that these passages depict the new exodus as "a new creation of Israel in wondrous prosperity."[21] The announcement of Israel's liberation and re-creation dominates Isaiah 40–55. But it is a new creation of a different sort that is promised in Isaiah 65 and 66.

Isaiah 65 and 66: a new heaven and new earth

> Behold, I [will] create new heavens and a new earth. The former things will not be remembered, nor will they come to mind. But be glad and rejoice forever in what I will create, for I [will] create Jerusalem to be a delight and its people a joy.   (Isa. 65.17–18)

> "As the new heavens and the new earth that I make [will] endure before me," declares the LORD, "so will your name and descendants endure."   (66.22)

The classic expression of cosmic new creation in the biblical tradition is found in the concluding chapters of the book of Isaiah.[22] Although a minority argue that this dramatic announcement of a new cosmos is intended simply as "language of exaggeration," and denotes only the renewal of God's people,[23] this is difficult to maintain. As the following

---

[19] Mckenzie's summary of "former things" in 41.21–29 (1968: 35).

[20] Westermann (1969: 127–29).   [21] Stuhlmueller (1970: 64).

[22] Compare the comments of Hanson (1975: 155–61), Black (1976: 15), D. M. Russell (1996: 69–77).

[23] Citing Westermann (1969: 408). Similarly Reumann (1973: 88), Black (1976: 15), and Emerson (1996: 95) in relation to 65.17. Whybray (1975: 266–67) argues that the reference to a new heaven and earth in 65.17 is secondary. Equally implausible is the interpretation of Watts (1987: 354), who translates הארץ, in these passages as "the land," and believes it refers to "agricultural fertility." Used in conjunction with השמים, this phrase can only mean "the heavens and *earth*."

chapter will show, these passages were certainly understood cosmologically in later Jewish and Christian literature. A more balanced position is stated by Russell: "The announcement of the new heavens and a new earth [in Isaiah 65–66] represents in the most comprehensive terms the work of salvation embracing both the faithful servants and their world."[24]

In continuity with chapters 40–55, the new event of Isaiah 65.17 is contrasted with "the former things" (ראשׁות), which "will no longer be remembered." Yet whereas earlier chapters focused on the transformation of God's people, with creation playing a supportive role (e.g. 43.18), the situation in chapters 65 and 66 is reversed. Here, creation itself takes center stage, with God's people and God's city being swept up in the ovation of praise to the Creator (בורא, 65.17, 18; cf. 42.5; 43.1, 15).

Summarizing the discussion thus far, the Isaianic motif of new creation is both anthropological and cosmological in scope. It includes God's people and God's world. Addressing the needs of a community in exile, it speaks of a transformed people (40–55) in a transformed universe (65–66). Complementing the Isaianic emphasis on a renewed community – perhaps even undergirding it – was the vision of Jeremiah and Ezekiel.

Jeremiah: a new covenant

"The time is coming," declares the LORD, "when I will make a new covenant with the house of Israel and with the house of Judah. It will not be like the covenant I made with their forefathers . . . I will put my law in their minds and write it on their hearts. I will be their God, and they will be my people. No longer will a man teach his neighbor, or a man his brother, saying, 'Know the LORD,' because they will all know me, from the least of them to the greatest," declares the LORD. "For I will forgive their wickedness and will remember their sins no more."
(Jer. 31.31–34)

Jeremiah's promise of a new covenant is certainly one of the more memorable prophecies of the Old Testament as far as Christian readers are concerned, and has the distinction of being the lengthiest Old Testament citation in the New Testament (Heb. 8.8–12; cf. Luke 22.20; 1 Cor. 11.25; 2 Cor. 3.6; Heb. 9.15; 12.24). Its significance in Jeremiah can hardly be overestimated, in that it provides the solution to the grim dilemma so

---

[24] D. M. Russell (1996: 75).

prominent in the preaching of the prophet himself.[25] As most agree, the newness of the new covenant announced by Jeremiah lies in its inwardness, being written *on the heart* rather than on tablets of stone.[26] As Bright observes, "No Prophet stressed more strongly than he the native corruption of the heart . . . or more earnestly insisted upon the need of an inward cleansing, a radical inner change."[27] It is only reasonable that Jeremiah's perception of the *plight* decisively informed his presentation of the *solution*.

Israel's wicked heart

"Judah's sin," proclaimed Jeremiah, "is engraved with an iron tool, inscribed with a flint point on the tablets of their hearts" (17.1), and this verse can serve as the thesis statement of Jeremiah's theology of the heart. According to this prophet, "the heart is deceitful above all things, beyond cure" (17.9), and in desperate need of "circumcision" (4.4) and "cleansing" (4.6). Jeremiah's favorite description of his people's heart condition is "stubbornness of [an evil] heart" ([הרע-] לב שררות, 3.17; 7.24; 9.13; 11.8; 13.10; 16.12; 23.17), and it is this inner disposition which, according to Jeremiah, rendered Israel incapable of obedience: "But they will reply 'It is no use . . . each of us will follow the stubbornness of his evil heart' " (18.12). In Jeremiah's eyes, Israel was like "a wild vine" (2.21), "a ruined garment" (13.1–9), "dross-ridden silver" which could not be refined (6.28–30; cf. 2.22). Jeremiah's conviction was that sin was no longer a matter of periodic disobedience, but of intrinsic nature: "Can the Ethiopian change his skin, or the leopard its spots? Neither can you do good who are accustomed to doing evil" (13.23; cf. 4.22; 8.22; 5.1–5). The mountain springs run in their course (18.14), the oceans know their boundaries (5.22–23), the birds of the air observe their time of migration (8.7a), "but my people do not know the requirements of the Lord" (8.7b), says the prophet. Jeremiah's accusation is that, unlike the rest of the created order, Israel's fundamental instincts were contrary to God's intention, and in view of these texts, Potter reasons that, "the New Covenant written on the heart seems the answer to this problem of human nature."[28]

---

[25] Against the extreme views of Nicholson (1970) and Carroll (1986), there is no reason to deny that the authentic voice of Jeremiah can be heard throughout the pages of the book which bears his name. See the major commentaries of Bright (1965), J. A. Thompson (1980: 3–125), Holladay (1988: 10–24), Craigie, Kelley, and Drinkard (1991: xxxi–xxxvii).

[26] Von Rad (1965: 213), Zimmerli (1978: 205), J. A. Thompson (1980: 581), Carroll (1986: 611), Clements (1988: 190–92), McKane (1996: 818), etc.

[27] Bright (1965: lxx), speaking for many.

[28] Potter (1986: 351), following Weippert (1979: 336–51). Similarly von Rad (1965: 216, 269), Gowan (1986: 70–72), and others.

Israel's "organized hypocrisy"[29]

Closely related to Jeremiah's analysis of Israel's "heart" was his strident condemnation of the religious activity of his people, issuing, as he saw it, from insincere motives: "'Judah did not return to me with all her heart, but only in pretense,' declares the Lord" (3.10). Jeremiah's infamous Temple sermon (7.1–29; 26.1–24) consisted of a scornful derision of the worshipers at the Temple as they proclaimed, "This is the Temple of the Lord!"; to which Jeremiah called back, "You are trusting in deceptive words that are worthless!" (7.8). Jeremiah's insistence on the priority of the internal over the external permeates his proclamation, and for that reason is a major topic in the secondary literature:[30]

> In those days . . . men will no longer say, "The ark of the covenant of the LORD." It will never enter their minds or be remembered; it will not be missed, nor will another one be made. (Jer. 3.16)

> What do I care about incense from Sheba or sweet calamus from a distant Land? Your burnt offerings are not acceptable; your sacrifices do not please me. (6.20)

> Go ahead, add your burnt offerings to your other offerings and eat the meat yourselves! For when I brought your forefathers out of Egypt and spoke to them, I did not give them commands about burnt offerings and sacrifices, but I gave them this command: Obey me and I will be your God and you will be my people.
> (7.21–22; cf. 11.15)

Jeremiah goes so far as to declare circumcision itself irrelevant (9.25–26; see chapter 11), which is further evidence of his conviction that "external practice is no substitute for inward obedience."[31] Connecting this important theme with Jeremiah's announcement of a new covenant, Southwell remarks, "this last idea is a favorite of Jeremiah, for whom true religion consists not in external and ritual observance of law or cult, but in personal and intimate knowledge of God."[32]

The plight and the solution

Any consideration of Jeremiah's analysis of the human condition inevitably involves language like "tremendous bondage,"[33] "ein stark

---

[29] Jeremiah's assessment of the religious establishment according to Skinner (1922: 175).
[30] See Skinner (1922: 165–84), Buis (1968), Weinfield (1976: 17–56), K. Koch (1980: 13–80), J. A. Thompson (1980: 67–71).
[31] J. A. Thompson (1980: 97).   [32] Southwell (1982: 83).
[33] Von Rad (1965: 216).

formulierter anthropologischer Pessimismus,"[34] "the radical evil in man,"[35] "a virtual degradation of human nature,"[36] "l'incapacité radicale de l'homme,"[37] and so on. Indeed, as John Bright candidly admits, "One who reads the book of Jeremiah ... and ponders his message, is likely to come away depressed,"[38] and against this backdrop, Jeremiah's new covenant is all the more significant. Jeremiah foresees a time when, apart from any human initiative, God's will would be implanted in the heart, thus enabling obedience:

> If God's will ceases to confront and judge men from outside themselves, if God puts his will directly into their hearts, then, properly speaking, the rendering of obedience is completely done away with, for the problem of obedience only arises when man's will is confronted by an alien will ... What is here outlined is the picture of a new man, a man who is able to obey perfectly because of a miraculous change in his nature.[39]

In keeping with von Rad's appraisal, and in stark contrast to Jeremiah's description of the plight, the language that surfaces in connection with Jeremiah 31.31–34 (the solution) typically involves phrases like "an anthropological restructuring – a renewal of man himself,"[40] "rénovation intérieure,"[41] "spiritual metamorphosis,"[42] "a complete transformation,"[43] "a new humanity,"[44] and so on. According to Helga Weippert, "Daß im Wort vom neuen Bund die Verheißung, Jahweh werde sein Gesetz ins Herz schreiben, eine so tiefgreifende Veränderung des Menschen anzeigt, *daß man von einer Neuschöpfung sprechen darf*, hat uns der Weg entlang ausgewählter Texte aus dem Jeremiabuch nahegelegt."[45]

But Jeremiah was not alone among his contemporaries in proclaiming that God would one day re-create his people from the inside out. Ezekiel had a similar expectation, corroborating and extending the analysis of his counterpart in Jerusalem.

Ezekiel: a new heart and a new spirit

I will give them an undivided heart (לב אחד) and put a new spirit (רוח חדשה) within them; I will remove from them their heart of

---

[34] Weippert (1979: 344). Similarly Bright (1965: xlv), K. Koch (1980: 19).
[35] Eissfeldt (1966: 359).   [36] Polk (1984: 42)   [37] Buis (1968: 10).
[38] Bright (1965: lxi).   [39] Von Rad (1965: 213–14).   [40] K. Koch (1980: 66).
[41] Buis (1968: 4).   [42] Weinfield (1976).   [43] Heschel (1962: 129).
[44] Gowan (1986: 81).   [45] Weippert (1979: 347), my emphasis.

stone and give them a heart of flesh. Then they will follow my
decrees and be careful to keep my laws. They will be my people
and I will be their God.   (Ezek. 11.19–20; cf. 18.31)

I will give you a new heart (לב חדש) and put a new spirit (חדשה
רוח) in you; I will remove from you your heart of stone and give
you a heart of flesh. And I will put my Spirit (רוחי) in you and
move you to follow my decrees and be careful to keep my laws.
                                                            (36.26–27)

Like Jeremiah, the prophet Ezekiel looked forward to the day when Israel
would receive "new life from a new creative act of God,"[46] and his description of this event is remarkably similar to that of Jeremiah. Both prophets
spoke of a future inner renewal in which God would take the initiative
and accomplish through his people what they had failed to do themselves:
"I will put my Spirit in you *and move you to follow my decrees*" (36.27).
Moreover, both prophets make the heart (לב) the focal point of this coming renewal, and Ezekiel's "new heart/spirit" is commonly equated with
Jeremiah's "new covenant."[47] This equation is strengthened by the fact
that Ezekiel also promises a new "everlasting covenant" (16.60; 37.26;
cf. 34.25).[48] Given their similar descriptions of the solution, it should
come as no surprise that these prophets also shared a common view of
Israel's plight.

Israel's adulterous heart

Then in the nations where they have been carried captive, those
who escape shall remember me – how I have been grieved by
their *adulterous hearts* . . . which have lusted after their idols.
                                                            (Ezek. 6.9)

The "adultery" of Israel, according to Ezekiel, was her idolatry, and this
prophet depicts in unseemly and lurid detail the entire history of his people
as one continuous act of unbridled promiscuity. The historical surveys of
chapters 16, 20, and 23 would cause most to blush, and are intended to

[46] Werner Schmidt's description of Ezekiel's "new heart/spirit" texts (1979: 255).
[47] See, e.g., von Rad (1965: 235), Eichrodt (1967: 58 n. 5), Buis (1968: 4), Schoefield
(1969: 195), Weinfield (1976: 31), Zimmerli (1978: 212), K. Koch (1980: 111), Cody (1984:
173), Gowan (1986: 2–3).
[48] It is not clear if these correspondences suggest literary dependence (so von Rad [1965:
235], Holladay [1989: 81–85]) or if they should be explained simply in terms of a shared
assessment of Israel's condition (so K. Koch [1980: 85]).

demonstrate "the radical corruption of the nation."[49] But Ezekiel is not content to condemn only Israel's high places and city shrines (16.2–26). Rather, he fastens his attention on the heart as the seat of idolatry, refusing to ignore the "idols in their hearts" (גלוליהם על־לבם, 14.3):

> As for those whose hearts are devoted to their vile images and detestable idols, I will bring judgment down on their own heads.
> (Ezek. 11.21)

> Son of man, these people have set up idols in their hearts, and put wicked stumbling blocks before their eyes. (14.3; cf. 14.4)

> When any Israelite or any alien living in Israel separates himself from me and sets up idols in their heart . . . I the Lord will answer that person myself. (14.7)

> For their hearts are devoted to their idols. (20.16)

This studied repetition underscores Ezekiel's conviction regarding Israel's inner disposition toward idolatry, and allows the prophet to point his finger at the very center of the human person, the heart. Not unlike Jeremiah's condemnation of Israel's fundamental instincts, Ezekiel offers a genealogical basis for the errancy of his people

> This is what the Sovereign LORD says to Jerusalem: Your ancestry and birth were in the land of the Canaanites; your father was an Amorite and your mother a Hittite. (Ezek. 16.3)

Israel's hardened heart

Ezekiel's most persistent charge against his people is that they are "a rebellious house" (בית המרי), a phrase that occurs some thirteen times in the book of Ezekiel, along with many similar expressions:

> Son of Man, I am sending you to the Israelites, to a rebellious nation that has rebelled against me; they and their fathers have been in revolt against me to this very day. (Ezek. 2.3)

> Son of man, you are living among a rebellious people. They have eyes to see but do not see and ears to hear but do not hear, for they are a rebellious people. (12.2)

> Say to this rebellious house, "Do you not know what these things mean?" (17.12)

---

[49] Zimmerli (1979: 58).

Israel's rebelliousness is twice linked to a "hardened" (חזק, 2.4) or "calcified" (קשה, 3.7) heart, which is the reason why Yahweh is determined to make Ezekiel equally obdurate:

> But I will make you as unyielding and hardened as they are. I will make your forehead like the hardest stone, harder than flint. Do not be afraid of them or terrified by them, though they are a rebellious house.   (Ezek. 3.8–9)

This also explains why a heart transplant was the only remedy available: "I will remove from you your heart of stone and give you a heart of flesh" (11.19; 36.26). According to Schoefield, "The disease of the nation is so malignant . . . drastic surgery is needed."[50]

The plight and the solution

Much more could be said of Ezekiel's scathing denunciation of his people, but in view of his ideological kinship with Jeremiah, and his similar appraisal of Israel's plight, it should come as no surprise that his evaluation of Israel's condition is summarized in language comparable to what we saw earlier: "a degenerated reason is therefore a theme that permeates Ezekiel's anthropology,"[51] "the radical wrongness . . . of human nature,"[52] "[Israel's] deep-seated inability to obey,"[53] and so on. Given that Ezekiel 36.26–27 and Jeremiah 31.31–34 are regarded by many as parallel passages, Ezekiel's presentation of the solution likewise evokes similar language: "transformed humanity,"[54] "new being,"[55] "renewal,"[56] "re-creation,"[57] and so on. According to both Preuss and Hals,[58] Ezekiel 36 depicts God's future work in the hearts of his people as a kind of "new creation" which, arguably, is a very adequate summary of the message of these passages.

Summary and conclusions

Reiterating the limited scope of this opening section, the preceding analysis offered only an overview of the motif of new creation in the later

---

[50] Schoefield (1969: 205).   [51] K. Koch (1980: 111).   [52] Gowan (1986: 69).
[53] Von Rad (1965: 229).   [54] K. Koch (1980: 108), Gowan (1986: 59–96).
[55] Zimmerli (1983: 263).   [56] Werner Schmidt (1979: 255), Newsome (1984: 136).
[57] Von Rad (1965: 235), Gowan (1986: 69–72). According to Allen (1994: 179), Ezekiel 36 promises that God will "remake their human nature."
[58] Hals (1989: 262), Preuss (1992: 274).

prophets. While necessarily brief, this survey was sufficient to demonstrate three distinct patterns of thought, each of which could be adequately summarized with the maxim "new creation."

Employing the phrase "former things/new things" – a maxim with a fairly wide field of reference – Isaiah 40–55 depicts Israel's impending release from captivity as a second exodus, "a new creative redemption."[59] Klause Kiesow, in his study of exodus texts in Isaiah 40–55, describes this event as "die rettende Zuwendung Jahwehs, die...Leben in Fülle schenkt,"[60] and this summation nicely exposes the theological depth implicit in this exodus symbolism. Moreover, this imagery is embedded in a context that suggestively unites "creation" terminology with "redemption" terminology, and the implications of this potent alliance are underlined by Watts:

> The vision relates these salvation-words [גאל, ישע] to strong creator-words...to shape a theological pattern that has dominated biblical thought on salvation from that time on, even when it came to involve spiritual and individual issues widely separated and only metaphorically similar to the need for physical group rescue and restoration evidenced in the Exodus and the Exile.[61]

In the final chapters of the book of Isaiah, the vision expands to include heaven and earth. God's people are promised not simply "a land flowing with milk and honey," but a world that is in tune with the purpose of its maker. The book of Isaiah, then, contains two different, but not unrelated expressions of the motif of new creation, and to these should be added the perspective of Jeremiah and Ezekiel.

With respect to their new-creation motif, Jeremiah and Ezekiel can be treated together, and their presentation of this theme is as different from that in the book of Isaiah as was the situation these prophets addressed. Citing von Rad again,

> For these prophets the hardest problem lies in the realm of anthropology – how can this "rebellious house," these men "of hard forehead and a stubborn heart" (Ezek. 2.3–4), who are as little able to change themselves as an Ethiopian can change the colour of his skin (Jer. 13.23) – how can these be Yahweh's people?[62]

Responding to this situation, Jeremiah and Ezekiel looked forward to the day when God would re-create his people from the inside out. In

---

[59] Stuhlmueller (1970: 143).   [60] Kiesow (1979: 78).
[61] Watts (1987: 106).   [62] Von Rad (1965: 269).

proclaiming a new (interior) covenant, a new heart, and a new Spirit, these prophets effectively planted the flag of hope in the rebel outpost of Jerusalem, insisting that Israel's real problem was not the enemy camped outside the walls, but the enemy entrenched within. In the discussion of the message of Ezekiel, I was noticeably silent about the crucial theme of the infusion of a new Spirit, preferring to take this up at a later point (chapter 7). Yet even from the analysis thus far, we can see the logic of Werner Schmidt's decision to connect Ezekiel's new Spirit with Jeremiah's new covenant and treat both under the heading, "Wende und Neuschöpfung durch den Geist."[63]

[63] Werner Schmidt (1984: 172).

3

NEW CREATION IN APOCALYPTIC JUDAISM: *JUBILEES*

From the table in the corner they could see a world reborn.

Les Misérables

Jubilees: a case study

As "one of the most important documents in the history of the Jewish religion,"[1] the book of *Jubilees* provides an immensely valuable introduction to the issues and ideas which shaped the "Judaism" of the pre-Christian era.[2] Written either just prior to the Maccabean uprisings, or sometime early in the Maccabean era,[3] *Jubilees* offers a commentary on the tumultuous events of this period from a perspective closely related to that of the Hasidim, those pious defenders of the law who rallied to the support of Mattathias and his sons against the encroachments of Hellenistic culture.[4] *Jubilees'* use of Enochian material,[5] along with its obvious

---

[1] Zeitlin (1939/40: 30). Similar comments are made by Charlesworth (1981: 143) and Holder (1994: 119).

[2] The term "Judaism" should be taken in its broadest sense, denoting the full diversity of faith and practice in the period.

[3] Although earlier writers dated *Jubilees* closer to 100 BC (e.g. Charles, F. Martin, Schürer, Testuz), recent scholarship has adjusted this to c. 168–140 BC. Cf. VanderKam (1977: 207–85), Berger (1981: 300), Nickelsburg (1984b: 101–3), Wintermute (1985: 43–44), Vermes in Schürer (vol. III.1, 1986: 313).

[4] See 1 Macc. 2.41–48; 7.8–17; 2 Macc. 14.6. The link with the Hasidim is made by Nickelsburg (1972: 46–47), VanderKam (1977: 251), Berger (1981: 298), Wintermute (1985: 44), and Vermes in Schürer (vol. III.1, 1986: 315), though it remains only a reasonable conjecture. Given the probable link between the Hasidim and the Essenes, those who prefer to speak of *Jubilees'* "proto-Essene" character (cf. VanderKam [1977: 283], Charlesworth [1981: 143], Endress [1987: 245], Nickelsburg [1991: 79]) are affirming nothing substantially different.

[5] *Jubilees* interpolates Enochian traditions in several places, the most noteworthy being 4.17–24. On this see Charles (1902: xliv), F. Martin (1911: 325–26), and VanderKam (1978). On the more contentious claim that later portions of *1 Enoch* rely on *Jubilees*, see Milik (1976: 255).

importance to the sectaries at Qumran,[6] attests to its broader relevance and influence and renders it an ideal specimen for examination. Moreover, its length and literary integrity permit a more confident evaluation of its themes, especially in comparison with the composite work of 1 Enoch.[7] Finally, if any weight at all can be attached to the traditional connection made between the Hasidim of the Maccabean era and the Pharisees of the New Testament era,[8] and if any book can claim to illuminate the perspective of the pre-Christian Paul, the Pharisee par excellence (Phil. 3.5; cf. Acts 23.6; 26.5), *Jubilees* is that book.

Using *Jubilees* as a representative work of apocalyptically oriented Judaism, the goal in this section will be to understand new creation within the argument of this book and, by implication, within the apocalypses more generally. Because the main interest is in the book of *Jubilees*, the burden of corroborating evidence from other sources will be borne by the footnotes. I will justify this approach more fully in what follows, after clarifying the relationship between *Jubilees* and apocalyptic.

Jubilees as apocalyptic

The book of *Jubilees* is among those works "usually named as Palestinian Jewish apocalypses,"[9] though this common classification has been variously nuanced.[10] And while there is much "semantic confusion"

[6] In addition to the numerous fragments of *Jubilees* found at Qumran, the author of the Damascus Rule cites *Jubilees* as authoritative (CD 16.2–4); see VanderKam (1977: 255–82).

[7] The eccentric and complex multi-redactional hypothesis of Davenport has been uniformly rejected by subsequent research: Sanders (1977: 386–87), Berger (1981: 301), Münchow (1981: 43), VanderKam (1981), Nickelsburg (1984b: 102).

[8] See, e.g., D. S. Russell (1967: 62–68, 159–60), Schürer (vol. II revised, 1979: 400–1), Efron (1987), Kampen (1988), Hengel (1991: 44–45).

[9] Sanders (1983: 456). A sampling of those who list *Jubilees* as apocalyptic include G. I. Davies (1978), Carmignac (1979: 3–33), Greunwald (1979: 105), Rowland (1982: 51–52), Collins (1984: 7–9), Cohen (1987: 196), Endress (1987: 5), Nickelsburg (1991: 73), Holder (1994: 119–21), Kugel (1994).

[10] Some regard *Jubilees* as apocalyptic in theological orientation, though not in literary form (D. S. Russell [1964: 54], Berger [1981: 279–85], Mell [1989: 152]), while others regard it as a mixed genre (Testuz [1960:11–12], Münchow [1981: 43–44]). After listing six typical features of apocalyptic that *Jubilees* shares with this genre, Wintermute objects to this classification on the basis that Jubilees does not have (1) "bizarre imagery," (2) "limited esoteric appeal," and (3) "preoccupation with the type of eschatology characteristic of apocalyptic" (1985: 37). Since Rowland's work (1982: esp. 1–72), objections (1) and (3) are no longer tenable, while (2) is hardly an essential feature of apocalyptic, even if one grants its legitimacy. Stone's warning against this simple "list" approach is apposite: "Indeed the 'truly apocalyptic' apocalypses are the exception rather than the rule" (1991: 408).

surrounding the current use of the word *apocalyptic*,[11] as Tigchelaar points out, "the one point most scholars agree on is the existence of a genre apocalypse."[12] Accordingly, the use here of the term "apocalyptic" will be in specific reference to the genre, or to ideas particularly prominent in the apocalypses. A brief discussion of apocalyptic technique in the book of *Jubilees* will both introduce the message of this book and set the stage for the analysis of its new-creation motif.

Divine disclosure and the decoding of history

The first and most foundational claim of the book of *Jubilees* concerns its revelatory nature: "This is the account of the division of days ... and their jubilees throughout all the years of the world *just as the Lord told it to Moses*" (prologue).[13] Most of the opening chapter is aimed at supporting this central assertion, which must be firmly established if the author's claim to unveil the meaning of history is to appear credible. The book opens on Mount Sinai, with Moses receiving the two stone tablets from the Lord. But instead of Moses then descending to the children of Israel encamped below, as in the Exodus account (Exod. 31–32), the book of *Jubilees* tells the story this way: "And then [God] said to him, 'Pay attention to all the words which I tell you on this mountain. Write them in a book so that [Israel's] descendants might know that I have not abandoned them'" (1.5; cf. *1 Enoch* 82.1–3). By "Israel's descendants," the author certainly has in mind his/her own contemporaries,[14] thus divulging at the outset the purpose of this revealed history: to offer hope to the present generation of Israelites enduring the crisis of foreign domination and political turmoil. Indeed, the tendentious rewriting of Israel's history that follows is actually intrinsic to this genre, as Rowland points out:

> Thus apocalyptic, whose main concern was the revelation of the divine mysteries, could in no sense be complete without offering some kind of total view of history. An orientation towards

[11] Citing Stone (1991: 405). See also Barker (1978: 324–29), R. L. Webb (1990: 115–26), Matlock (1996).

[12] Tigchelaar (1996: 11).

[13] The claim of direct revelatory experience is commonplace in the apocalypses: *1 Enoch* 1.1–3; 17–19; 37.1; 72.1; 83.1; 108.15; *2 Enoch* 1.1–6; *Apoc. Zeph.* 1.1; 4 Ezra 4.31; 6.18–19; 9.1; 10.38; 14.37–48; *Syr. Bar.* 36–40; 53.1. On the importance of the revelation of mysteries in apocalyptic see, e.g., Rowland (1982), Stone (1984: 427–33), Vermes in Schürer (vol. III.1, 1986: 242–43) and D. S. Russell (1992: 60–102). Unless otherwise indicated, citations from *Jubilees* will be taken from Wintermute in *OTP* vol. II.

[14] So Davenport (1971: 19–21), Berger (1981: 312).

the future alone would have given a theological picture which minimized divine control of history in the present. The extent of apocalyptic's debt to the past is manifested in the way in which the divine activity through history is so consistently portrayed in the historical reviews contained in the apocalypses. To that extent the mantle of earlier historiography has fallen on the apocalypticists.[15]

The choice of Moses as the medium for this revelation invested the message with authority, while also giving the impression that the present historical circumstances had been foretold long ago and that everything was still proceeding according to the divine plan.[16]

Apology and historiography

The author's interest in current affairs is betrayed in a number of ways, some more subtle than others. Although purporting to recount the biblical events from creation to Sinai, *Jubilees'* sometimes imaginative retelling of Genesis is characterized by expansions, deletions, insertions, and other modifications aimed at contemporizing the biblical text and relating it to the present predicament.[17] Martin's judgment that, "L'histoire n'est donc pour lui que le prétexte ou plutôt le cadre de cette double apologie"[18] is borne out by even a cursory reading of the text. A few examples should suffice.

Adam and Eve. In Genesis 3, the story of Adam and Eve sewing fig leaves together to cover themselves is told without further comment, but note the principle that the author of *Jubilees* draws: "Therefore, it is commanded in the heavenly tablets to all who know the Law that they should cover their shame and they should not go about naked as do the gentiles" (3.31; cf. 7.7–13, 20; 48.19). The infamous events of Jason's highpriesthood (174–169 BC), his program of Hellenistic reform involving, among other things, the construction of a gymnasium where

---

[15] Rowland (1982: 145). See also G. I. Davies (1978), Müller (1978: 224–44), and Hall (1991). Historical summaries are a regular feature of the apocalypses and related literature: Dan. 7–12; *1 Enoch* 83–90; 91.12–17; 4 Ezra 3.1–27; 11–12; *Syr. Bar.* 35–40; 53–74; *Apoc. Abr.* 21–32. Cf. *Sib. Or.* 3.97–161.

[16] On this aspect of pseudonymity, see Rowland (1982: 67–69), Collins (1984: 30), Mell (1989: 117–18), D. S. Russell (1992: 67–68).

[17] Of the numerous discussions of *Jubilees'* hortatory technique, especially insightful are F. Martin (1911: 321–44), Endress (1987), Hall (1991: 31–47), VanderKam (1993 and 1994), and Syren (1994).

[18] F. Martin (1911: 322).

Jewish men exercised naked like their Greek counterparts[19] is transparent in this warning and is regularly noted in the secondary literature.[20]

Jews and Gentiles. The intermingling and intermarriage of Jews and Gentiles is also of grave concern to the author, and nowhere is this more apparent than in the retelling of Dinah's rape (see Gen. 33.18–34.31).[21] The principal modifications of the biblical narrative serve the purpose of increasing the guilt of the Shechemites while justifying the brutality of Simeon and Levi. Omitted from the Genesis account are (1) the circumstances of Dinah's abduction ("she went out to visit the women of the country," Gen. 33.2), which might be taken as frivolity on the part of the young girl,[22] (2) Jacob's negotiations with the Shechemites, which took for granted complex social and political intercourse between Jews and Gentiles, and (3) the circumcision of all the male Shechemites (Gen. 33.13–24), which rendered their subsequent slaughter all the more dubious. Interpolated into the biblical narrative is the statement concerning Dinah's age ("and he defiled her, though she was little, only twelve," 30.2), and the implication that all the men of Shechem somehow participated in the defilement (30.3).[23] These additions intensify and widen the guilt of the Shechemites, further preparing the ground for the author's main point: the provocative likening of intermarriage to the defilement of rape:

> And it is a reproach to Israel, to those who give and those who take any of the daughters of the gentile nations because it is a defilement and it is contemptible to Israel. And Israel will not be cleansed from the defilement if there is in it a woman from among the daughters of the gentiles or one who has given any of his daughters to a man who is from any of the gentiles.
>
> (30.14–15)

Even more shocking is the adulation heaped upon Simeon and Levi for their treacherous butchery of the Shechemites – quite unlike the biblical account (cf. Gen. 49.5–7):

---

[19] See 1 Macc. 1.10–14; 2 Macc. 4.7–20; Josephus, *Ant.* 12.1.

[20] E.g., Charles (1902: 29), Testuz (1960: 112), VanderKam (1977: 245–47), Berger (1981: 300), Schwarz (1982), Wintermute (1985: 46), Vermes in Schürer (vol. III.1, 1986: 311).

[21] See the discussions in F. Martin (1911: 333–35), Endress (1987: 120–54); see also the more general treatment of this theme by Schwarz (1982).

[22] Josephus seems to take it this way (*Ant.* 1.337), as did later writers, according to Endress (1987: 124).

[23] So Berger (1981: 470), and Endress (1987: 124–25).

And it was a righteousness for them and it was written down for them for righteousness. And the seed of Levi was chosen for the priesthood and levitical orders to minister before the Lord always just as we [angels] do. And Levi and his sons will be blessed forever because he was zealous to do righteousness and judgment and vengeance against all who rose up against Israel.

(30.17–18; cf. 20.1–5)

This blessing amounts to a divine sanction for the eradication of all who would oppose the faith and practice of Israel (i.e., the Gentiles),[24] and fully justifies Testuz's description, "extrêmement violent," in reference to *Jubilees'* prohibition of intermarriage.[25] It would be going beyond the evidence to argue, as some have, that *Jubilees'* consistent elevation of the levitical priesthood was intended as propaganda for the military campaigns of the (priestly) Maccabean leadership,[26] but it is nonetheless true that the sentiments expressed in *Jubilees* echo the concerns which prompted the Maccabean uprisings, and that those promoting the Hasmonean cause would have found this book a very pleasant read.

Jacob and Esau. Exhibiting more finesse (and cunning), the subtle changes made to the exchange between Isaac and Jacob in Genesis 27 are particularly noteworthy.[27] Rather than having Isaac first ask his son, "Who are you?," to which Jacob falsely replies "I am Esau, your firstborn" (Gen. 27.18–19), *Jubilees* simply has Jacob enter with the greeting "I am your son" (26.13). Equally coy is Jacob's response when asked directly by his father, "Are you my son Esau?" To this Jacob replies, "I am your son" (26.19; contrast with Gen. 27.24).[28] These alterations are part of an

---

[24] *Jubilees* provides a rich storehouse of "Decknamen," encrypted names, which Volz (1934: 83–84) reminds us is typical of the literature of the period. The material from Qumran is the best illustration of this technique. Although *Jubilees* 30 decodes "the Shechemites" for the reader (= Gentiles, 30.7–23; see also the Raphaim = Ammonite decoding of 29.9–11), most are left encrypted and are capable of a number of contemporary allusions, e.g., Esau and the Edomites (especially chapters 35–38); the Philistines (24.27–33); the Kittim (24.28–29); the Canaanites (25.1–10); the Amorites (34.1–9), etc.

[25] Testuz (1960: 113). Note also 22.20; 25.1–10; 27.10.

[26] E.g., Charles (1902: lxxiii), F. Martin (1911), and Meyer (1938, according to Berger [1981: 300]); cf. also Wintermute (1985: 44–45). The priestly descent of the Maccabees was well established. According to 1 Macc. 2.1 and Josephus, *Ant.* 12. 265, Mattathias was of the priestly family of Joarib (1 Chron. 24.1–7; Neh. 11.10). On the priestly claim of the Hasmoneans see 1 Macc. 2.54; 12.5, 20; 13.36; 14–16; Josephus, *Ant.* 12. 265; 16.187; 20.238, and *Vita* 1–6, where Josephus traces his own priestly lineage through the Hasmoneans.

[27] See F. Martin (1911: 332) for a more detailed discussion.

[28] Moreover, according to *Jubilees*, Jacob's charade succeeded because "the change was from heaven in order to distract his mind" (26.18).

elaborate program of subordinating Esau to Jacob, which almost certainly reflects current Jewish–Idumean hostility.[29]

If these modifications evince some degree of literary dexterity on the part of the author, others are less discreet. Compare the final words of Esau's blessing in Genesis with those in *Jubilees*:

Genesis 27.40	Jubilees 26.34
And by your sword you shall live and you will serve your brother. But when you break loose you will break his yoke from your neck.	And by your sword you shall live and you will serve your brother. And it will happen that when you become great and you will remove his yoke from your neck, *that then you will surely sin completely unto death, and your seed will be rooted out from under heaven.*

Finally, given the historical context, one cannot help but sense that *Jubilees'* creative speculation concerning the ultimate demise of Esau was penned with great satisfaction by the author: "Then Jacob [= Israel] bent his bow and let fly an arrow and shot his brother Esau [= Idumea] in the right breast, and killed him" (38.2). The account in 1 Maccabees makes deciphering these "Decknamen" light work: "And Judas made war on the descendants of Esau in Idumea . . . He dealt them a heavy blow and humbled them and despoiled them" (5.3).

To these examples could be added numerous excursuses on the importance of circumcision (15.25–34; 20.3), keeping the Sabbath (2.7–33; 50.1–13), the Jewish right to Palestine (chapters 8–10), and so on, all of which serve the purpose of exhorting the Jewish people to remain faithful to their ancestral religion even in the face of political subjugation and cultural-religious annihilation. These illustrations and this historical backdrop are not contested, but they are highlighted here in order to focus attention on the attendant crisis which produced this book and allowed this genre to flourish. Collins rightly observes that "it is generally agreed that apocalypse is generated by social and historical circumstances,"[30] so any investigation of the book of *Jubilees* must also be an inquiry into the historical-cultural milieu of this apocryphon.

---

[29] See 1 Macc. 5.1–6; Josephus, *Ant.* 327, and the discussions of, e.g., VanderKam (1977: 230–38), Endress (1987: 85–119), Syren (1994).

[30] Collins (1984: 18). This is one of the foundational premises of Körtner's recent theology of apocalyptic: "The hermeneutical key to the apocalyptic understanding of existence . . . is world anxiety" (1995: 21). See also Hanson (1975).

The significant details of this period of Jewish history are well known, and tell the story of political turmoil, religious oppression, apostasy, guerilla warfare, and general social upheaval.[31] Few, if any, would argue with Christopher Rowland's emphasis on the importance of apocalyptic in providing "coherence and significance to existence in the present, when historical circumstances offered only perplexity and despair."[32] This concern to instill some sense of order even in the midst of chaos lies at the heart of the "historical" apocalypses and their glorious vision of a "new creation,"[33] and merits specific attention before I examine the particular expression of this motif in the book of *Jubilees*.

Hope and despair

Apocalyptic has been called "the literature of the oppressed" – a designation which is particularly sensitive to the historical contexts and literary tone of much of this material.[34] From the time of Paul Volz, perhaps the greatest writer on early Jewish eschatology, who identified *Pessimismus* as "the fertile soil" (*der Nährboden*) of apocalyptic,[35] the term "pessimism" has been regularly employed to describe the outlook of those associated with this genre.[36] Consider, for example, the way the author of *Jubilees* depicts the current state of the Jewish people as (s)he saw it:

> For calamity follows on calamity, and wound on wound, and tribulation on tribulation, and bad news on bad news, and illness

[31] Primary sources for the period are 1 Maccabees; Josephus, *Ant.* 12–14; *JW* 1–2.

[32] Rowland (1982: 22).

[33] The distinction between historical apocalypses (Daniel 7–9; *Syriac Baruch*, 4 Ezra, *Jubilees*, the *Apocalypse of Weeks* [*1 Enoch* 93], the *Animal Apocalypse* [*1 Enoch* 85–90], Revelation) and those focusing on other-worldly journeys (*The Book of the Watchers* [*1 Enoch* 1–36], *The Astronomical Book* [*1 Enoch* 72–82], *T. Levi, 3 Baruch, 2 Enoch, the Apocalypse of Zephaniah*) is frequently made, though the boundaries should not be construed rigidly (e.g., the *Testament of Abraham* combines both). It is important to bear in mind that the motif of new creation occurs almost exclusively in the eschatological material of the historical apocalypses.

[34] A phrase found in D. S. Russell (1964: 17), Collins (1984: 7), and elsewhere. Compare James Charlesworth's assessment of the material of the OT pseudepigrapha: "Almost all of the literature is anthropocentric in that it evolves out of humanity's distress" (1985: 67).

[35] Volz (1934: 8). Note also the prominence of the word in his table of contents (V).

[36] E.g., Rowley (1947: 35), Rist (1962: 158), D. S. Russell (1964: 104, 267), Hanson (1975: 11–12), Münchow (1981: 21, 77, 90), Vermes in Schürer (vol. III.1, 1986: 243), Mell (1989: 117), Aune (1993: 26), etc. Quite often this valid observation is overextended and made to apply to the apocalypticist's view of the historical process *per se*, and not merely to the present period of distress. Rowland (1982: 23–48) provides an important corrective to this overstatement, though without denying the point being made here. Note his observation on page 38: "There is little doubt that the hope for the future in Judaism was closely allied to a pessimistic view of the state of the world in the present."

on illness, and all such painful punishments as these, one after
another – illness, and disaster, and snow, and frost, and ice, and
fever, and chills, and torpor and famine, and death and sword,
and captivity, and all kinds of calamities and pains.   (23.13)[37]

Although Baudry's assessment requires qualification, passages like this
offer substantiation for his conclusion that "une vision pessimiste se
dégage du livre des Jubilés."[38]

The historical crisis of intertestamental Jewish history would have been
felt all the more acutely by those who recalled the hopeful vision of the
prophets, as the apocalyptic writers certainly did, and it is entirely conceivable that the apocalypses themselves were partly intended to mitigate
the discrepancy between (authoritative) prophecy and historical reality.
In the same way that attributing the apocalypse to a venerated figure of
Israel's past served to create the impression of God's continued control, so
too the periodization of history so typical of the apocalypses contributed
to a sense of God's sovereignty over human affairs and an orderly unfold-
ing of the divine plan.[39] This longing for order is taken to an extreme by
the author of *Jubilees*, who organizes the entirety of Israel's history into a
perfectly symmetrical system of "sevens," in which every feast and every
day of the week fell on the same date that it had in every previous year.[40]

But if the writers of the apocalypses viewed their *present* circumstances through dark lenses, their vision of the future was markedly different and served as a foil to the woeful picture painted elsewhere.[41]
Indeed, while eschatology need not be considered the *raison d'être* of
the apocalypses, in those oriented toward discerning God's purpose in
human history it was integral to their message. Volz himself is careful to
make the connection between the present dilemma and the future hope
explicit: "Nur durch den Gedanken an das Jenseits wird das jetzige Leben

[37] The author locates himself within the final period of distress, not, as Charles thought
(1902: lxxvii), within the new age. See F. Martin (1911: 522, 529), Testuz (1960: 169, 177),
Davenport (1971: 72–79), Berger (1981: 282, 440), Münchow (1981: 56, 60). For equally
morose appraisals see, e.g., *1 Enoch* 91.5–9; 102.4–11; 106.18–19; 108.9–10; *2 Enoch*
10.4–6; 34.1–3; 50.2–4; 66.6; 70.5–7; *4 Ezra* 4.23–25; 5.2–3, 28–29; 7.12–16; *Syr. Bar.*
3.1–3; 10.6–19; 11.4–7; 50.13–16; 73.2–4; 78.5; 80.1–7; 82.1–9; 83.4–9. Note also the
words of the dying Mattathias: "Arrogance and outrage are now in the ascendant; it is a
period of turmoil and bitter hatred" (1 Macc. 2.49).
[38] Baudry (1992: 171). So too Münchow (1981: 61).
[39] See Dan. 7–9; *1 Enoch* 10.12; 83–90; 93; *2 Enoch* 33.1–2; *Syr. Bar.* 27–30; 48.1–3;
53–74; *Apoc. Abr.* 29.1–3, 15–21; *T. Levi* 16–18; *Sib. Or.* 3.97–161.
[40] On this see Charles (1902: xv), Testuz (1960: 121–64), Jaubert (1965: 15–30), Berger
(1981: 282–83).
[41] This point has been given special emphasis by Rowland (1982: 156–89), and D. S.
Russell (1992: 14–15).

erträglich."[42] In fact, although the apocalypses themselves are hardly ho-
mogeneous in content and structure, and offer a variety of pictures of
God's future dealings with Israel and the nations, the primary *intent* of
the eschatological material in this diverse body of literature remains con-
stant: to offer hope to the present generation through the promise of
ultimate deliverance and vindication. And while the motif of new creation is also variously enunciated and conceived,[43] as part of the stock of
eschatological symbols common in the period, it too had a very regular
and consistent function within the apocalyptic paradigm. As the most
radical and comprehensive eschatological image available, new creation
was held out as the supreme solution to the dilemma as it was perceived
by these writers. This point is not disputed and will be illustrated through
primary source material later in this discussion. For the moment, Vermes'
summary will suffice: "Even when there was no immediate hardship or
oppression, a pessimistic assessment of affairs still constituted the motive for writing. The existing situation, the present condition of the chosen
people, stood in glaring contrast to their true destiny. A complete revolution must come and soon. Such is the conviction expressed in all these
writings."[44] It constitutes no depreciation of the diversity of the material,
then, to speak of the "typical function" of the motif of new creation in
the apocalypses, and to illustrate this through a detailed examination of
one work representative of this genre.

In keeping with the above analysis, and serving as a methodological
preface to the ensuing discussion, Michael Stone's observation on "cosmic
redemption" in the Second Temple period deserves special emphasis:

---

[42] Volz (1934: 8).

[43] The precise phrase "new creation" occurs only rarely in the literature of the period
(*1 Enoch* 72.1; *Jub.* 1.29; 4.26; *Syr. Bar.* 44.12), though the idea is also present in texts
which describe a new heaven and earth (*1 Enoch* 91.15–16; *Lib. Ant.* 3.10; Rev. 21.1–5),
and sometimes implicit in the notion of cosmic destruction (4 Ezra 7.31; *2 Enoch* 70.9–10;
Apoc. Zeph. 12.5–8; *Sib. Or.* 4.186; 3.92; 7.118–49; *As. Mos.* 10.1–10; cf. 4 Ezra 6.25; 1QH
3.29–34; *Syr. Bar.* 21.17; 40.3). More common is the thought that creation will be renewed
or transformed (*1 Enoch* 45.4–5; *Jub.* 1.29; 23.26–31; *Syr. Bar.* 32.6; 49.3; 57.2; 4 Ezra
6.13–16; 7.75–80; *Apoc. Abr.* 17.14; *Lib. Ant.* 6.3; 32.17; *Sib. Or.* 5.271–74; 3.670–760).
Many texts, however, are ambiguous (*2 Enoch* 65. 4–10; 4 Ezra 7.50; *1 Enoch* 71.15; 1QH
11.9–14; 13.11–12; 1QS 4.23–26), and we also find both ideas combined in a single work
(compare *Syr. Bar.* 44.12 with 32.6; 4 Ezra 7.31, 50 with 6.13–16 and 7.75; *Lib. Ant.* 3.10
with 6.3 and 32.17). This fluidity should not be construed as inconsistency, but merely as
evidence for a variety of ways of articulating the ultimate eschatological reality. We might
say that the more general hope for a new age (4 Ezra 7.112–14; 8.52; *2 Enoch* 33.11;
50.2; 62.1; *Life of Adam and Eve* 51; *Syr. Bar.* 14.13; 15.7–8) is sometimes given concrete
expression in the idea of a new or renewed creation (see *2 Enoch* 65.4–10 and compare
4 Ezra 7.75 with 7.112–14).

[44] Vermes in Schürer (vol. III.1, 1986: 243). Similar evaluations abound: D. S. Russell
(1964: 284), Hanson (1975: 405–6), Greunwald (1979: 89), Cohen (1987: 98–99, 196–97).

"One way of describing redemption is to search to characterize the quandary or condition from which redemption is sought. *The nature of the redemption is a correlative of the nature of the quandary.*"[45] In other words, given the importance of *the plight* in determining the formulation of *the solution*, any examination of new creation in Jewish apocalyptic must concentrate on the nature of the dilemma as it was perceived by these writers. Accordingly, the following analysis will pay close attention to how the author of the book of *Jubilees* depicts the plight from which redemption is sought. Only in this way can the solution, "new creation," be adequately apprehended.

New creation

Central texts

The phrase "new creation" occurs twice in the book of *Jubilees*, in 1.29 and 4.26,[46] though it is important that these texts are not studied in isolation from the work as a whole;[47] for while a more liberal use of this terminology might increase the raw material for the present exegesis, there is certainly no lack of an interpretive framework for this important motif. Two considerations will guide the analysis. First, while a satisfactory literary-critical study of the book of *Jubilees* has yet to be written, the work that has been done on this book consistently regards the opening chapter as an epitome of the book as a whole.[48] In Hall's view, the eschatological material of chapter 1 "serves as a powerful and winning proem" divulging the key issues of the book, and it is not insignificant that the motif of new creation is introduced here. As the theme of the final verse of the opening chapter, the announcement of an impending cosmic renewal brings this eschatological preface to a crescendo while casting its shadow the length of the book. Klaus Berger is perfectly justified in claiming that the whole of *Jubilees* provides the background to this crucial verse.[49]

---

[45] Stone (1991: 446), my emphasis.
[46] Unfortunately, this material is not extant in Greek, Hebrew, Latin, or Aramaic. VanderKam (1989) has conveniently collected the surviving material, providing parallel columns of the Ethiopic text and Greek/Aramaic (etc.) fragments.
[47] As do G. Schneider (1959) and Mell (1989).
[48] E.g., Testuz (1960: 174–75), Davenport (1971: 21), Berger (1981: 279), Münchow (1981: 44), Mell (1989: 153), Hall (1991: 44), VanderKam (1993: 118).
[49] Berger (1981: 279). Consequently, my analysis will focus on this passage. While the second mention of new creation (4.29) underscores the importance of this idea to the author, its parenthetical nature allows it little contribution beyond this.

Second, in every estimation the central eschatological passage in the book of *Jubilees* is the lengthy dissertation in chapter 23,[50] a passage which sheds valuable light on the same material in chapter 1. And while the phrase "new creation" does not occur in chapter 23, many regard 23.26–31 as a commentary on the new-creation motif of 1.29 and 4.26,[51] and if this judgment is even partially correct, any examination of this theme in the book of *Jubilees* must incorporate this vital supplementary material.[52] A comparison of 1.7–29 with 23.11–31 will demonstrate their complementary nature and establish the main line of enquiry in the following sections.

A thematic synopsis of *Jubilees* 1.7–29 and 23.11–32

Although different in arrangement, both *Jubilees* 1.7–29 and 23.11–32 employ the familiar pattern of thought, sin→ judgment→ repentance→ restoration.[53] These passages are too lengthy to reproduce in their entirety here, but I can summarize their content under the aforementioned rubric.

Sin: rebellion and stubbornness (1.7, 22; 23.16–17), idolatry (1.8, 9, 10, 11), disregard for the law (1.9, 10, 14; 23.16, 19), adopting Gentile practices (1.8, 23.14), disregard for the sanctuary (1.10; 23.21), moral decay (23.14–15, 16–17, 21).

Judgment: general affliction (1.8; 23.12–13, 15, 22, 23), foreign domination (1.10, 13, 19; 23.22–23, 24), exile (1.13, 15; 23.22), demonic oppression (1.20, 25; 23.29), physical degeneration (23.11, 15, 25), war (23.20–21), corruption of nature (23.18).

Repentance: seeking God (1.15, 23), return to the law (1.23–24; 23.26).

Restoration: return from exile (1.15), restoration of national identity (1.16; 23.30), restoration of temple cult (1.17, 29), moral renewal (1.15–18, 20, 22, 23–25; 23.26), divine presence (1.17–18, 25–28), physical longevity (23.27–28).

New creation:
... from [the time of creation until] the time of the New Creation
   when the heavens, the earth, and all their creatures will be renewed like the
   powers of the sky and like all the creatures of the earth,

---

[50] So Charles (1902: lxxxvii–lxxxix), Volz (1934: 28), Testuz (1960: 64), Davenport (1971: 1–2), Münchow (1981: 54), Rowland (1982: 167), Kugel (1994: 322).

[51] Charles (1902: 9, 150–51), F. Martin (1911: 527), Volz (1934: 28, 30), Davenport (1971: 45).

[52] This observation is directed against G. Schneider (1959) and Mell (1989), both of whom ignore the import of chapter 23 in relation to the motif of new creation.

[53] On this see Berger (1981: 440), Endress (1987: 51–62), Nickelsburg (1991: 77–78).

until the time when the temple of the Lord will be created in Jerusalem on Mt. Zion (1.29).[54]

The correspondences between the two passages are obvious, though it is striking that *Jubilees* 23 makes no explicit mention of a new or renewed creation. Offered as a concise summary of the deliverance described in the preceding verses, "new creation" in 1.29 articulates the hope for a complete reversal of the present crisis. In the intercessory prayer of Moses which interrupts the discourse (1.19–21), this dilemma is itemized in terms of three specific factors: sin, Satan, and the Gentiles:

And Moses fell upon his face, and he prayed and said, O Lord, my God, do not abandon your people and your inheritance
> *to walk in the error of their heart.*
And do not deliver them
> *into the hand of their enemy, the gentiles*, lest they rule over them and cause them to sin against you . . .
And do not let
> *the spirit of Beliar rule over them to accuse them* before you and ensnare them from every path of righteousness.

Not surprisingly, this situation is reversed in the eschatological renewal described in chapter 23:

And in those days,
> *children will begin to search the law*, and to search the commandments and to return to the way of righteousness . . .
> *And there will be no more Satan* nor any evil one who will destroy . . .
> *And they will drive out their enemies* (26–30).

This three-dimensional portrayal of the plight not only summarizes the perspective of chapters 1 and 23, it also provides the fundamental point of departure for the historical review contained in the remainder of the book. Because the author's perception of the problem directly informed his/her formulation of the solution, the ensuing analysis will also focus on the plight.

Sin, Satan, and the Gentiles

While the general contours of the plight are easily discernible from the two major eschatological passages, the proportions of each constituent

---

[54] VanderKam's translation (1989: 7), following Stone's reconstruction of the opening line (1971: 125–26), which is also adopted by Berger (1981) and Wintermute (1985).

and their relationship to the whole are fully disclosed only in the revealed history which surrounds this material. As the story of Israel's predicament is (fore)told, a very clear priority emerges within this triad, with Satan and the Gentiles bearing the primary weight of responsibility, and human depravity (individual or corporate) usually explained in relation to one of these.

Satan: the enemy of Israel. The "demonic clutter" of apocalyptic literature is well known,[55] and the activities of Satan, demons, and the angelic realm are notably emphasized in the early apocalypses of *1 Enoch* and *Jubilees*.[56] The author of *Jubilees* provides unique information on, among other things, the classes of angels (2.2, 18; cf. 1.25), their circumcised state (15.26–27), the work of "guardian" angels (15.31–32), and even the creation of the angelic host (2.2), an incident not previously accounted for in the surviving literature.[57] But *Jubilees'* most important contribution lies in its portrayal of the work of Satan and his cohorts, which plays a constitutive role in the strategy of this apocalypse.

Particularly eye-catching are the "corrections" which the author makes to the biblical text in an attempt to iron out its theological wrinkles while implicating the demonic realm. According to *Jubilees* it was Satan, not Yahweh or his angel, who was responsible for the near sacrifice of Isaac (17.16; 18.12), who planned to slay Moses on his way to confront Pharaoh (48.1–4; cf. Exod. 4.24–25), who killed the firstborn of Egypt (49.2–4), and who hardened Pharaoh's heart (48.9). More importantly however, the author of *Jubilees* blames these spiritual forces of evil for the introduction of astrology (8.3), disease (10.11–12), war (11.2–6), idolatry (11.4; cf. 1.11), slavery (11.3), murder (11.2–4), poverty (11.9–13), transgression of the law (7.27–29; 15.33–34), and all manner of evil:

> And cruel spirits assisted [the sons of Noah] and led them astray so that they might commit sin and pollution. And the prince, Mastema, acted forcefully to do all of this. And he sent other spirits to those who were set under his hand to practice all error and sin and all transgression, to destroy, to cause to perish and to pour out blood on the earth. (11.5)[58]

---

[55] Citing Charlesworth (1985: 66).

[56] See, e.g., F. Martin, (1911: 510–19), D. S. Russell (1964: 235–62), Rowland (1982: 78–12), Mach (1992). 4 Ezra is a notable exception.

[57] So VanderKam (1994: 307).

[58] Cf. 7.27; 10.1–5; 12.20; 4Q286 Frag. 7, 2.1–12. On the activities of Satan and the demonic realm cf. *1 Enoch* 9.6–7; 10.8; 13.2; 19.1; 40.7; *Apoc. Mos.* 7; *Mart. Is.* 1.8–2.6; *Apoc. Abr.* 13–14; *T. Jud.* 19; *T. Dan* 5–6; *T. Ben.* 6–7; 4Q286; 11Q11 1–5; 4Q510; 4Q390.

In the author's view, Satan exerts a legitimate and divinely granted authority over humanity (10.7–8; cf. *Apoc. Abr.* 23), so even the patriarchs Noah, Moses, and Abraham are obliged to pray for deliverance from his rule: "And [Abram] prayed . . . 'Save me from the hands of evil spirits which rule over the thought of the heart of man, and do not let them lead me astray from following you' " (12.20).[59] Charlesworth's description of humanity as "a helpless pawn" before these dark powers is an apt summary of the book of *Jubilees*.[60]

But the demonic realm is not only credited with ensuring the *dominance* of evil in the world, it is also held accountable for the *origin* of evil in the world, which the author traces to the story of the "watchers," those angels who united with human females (Gen. 6.1–5).[61] This explanation, of course, is hardly unique to *Jubilees*,[62] but its significance lies in the fact that in *Jubilees* it completely eclipses the story of Adam and Eve in the garden. Whereas the sin of Adam brings about the loss of edenic harmony and little more (3.17–31), note the consequences of the sin of the watchers:

> And injustice increased upon the earth, and all flesh corrupted its way; man and cattle and beasts and birds and everything which walks on the earth. And they all corrupted their way and their ordinances, and they began to eat one another. And injustices grew upon the earth and every imagination of the thoughts of all mankind was thus continually evil.   (5.2)

The author later describes the sin of the fallen angels as the "beginning of impurity" (7.21), and the weight which is placed on this event justifies Baudry's assessment: "Le récit, manifestement étiologique, permet d'expliquer les maux qui continuent à frapper les hommes, et dans ce cas,

[59] Cf. 1.20; 10.3–6; 19.28; 11QPs[a] 19.15. Although the author asserts in one place that Israel is not under the spirits as are the nations (15.31–32), it is clear that Israel has allowed itself to be drawn into such subjugation, which renders them all the more guilty (cf. 6.26–27; 10.1; 19.28). Similarly Testuz (1960: 84), Münchow (1981: 60).

[60] Charlesworth (1985: 66).

[61] Baudry's study (1992) of original sin in the OT pseudepigrapha is essential reading on the subject. Of the three explanations commonly offered for the presence of evil (Adam, human depravity, and demons), Baudry shows how the story of the watchers is preeminent in most of the literature, and supremely important in the early apocalypses of *1 Enoch* and *Jubilees*. The anthropological explanation is championed by 4 Ezra (less so in *2 Enoch*) while the Adamic solution is prominent in *Syriac Baruch* and the *Life of Adam and Eve*. Similar conclusions are reached by A. L. Thompson (1977).

[62] See *1 Enoch* 6–16; 64; 67.4–7; 69; 86–88; *2 Enoch* 7.1–4; 18.1–3; *3 Enoch* 28–29; *T. Reub.* 5.6–7; *T. Naph.* 3.5; *Sib. Or.* 1.87–124; CD 2.18; 1QapGen 2.1; 4Q510; 4Q525; 4Q545.

sans avoir recours au péché d'Adam."[63] So devastating were the consequences of the sin of the watchers, that *Jubilees* has God renewing the entirety of creation shortly thereafter: "And he made for all his works a new
and righteous nature so that they might not sin in all their nature forever,
and so that they might all be righteous, each in his kind, always" (5.12).[64]

Given the author's belief that the present order was the domain of
Satan, his vision of the ideal state and of the future world, repeated like
a refrain throughout the narrative, is almost predictable: "And there was
no Satan and there was no evil" (40.9).[65]

The Gentiles: "le mot abhorré."[66] But the world was not only cluttered
with demons, it was also populated with Gentiles, and the author spares
no ink in his demand that Israel "be separate from the Gentiles . . . because
all of their deeds are defiled, and all of their ways are contaminated, and
despicable, and abominable" (22.16).[67] I have already discussed *Jubilees'*
retelling of Dinah's rape, which provided a divine mandate for the ex-
termination of the Gentiles, and briefly mentioned the "code names"
employed by the author in his anti-Gentile polemic (Sodom, Canaan,
the Edomites, the Philistines, etc.), and to these should be added certain
ethical expressions used to designate non-Jews: "children of destruction" (15.26; cf. 20.6), "children of perdition" (10.3), "sons of Beliar"
(15.33–34), "the enemy" (1.19; 23.30; 24.29; 30.17), "sinners" (16.5–6;
22.23, 24; 24.28), "idol worshipers" (22.22), or simply "the hated ones"
(22.22).

One selection from the narrative perfectly illustrates the author's dis-
dain for all things Gentile. The lengthy and moving account in Genesis
of Abraham interceding for Sodom, bargaining with God in an attempt
to spare the city, is entirely omitted by the author of *Jubilees*. We are
given only a summary record of Sodom's sin and destruction, and are

---

[63] Baudry (1992: 171). So too, F. Martin (1911: 545), Testuz (1960: 83, 198), Berger
(1981: 282), Münchow (1981: 60), Wintermute (1985: 47).

[64] Although Charles emended this text to give it an eschatological reference, "And he
shall make . . ." (1902: 44–45), most regard this correction as unnecessary: F. Martin (1911:
509), Volz (1934: 30, 337), Davenport (1971: 48), Berger (1981: 15), VanderKam (1989:
33). Similar traditions concerning God's renewal of creation after the fall are transmitted
by Philo (*Vita Mos.* 2.59–65), Josephus (*Ant.* 1.75), *1 Enoch* 10.7–8, and *2 Enoch* 70.9–10.

[65] Cf. 23.29; 46.2; 50.5; *1 Enoch* 69; *T. Lev.* 18.12; *T. Dan* 6.4; *Apoc. El.* 5.36–39;
As. Mos. 10.1; 1QM 1.5; 4QPs 10.5–14; Rev. 20.2.

[66] F. Martin's phrase summarizing *Jubilees'* attitude toward Gentiles (1911: 528).

[67] The anti-Gentile polemic in *Jubilees* is severe, and often commented on in the secondary literature. See Charles (1902: lv–lvi), F. Martin (1911: 528), Davenport (1971:
72–73), Wintermute (1985: 47), Endress (1987: 236–38). Solomon Zeitlin, a Jewish scholar,
remarked that "the book is permeated by a chauvinistic spirit" (1939/40: 30), though such
appraisals need to be read against the historical backdrop sketched above.

left with the distinct impression that the author did not entirely approve of Abraham's concern for this wicked Gentile city (cf. *Jub.* 16.5–6 with Gen. 18.16–19.29).[68]

In the same way that Satan and the demonic realm exercised dominion over Israel and led them astray, so too did the Gentiles (1.9–10, 19; 6.35; 12.29; 15.34; 21.21–24) who, "because of all the evil of pollution of their errors . . . have filled the earth with sin and pollution and fornication and transgression" (9.15).[69] In his/her more charitable moments, the author envisions only the eschatological triumph of Israel over the nations: "And I shall give to your seed all of the land under heaven and they will rule in all nations as they have desired. And after this all of the earth will be gathered together and they will inherit it forever" (32.19; cf. 7.11–12; 19.18–19; 22.11–12; 23.29–30; 31.18–19; 38.14). More typical, however, is language of destruction:

> [And they shall be]
> . . . destroyed and annihilated from the earth and uprooted from the earth (15.26)
> . . . uprooted and destroyed from the earth and they shall be cursed.   (31.20; cf. 15.34; 20.4; 22.20; 26.34; 31.17, 19–20)

In chapter 24 the author fabricates an elaborate speech of denunciation and places it on the lips of Jacob. Although formally a curse against the Philistines, no one questions its wider contemporary application:[70]

> And no remnant will be left to them, nor one who escapes on the day of the wrath of judgment; because all of the Philistine seed is (destined) for destruction and uprooting and removal from the earth. And, therefore, there will not be any name or seed which remains upon the earth for any of the Caphtorim. Because if they go up to heaven, from there they will fall; and if they are set firm in the earth, from there they will be torn out . . . and neither name nor seed will be left for them in all the earth, because they shall walk in an eternal curse.   (24.30–32)

[68] As 16.6, 20.1–8 and 22.22 reveal, the wickedness of Sodom and its final destruction is intended by the author as a reference to the moral character and ultimate demise of *all* Gentiles. Cf. the prophecy in *T. Naph.* 4.1: "And you will stray from the Lord, living in accord with *every wickedness of the gentiles* and committing *every lawlessness of Sodom.*"

[69] Although ostensibly an admonishment to Noah's sons, this verse actually has in view the territorial ambitions of contemporary foreign powers. See Volz (1934: 238), Berger (1981: 375), and compare the language of 6.35; 21.19–22; 22.16–23.

[70] See, e.g., Charles (1902: 155), Berger (1981: 447), Wintermute (1985: 104), Sanders (1992: 291–92).

The author of *Jubilees* says nothing of the repentance of any Gentile, nor gives any hint that they could be included as proselytes within God's people. Testuz concludes that, according to *Jubilees*, "[un Gentil] est et reste un Gentil, soumis aux démons, vivant dans le péché, l'impureté, le sacrilège, et condamné irrémédiablement à la destruction."[71] The cumulative evidence suggests that the author hoped for an eschaton that was entirely Gentile-free:

> And for all of those who worship idols and for the hated ones [= Gentiles], there is no hope in the land of the living; because they will go down into Sheol. And in the place of judgment they will walk and they will have no memory upon the earth. Just as the sons of Sodom were taken from the earth, so too all of those who worship idols shall be taken away. (22.22)

Not surprisingly, *Jubilees'* insistence on the final demise of the nations and the ultimate triumph of Israel was succinctly presaged in the eschatological material of the opening chapter: "And they [Israel] shall be the head and not the tail" (1.16).[72]

New creation: anthropological renewal

Although rarely noted in the monographs, articles, and theses dedicated to exploring the background to Paul's new-creation statements, the motif of new creation has an anthropological as well as a cosmological expression in apocalyptic, and the book of *Jubilees* in particular, and only prejudicial selectivity can account for its omission in the secondary literature. Both major eschatological passages promise an anthropological renewal in the eschaton, though each has its own distinct focus. Chapter 1 speaks of a moral renewal expected in the new age, while chapter 23 looks forward to physical renewal and increased longevity, as in the period before the sin of the Watchers (see 23.8–10).

Moral renovation

The promise of moral renewal in the eschaton is a familiar theme in prophetic-apocalyptic Jewish literature, though it is normally expressed in terms of the expansion of righteousness and/or the elimination of evil:[73]

[71] Testuz (1960: 74).
[72] A biblical saying denoting a position of dominance (cf. Deut. 28.13, 44; *1 Enoch* 103.11; 11Q19 59.20–21).
[73] See Koenig (1971).

> And every iniquitous deed will end, and the plant of righteousness and truth will appear forever.   (*1 Enoch* 10.16)

> Thenceforth nothing that is corruptible shall be found . . . and all evil shall disappear.   (*1 Enoch* 69.29)

> Bad government, blame, envy, anger, folly, poverty will flee from men . . . and every evil in those days.   (*Sib. Or.* 3.377–80)

> And this will be the sign that this is going to happen. When those born of sin are locked up, evil will disappear in front of justice.   (1Q27 1.5)

> and a judgment of vengeance to exterminate wickedness . . . and there will be purity amongst those purified.   (4Q511 35.1–3)

> Sinful indulgence has come to an end, unbelief has been cut off, and righteousness has increased and truth has appeared.   (4 Ezra 7.114)

Passages of this variety could be multiplied a hundredfold,[74] but the (near) uniqueness of *Jubilees* 1 lies in its emphasis on the *inwardness* of the renovation expected in the age to come:

> But after this they will return to me in all righteousness and with all of their heart and soul. And I shall cut off the foreskin of the heart of their descendants. And I shall create for them a holy spirit, and I shall purify them so that they will not turn away from following me from that day and forever.   (1.23)

Descriptions of a glorious outer transformation, "garments of unending light," and so on, are more common in the literature of the period,[75] but rarely is the notion of a profound inner transformation accentuated, as Gowan points out: "Jewish literature does occasionally speak of a new heart/spirit, etc., but the notions of a drastic internal change are not developed."[76]

---

[74] Cf. *Jub.* 4.26; 50.5; *1 Enoch* 5.8–9; 49.2–3; 50.1–5; 56.8; 91.11–17; 92. 4–5; 100.5; *2 Enoch* 65–66; *T. Dan* 6.6; *Pss. Sol.* 17.21–46; *Syr. Bar.* 73.4–5; 4 Ezra 6.27–28; 7.112–14; 1QS 4.20–23; 4Q300 3.1–6; 4Q171, etc.

[75] See *1 Enoch* 38.4; 50.1; 90.37–39; 108.11–13; *Syr. Bar.* 51.1–3; *2 Enoch* 22.8–10; 66.7; *3 Enoch* 12.1–2; *As. Is.* 9.8–10; 1QS 4.6–8, 22–23; 1QM 1.8; CD 3.20; 4Q504 8.1–5; 4Q548; 1QSb 4.25–28; Wisd. 3.7. Cf. Rom. 8.23; 2 Cor. 5.4; Phil. 3.21.

[76] Gowan (1986: 79). The clearest examples of inner renewal in the eschaton come from *T. Judah* 24 and *T. Levi* 18, both of which may reflect Christian influence (so de Jonge [1975: 210–19]). Less pronounced are 4 Ezra 6.25–28; *Apoc. Mos.* 13.5; *Ep. Bar.* 2.30–35; *T. Dan* 5.11; 1QS 4.19–23; 4Q521 frag. 2, col. 2; Descriptions of a present inner renewal

In comparison with the prophetic material surveyed in the previous section, and the eschatological renewal envisioned by the latter prophets (chapter 2), two important differences are immediately apparent. First, unlike Jeremiah and Ezekiel, who believed Israel was hardened beyond repentance, the author of *Jubilees* fully expects Israel to amend its ways and rededicate itself to God and Torah. Note the sequence of events envisioned in 1.15:

Cause		*Effect*
And afterwards they will turn to me from among the nations with all their heart and with all their soul and with all their might.	→	*And I shall gather them from the midst of all the nations.*
And they will seek me	→	*so that I might be found by them.*
When they seek me with all their heart and with all their soul,	→	*I shall reveal to them an abundance of peace in righteousness.*

The same sequence is outlined in 1.22–23:

Cause		*Effect*
And they will not obey until they acknowledge their sin and the sins of their fathers. But after this they will return to me in all righteousness and with all of their heart and soul.	→	*And I shall cut off the foreskin of their heart.*

Quite unlike Jeremiah, and Ezekiel, the book of *Jubilees* makes God's re-creative activity *contingent* upon Israel's return rather than *enabling* that return, and this suggests a more optimistic anthropology than we observed in the previous section.[77]

Second, in spite of the prophetic expectation of an eschatological outpouring of God's Spirit (see chapter 8), the author of *Jubilees* allows no role for the divine Spirit in the eschaton. This assertion might seem questionable in light of the prayer of Moses in 1.21 (cf. 1.23), but this text does not describe an outpouring and infusion of the *divine* Spirit, but a renewal of the *human* spirit, as every translation acknowledges.[78] On closer inspection, 1.21 appears to be a conscious recollection of the

---

are frequent in the literature from Qumran: 1QH; 1QS 3.3–10; 4Q434, 436, 437. Cf. also 4 Ezra 8.53; *Jos. As.* 8.9 (chapter 4).

[77] This optimistic anthropology is especially evident in 5.12, where the author explains that God gave "a new and righteous nature" to all of his creation after the sin of the watchers.

[78] The passage is never translated as a reference to the divine Spirit.

prayer for moral renewal found in Psalm 51:[79]

Psalm 51.12		Jubilees 1.21
Create in me a clean heart, and renew a right spirit in me.	→	Create a pure heart and a holy spirit for them.

Although the divine Spirit is not the agent effecting this inner transformation, "new creation" is a thoroughly appropriate designation for what the author describes, as Sjöberg attests: "In Jub wird diese Erneuerung des Herzens und des Geistes der Menschen nun ausdrücklich als eine Neuschöpfung bezeichnet."[80]

Physical rejuvenation

Whereas chapter 1 concentrates on the inner moral renewal of the age to come, chapter 23 highlights the restoration of physical strength and longevity. As before, this physical renewal is predicated upon a prior return to the law:

Cause		Effect
And in those days children will begin to search the law, and to search the commandments and to return to the way of righteousness. (23.26)	→	*And the days will begin to increase and grow longer among those sons of men . . . until their days approach a thousand years.* (23.27)

Accompanying this somatic renewal are healing, peace, the elimination of Satan, and the expulsion of Israel's enemies (29–30). This period of physical longevity and earthly bliss has many parallels in related literature of the period,[81] and is enunciated by the author in terms which are evocative of his/her earlier promise of a new creation. The relationship between the two passages has been variously construed, and is not without relevance as I consider the cosmological dimension of this motif.

New creation: cosmological transformation

I noted earlier that despite the similarities between chapter 1 and chapter 23, the latter passage makes no mention of a new creation, even though the motif seems intrinsic to the author's eschatological hopes. Most writers assume that the author envisions a gradual transformation of the earth

---

[79] Correctly Charles (1902: 6), G. Schneider (1959: 80). Cf. Vos (1973: 51).

[80] Sjöberg (1950: 71). So too Testuz: "Il y aura . . . une nouvelle création de la nature entière, comme du coeur des hommes" (1960: 198).

[81] E.g., *1 Enoch* 5.9–10; 10.17–22; *2 Enoch* 65.8–11; *Syr. Bar.* 73–74; 1QS 4.6–8; *Sib. Or.* 3.741–61; Isa. 65.17–25.

(chapter 23) which ultimately leads to a new or renewed creation (1.29; 4.26).[82] Alternatively, it might be possible that "new creation" in *Jubilees* functions more as a cipher for eschatological bliss, not unlike the phrase "the day of great peace" (23.30; 25.20; 31.19). On this reading, the renewals described in chapters 1 and 23 are not consecutive, but equivalent; both articulate in different imagery the final victory of Israel and the ultimate redemption of the created order. Although not precise in every detail, the correspondences between 1.29 and 23.27–31 lend support to this fresh interpretation:[83]

	Jubilees 1.29 Until the day of the New Creation . . .	*Jubilees* 23.27–31 until their days approach a thousand years . . .
Renewal of the natural order	when the heaven and earth and all their creatures shall be renewed according to the powers of heaven and according to the whole nature of earth,	And there will be no old men and none who is full of days. Because all of them will be infants and children.
Expulsion of the Gentiles	until the sanctuary is created in Jerusalem and upon Mt Zion[84]	And they will drive out their enemies . . . and they will see all of their judgments and all of their curses among their enemies . . . and they will know that the Lord is an executor of judgment.
Blessing, peace, healing	And all of the lights will be renewed for healing and peace and blessing for all of the elect of Israel.	. . . all of their days will be days of blessing and healing. And the Lord will heal his servants and they will rise up and see great peace.

Even though new creation in 1.29 is immediately described in terms of the renewal of the natural order, which is remarkably similar to 23.27–28,

[82] Charles (1902: xiv), D. S. Russell (1964: 292), Davenport (1971: 45, 78). Cf. F. Martin (1911: 527–30), Testuz (1960: 171–72).

[83] Although this position has not been developed previously, writers on *Jubilees* often discuss these passages together as if they were parallel texts, and the interpretation offered here is at least hinted at in the comments of F. Martin (1911: 527), Davenport (1971: 45), and Nickelsburg (1991: 78, 94–95).

[84] I suggest that in light of the events surrounding the Maccabean uprisings, the desecration of the sanctuary and the military campaigns of Judas to retake the Temple area (1 Macc. 3.42–4.60), it is very likely that *Jubilees'* anachronistic concern for the re-establishment of the sanctuary (25.21; 31.14; cf. 4.26) reflects a military objective as well as a cultic-religious aspiration. See also 1QpHab 12.

the evidence for equating the two renewals is not decisive. What is clear, however, is that in the central eschatological passage of the book the hope for a renewed heaven and earth recedes behind dreams of a national and military resurgence, and it is very likely that the two eschatological visions were not sharply distinguished by the author. Indeed, on either reading, new creation in *Jubilees* is intimately connected with the defeat of the earthly and demonic powers responsible for Israel's predicament, and this is entirely consistent with the primary function of the eschatological material in the apocalypses.

New creation: restoration and reversal

Eschatology and the apocalyptic paradigm

I spoke earlier of the "apocalyptic paradigm" and argued that the primary role of eschatology and the motif of new creation within this paradigm was to enable the suffering elect of Israel to make sense of their present circumstances through the promise of ultimate redemption and vindication. The literature of the period provides an enormous amount of illustrative material in support of this point, which, as far as I am aware, is not controversial. In addition to the elimination of Satan and evil which I noted earlier, the visionaries of the period dreamt of the day when the yoke of Gentile oppression would be finally broken, and this hope, understandably, figured prominently in their descriptions of the day of judgment and the age to come. The eschatological material of *1 Enoch* is saturated with this idea:

> From that time, those who possess the earth will neither be rulers nor princes ... At that moment kings and rulers shall perish, they shall be delivered into the hands of the righteous and holy ones.
> (*1 Enoch* 38.4–5)

> In those days the kings of the earth and the mighty landowners will be humiliated.   (48.8)

> They are preparing these [chains] for the kings and potentates of the earth in order that they may be destroyed thereby ... and the righteous ones will have rest from the oppression of sinners.
> (53.6–7)

> On that day, all the kings, the governors, the high officials, and all those who rule the earth shall fall down before him ... he will deliver them to the angels for punishments in order that

vengeance shall be executed on them – oppressors of his children
and his elect ones. (62.9–12)

Those waters shall become in those days a poisonous drug . . .
unto the kings, rulers, and exalted ones. (67.8)

Similarly, the writer of *Syriac Baruch* speaks of the day when "all those
who now have ruled over you . . . will be delivered up to the sword" (72.6),
while the psalmist believes the Davidic messiah will come "to destroy
unrighteous rulers, to purge Jerusalem from gentiles" (*Pss. Sol.* 17.22).
According to the *Apocalypse of Abraham*, God's anointed "will summon
[his] people, humiliated by the heathen. And [he] will burn with fire those
who mocked them and ruled over them in this age" (31.1–2). Many more
such texts could be cited, but that would be to belabor the obvious.[85] The
judgment and eradication of the earthly powers that harassed Israel during
the present age were so important to these visionaries that the coming age
could be described simply as "the age of peace" (4QTNaph 2.5) or "eternal
peace" (*Syr. Bar.* 73.1; *T. Dan* 5.11), or "great peace" (*Sib. Or.* 3.755;
Jub. 23.30; 25.20; 31.20), in which the righteous will hear "a voice of
rest from heaven" (*1 Enoch* 96.3). On this day "the sword will cease in
the earth" (4Q246) because God himself "will remove the sword that has
threatened since Adam" (*T. Lev.* 18.10), and there will be "no more iron
for war, nor shall anyone wear a breastplate" (*1 Enoch* 52.8–9). "From
that time on," writes the visionary, "the righteous ones shall sleep a restful
sleep, and there shall be no one to make them afraid" (*1 Enoch* 100.5).[86]

The prominence of this hope for eschatological redemption and national vindication in the apocalypses has prompted E. P. Sanders to
suggest that the themes of *restoration* and *reversal* are not only "characteristic" of apocalyptic, but also "generative" of these works, in that "the
authors intended to promise restoration from present oppression."[87] While
this proposal fits less easily with the apocalypses that focus on other-
worldly journeys, it is certainly relevant to the historical apocalypses,
which were concerned to provide hope for those enduring desperate
times. The apocalyptic hope for a new creation should be interpreted

[85] A further sampling of passages would include *1 Enoch* 49.2; 60–63; 94–100; *2 Enoch*
66.6; *Syr. Bar.* 13; 80–83; *Sib. Or.* 295–400; 1Q27 1.3–11; 4Q171 2–3; 4Q161; *T. Mos.*
10.2; 4 Ezra 6.19, etc.

[86] See also 1 Macc. 14.11; *Arist.* 291; *Sib. Or.* 3.780; *T. Levi* 18.5; 1QM 1.9; 4Q431
1.1–9.

[87] Sanders (1989: 458–59), who follows in the steps of Volz: "Weil es nun im Diesseits
gerade umgekehrt ging, als man nach dem Recht hätte sollen, so bringt der eschatologische
Akt der Vegeltung eine völlige Umkehrung des Bisherigen . . . es geschieht eine Umwand-
lung für die Heiligen und Auserwählten" (1934: 126).

within this pattern of thought, *restoration* and *reversal*, and in keeping with the eschatological material cited above, is usually explicitly set in antithesis to the present crisis and the oppression of foreign domination.

New creation and the apocalyptic paradigm

François Martin correctly points out that in the opening chapter of *Jubilees* the promise of a new creation (1.23–29) follows, "à peu près sans transition l'annonce de ci qui adviendra après la captivité" (1.7–21),[88] and this is what we would expect given the purpose of the book just disclosed: "And the Lord revealed to him both what was in the beginning and what will occur in the future . . . and he said, 'Set your mind on every thing which I shall tell you on this mountain, and write it in a book *so that their descendants might see that I have not abandoned them . . .* ' " (1.5). And as we saw earlier, in the eschatological material of chapter 23 the renewal of the natural order is virtually coterminous with the realization of political and military ambitions.

The *Apocalypse of Weeks* (*1 Enoch* 91–93) speaks of a day of judgment when "the first heaven shall depart and pass away – a new heaven shall appear" (91.16). This "eternal judgment" (91.10, 15) and cosmic transformation are necessary because of the situation described in the preceding verses:

> For I know that the state of violence will intensify upon the earth; a great plague shall be executed upon the earth; all forms of oppression will be carried out and everything shall be uprooted and every arrow shall fly fast. Oppression shall recur once more and be carried out upon the earth . . . In those days, injustice shall be cut off from its sources of succulent fountain and from its roots – likewise oppression together with deceit; they shall be destroyed from underneath heaven. All that which is common with the heathen shall be surrendered; the towers shall be inflamed with fire and be removed from the whole of the earth . . . and those who design oppression and commit blasphemy shall perish by the knife.   (91.5–11)

The key words of this macabre oracle are "oppression," "injustice," and "the heathen," and it is precisely this grim triad which will be vanquished by the coming of the new world.

---

[88] F. Martin (1911: 527 n. 10).

As illustrated earlier, the *Similitudes of Enoch* (*1 Enoch* 37–71) have much to say in judgment of the rulers and potentates who have oppressed Israel, so it is perfectly fitting that its vision of the new creation is explained as a day of "peace" for the elect: "And I will transform heaven and make it an eternal blessing and light. And I will transform the dry ground and make it a blessing . . . for I have seen, and have satisfied with peace my righteous ones" (45.5–6).[89]

In the apocalypse of 4 Ezra, the anthropological dilemma receives special emphasis (3.20–27), but it is the question of Gentile oppression that leads to the statements about the new creation (7.30–32, 47, 50, 75). In 6.55–59 Ezra asks,

> As for the other nations which have descended from Adam, you have said that they are nothing, and they are like spittle . . . And now, O Lord, behold, these nations which are reputed as nothing domineer over us and devour us . . . If the world has indeed been created for us, why do we not possess our world as an inheritance? How long will this be so?

This prompts the Angel Uriel to reveal that the earth itself will experience a death and rebirth following the death of the messiah (7.26–31), in which "the corruptible shall perish" (7.31). Ezra then refers to this as the renewal of creation (7.75), and every indication suggests that this doctrine was articulated as a response to Ezra's question about continued foreign domination.

A similar connection is made in *Syriac Baruch*. In chapter 31, the legendary scribe of Jeremiah exhorts his compatriots, "Do not forget Zion but remember the distress of Jerusalem. For behold the days are coming that all that has been will be taken away to be destroyed, and it will become as though it had not been" (31.5). This leads to a prediction concerning the destruction of Jerusalem and the subsequent glorification of the Temple (32.1–4), and the concluding admonition: "We should not, therefore, be so sad regarding the evil which has come now . . . For greater than the two evils will be the trial when the Mighty One will renew his creation" (32.5–6).

The renewal of creation is elsewhere linked to foreign domination in *Syriac Baruch* (e.g., 44.2–15; 57.2 with chapters 72–74), and in one of the final chapters of this apocalypse the writer elaborates on the great eschatological reversal of fortunes which will come:

---

[89] Translation by Charles in Sparks (1984).

And we should not look upon the delights of the present nations,
but let us think about that which has been promised to us regarding the end . . . The end of the world will then show the great
power of our Ruler, since everything will come to judgment . . .
> For all sorts of health which exist now will be changed into
> illness.
> And every might which exists now changes into weakness
> and every power that exists now changes into miseries,
> and every youthful energy changes into old age and consum-
> mation.
> And every beauty of gracefulness which exists now changes
> into withering and ugliness.
> And every infantile pride which exists now changes into low-
> liness and shame . . .   (83.5–23)

Although I could draw on other illustrative material, one final passage
will have to suffice. The *Assumption of Moses* promises a day when
God's kingdom "will appear throughout his whole creation," when "the
devil will have an end," and when "sorrow will be led away" (10.1).
Verses 3–6 then describe a great cosmic destruction in which the earth,
sun, moon, and stars are decimated. Bracketing this eschatological
cataclysm as a kind of interpretive inclusio are the words, "Yea he will at
once avenge them of their enemies" (10.2) . . . "In full view he will come
to work vengeance on the nations" (10.7).

Summary and conclusions

While my aims in this section have been modest, the foregoing analysis
will have important implications as I attempt to compare and contrast
the motif of new creation in Paul and apocalyptic. One conclusion that
should be highlighted at this point concerns the very real expectation of a
profound anthropological renewal in the world to come. As an eschatological theme, new creation has both a cosmological and an anthropological
nuance in apocalyptic Judaism, and any alleged *traditionsgeschichtliche*
evaluation of this motif in Paul's letters must take both into account.

The most important conclusion, however, relates to the function of the
new-creation motif within the apocalyptic paradigm. The examination of
Jubilees, supplemented through corroborating material, has shown that
new creation in apocalyptic was formulated in response to the dilemma
as it was perceived by these writers. Particularly important in their analysis of the plight was the oppressive dominion of Satan and the Gentiles,

and the book of *Jubilees* represents an especially eloquent statement of this position. Battling both earthly and heavenly forces, the apocalyptic visionaries felt the cosmos itself closing in around them, and it is hardly surprising that their picture of the future was that of a completely transformed universe.

While not completely unaware of the enemy within, "the evil inclination" which prevented complete obedience, this notion does not receive the attention in pre-AD 70 apocalyptic literature that it did later. Vermes remarks that "In the domain of apocalypticism . . . the central theme is often the revelation of the ultimate triumph of justice over the wicked secular powers,"[90] and this evaluation is supported by the preceding analysis. When the plight is perceived primarily in terms of extrinsic factors, political and demonic oppression, it follows that the solution will be similarly conceived: a newly created cosmos. It is this hope which animated the eschatological vision of the apocalyptic writers, and nowhere is this perspective more clearly enunciated than in the closing chapters of Revelation: "Then I saw a new heaven and a new earth . . . and God will wipe every tear from their eyes, and death, and mourning, and crying, and pain will be no more."

[90] Vermes in Schürer (vol. III.1, 1986: 241).

4

NEW CREATION IN DIASPORA JUDAISM:
JOSEPH AND ASENETH

> The theme of death and rebirth, of course, has other symbolic
> functions: the initiates die to their old life and are reborn to
> the new. The whole repertoire of ideas concerning pollution and
> purification is used to mark the gravity of the event and the power
> of ritual to remake a man – this is straightforward.
>
> Mary Douglas, *Purity and Danger*

Plot summary

The story of *Joseph and Aseneth*, a Hellenistic romance of Diaspora
Judaism,[1] takes as its point of departure the curious statement of Genesis
41.45: "Pharaoh gave Joseph the name Zaphenath-Paneah and gave him
Aseneth, daughter of Potiphera, priest of On to be his wife." The marriage
of a venerated patriarch to the daughter of a pagan priest would have
certainly raised a few (Jewish) eyebrows and invited explanation. Such
an explanation would be all the more relevant if also employed to address
specific concerns within the author's community.

With these twin goals in mind, *Joseph and Aseneth* tells the story
of a beautiful, if high-minded, Egyptian virgin (Aseneth) who spurns the
suggestion of her father that she marry Joseph, "the powerful one of God"
(4.7),[2] insisting that only Pharaoh's firstborn is her equal. Aseneth's pride
is soon turned to shame when Joseph arrives in his golden chariot, royal
attire, and angelic splendor (5.1–7). Further humiliation awaits the love-
struck Egyptian when Joseph refuses her kiss of greeting and offers her
instead a sermon on the inappropriateness of a God-fearing man whose

---

[1] On this genre classification see Philonenko (1968: esp. 43–48), Burchard (1970:
66–81), West (1974: 70–81), Kee (1983: 394), Chesnutt (1995: 35–92), Wills (1995:
170–84), Barclay (1996: 204–216).

[2] The Greek text, chapter and verse divisions are those of Burchard (1996: 163–209). The
English translation given here follows Burchard (*OTP*) closely, only occasionally diverging
from his text.

lips bless the living God kissing a "foreign woman" whose lips bless lifeless idols (8.5). Seeing Aseneth's dejection, Joseph prays that God would re-create her by his Spirit and that she might one day be numbered among God's people (8.9). What follows (chapters 9–13) is a lengthy prayer and confession of sin by Aseneth which leads to a visitation from "a man from heaven . . . the chief of the house of the lord" (14.3–7). After a number of mysterious rituals symbolizing Aseneth's new status, the first act of the drama is brought to a fitting consummation in Aseneth's marriage to Joseph (chapters 20–21).

Chapters 22–29 are markedly different in content and theme, which has prompted Burchard to describe *Joseph and Aseneth* as a "Doppelnovelle."[3] This section concentrates on a plot by Pharaoh's son to kill Joseph and take Aseneth for his bride. The scheme is foiled through a number of mishaps and the romance concludes with Joseph reigning in Egypt on Pharaoh's throne for forty-eight years, with the beautiful Aseneth at his side.

Language, date, provenance, and character

While not every feature of *Joseph and Aseneth* is fully understood,[4] there is broad agreement on the important introductory issues of original language, date, provenance, and Jewish character. Christoph Burchard's early work on the textual and literary history of *Joseph and Aseneth* removed any doubt that the original language of this document was Greek.[5] Its date is usually fixed between 100 BC and AD 100, and Charlesworth accurately summarizes the consensus in describing *Joseph and Aseneth* as "roughly contemporaneous with the New Testament."[6] An Egyptian provenance is considered "ein weithin gesichertes Ergebnis der Forschung,"[7] as is its Jewish character. While *Joseph and Aseneth* clearly employs imagery and symbolism drawn from a pagan environment, thus expressing Jewish faith in a contemporary medium and thought-form, it is nonetheless true, as Goodman remarks, that "the ideas expressed [in *Joseph and Aseneth*] would be perfectly possible for any Jew."[8] The

---

[3] Burchard (1983: 592).

[4] The two most frequently discussed issues are the history-of-religions relationship between *Joseph and Aseneth* and the mystery cults (cf. Philonenko [1968: 53–109], Sänger [1980], Kee [1983: 394–413], Chesnutt [1995: 185–253]), and the precise significance of the meal formulas in 8.5, 9; 15.5; 16.16; 19.5 and 21.13–21. On this see the comprehensive survey of Burchard (1987: 102–34).

[5] Burchard (1965: 91–99).   [6] Charlesworth (1976: 42).   [7] Sänger (1979: 11).

[8] Goodman in Schürer (1986: 548–49). Cf. Burchard's earlier assessment: "Es gibt . . . in ihr kein Satz, der nicht jüdisch sein könnte" (1965: 99).

strong consensus on these issues includes Burchard, Denis, Charlesworth, Nickelsburg, Collins, Leaney, Goodman, D. S. Russell, Chesnutt, Barclay, and Feldman and Rheinhold,[9] and provides a solid foundation for the present analysis.[10]

Purpose and theme

In general terms, *Joseph and Aseneth* can be considered religious propaganda aimed at portraying Judaism in the best possible light. Attempts to identify the purpose of *Joseph and Aseneth* invariably focus on the theme of conversion,[11] and E. P. Sanders has gone as far as calling conversion "the *raison d'être*" of the story.[12] While not disputing the central role of Aseneth's conversion, it is important to distinguish between the *main theme* of the book, and the *reason(s)* for which it was written.

One of the central issues surfacing repeatedly throughout the narrative has to do with proper social intercourse between Jews and Gentiles. From the opening description of Aseneth as one who "had nothing similar [in appearance] to the virgins of the Egyptians, but she was in every respect similar to the daughters of the Hebrews" (1.5), it is clear that the tensions between two communities are in the foreground. Joseph's refusal to eat at the same table with his host (7.1), as well as his rejection of Aseneth's kiss

---

[9] Burchard (1965, 1983, 1985, 1987), Denis (1970: 40–48), Charlesworth (1976: 137–40; 1981: 291–92), Nickelsburg (1981: 158–63; 271–72; 1984a: 65–70), Collins (1983: 89–91; 211–18), Leaney (1984: 169–70), Goodman in Schürer (1986: 546–52), D. S. Russell (1987: 91–94), Chesnutt (1995: 80–85), Barclay (1996: 204–10), Feldman and Rheinhold (1996: 54).

[10] On the basis of alleged non-Jewish symbolism in *Joseph and Aseneth*, Holtz argued that its present form betrays a later Christian editor (1968: 482–97). Few (if any) have been persuaded. Holtz assumes a monolithic form of first-century Judaism in which "new birth" and "son of God" language was unknown. Such a paradigm is no longer tenable. More recently, Gideon Bohak (1996) has dated *Joseph and Aseneth* as early as 170 BCE, though his highly conjectural allegorical reading of *Joseph and Aseneth* has been heavily criticized by Chesnutt (1996). Moving in the opposite direction, Ross Kraemer (1998), has challenged each of the major tenets of the critical consensus: date, provenance, religious orientation, and textual history. Stricty speaking, Kraemer remains "steadfastly agnostic" (1998: 301) on the religious identity of the author, though she seems inclined toward a Christian origin of *Joseph and Aseneth* in the third or fourth century CE. While more substantive than Bohak's work, Kraemer's unbridled enthusiasm for (often strained) history-of-religions parallels severely compromises her conclusions, and has garnered critical comments by reviewers (Inowlocki [1999], Bauckham [2000], Bohak [2000], Chesnutt [2000]). While illuminating at many points, Kraemer's research does not warrant abandoning the very large consensus on the issues of the date, provenance, and religious orientation of *Joseph and Aseneth*.

[11] See, e.g., Sänger (1979: 11–36), Burchard (1983: 601), Nickelsburg (1984b: 65–71), Goodman in Schürer (1986: 548), R. C. Douglas (1988: 31–42), Chesnutt (1995: 264), Barclay (1996: 205), Feldman and Rheinhold (1996: 54), etc.

[12] Sanders (1976: 23).

(8.5–7), are explained on the basis of his convictions regarding proper Jew–Gentile relations: "for this is an abomination before the Lord God" (8.7; cf. 7.1). Joseph's description of Jews in contrast to Gentiles (8.5–6) is particularly pointed in that it not only dismisses all non-Jews as idolatrous, but also carefully delineates the proper object of a Jewish man's affection: "But a man who worships God will kiss his mother and the sister of his mother and the sister of his clan and family and the wife who shares his bed." Chesnutt's conclusion warrants attention: "The story is addressing vital social issues. The milieu of JosAsen evidently was one in which Jews lived in dynamic tension with gentiles and struggled to maintain a distinctive Jewish identity. The polluting effect of intermarriage and of table fellowship with gentiles was of grave concern to the author."[13]

Yet even with this caveat in place, there is little doubt that the central purpose of *Joseph and Aseneth* is conveyed through its elaborate and sophisticated portrayal of Aseneth's conversion to Judaism. John Barclay, and others, are correct to emphasize *Joseph and Aseneth*'s portrayal of conversion to Judaism as "a path to personal transformation,"[14] and there is no reason to restrict the author of this work to either individual or social concerns. The two are inextricably connected.

With this in mind, it is possible to identify one text as the thematic center of the book, in that all the major motifs used to portray Aseneth's conversion are concentrated here. This verse, 8.9, introduces the heart of the conversion cycle which, in turn, emanates centrifugally from this text. The passage consists of a prayer offered by Joseph who, after piously dismissing Aseneth's kiss of greeting on the basis of her status as a Gentile, is so moved by her anguish that he prays for the conversion of the smitten Egyptian. The length, sophisticated structure, and programmatic function of Joseph's prayer invite detailed analysis, and combine to focus the reader's attention on the primary theme of the conversion cycle: *conversion as a transforming event, whose defining feature is newness.*

New creation

The story of Aseneth's conversion spans the greater part of fourteen chapters (chapters 8–21), and the phrase most often invoked to summarize this

---

[13] Chesnutt (1988: 24).
[14] Barclay (1996: 215). Cf. Philonenko (1965: 147–53; 1968: 75–98), Kee (1983: 394–413). Kraemer downplays the significance of conversion in *Joseph and Aseneth*, preferring to depict the events of chapters 9–18 in terms of the practice of the adjuration of angelic beings. While certainly novel, Kraemer's analysis is hardly persuasive. See the reviews of Bauckham (2000) and Chesnutt (2000).

transforming event is "new creation."[15] As we shall see, the narrative itself is saturated with creation motifs and easily corroborates the comment of Douglas that in *Joseph and Aseneth* "creation and conversion become synonymous."[16] This judgment, however, cannot be taken for granted. The following analysis of the structure, terminology, and narrative development of Joseph's prayer will both confirm and more fully substantiate this assessment.

Joseph and Aseneth 8.9: translation and structure

A	Strophe A	1	**Lord,**
D		2	God of my father Israel,
D		3	the Most High, the Mighty of Jacob
R			
E	Strophe B	4	who gave life to everything (ὁ ζωοποιήσας τὰ πάντα)
S		5	and called them
S		6	from darkness to light,
		7	from error to truth,
		8	from death to life,
A	Strophe C	9	**You Lord**, bless this virgin,
P		10	renew her by your spirit, (ἀνακαινίζω)
P		11	refashion her by your hidden hand, (ἀναπλάσσω)
E		12	make her alive again by your life, (ἀναζωοποιέω)
A			
L	Strophe D	13	let her eat the bread of life
		14	and drink the cup of your blessing,
		15	number her with your people
		16	whom you chose before everything came to be,
		17	may she enter your rest
		18	which you prepared for your elect
		19	and may she live in your eternal life for ever and ever.

Joseph's prayer is bipartite, consisting of the address (strophes A and B) and the appeal (strophes C and D), each introduced by the vocative Κύριε. This structure is not uncommon in biblical prayers and reflects the author's conscious adoption of biblical (LXX) style.[17] The address is composed of

---

[15] See, e.g., Derrett (1985: 601), Burchard (1987: 107–8), Chesnutt (1995: 172–76). *Neuschöpfung* is the German equivalent: G. Schneider (1959: 261), Delling (1963: 31), Vos (1973: 69), Berger (1975: 233), Fischer (1978: 107, 111), Sänger (1979: 27). Similarly, Philonenko (1968: 61): "nouvelle création."

[16] R. C. Douglas (1988: 35). So too Burchard (1987: 108); Chesnutt (1995: 145): "Creation imagery is the language most often used to describe Aseneth's conversion."

[17] Compare, for example, 1 Kings 8.22–52; 2 Kings 19.15–19; Neh. 1.5–11; 9.6–37; Tobit 3.2; Add. Esth. 4.17b–h. On the imitation of biblical style in *Joseph and Aseneth* see

a series of divine predicates, two nominal (lines 2–3) and two participial (lines 4–5), the last being expanded by three prepositional phrases.

The structure of the appeal is less easily discerned. One might be tempted to treat the sequence of nine aorist imperatives (lines 9–19) as individual links in a long chain, though a good case can be made for a more purposeful arrangement. The vocative Κύριε and introductory appeal (line 9) are followed by a succession of ἀνα- verbs which clearly belong together, as their repetition in 15.5 confirms. Strophe D is more troublesome in that it lacks the kind of unifying feature so obvious in the strophe which precedes it. The bread and cup statements (lines 13–14) also belong together. The recurrence of the meal formulas in *Joseph and Aseneth* (8.5; 15.5; 16.16; 19.5; 21.21) renders this judgment beyond doubt. Further consideration of the meal formulas reveals that lines 15–19 belong with lines 13–14 and that lines 13–19 form a single strophe.

The meal formulas in *Joseph and Aseneth* are presented in two alternative forms, both reflecting the triadic nature of symbolism. Verses 8.5, 15.5, and 16.16 speak explicitly of bread, drink, and an anointing (χρίσμα). In 8.9, 19.5, and 21.21, however, the final element is replaced by a statement concerning Aseneth's union with God's people. This second group of texts is further united by a formulaic statement concerning the eternal nature of this union: εἰς τὸν αἰῶνα χρόνον (8.9; 19.5); εἰς τοὺς αἰῶνας τῶν αἰώνων (21.21; cf. 6.8). This corresponds to the "incorruptible anointing" (χρίσμα ἀφθαρσίας) of the former group of texts and is one of several features which unite these passages under the designation "meal formulas." Not previously noted, the alternating form of the third element of the meal formulas considerably illuminates the function of these difficult texts, and will be taken up later in this analysis.[18]

Strophes A and B: analysis and interpretation

Form-critical analysis. The address, though a traditional component, is hardly a mere preliminary to the petition.[19] As the biblical parallels make clear, the address anticipates the appeal in that it describes God in terms consistent with the petitioner's request. In prayers of this type the appeal not only echoes the themes of the address but often repeats its terminology. Note the following examples drawn from the Septuagint:

Delling (1978: 29–56) and Burchard (1983: 592–95). For biblical parallels to the structure of this petition see below.

[18] The history of interpretation of the meal formulas is conveniently surveyed by Burchard (1987: 109–17).

[19] Eighty percent of the lengthy prayer in Nehemiah 9 consists of the address.

	Address	Appeal
1 Kings 8.23–25	Κύριε ὁ θεὸς Ισραηλ . . . ὁ φυλάσσων διαθήκην σοῦ . . .	νῦν, κύριε ὁ θεὸς Ισραηλ . . . φυλάξον . . . ἃ ἐλάλησας
Tobit 3.2–3	Δίκαιος εἶ κύριε καί πᾶσαι αἱ ὁδοί σου ἐλεημοσύνη . . .	καὶ νῦν σὺ κύριε . . . μή με ἐκδικήσῃς ταῖς ἁμαρτίαις
Add. Esth. 4.17b–h	Κύριε, κύριε βασιλεῦ πάντῶν κρατῶν . . . οὐκ ἔστιν ὁ ἀντιδοξῶν σοι ἐν τῷ θέλειν σε σῶσαι τὸν Ισραηλ . . .	καὶ νῦν κύριε ὁ θεὸς ὁ βασιλεὺς φεῖσαι τοῦ λαοῦ σου

The logic of this arrangement is apparent, and further illustrations are not hard to find.[20] Aseneth's lengthy prayer in chapters 12–13 is similarly formulated, as is her brief entreaty in 27.10:[21]

	Address	Appeal
JosAs. 27.10	Κύριε ὁ θεός μου . . . ὁ ἀναζωοποιήσας με καὶ ῥυσάμενός με ἐκ τῶν εἰδώλων . . .	ῥῦσαί με ἐκ τῶν κειρῶν τῶν ἀνδρῶν τῶν πονηρῶν τούτων

This form-critical assessment has significant implications for the exegesis of this text, and allows me to conclude that the appeal cannot be fully apprehended apart from the address – and vice versa. Given the mutually illuminating character of this address–appeal pattern, an examination of the language and imagery of strophes A and B (the address) will prove critical for the interpretation of strophes C and D (the appeal).

Comparative Analysis. The description of God as the creator (line 4) is common in Jewish (and Christian) prayers of the period,[22] and the precise appellation ὁ ζωοποιήσας τὰ πάντα is also found on occasion.[23] Line 4 repeats verbatim Joseph's initial words of greeting to Aseneth ("May the God who gives life to all things [ὁ ζωοποιήσας τὰ πάντα] bless you" 8.3), and the author's determination to stress the thematic character of this idea has manifestly overridden any concern for narrative subtlety.

The prepositional phrases of lines 6–8 modify the verb καλέω (line 5) and describe the creator's call as one from darkness to light, error to

[20] See 2 Kings 19.15–19; Neh. 1.5–11; 9.6–37; Tobit 7.5–9; Judith 9.2–14.

[21] The language of Aseneth's prayer for rescue (ὁ ἀναζωοποιήσας με) can be compared to the psalmist's confession of thanks after experiencing deliverance: ἐζωοποίησάς με (Ps. 70.20).

[22] See, e.g., 2 Kings 19.5; Ps. 115.15; Isa. 37.16; Add. Esth. 4.17; Sir. 24.8; Bel. 5; Wisd. 9.1–2; 2 Macc. 1.24; 7.23; 3 Macc. 2.2; 4 Macc. 5.25; *Jub.* 12.19; 22.4; *1 Enoch* 84.2–3; *Syr. Bar.* 21.4; 1QH 16.8; *JosAs.* 12.1.

[23] Neh. 9.6; Dan. 4.37; 1 Tim. 6.13 (א, 𝔐).

truth, and death to life. Καλέω is occasionally used to describe God's creation of the cosmos,[24] though the clauses attached to it here restrict its focus to the individual. Indeed, the language of lines 6–8 can be properly designated *conversion language,* in that it reflects typical Jewish and (Jewish-)Christian diction to describe conversion.[25] The soteriological metaphors of light/darkness, error/truth, and death/life are so common in the literature of the period (and contemporary religious discourse as well) that I will cite only one text representative of each, and allow the footnotes to supply further illustrative material.

The most prevalent of these transfer metaphors is the movement from darkness to light, and Philo's portrayal of Abraham's rejection of the philosophy of Chaldeans as a "pure ray of light" which awakened him out of "profound darkness" (*Abr.* 70) is typical.[26] Klaus Berger's assessment of this widespread symbolism points out the kind of development and connections undergirding this imagery: "Die Erschaffung des Lichts als des ersten Schöpfungswerkes Gottes (Gen. 1.3) wird zum ätiologischen Mythos für den Vorgang jeglicher Bekehrung (2 Kor. 4.6). Es ist der Schöpfergott, der erleuchtet."[27]

The movement from error to truth is another common component of conversion language and is well attested, for instance, in the literature from Qumran. Here it is often linked with light and darkness terminology and contributes to the distinctive outlook of the sect:

> Those born of truth spring from a fountain of light, but those born of falsehood spring from a source of darkness. All the children of righteousness are ruled by the Prince of Light and walk in the ways of light, but all the children of falsehood are ruled by the Angel of Darkness and walk in the ways of darkness.
>
> (1QS 3.19–21)[28]

Describing God as "the one who gives life to the dead" was not without precedent,[29] and it is hardly surprising that it came to be employed as transfer terminology. Again, the sectaries at Qumran depicted entrance into their community in terms of life from death (1QH 3.19–23;

---

[24] Isa. 40.26; 41.4; 48.13–15; Wisd. 11.25; Philo, *Spec. Leg.* 4.187; Rom. 4.17.
[25] See Berger (1976: 541 n. 328), Sänger (1979: 26), Chesnutt (1995: 145–49).
[26] See also Philo, *Virt.* 179–80, 221; *T. Gad.* 5.7; 1QS 3.14–4.1; 4Q434; 4Q541; 4Q543; 4Q545–48, etc.; John 1.4; 8.12, etc.; Acts 26.18; 2 Cor. 4.6; Eph. 5.8; 1 Pet. 2.9; *1 Clem.* 59.2; *2 Clem.* 1.6; *Acts Thom.* 27–28.
[27] Berger (1994: 269).
[28] Cf. also 1QH 10.14–15; 11.27–28; 4Q280; 1Q28b 3.22–25; 4Q418 frag. 126, etc.
[29] See 2 Sam. 1.6; 2 Kings 5.7; 2 Esdr. 19.6 (Neh. 9.6); Tobit 13.2.

11.9–14), though a fuller use of this imagery is found in Christian literature.[30]

Contextual Analysis. The comparative material is illuminating, but for present purposes it is more important to note the way the author unfolds each of these ideas vis-à-vis the heroine of the story, Aseneth. The author intends to portray Aseneth's conversion as a movement from darkness to light, error to truth, and death to life, and this is accomplished with deft proficiency. Aseneth herself recognizes that the heavenly messenger was sent to rescue her "from the darkness" and to bring her up from the abyss (15.12). Those whose literary tastes are more refined will find deeper satisfaction in the way the author begins Aseneth's seven-day fast of repentance by observing that she wept "until the sun set ... and the night fell" (10.1), and ends this fast with the words, "And on the eighth day, behold, it was dawn and the birds were already singing" (11.1).

The error versus truth motif is developed largely through Aseneth's prayers of confession. Through these Aseneth admits her wickedness (πονηρός), her sin (ἁμαρτία), and her lawlessness (ἀνομία).[31] Aseneth's psalm of repentance in chapter 21 begins each of its eleven stanzas with the words "I have sinned (ἥμαρτον), Lord I have sinned; before you I have sinned much," and brings home the author's point with force. Aseneth's chief error was her idolatry (2.3; 3.6; 8.5–7; 11.8–9), and this, naturally, figures prominently in her prayers: "My mouth is defiled from the sacrifices of the idols and from the tables of the gods of the Egyptians. I have sinned Lord, before you I have sinned much in ignorance, and have worshiped dead and dumb idols. And now I am not worthy to open my mouth to you Lord" (12.5; cf 21.14). Everything that passed through Aseneth's lips was unclean and tainted with idolatry, her food (6.3–7; 12.4), as well as her speech (8.5; 21.13–14). Since Aseneth's sin is particularly associated with her lips, it is not insignificant that it is through Joseph's kiss that he imparts to her a "spirit of truth" (πνεῦμα ἀληθείας, 19.11).

The movement from death to life is also prominent in the conversion cycle and renders the title of Chesnutt's important monograph particularly apt: *From Death to Life: Conversion in Joseph and Aseneth.* This, in fact, is Aseneth's own description of her conversion (27.10; cf. 12.7–15; 21.14) as well as that of her father who, upon seeing the luminous visage of his newly converted daughter, "rejoiced and gave glory to God who gives life to the dead" (20.7). Aseneth begins her protracted lament of repentance

---

[30] E.g., John 5.21, 24; 1 John 3.14; Rom. 4.14, 24; 6.1–11; 7.1–4; Gal. 2.19–21; 5.15–16; 2 Cor. 5.14–17 (see chapters 6–9 below).

[31] Πονηρός: 6.3, 4, 5, 7; 12.4; 13.3; ἁμαρτία: 11.10, 11, 18; 12.3, 15; ἀνομία; 11.10, 17; 12.3.

by changing into "a black tunic of mourning" which she last wore the day she buried her brother (10.9; 13.3). This death-shroud is intended not only as a striking visual contrast to her post-conversion attire, which was "like lightning in appearance" (18.3), but also as a symbol of her death–life (i.e., conversion) experience.

"Life," in fact, may be the single most theologically evocative idea in *Joseph and Aseneth*. It finds expression in scores of different contexts and in at least six cognate forms.[32] It is the author's chief description of God (8.3, 5, 9; 11.10; 12.1; 20.7) and the fundamental gift imparted to Aseneth in her conversion (8.9; 16.14; 20.7; 21.21; 27.10). Moreover, in *Joseph and Aseneth* it is the πνεῦμα ζωῆς (16.14; 19.11; 21.21; πνόη ζωῆς, 12.1; 16.8) which effects transformation (8.9) and bestows life (16.14–16).[33]

The analysis presented above provides substantiation for Delling's assessment of the language of Strophe B: "Es ist deutlich, daß die beiden Partizipialsätze (bis φῶς) zunächst die natürliche Schöpfung meinen ... alsbald aber auf die geistige Neuschöpfung bezogen werden."[34] This will become even more evident as I turn my attention to Strophes C and D.

Strophe C: analysis and interpretation

Comparative analysis. If the address, laden as it is with transfer symbolism, foreshadows the appeal, I have good reason to expect that strophes C and D (the appeal) will elaborate and define the author's understanding of conversion, and I am not disappointed. The compound verbs which distinguish strophe C (ἀνακαινίζω, ἀναπλάσσω, ἀναζωοποιέω) are not often encountered in the literature of the period, though in their unprefixed forms they are common enough.[35] This same row of verbs is found in 15.5

[32] I have noted 44 occurrences in the following cognates: ζωή, ζάω, ζωοποιέω, ζωογονέω, ἀναζάω, and ἀναζωοποιέω. There may be others.

[33] There is an intriguing interplay between πνόη and πνεῦμα in *Joseph and Aseneth*. In each of its eight occurrences (12.1; 15.14; 16.8 [2x], 9 [2x], 11[2x]), πνόη may legitimately be translated "breath," yet without diminishing the allusive character of the word. Aseneth prays to the God who gives the "breath of life" to all his creation (12.1; cf. Gen. 2.7), and later receives a "spirit of life" (19.11). In chapter 16, where the honeycomb is first said to contain the "breath of life" (16.8), then later the "spirit of life" (16.11), the words πνόη and πνεῦμα are interchangeable. Moreover, while the phrases πνόη/πνεῦμα ζωῆς are never articular, nor unambiguously in reference to the divine Spirit, according to Joseph's prayer Aseneth's transformation will be accomplished through the *divine* Spirit, which the narrative portrays as effected by the πνόη/πνεῦμα ζωῆς.

[34] Delling (1963: 31 n. 4).

[35] Ἀναπλάσσω, and ἀναζωοποιέω are not found in the LXX, or the New Testament. Πλάσσω is the verb used in the LXX to translate יצר in Gen. 2.7, and it is regularly used thereafter to describe God's creation of humanity: Philo, *Op. Mund.* 137; Josephus, *Ant.* 1.32; 1 Tim. 2.13; *1 Clem.* 33.4; 38.3; *Barn.* 19.2; *Diogn.* 10.2. The use of ἀναπλάσσω to

where they are similarly followed by a meal formula and a statement concerning Aseneth's eternal union with God's people (15.6). Ἀναζωοποιέω occurs on its own in Aseneth's prayer in 27.10, so would appear to summarize the entire triplet.[36] While each of these verbs could be examined with profit independently, the author's main point in piling these ἀνα- ("again," "anew") clauses on top of each other relates to the controlling purpose of the conversion cycle: to depict conversion as *a completely transforming event, whose defining feature is newness.*

Contextual analysis. Once again, the narrative unfolds the prayer in a variety of images and symbols. Upon leaving Aseneth's home, Joseph remarks suggestively to Aseneth's father, Pentephres, "this is the day on which God began to make all his creatures" (9.5), and it is Aseneth's re-making that the following chapters describe. In 14.12 she is given a new linen robe and a new girdle, which is followed by a new name (15.7). Michael Mach correctly sees this as symbolic of Aseneth's change of identity and offers the concise commentary, "Sie ist nun eine andere."[37] More puzzling, though certainly to be understood in terms of this transformation motif, is the angel's proclamation that Aseneth is now a virgin and that her head has become like that of a young man (15.1). The angelic visitor then answers Joseph's prayer by assuring her that she will indeed be renewed (ἀνακαινίζω), formed anew (ἀναπλάσσω), and made alive again (ἀναζωοποιέω) "from this day" (ἀπὸ τῆς σήμερον, 15.5). E. P. Sanders is correct to underscore the realized soteriology of Aseneth's conversion, which is the presumption of the conversion cycle: "It is not said that the one who eats the bread and drinks the cup and is anointed with the ointment in *Joseph and Aseneth* will gain life, but rather that such a person has life. This is a motif which is missing, as far as I can see, in Palestinian Judaism."[38]

The portrayal of Aseneth's conversion as a new act of creation takes other, less obvious forms as well. Aseneth's fast of repentance lasts seven days, which probably alludes to the seven-day creation narrative of Genesis 1. The cosmos itself mirrors Aseneth's experience as the morning star rises in response to her repentance (14.1; cf. 2 Pet. 1.19; Rev. 2.28; 22.16). Like the application of ζωοποιέω to Aseneth's conversion

describe the re-creation of an individual upon conversion in *Joseph and Aseneth* follows logically from this. It is used similarly in *Barn.* 6.11, 14 and *2 Clem.* 8.2. For ἀναζωοποιέω see 15.5, 27.10; *T. Abr.* 18.11. Ἀνακαινίζω (= ἀνακαινόω) and ἀνακαίνωσις make several important appearances (Rom. 12.2; 2 Cor. 4.17; Col. 3.10; Heb. 6.6) and, as in *JosAs.* 8.9, are often associated with the Spirit: Ps. 104.30 (LXX); Titus 3.5; *Barn.* 6.11; *Herm. Vis.* 3.8.9; *Herm. Sim.* 8.6.3.
[36] So Mell (1989: 234).   [37] Mach (1992: 269).   [38] Sanders (1976: 43).

(20.7) – a verb elsewhere applied only to the created order (8.3, 9, 12.1) – these literary devices allow the author to parallel God's first creative act with his new creative act (conversion) making the former a metaphor for the latter.

Excursus: honey in the conversion cycle

Perhaps the most perplexing feature of the conversion cycle is the mysterious honeycomb of chapter 16. Located at the heart of the conversion cycle, its importance within the narrative requires that it be given separate treatment.[39] In this chapter we find Aseneth preparing a meal for an angelic visitor who has come in response to her tears of contrition. The entire episode, however, is shrouded in dark symbolism and opaque imagery (magically appearing honey, a glowing hand, angelic bees, a bloody cross, and so on), the clues to which are probably forever buried in the sands of antiquity. The interpretation of this imagery is notoriously difficult, and James Charlesworth admits that this passage has "utterly defied" all attempts to decode it.[40]

The consensus: honey symbolizes manna. But for all the mystery and guesswork which surrounds the interpretation of *Joseph and Aseneth* 16, it is possible to speak of a consensus regarding one element of this chapter, the significance of the honey. Marc Philonenko put the matter succinctly: "Il ne peut s'agir que de la manne."[41] Equating the honeycomb (κηρίον μελίσσης, 16.2) with the manna fed to the Israelites in Exodus 16 is reasonable given the (certainly deliberate) similarities in the way the two are described (compare Exod. 16.14, 31 with *JosAs.* 16.8). So confident is Burchard in the singular importance of this connection that he can refer to the honeycomb alternatively as manna.[42] Michael Mach extends the honey = manna equation to the point of saying, "Wer Jude werden will, hat nach Meinung des Verfassers die grundsätzliche Erfahrung Israels in der Wüste nachzuholen."[43]

While it cannot be denied that *Joseph and Aseneth* 16.8 contains some kind of an allusion to the manna of Exodus 16, it is questionable whether this connection is solely determinative for its interpretation. Exodus motifs are hardly conspicuous in *Joseph and Aseneth*;[44] this book does not

---

[39] For a more detailed presentation of this argument, see Hubbard (1997: 97–110).
[40] Charlesworth (1985: 25).   [41] Philonenko (1968: 96).
[42] Burchard (1987: 114–17).   [43] Mach (1992: 272).
[44] Cf. Chesnutt (1995: 147 n. 62).

mention manna, and this chapter does not rely on exodus, or second-exodus traditions. Yet if the significance of the honey cannot be apprehended exclusively on the basis of Exodus 16, where does its significance lie?

A counter-proposal: honey symbolizes new birth. The answer to this riddle may be provided by the *Epistle of Barnabas*. Indeed, the potential for comparison between *Joseph and Aseneth* and *Barnabas* is significant in that, if the scholarly consensus can be trusted, both were written at roughly the same time and from roughly the same place.[45] We need not suppose that the two authors rubbed shoulders in the markets of Alexandria, but if Christoph Burchard's dating of *Joseph and Aseneth* in the reign of Trajan (AD 98–117) is correct, they may well have been contemporaries. Further, it is often argued that *Barnabas* is of Jewish-Christian origin and this renders any literary-conceptual connection with *Joseph and Aseneth* of great interest.[46]

The passage which most illumines the present discussion is *Barnabas* 6.8–7.2. This text, overlooked thus far in the interpretation of *Joseph and Aseneth* 16, is the only extant ancient source which combines the peculiar renewal language of *Joseph and Aseneth* 8.9 and 15.5 (ἀνακαινίζω, ἀναπλάσσω, [ἀνα]ζωοποιέω) with a specific reference to the consumption of honey. As it stands, the passage appears to be a digression from the main theme of suffering, and represents an allegorical interpretation of the "good land" texts of Exodus 33.1–3; Leviticus 20.24; Deuteronomy 6.18, and so on. In interpreting the meaning of "a land flowing with milk and honey," the author comments: "Since he has made us new (ἀνακαινίσας ἡμᾶς) by the remission of sins, he has made us another sort [of person], as though we had the souls of children, indeed, as though he were creating us afresh" (ἀναπλάσσοντος αὐτοῦ ἡμᾶς; 6.11).

The author goes on to speak of the re-creation of pre-fall Adam, quoting the dictum "the last things shall be as the first" (6.12–13), and then further relates this latter-day re-creation (ἀναπλάσσω, 6.14) to the prophecies of Ezekiel 36. In 6.17 the author again asks, "What then is the milk and the honey?," and explains: "You see an infant is first made alive

---

[45] Most date *Barnabas* between AD 80 and 130 and believe it to be of Alexandrian origin. See the extensive discussions by Kraft (1965: 39–56) and Paget (1994: 9–42).

[46] William Horbury (1992: 315–45) has forcefully argued for a Jewish-Christian origin of *Barnabas*. He considers it "a Christian sub-section of Jewish literature" (145). The most persistent exponent of this view is L. W. Barnard, most recently in his *ANRW* article on the subject (1993: 159–207). Paget (1994: 7–9) gives a balanced discussion of the issue and decides, with hesitation, against a Jewish-Christian authorship.

(ζωοποιέω) by honey, then by milk.[47] In the same way we, who are made alive (ζωοποιέω) by faith in the promises and the word, shall live, ruling over the earth."

New birth and new creation imagery in contemporary litera-ture. The practice of feeding honey to a newborn (cf. Isa. 7.15) is well documented in antiquity and should probably inform interpretation of the honey in *Joseph and Aseneth* 16.[48] It is clear that both authors understood conversion as a kind of new creation, and this points to a common trans-fer metaphor of the period. The fusion of the ideas of new creation and new birth that we see in *Barnabas* and *Joseph and Aseneth* is predictable given the terminology involved, and is best illustrated by Titus 3.5, where παλιγγενεσία and ἀνακαίνωσις stand side by side as synonyms.[49] This should probably be related to the way natural birth is sometimes described as creation *ex nihilo*. Philo, for instance, speaks of birth as the process by which that which had no existence is brought into being (δι' ἧς τὸ μὴ ὂν ἄγεται πρὸς τὸ εἶναι – *Virt.* 130), and elsewhere he describes the creation of the cosmos in identical language.[50] The Maccabean author is more explicit. In an attempt to strengthen her son who is about to be martyred, the courageous mother of 2 Maccabees 7 reminds him of how she carried him in her womb and concludes, "I implore you my child, look at the heavens and earth and everything in them, and realize that it was not from existing materials (οὐκ ἐξ ὄντων) that God made these things, *and humanity is brought into being in the same way*" (2 Macc. 7.28).

This text is particularly instructive in that the creation of the cosmos is deemed to be a fitting analogy to natural birth, and both are said to occur *ex nihilo*. Given this close association between creation and birth, it is no surprise that new *creation* would likewise be thought of as new *birth*.

---

[47] My translation leaves the idiom in place. Kraft (1965: 100–1) translates the clause, "Because the infant is *initiated into life* first by honey," while Kirsopp Lake (LCL, 1976: 363) renders it, "because a child is first *nourished* with honey"; the emphases are mine. In both *Joseph and Aseneth* and *Barnabas* the honey is described as that which imparts life. A comparison of the two suggests we are dealing with an idiom and resolves this curious attribute of the honey in *JosAs.* 16.14–16: the substance commonly associated with new life is idiomatically described as producing that life.

[48] See the texts and literature cited in BAGD (under μέλι) and by Hans Windisch (1920: 338). The association of honey with infants in ancient societies is regularly noted in the literature on *Barn.* 6.17.

[49] Although somewhat dated, the most important discussions of this language remain those of Adolf von Harnack (1918: 97–143) and Erik Sjöberg (1950: 44–85).

[50] See *Spec. Leg.* 4.187; *Op. Mund.* 81; *Vit. Mos.* 2.100.

New birth and its thematic development in Joseph and Aseneth. The parallels between *Barnabas* and *Joseph and Aseneth* point strongly in the direction of seeing Aseneth's consumption of honey as a symbol of her new birth.[51] Once again, however, the narrative itself invites us to make this connection. The glorious portrayal of Joseph's arrival at Pentephres' house (5.4–11) prompts Aseneth to conclude that "the sun from heaven" has arrived on its chariot and that Joseph must be divine (6.3). His royal attire and luminous countenance lead Aseneth to reason, "Joseph is a son of God. For who among men on earth could beget (γεννάω) such beauty, and what womb could give birth (τίκτω) to such light?" (6.4). The author's point, which will be developed later in the conversion cycle, is that divine radiance is an expression of divine birth. It is not surprising, then, that following Aseneth's consumption of honey, her transformed beauty parallels the description of Joseph: "And they saw Aseneth as a vision of light, and her beauty was a heavenly beauty" (20.6; cf. 18.9).

Depicting Aseneth's conversion as new birth resolves another tension in the narrative introduced in 7.5, as Joseph recalls the words of his father: "For Jacob would say to his son Joseph and all his sons, 'My children, guard strongly against associating with foreign women.'" Hence, Joseph's rejection of Aseneth's kiss is explained on the basis that Aseneth is a foreigner (8.5), and that the devout Jew will kiss only his "sister" and wife (8.6).[52] Upon converting, however, Aseneth is no longer the daughter of Pentephres, but "the daughter of the Most High" (21.5), so is worthy of a Joseph's kiss (19.11). Chapter 16's portrayal of Aseneth's conversion as new birth is the necessary fulfillment of these motifs, epitomized by Joseph's prophetic word in 7.8: "She is a sister to me, and I love her from today as my sister." So, quite apart from the symbolic honey of chapter 16, the author clearly intends his/her readers to see the proselyte as a full member of the Jewish family with all the privileges and responsibilities of ethnic Jews. Aseneth's change of status from "foreigner" to "sister" furthers the author's point that conversion is in fact *new birth into a new family.*

Further, as we look specifically at chapter 16, it is clear that some kind of regenerative significance must be attached to the honey. It is eaten only

---

[51] This analysis of Aseneth's conversion and transformation, based on concrete literary affinities with *Barnabas*, demonstrable socio-cultural precedent, and clear contextual warrant, should be contrasted with Kraemer's more speculative reliance on later Hekhalot traditions (1998: 111–54).

[52] The Greek text reads, τὴν ἀδελφὴν τὴν ἐκ τῆς συγγενείας αὐτοῦ (8.5). This extended use of "sister" to designate a spouse or a female Israelite is well attested (Song Sol. 4.9, 10; 5.1; Tobit 7.8, 11, 15; cf. *Jub.* 25.3; 1 Cor. 9.5), and anticipates Aseneth's future status as Joseph's "sister" and wife.

by those who repent (16.14), and as 15.7 has just explained, all who repent are made anew (ἀνακαινίζω) by the angel Repentance. More importantly, the honeycomb is called "breath of life" (16.8; cf. 12.1–2), "spirit of life" (16.14; cf. 8.9), and "comb of life" (16.14), and imparts youthful vitality:

> Behold, from today your flesh will flourish like flowers of life from the ground of the Most High, and your bones will grow strong like the cedars of the paradise of delight of God, and untiring powers will embrace you, and your youth will not see old age and your beauty will not fail for ever.   (16.16)[53]

New birth and initiation. Finally, students of comparative religions, especially those with an interest in initiation rites, will not fail to notice that this interpretation of the honey incident in *Joseph and Aseneth* corresponds precisely to the initiatory symbolism observed by ethnologists and anthropologists in countless settings and cultures throughout the globe.[54] A more detailed discussion of initiatory symbolism will be offered later (chapter 5), but for the moment it is sufficient to note that the elaborate description of conversion in *Joseph and Aseneth* allows it to be scrutinized under Arnold van Gennep's rubric as a rite of passage. Be it puberty rites of primitive societies, or initiation rites of religious organizations and secret sects, a common repertoire of mythical ideas is employed in these ritual dramas to illustrate the neophyte's passage from one status to another, the most prominent being death and rebirth. The new status of the initiate can be pictured in a variety of ways (a new name, new clothing, etc.) as can be the initiate's new birth, all depending on indigenous symbols.[55] The initiate may pass through the legs of a woman, suckle, eat the food of a infants, or perform other infant-like behavior.[56] *Joseph and Aseneth* has, in fact, been examined through the lens of anthropological research, but only in order to demonstrate its general coherence to van Gennep's tripartite structure of initiatory rituals.[57] It

[53] In this connection, the textual variant at Luke 24.42, which has Jesus consuming honey during one of his post-resurrection appearances is noteworthy. Does this later addition reflect the use of honey in the baptismal and eucharistic rituals of the ancient church, or do both attest to the association of honey with new life in antiquity? This variant was brought to my attention by Professor Christopher Rowland.

[54] The literature on initiation rites is vast, but more than enough comparative data can be culled from the basic texts: van Gennep (1960), Eliade (1961, 1965a, 1965b), Bleeker (1965b), La Fontaine (1985). See further literature cited in chapter 5.

[55] The universality of initiatory symbols is explored by Mary Douglas in *Natural Symbols* (1970).

[56] Details are provided by van Gennep (1960: 29–38, 92–95), Eliade (1965a: 28), V. Turner (1967, 1977), La Fontaine (1985: 66–67, 88–91).

[57] R. C. Douglas (1988: 31–42); cf. Philonenko (1965).

is clear that much more work could be done here, but for present purposes it will suffice to note that seeing Aseneth's consumption of honey as indicative of her new birth locates this symbolism within a larger, universal pattern of symbolic expression replete with illustrative parallels from the study of the phenomenology of religion. Before moving on to strophe D, a bit more should be said about Exodus imagery and its use in *Joseph and Aseneth* 16.

Exodus 16 once more. The language of *Joseph and Aseneth* 16.8 makes it fairly clear that Exodus 16 was not far from the author's mind. The manna of Exodus is described as dew (16.13), white in appearance and tasting of honey (16.31), and these are all picked up by the author of *Joseph and Aseneth*. Yet the transformative, regenerative effects associated with the honey-cake of *Joseph and Aseneth* are difficult to derive from the Exodus narrative and this suggests that the background to this imagery might be more complex than previously allowed. It is conceivable that this clear literary allusion to Exodus 16 might not provide all the necessary clues for the interpretation of the honey in *Joseph and Aseneth* 16, and in that case we would be justified in looking elsewhere to discern its fundamental import. This point is illustrated by considering a Coptic text, *Historia Pachomii et Theodori*. The text itself is late and is cited here only by way of illustration, though its Egyptian provenance may make it relevant to *Joseph and Aseneth* and *Barnabas*.[58]

> ... vision (horama), and he remembered that which he had beheld in the vision (horama) from the lord, on the day whereon he was being instructed towards becoming a Christian; how he had beheld in that revelation the dew of heaven descending upon him, (how) afterwards it had collected and had become a cake of (honey ...) and it fell (upon the ground) ... As for him he was informed by the Spirit (pneuma) that 'this (cake of honey) that did (collect) in (thy hand) and fall upon the (ground, these [sic]) are the gifts (charismata) that came to thee from the Lord. And they shall come also unto thy brethren, that is, the earth. When they shall have become born again, being cleansed from (all) pride (of heart) ... '

[58] The Coptic text, along with the English translation presented here and text-critical notes can be found in Crum (1913: 140–41). On the basis of paleography, Crum concludes "It is still necessary vaguely to assign [these texts] to about the 7th century" (p. v). The English text is also cited by Berger (1975: 235).

Not unlike *Joseph and Aseneth*, the honey-cake in this passage is a symbol of the Spirit and new birth, but the imagery is certainly borrowed from Exodus 16. With this text as an analogy, we may conjecture that within the Jewish milieu of *Joseph and Aseneth* it would have been quite easy, perhaps even common, to clothe a contemporary symbol in biblical imagery, yet not intend its meaning to be derived solely from the biblical context. This is precisely what is happening in the text above and in *Barnabas* 6, and this scenario allows us to read *Joseph and Aseneth* 16 with a deeper appreciation of the multivalent symbolic world of its first-century readers. To be sure, the *Epistle of Barnabas* and *Joseph and Aseneth* are more different than alike, but this only renders their identical portrayal of conversion all the more conspicuous.

Recapitulating briefly, understanding Aseneth's consumption of honey as indicative of her new birth finds support in contemporary parallels (*Barn.* 6), the thematic development of the narrative itself, and is of a piece with initiatory symbolism generally. Feeding honey to a newborn was a common practice in antiquity, and it is very likely that the first readers of *Joseph and Aseneth* would have perceived the significance of this act far more easily than we moderns do. Most importantly however, when Aseneth's consumption of honey is seen to be indicative of her rebirth into the people of God, chapter 16 is more firmly anchored in the flow of the narrative in that the honey episode is seen to be a further development of the dominant theme of the conversion cycle: *conversion as a transforming event, whose defining feature is newness.*

Strophe D: analysis and interpretation

Strophe D concludes Joseph's prayer with the request that Aseneth be allowed to "eat the bread of life" (line 13), "drink the cup of blessing" (line 14), and that she be numbered with God's people (lines 15–19). The significance of these "meal formulas," as they are called, is widely debated, though most of this complex discussion is not germane to the present analysis.[59] While the following observations would fit comfortably with a number of interpretations of the meal formulas, they are especially well suited to the recent interpretation of Randall Chesnutt: "It seems most likely that this high evaluation of the daily meal and the concern for the

---

[59] The essential question is whether these meal formulas reflect the practice of an initiatory meal associated with conversion to a (sectarian) Jewish community (so, for example, Holtz, Kee, Philonenko), or whether they allude, more broadly, to normal Jewish meals (Burchard [1965, modified in 1987], Jeremias, Sänger) and/or the entire Jewish way of life (Collins [1983], Chesnutt [1995]).

maintenance of purity in table fellowship is what gave rise to the representative use of meal language in *Joseph and Aseneth* to express Jewish identity vis-à-vis Gentile existence."[60]

Building on Chesnutt's thesis, it is crucial to recognize the triadic nature of *each occurrence* of the meal formula, as I argued earlier, and also to see that the final element of the formula emphasizes Aseneth's eternal union with God's people. Although an explicit reference to an "incorruptible anointing" does not follow the "bread" and "cup" statements in 8.9, 19.5, and 21.21, it is very likely that this χρίσμα ἀφθαρσίας (8.5, 15.5, 16.16) does have a counterpart in these other passages, as the following illustrates:

8.5; 15.5; 16.16	8.9	19.5	21.21
ἄρτον ζωῆς	may she eat the bread of life	he gave me bread of life	he gave me bread of life
ποτήριον ἀθανασίας	may she drink the cup of blessing	and a cup of blessing	and a cup of wisdom
χρίσμα ἀφθαρσίας	may she be numbered among your people	and he said 'I have given you for a bride to Joseph	and I became his bride
	εἰς τὸν αἰῶνα χρόνον	εἰς τὸν αἰῶνα χρόνον'	εἰς τοὺς αἰῶνας τῶν αἰώνων

If this analysis is correct, it is inaccurate to speak of the "dyadic" and the "triadic" nature of the meal formulas, as does Chesnutt.[61] The "imperishable" or "incorruptible" (ἀφθαρσία) nature of the anointing in 8.5, 15.5, and 16.16 is undoubtedly picked up in the αἰῶνα clauses of 8.9, 19.5, and 21.21. The χρίσμα character of this final element alludes to the sacred quality of this union, aptly portrayed through the imagery of marital union in 19.5 and 21.21. This sacred dimension of Aseneth's conversion is connected with the biblical practice of anointing to sacred office (Exod. 28.41; Lev. 8.12; 2 Sam. 2.7; 1 Kings 19.16; Ps. 88.21 [LXX], etc.), and is explained more fully in chapter 15 by Aseneth's angelic visitor. After affirming point by point the details of Joseph's prayer that Aseneth be "renewed," "formed anew," "made alive again," and that she "eat the bread of life," "drink the cup of immortality," and be anointed with an "incorruptible anointing" (15.5), the Angel then adds the following words of explanation:

---

[60] Chesnutt (1995: 133).   [61] Chesnutt (1995: 129).

And your name shall no longer be called Aseneth, but your name shall be City of Refuge (πόλις καταφυγῆς) because in you many nations will take refuge (καταφεύξονται ἔθνη πολλά) with the Lord God, the Most High, and under your wings many peoples trusting in the Lord God will be sheltered, and behind your walls will be guarded those who attach themselves to the Most High God in the name of repentance. (15.7)

Aseneth's renaming, and the commentary thereon, is a citation of Zechariah 2.15 (LXX) which predicts the eschatological conversion of the Gentiles.

Rejoice and shout, O daughter of Zion! For behold I am coming to you and I will dwell in your midst, says the Lord. And many nations will take refuge (καταφεύξονται ἔθνη πολλά) with the Lord in that day (ἐν τῇ ἡμέρᾳ ἐκείνη) and they will be as a people to him and they shall dwell in your midst. (Zech. 2.14–15)

In applying this text to Aseneth's conversion, the full implications of this event are revealed. The author's change of ἐν τῇ ἡμέρᾳ ἐκείνη (Zech. 2.15) to ἀπὸ τῆς σήμερον (*JosAs.* 15.5; cf. 7.8) allows us to speak of a realized eschatology, in addition to the more obvious realized soteriology mentioned earlier. Moreover, Aseneth herself is shown to have typological status, and becomes a prototype and first fruits of proselytes to come. Her change of name and marriage to the patriarch Joseph are indicative not only of her membership in a new community, these symbolic acts also elevate her to the level of a Matriarch for the Gentiles. As with the name change of Abraham and Sarah (Gen. 17), Aseneth's new name, "City of Refuge," ascribes a corporate significance to her conversion and justifies Burchard's observation: "Aseneth ist das Zion der Proselyten."[62]

Summary and conclusions

While more could be said about Aseneth's conversion and the literary technique of the author of *Joseph and Aseneth* in describing that conversion, the foregoing examination has sufficiently exposed the vital issues relevant to this study. Of primary importance for the subsequent analysis is *Joseph and Aseneth*'s elaborate and vivid portrayal of conversion as new creation. As Burchard observes, "the phrase itself is absent, but it seems to be an appropriate term to cover the fundamental

---

[62] Burchard (1965: 119).

transformation both spiritual and physical which is ascribed to Aseneth in a variety of ways."[63] The ancillary motifs which support this representation are equally relevant, and depict this event as a movement from darkness to light, error to truth, and, most importantly, death to life. This is typical transfer terminology, or "conversion language," as is the new-birth imagery symbolized in Aseneth's consumption of honey. Moreover, the agent effecting Aseneth's new creation is the Spirit, whose principal function in the narrative is to impart *life*. The realized soteriology so prominent in the work is rendered even more provocative through the author's frequent use of cosmic imagery to illustrate Aseneth's conversion. While the focus of the narrative remains on Aseneth, creation symbolism provided the author with a powerful analogy to conversion, once again illustrating the dynamic interplay between creation and redemption.

But *Joseph and Aseneth*'s portrayal of conversion as new creation was not intended simply as an exploration of the theological profundities of conversion, but was meant to address crucial issues facing the author's community. As noted earlier, *Joseph and Aseneth* reveals a social and religious milieu in which the status of proselyte was in question and where Jews and Gentiles lived in dynamic tension.[64] Through her conversion, Aseneth becomes "a daughter of the most High" (21.4) and a suitable marriage partner for Joseph. It overturns her "strange woman" status (7.5) and makes her a full member of the Jewish community. The primary reason for presenting conversion as new creation was to address vital social concerns, specifically, the relation of the convert to the *ethnic* Jewish community.

Taking a cue from the thematic center of the book, 8.9, I have emphasized *newness* in my discussion of the conversion cycle, but I could have easily expressed this idea negatively, and spoken of Aseneth's conversion as a "total break" with her past.[65] There is narrative warrant for such an approach, and Philonenko articulates this point of view: "Sa conversion n'en est que plus éclatante et marque une rupture totale avec le paganisme auquel elle prétendait rester attachée."[66] Whether enunciated positively or negatively, new-creation symbolism is well suited to emphasize a complete break with the past and the newness of the convert's condition. It connotes not only the idea of a new individual in a new community, it also betokens a repudiation of the convert's former value system and way of

---

[63] Burchard (1987: 108).   [64] On this, see Chesnutt (1988).
[65] Citing Barclay (1996: 206). Similarly Chesnutt (1995: 175–76).
[66] Philoneko (1968: 52).

life. As such, it is the ideal expression to apply to Jewish converts from a pagan environment, as Burchard acknowledges: "As to *JosAs.*, it should be noted that 'new creation' is for Gentiles only."[67]

Finally, I conclude by reiterating what Nickelsburg has called "the prototypical nature of Aseneth's conversion."[68] According to Barclay, Aseneth is held up as the "paradigmatic convert,"[69] and this assessment is a valid interpretation of the lofty words of blessing pronounced by Aseneth's angelic visitor: "Because in you many nations will take refuge with the Lord God, the Most high" (15.7).

Joseph and Aseneth may be unique among the extant works of Diaspora Judaism in its lavish and detailed literary presentation of conversion as new creation, but we need not suppose that this imagery was without precedent, or in any sense unusual. Just the opposite may be true, as Chesnutt argues: "The conversion of Aseneth as reported in *Joseph and Aseneth* is probably more representative of Jewish proselytism in the Hellenistic world than has previously been supposed."[70] To be sure, there is an element of conjecture in this judgment, but it remains true that depicting conversion as new creation was current in at least one strand of first-century Diaspora Judaism, and it would be remarkable if *Joseph and Aseneth* represented the sole occurrence of this symbolism.

Summary of part I

The preceding analysis sets the stage for the subsequent argument primarily by outlining the rich diversity of new-creation imagery in the literature of Second Temple Judaism. This diversity has a clear precedent in the eschatological visions of the later prophets, and in each instance, the motif of new creation stands in antithesis to the perceived dilemma of the writer, making a correct appraisal of the plight crucial for a correct appraisal of the solution.

Jubilees and *Joseph and Aseneth* provide illuminating illustrations of this point. Although new creation has both anthropological and cosmological dimensions in *Jubilees*, the cosmological horizon receives more emphasis, and this observation is even truer of the apocalyptic genre taken as a whole. Here the "plight" was intimately associated with the historical situation of foreign domination, which was exacerbated through the harassment and enticement of the evil angelic realm. To the apocalyptic

---

[67] Burchard (1987: 108).

[68] Nickelsburg (1984a: 70). Similarly Philonenko (1968: 55), Burchard (1983: 601), Collins (1983: 217).

[69] Barclay (1996: 214).   [70] Chesnutt (1995: 255–56).

visionaries, the answer came in the form of the destruction of the political and spiritual agents of evil, and the reconstitution of the entire created order. In *Joseph and Aseneth* however, the issue to be resolved was how a pagan, born in sin and nurtured in idolatry could ever become a full member of the family of God. The solution of this community was that the proselyte was re-created by the Spirit of God, so all prior involvements were irrelevant. Both *Joseph and Aseneth* and *Jubilees* contain a morose estimation of the plight from which redemption is sought, and both employ new-creation imagery in response. However, a pessimistic appraisal of the human condition (*Joseph and Aseneth*) called for a different solution than a pessimistic appraisal of the historical situation (*Jubilees*), and this observation provides a fitting introduction to the treatment of new creation in Paul's letters.

PART II

**From death to life: new creation in the contours
of Paul's thought**

This study, as noted in the introduction, is essentially an argument about
context. Without a specific literary-conceptual framework to provide definition and texture, words remain intangible and amorphous entities capable of any number of meanings. Understanding an idea in its native
environment means becoming acquainted with a whole host of other
ideas indigenous to that environment. It is this conceptual network which
furnishes the definitional boundaries of an idea and, to a great extent,
determines its content. In what follows I attempt to place Paul's new-
creation statements in the theological context in which they are found,
his death–life symbolism. Within this theological matrix – surely one of
the most important in Paul – a number of ideas occur with remarkable
consistency, and it is these, I will argue, which add content and clarity to
Paul's allusive καινὴ κτίσις.

The dominant symbolism of these texts, dying and rising with Christ,
has been the subject of several distinguished monographs and numerous
shorter studies,[1] and an exhaustive treatment is certainly not offered here.
This present study will be limited in two important ways. First, I shall take
as the starting-point the classification proposed by Robert Tannehill, who
identified two essential varieties of death–life passages in Paul: those in
which dying and rising with Christ form the basis of the new life, and those
in which it expresses the structure of the new life.[2] The primary focus of
chapters 6, 7 and 9 will be an examination of those passages which fall
into the former category (Rom. 6.1–14; 7.1–6; Gal. 2.19–20), as it is to
this family of texts that 2 Corinthians 5.17 and Galatians 6.15 belong.[3]
Second, since a detailed exegesis of each text is beyond the scope of this

---

[1] Most notable are those of Tannehill (1967), Siber (1971), and Wedderburn (1987).

[2] Tannehill (1967). Wedderburn's study corroborates this basic division, though he pre-
fers to speak of "life *through* death" and "life *in* death" (1987: 360–92). This more concise
terminology will also be employed.

[3] Other texts making use of this motif will be incorporated at relevant points in the
discussion.

study, I will concentrate only on those structural and thematic elements deemed relevant to the present investigation. This self-denying ordinance is intended to concentrate attention on the central task of elucidating Paul's new-creation statements.

Death–life symbolism, however, is hardly original to Paul and the wider religious context sheds valuable light on the same imagery in Paul's letters. This material is especially important for establishing the focus and orientation of death–life symbolism, as the exegesis of the relevant texts will confirm. Working from the general to the specific, I look first at death–life symbolism through the lens of socio-religious anthropology and then at its particular application in Paul. In part III I will examine 2 Corinthians 5.17 and Galatians 6.15 specifically, locating these texts in their epistolary context as well as the broader theological context outlined here.

5

FROM DEATH TO LIFE: INSIGHTS FROM CULTURAL ANTHROPOLOGY

> Everywhere we decipher the same mystery of death to the secular
> condition, followed by resurrection to a higher mode of being.
>
> Mircea Eliade, *Images and Symbols*

"Death" and "life" constitute, arguably, the most fundamental categories
of human existence. Not surprisingly, they occur with predictable regu-
larity in religious symbolism from culture to culture. The goal of this introductory section is to provide the backdrop against which Paul's death–
life statements gain fullest clarity. Specifically, I will demonstrate the
importance of interpreting this symbolism within the broader category of
"life-crisis rituals," which anthropologists and ethnologists have scrutinized and evaluated for nearly two centuries. Situating Paul's symbolism
within this larger, universal pattern of symbolic expression will serve to
orient the exegesis of the relevant texts, while also providing a methodology for interpreting Paul's religious symbolism generally. Specialists in
the phenomenology of religion can offer valuable help to New Testament
exegetes in the interpretation of religious imagery. Where exegetes atom-
ize, comparative religionists synthesize. Both are crucial, but if exegetes
neglect the whole, their understanding of the parts is likewise diminished.

Rites of passage

The work of Arnold van Gennep

The name of Arnold van Gennep is virtually synonymous with rites of passage. His seminal study of the subject early in the twentieth century was
both ground-breaking on the theoretical level, and noteworthy on the popular level: it is one of only a handful of technical monographs which can
claim to have established a popular idiom in a variety of languages.[4] The

---

[4] On the influence of van Gennep see Kimball (1960: v–xix; 1968: 113–14), Eliade
(1965b: 1), M. Douglas (1966: 114–15), V. Turner (1967: 94; 1968: 520–26), Leach

genius of this contribution lies in its simplicity and comprehensiveness. Van Gennep observed that every ritual of transition, be it puberty rites of primitive cultures, initiation rites of religious organizations and secret societies, or marriage and funerary rites, exhibits the same tripartite structure: "preliminal rites (rites of separation), liminal rites (rites of transition), and postliminal rites (rites of incorporation)."[5] Having described an individual's life in terms of "a series of passages," van Gennep suggests that the purpose of these ceremonies "is to enable the individual to pass from one well-defined position to another, which is equally well-defined."[6]

Van Gennep's classification has been all but universally accepted, as La Fontaine's conclusion illustrates: "ethnographic evidence has demonstrated over and over again in different parts of the world the validity of van Gennep's assertion that this tripartite structure was to be found in all rituals of transition."[7] Van Gennep's schema has been particularly helpful in understanding that family of life-crisis rituals known as initiation rites, which, for example, mark the transition from childhood to adulthood, or entrance into a religious community.[8]

As noted above, the purpose of these rites, in their various forms, is to indicate a transition from one state to another, both social and personal. Circumcision for example, when performed as a male puberty rite, marks the boy's transition to manhood, as well as his incorporation into a new social structure. Hence, Victor Turner can say that these ceremonies "detach ritual subjects from their old places in society and return them, inwardly transformed and outwardly changed to new places."[9] Eliade's assessment is similar:

(1968: 521), T. Turner (1977: 53–70), La Fontaine (1985: 24–31), Helander (1986: 117–18), Pentikäinen (1986: 1–2), R. C. Douglas (1988: 31–32), Houseman (1993: 212), M. Hamilton (1995: 132–33).

[5] Van Gennep (ET 1960: 11; first edition, 1909). Though he notes that not all are equally elaborated in every system.

[6] Van Gennep (ET 1960: 2–3).

[7] La Fontaine (1985: 25). Similar comments are made by V. Turner (1977: 53), Houseman (1993: 212). T. Turner (1977: 53–70) devotes the whole of his article to the importance of van Gennep's model.

[8] In addition to the vast amount of fieldwork that has been done on primitive societies, van Gennep's analysis has shed light on such diverse material as Greek and Egyptian mystery religions (Bleeker [1965b: 49–58], Eliade [1965a: 107–15], Dowden [1989]), modern secret societies such as the Masons (La Fontaine [1985: 38–57]), the Jewish-Diaspora document of *Joseph and Aseneth* (R. C. Douglas [1988: 31–42]; cf. Philonenko [1965: 147–53]), various aspects of Christian rituals (Antweiler [1965: 233–42], Grainger [1988]), modern evangelical and pentecostal movements (Helander [1986], Holm [1986]), gnosticism (Gihilus [1984], Bianchi [1986: 45–61]), as well as contemporary literary works (Eliade [1965b: 12–14]).

[9] V. Turner (1977: 36). Compare the analysis of Leach (1968: 525): "Ritual action . . . serves to express the status of the actor vis-à-vis his environment, both physical and social; it may also serve to alter the status of the actor."

Par initiation on comprend généralement un ensemble de rites et
d'enseignements oraux, au moyen desquels on obtient une modification radicale du statut religieux et social du sujet à initier.
Philosophiquement parlant, l'initiation équivaut à une mutation
ontologique du régime existentiel. A la fin de ses épreuves, le
néophyte jouit d'une toute autre existence qu'avant l'initiation:
il est devenu un *autre*.[10]

The association of life-crisis rituals with a change of status is so common in the literature on this subject that I need not linger over the matter.[11]
Of more interest in the present discussion is the symbolism used to express this transfer, particularly that of the liminal period, which draws on
physiomorphic imagery or "the biology of death."[12]

Death and life

Van Gennep's observation that "momentary death" was a "general theme
of magical as well as religious initiation"[13] has been substantiated and
illustrated by countless case studies.[14] Thus, Eliade can state matter-of-
factly, " 'Initiation' means, as we know, the symbolic death and resurrection of the neophyte."[15] The means of depicting the initiate's death varies
from group to group, depending on indigenous imagery,[16] but the concept
is always present. Equally prominent in life-crisis rituals is the idea of
new birth.[17] As with resurrection, it is symbolized in a variety of ways:
the initiate may pass through the legs of a woman, suckle, eat the food
of infants, or perform other infant-like behavior.[18] Whereas "death" is the
invariable element in the equation, new birth and resurrection appear to
be alternative ways of expressing the "life" side of this equation. This is

[10] Eliade (1965b: 1–2).
[11] See van Gennep (ET 1960: 110), V. Turner (1967: 93; 1968: 577; 1969: 166–203),
La Fontaine (1985: 16, 64, 82), Dowden (1989: 7); Houseman (1993: 212–17).
[12] V. Turner (1967: 96).   [13] Van Gennep (ET 1960: 110).
[14] See the material compiled by Eliade (1965a) and La Fontaine (1985).
[15] Eliade (1961: 49). Similar comments are made by M. Douglas (1966: 96), La Fontaine
(1985: 103), Dowden (1989: 36).
[16] The initiate may be buried (Eliade [1965a: 31], V. Turner [1967: 96]), painted black,
identified with dead ancestors (V. Turner [1977: 37]), made to travel through underground
passages (Eliade, 1965a: 41–60), etc. For Paul, the initiate's death and resurrection were
symbolized in baptism (Rom. 6.2–3).
[17] On new birth in life-crisis rituals see, e.g., van Gennep (ET 1960: 31, 105), Eliade
(1965a: 28, 60–72), V. Turner (1967: 52, 96; 1968: 576), La Fontaine (1985: 64–66),
M. Hamilton (1995: 135).
[18] La Fontaine (1985: 66–67, 88–91). Further details can be found in Bettelheim (1955:
214–23), van Gennep (ET 1960: 29–38, 95), Eliade (1965a: 28), V. Turner (1967: 52;
1977: 37).

one of Mary Douglas' points in speaking of a "repertoire" of symbols: "The theme of death and rebirth, of course, has other symbolic functions: the initiates die to their old life and are re-born to the new. The whole repertoire of ideas concerning pollution and purification are used to mark the gravity of the event and the power of ritual to remake a man – this is straight-forward."[19]

The ubiquitous nature of this symbolism led Douglas in a later work to speak of "natural symbols";[20] and La Fontaine speaks of "universal symbols," by which she means that "all rituals use a similar repertoire of concepts."[21] Van Gennep was aware of the global character of his schema and the related symbolism and suggested that the striking similarities issue from the fact that all initiation rites share a common goal.[22] A transition from one state to another could hardly be better epitomized than by the physiomorphic imagery of death and rebirth/resurrection. Van Gennep's suggestion has been amply confirmed, and particularly by the consensus statement of an international congress of anthropologists, which defined the purpose of initiation rites as "the attainment of something 'new.' "[23] In discussing the aims of life-crisis rituals Ugo Bianchi put the matter succinctly: "Every initiatory ritual – more exactly, every concept of 'novelty of life' – is a ritual or concept of death and rebirth."[24] As I turn to consider other facets of initiatory symbolism, it will be helpful to keep in mind the essential aim of this ritual drama: the attainment of *newness of life*, to use the Pauline idiom (Rom. 6.4).

Transformation

The word encountered most often in discussions of life-crisis rituals is *transformation*.[25] This is not surprising given the goal of initiation, and most of the related symbolism in life-crisis rituals is directed specifically toward articulating the transformative nature of the ceremony. Phrases like "ontological transformation,"[26] "metamorphosis,"[27] "becoming another,"[28] attaining "true human existence,"[29] becoming "a new

---

[19] M. Douglas (1966: 96).   [20] M. Douglas (1970).

[21] La Fontaine (1985: 13). Dowden (1989: 192) remarks that initiation rites form "an essential part of human nature."

[22] Van Gennep (ET 1960: 114).   [23] Bianchi (1986: iv).   [24] Bianchi (1986: 58).

[25] Although found in virtually all of the literature cited in this study, the term is especially prominent in the works of Eliade, La Fontaine, and V. Turner. In addition, see T. Turner (1977: 53–58) who devotes several pages to the meaning and significance of the word "transformation" in discussing initiation rites.

[26] Eliade (1965b: 1), V. Turner (1967:101), B. Lincoln (1981: 104).

[27] Houseman (1993: 216–17).   [28] Eliade (1965b:1).

[29] Bleeker (1965a: 20), Eliade (1965a: xiii), Pentikäinen (1986: 7).

man,"[30] "Leben in Fülle,"[31] and "new creation,"[32] are but a small sampling of expressions used by anthropologists and comparative religionists to capture the essence and aim of these death–life dramas. In Victor Turner's view, initiatory rituals "refashion the very being of the neophyte,"[33] which, in turn, equips the individual to function in the new community of which he or she becomes a part.

Ritual suffering

Particularly important in the ritual drama are the ordeals which the initiate must suffer during the liminal period. Again, these take a variety of forms, ranging from severe to comical, but are always an essential part of the process.[34] Their significance is twofold: personal and social. Regarding the former Turner says that "the neophyte is ground down to be fashioned anew, and endowed with additional powers to cope with their new situation in life."[35] The social dynamic of these ordeals is emphasized by Hamilton who, synthesizing the results of much fieldwork, concludes, "all these theorists, however, emphasize the role of initiation rites in radically breaking identifications and creating new allegiances and orientations by the use of dramatic and traumatic means."[36] Hence, the effect of the suffering and ritual death of the initiate in the liminal period can be summarized by the words *empowerment* and *demarcation*.

Empowerment

"No initiation known to us," writes Mendelson, "leaves the individual less powerful than he was before."[37] This empowerment serves the important purpose of enabling the individual to act in a manner appropriate to their new status, a fact repeatedly emphasized by anthropologists.[38] To cite Turner, "out of their mundane structural context [the initiates] are, in a sense, 'dead' to the world . . . then later refashioned into specific shapes compatible with their new post-liminal duties."[39] The rejuvenation and

---

[30] Bleeker (1965a: 20).   [31] Antweiler (1965: 242).
[32] Hoens (1965: 77), Dowden (1989: 7).
[33] V. Turner (1969: 103).
[34] La Fontaine (1985: *passim*). Cf. van Gennep (ET 1960: 75), Eliade (1961: 82–83; 1965a *passim*), Houseman (1993: 209).
[35] V. Turner (1967: 101).   [36] M. Hamilton (1995: 133).
[37] Mendelson (1965: 215).
[38] E.g., Eliade (1965a: *passim*), La Fontaine (1985: 64, 115, *passim*), Houseman (1993: 207), M. Hamilton (1995: 129).
[39] V. Turner (1977: 37).

empowerment of the initiate is directed specifically toward ethical behavior and becomes "a means by which the society or group upholds central moral values and principles and preserves the moral order."[40] Houseman's work stresses the responsibility of the individual in living in accordance with the change enacted in the ritual: "In as much as these transformations provide the necessary (and sometimes sufficient) grounds for legitimately undertaking certain distinctive activities, claiming certain privileged rights and responsibilities, etc., the issue of the participants' commitment to these changes is a particularly crucial one."[41] In other words, the imperative is rooted in the indicative in that the death–life ritual effects "the transformation of raw human material into socially responsible persons."[42]

The agent of such empowerment is not always made explicit, though Eliade has shown that this "sacred power" is often bestowed by the deity.[43] Indeed, identification with a deity, dead ancestors, or other supernatural power is a regular theme of the liminal period.[44] In terms of male puberty rites, Eliade points out that it is the deity that both performs the rite and resuscitates the novice.[45] The significance of the divine being in the liminal phase is sometimes understood in reference to the "life" side of the death–life drama: the initiate comes into contact with "the primordial generative powers of the universe"[46] and is permanently changed as a result. At other times, however, it is the "death" side of the drama which the presence of the deity explicates: "Initiatory death is thus the repetition of the death of the Supernatural Being ... since the primordial drama is repeated during the initiation, the participants in an initiation also imitate the fate of the Supernatural Being: his death by violence."[47]

Demarcation

The second effect of the suffering and ritual death of the initiate is to incorporate him/her into a new community, a community of those similarly transformed. La Fontaine's work is especially important here, though

[40] M. Hamilton (1995: 129). Cf. van Gennep (ET 1960: 182), V. Turner (1967: 108; 1969: 103), Pentikäinen (1986: 7). Eliade makes the point that the initiates are "indefinitely re-animated and enriched with new values" (1965a: 113).

[41] Houseman (1993: 207).

[42] La Fontaine (1985: 115). Note the way the indicative–imperative dynamic is expressed by Bernardi (1986: 81), who maintains that initiatory rituals "create a cognitive order at the same time as they promote a social order."

[43] Eliade (1965a: 72).   [44] Eliade (1965a: xiv–xv, 17–24, 37), V. Turner (1967: 98).

[45] Eliade (1965a: 21–24).   [46] V. Turner (1968: 577).   [47] Eliade (1965a: 131).

this point is often made in the literature. She writes, "Initiation defines boundaries, between members of a group and outsiders, between different statuses and between contrasted ideas . . . the initiates are not only transformed, but gain status."[48] This new social status entails obligations and responsibilities within the new community and serves to create "a loyal group, a cohesive social force."[49] This radical break with one's former life is often symbolized by stripping off old garments and being clothed with new.[50]

In discussing initiatory rites of secret societies and religious sects,[51] the notion of "change of status" – personal and social – might be more accurately described as "status reversal."[52] Those who occupy a high social position have their status stripped away, as do those who occupy a low social position. La Fontaine's emphasis lies on the role of such societies in attracting "the politically weak, the unsuccessful and marginal members of society." In her view, these groups offer "another way of obtaining the power and esteem that they are denied by their social position."[53] Turner, however, perceives the significance of the ritual for both groups: "The structurally inferior aspire to symbolic structural superiority in ritual; the structurally superior aspire to symbolic communitas and undergo penance to achieve it."[54] If Turner is correct, his analysis might shed light on the social function or, "plausibility basis" of Paul's death–life language,[55] especially his new-creation statements in Galatians and 2 Corinthians.

Betwixt and between

Perhaps the most intriguing – and at the same time, perplexing – aspect of life-crisis rituals was described by Turner in his pioneering essay "Betwixt

[48] La Fontaine (1985: 16). Cf. V. Turner (1968: 576), Dowden (1989: 193–202), Houseman (1993: 212).

[49] La Fontaine (1985: 78).

[50] On the significance and frequency of ritual nudity in initiation rites see van Gennep (ET 1960: 106), V. Turner (1968: 576; 1977: 37), La Fontaine (1985: 98), Dowden (1989: 31), Houseman (1993: 209–12),

[51] At this point, the difference between *initiation* and *conversion* should be made explicit. Whereas initiation usually involves a movement from one group to another *within* the dominant social structure, conversion generally entails a movement into a group which stands (in some sense) *outside* the dominant social structure. See R. C. Douglas (1988: 32).

[52] On this see V. Turner (1969: 166–203), but note B. Morris' critique of Turner on this point (1987: 252–63).

[53] La Fontaine (1985: 82).   [54] V. Turner (1969: 203).

[55] Here I cite Theissen (1992: 187), who defines *plausibility basis* as "the social conditions and factors which allow a conviction to seem obviously tenable."

and Between: The Liminal Period in Rites de Passage."[56] Once again Turner builds on the work of van Gennep, but his exposition of this phenomenon achieved a penetration lacking in the work of his predecessor. Turner's essential insight concerns the ambiguous "neither-nor," "both-and" status of the individual in the liminal period. He writes: "The essential feature of these symbolizations is that the neophytes are neither living nor dead from one aspect, and both living and dead from another. Their condition is one of ambiguity and paradox, a confusion of all the customary categories."[57]

The condition of being "neither one state, nor the next"[58] is commonly expressed in terms of transcending sexual barriers, so that the liminal person becomes "neither male nor female" or sometimes both.[59] Eliade summarizes the import of this imagery by observing, "All these images express the necessity of transcending 'pairs of opposites,' of abolishing the polarities that beset the human condition, in order to reach the ultimate reality."[60]

Those familiar with Paul's death–life symbolism will no doubt hear numerous echoes at this point. Paul's insistence on being "both living and dead" (Gal. 2.19–20; 2 Cor. 4.10–12; 6.9), his dissolution of gender barriers (Gal. 3.28), his attempt to transcend the "pairs of opposites"[61] which confronted him ("neither circumcision, nor uncircumcision, but *new creation*"), all bear a striking resemblance to the death–life symbolism encountered in initiatory rituals throughout the world. Again, the integrity of each tradition must be firmly maintained, especially against the tendency of some to homogenize the material too quickly. On the other hand, Paul's soteriological imagery belongs to a larger matrix of religious symbolism, and, as such, is not without analogy.

The cosmic simile

One other aspect of initiatory symbolism demands consideration, and its import with regard to this study could hardly be overestimated. It is not

---

[56] First published in *The Proceedings of the American Ethnological Society* (1964). On the importance of this essay see T. Turner (1977: 54–55), Pentikäinen (1986: 4–5), B. Morris (1987: 253–63), R. C. Douglas (1988: 32–34).

[57] V. Turner (1967: 96–97). Cf. T. Turner (1977: 37).

[58] M. Douglas (1966: 62). Cf. La Fontaine (1985: 117–40), M. Hamilton (1995: 134).

[59] V. Turner (1967: 98). The sexlessness of those in the liminal period is often discussed in the literature: van Gennep (ET 1960: 114–15, 172), Bettelheim (1955: 212–13), Dowden (1989: 65), Houseman (1993: 212).

[60] Eliade (1961: 84).

[61] Note how J. L Martyn (1985: 410–24) uses exactly the same phrase in his exegesis of Gal. 6.15.

uncommon to find cosmic imagery used in connection with life-crisis rituals,[62] and Eliade has made a special point of addressing the issue. In his view, the cosmogony provides the quintessential illustration of the central purpose of the death–life drama: the new creation of the initiate: "The cosmogenic myth serves as the paradigm, the exemplary model for every kind of making. Nothing better ensures the success of any creation (a village, a house, a child) than the fact of copying it after the greatest of all creations, the cosmogony."[63]

In drawing together the birth and creation language so prevalent in initiatory ritual Eliade concludes, "The newness of the spiritual life, its autonomy, could find no better expression than the image of an 'absolute beginning,' images whose structure is anthropocosmic, deriving at once from embryology and cosmology."[64]

Excursus: Paul and new birth

The preceding material has emphasized the importance of *new birth* in initiatory symbolism, and this raises the question of new-birth imagery in Paul. Albert Schweitzer was particularly keen to insist that "in Paul we find only Resurrection-mysticism and not also Rebirth-mysticism,"[65] and this view is frequently advocated today.[66] Against this, however, stand such texts as Galatians 4.29, the punch line of the Sarah and Hagar allegory: "Just as in that time the one born κατὰ σάρκα persecuted the one born κατὰ πνεῦμα, so also today." Paul's point is not that Isaac was born κατὰ πνεῦμα, but that believers are. He reads his perception of Christian experience into the Genesis narrative and defines it as new birth by the Spirit. Further, it is difficult to ignore Paul's fondness for birth metaphors. According to Paul, the result of reconciliation is not a mature individual, but a newborn infant (1 Cor. 3.1–3; 1 Thess. 2.7–12; cf. Titus 3.5). Paul refers to Onesimus as his child "begotten while in chains" (Phlm. 10), and the Corinthians as his children "begotten through the gospel" (1 Cor. 4.15; cf. 2 Cor. 6.13). The Galatians, who Paul feared were abandoning his gospel, were addressed as "My children, for whom *again* I am in the pains of childbirth . . . " (4.19). Most importantly, however, when Paul searches for a word to describe his own conversion,

---

[62] See the discussions in Eliade (1961: 83–85), V. Turner (1967: 99), B. Lincoln (1981), R. C. Douglas (1988).

[63] Eliade (1965a: xii).   [64] Eliade (1965a: 60).

[65] Albert Schweitzer (1931:15). See pp. 13–15, 119–20, and 138 for Schweitzer's elaboration.

[66] E.g., Wedderburn (1987: 62, 388), Mell (1989: 310 n. 118).

the term he chooses, ἐκτρώμα (1 Cor. 15.8), depicts a birth experience of the most violent and traumatic kind. Like Shakespeare's Macduff, he saw himself as one "untimely ripped" from his mother's womb, so it is hardly surprising that new-birth imagery should punctuate his letters. To be sure, Paul's symbolic landscape was dominated by the cross, so his favorite physiomorphic imagery (death–life symbolism) has this event at its center. Yet it is equally clear that Paul understood coming to faith in Christ as an experience of new birth, and this cannot be denied without excising a significant amount of material from Paul's letters.

This point is not merely academic. Ulrich Mell, for instance, warns against seeing any ontological connotation in καινὴ κτίσις because, "der Begriff und die Vorstellung einer Wiedergeburt bei Paulus selbst nicht vorkommen."[67] If the argument presented above is correct, Mell's warning may not be appropriate. Mell does, however, introduce the crucial issue of the interpretation of religious symbolism and the relationship between Paul's various soteriological metaphors.

Interpreting religious symbolism

If anthropological fieldwork has yielded a rich source of comparative material to draw on, anthropological theorists have been equally help-ful in providing methodological guidelines for the interpretation of reli-gious symbolism. The crucial issue here has to do with the relationship between the various symbols in any given symbolic network, and the importance of the whole for the interpretation of the parts. Eliade, for ex-ample, stresses the multivalency of symbolic expression and, hence, the necessity of recognizing interdependency within the variety of images: "It is therefore the image as such, as a whole bundle of meanings, that is *true*, and not any *one* of its meanings, nor one alone of its frames of reference."[68] Eliade may exaggerate, but his point is well taken. There is an intrinsic connectednesss in any symbolic web which resists attempts to isolate, remove, and analyze individual strands. Further, as Turner points out, the *parts* have to be interpreted in light of the *whole* if any coherent structure is to emerge. In his article on "Myth and Symbol" he writes, "The specific initiation rite or myth must also be examined as a compo-nent of a total system of religious beliefs and practices . . . the principles and themes underlying these must be related to those found in other parts of the total religious system."[69]

---

[67] Mell (1989: 310 n. 118).   [68] Eliade (1961: 15), his emphasis.
[69] V. Turner (1968: 578).

Both of these points have also been emphasized by Gerd Theissen in his essay "Soteriological Symbolism in the Pauline Writings."[70] In Theissen's view Paul depicts redemption by means of sociomorphic interaction symbolism (images drawn from the social sphere) and physiomorphic transformation symbolism (images drawn from the organic and biological spheres). A detailed description of his perceptive analysis will not be attempted here,[71] though my dependence on Theissen's work will be evident in what follows. The present concern is to note the way Theissen prepares the ground for his interpretation of Paul's soteriological symbolism by making precisely the same points as those made by Eliade and Turner. After discussing the virtues of a synchronic approach to Paul's symbolism, Theissen writes, "it is conceivable that the intention of Pauline soteriology can be found not in any single symbolism or any individual themes but in a network of all the symbols."[72] Yet this does not entail synthesis to the exclusion of analysis, as Theissen goes on to say: "for it is only the disclosure of a network of relationships between the units that permits us to distinguish clearly from one another the different elements in the imagery. *Element and structure determine each other mutually.*"[73]

Summary and conclusions

The importance of laying this methodological foundation will be apparent. 2 Corinthians 5.17 and Galatians 6.15 belong to that species of physiomorphic transformation symbolism issuing from the biological analogy of death and life. As such they are part of a larger family of passages – widely diverging in context – which exhibit a similar structure and have a similar focus. Paul's death–life symbolism should serve as part of the interpretive framework for his new-creation statements, though scholarly writing on these texts has yet to come to terms with this.

Another conclusion to be drawn from the previous discussion is that Paul's physiomorphic transformation symbolism does not consist solely of the categories outlined by Theissen, but also includes new-birth symbolism. To be sure, the centripetal nature of the death of Christ had the effect of drawing most of Paul's imaginative symbols into its vortex. However, his experience of the Spirit of the risen Christ was powerful

---

[70] Theissen (1992: 152–86).   [71] For such a description see Beker (1980: 256–60).
[72] Theissen (1992: 162). The strength of von Harnack's still valuable essay ("Die Terminologie der Wiedergeburt und verwandter Erlebnisse in der ältesten Kirche," 1918) is that he recognized the synonymity of this diverse terminology and saw it as a witness to the "Jubelruf" of renewal which reverberated throughout the literature of early Christianity.
[73] Theissen (1992: 162), my emphasis.

enough to establish an independent foothold in the apostle's thought, and this regenerative encounter he likens to new birth. Hence, it is not insignificant that "Spirit" and "life" are virtual synonyms in Paul. Given the presence of new-birth symbolism in Paul's letters, it is necessary to reckon with another "life" metaphor in discussion of Paul's death–life/new-creation symbolism.

Further, death–life symbolism has a fairly common currency in comparative religious studies and this wider context will prove helpful as I consider its peculiar expression in Paul's letters. It must be emphasized again that the primary context for the explication of Paul's religious symbolism must be Paul's letters themselves, along with the historical-social contexts in which they were penned. However, placing Paul's symbolism within the broader framework of religious phenomenology should lead to a better-informed exegesis. Before I turn my attention to Paul's death–life statements, a brief summary of the main points of chapter 5 is in order.

The purpose of initiatory rituals and symbolism is to mark a transition from one state to another. This is done through the (ubiquitous) imagery of death–resurrection/new birth. The death–life drama includes ritual suffering, which has the purpose of both empowering the individual for his/her new responsibilities and at the same time clearly demarcating them from those who have not been so initiated. The transformative nature of the death–life drama is further advanced by identification with supernatural powers, ritual nudity and re-clothing, and cosmic imagery. As such, death–life rituals are oriented toward the individual, so much so that Mendelson could write, "[initiation] seems to me so much tied to the intimate development of the individual that it is hard to say exactly in what way it is a part of any given social structure or organization."[74] Yet the social implications of initiatory ritual need not be doubted. "Through death to maturity,"[75] is Turner's concise synopsis of the death–life drama, and it is through these rituals that the moral expectations of the community are grounded in an event of transformative significance. According to Dowden, "a new creation takes place and initiates perform a transition into a new adulthood."[76]

---

[74] Mendelson (1965: 214).   [75] V. Turner (1967: 73).   [76] Dowden (1989: 7).

6

NEWNESS OF LIFE: ROMANS 6.1–11

> Reales Sterben ist notwendig... für die neue Existenz nach
> Paulus.   Herbert Braun, "Das 'Stirb und Werde'"

The transition from puberty rites of primitive societies to Paul's death–
life symbolism is neither as abrupt nor as novel as might first appear. In
fact, the connection has been noticed before, though previous discussions
have focused exclusively on Romans 6 and the relationship between Paul's
view of baptism and that of Hellenistic mystery religions.[1] The general
synthesis of initiatory symbolism offered in chapter 5, while written independently of A. J. M. Wedderburn's treatment, dovetails nicely with his
survey of "life through death" in Greco-Roman mystery religions. One
of his conclusions with respect to Romans 6 is particularly noteworthy:

> Thus it is true that "life through death" is attested in the mystery-
> rites and that this would provide an analogy to Paul's teaching
> on baptism and one which would lie close to hand... But its
> presence in the mysteries would be only one analogy among
> several and, moreover, it could be argued that the idea lay near
> to hand in any rite of passage, and was therefore a natural image
> to use in the context of an explication of the Christian initiatory
> rite.[2]

James Dunn, assessing the affinities between Lucius' initiation into the
Isis cult and Romans 6.3–4, reaches a similar conclusion:

> Set against a still broader background, we may cite the al-
> most universal instinct which finds expression in "rites of pas-
> sage," when an experience of "liminality" seems to be part of
> the transition and the imagery of "new birth" naturally comes

---

[1] King (1977), Wedderburn (1987: 363–92).
[2] Wedderburn (1987: 379–80).

to mind ... The similarities between Apuleius and Romans at this point, therefore, is best explained by recognizing both as independent expressions of this same broader instinct, where only a small stock of metaphors is adequate to describe this kind of radically transforming experience known to Lucius and Paul.[3]

Both of these authors, and Wedderburn in particular, have helped to prepare the ground for the approach taken here. The basic structure and effects of Paul's death–life symbolism are echoed wherever we see the human soul aspiring to newness of life. However, as these "broader instincts" pass through Paul's Christological prism they are refracted in unprecedented ways. For Paul, death is not simply the means to life but also *true* life's defining feature: "Always carrying about the dying of Jesus in our bodies so that the life of Jesus might also be manifest in our bodies" (2 Cor. 4.10; cf. 4.11; 6.9). Further, the Christian's death takes place *with Christ* and is somehow related to the historical event of the crucifixion: "You have become united to the very likeness of his death" (Rom. 6.5); "One died for all, therefore all died" (2 Cor. 5.15). As I turn to consider the Pauline material, I will leave behind the history-of-religions parallels in order to allow the apostle's voice to be heard distinctly. Yet resonances between the two will no doubt also be heard.

Context

Romans 6.1–11 is located within the larger unit of 5.12–8.39. Romans 5.1–11 summarizes the first major section of the letter (Δικαιωθέντες οὖν ἐκ πίστεως, 5.1), making 5.12–21 "both transitional and pivotal."[4] Drawing firm lines of division in Paul's argument at this point is difficult (and perhaps artificial), though two considerations warrant taking 5.1–11 with what precedes rather than what follows. Διὰ τοῦτο ("For this reason," 5.12) is best understood to signal a development in thought,[5] and probably

---

[3] Dunn (1988: 310). Cf. Wedderburn's judgment, "the similarities between the Isiac initiation of Lucius and Paul's teaching on baptism boil down to a general analogy: there is a symbolic death and salvation graciously bestowed in the form of a new birth or a new creation" (1987: 380).

[4] Morgan (1995: 38).

[5] Correctly noted by Schlier (1977: 159), Leenhardt (1961:140), Wilckens (1980: 314). Though against Lagrange (1950: 105), Barrett (1957: 110), and Schlier (1977: 159), it is unlikely to be *merely* a transitional particle, with no real connection to what precedes; it does not function this way elsewhere in the New Testament. On διὰ τοῦτο see Moo

builds on the argument of 1.16–5.11 as a whole,[6] which has been summarized in 5.1–11.[7] Further, 5.1–11 is linked to what precedes by the motif of boasting which was introduced in 2.17–23, stated formally in 3.27 ("Where then is boasting?"), further developed in 4.2 and 5.2–3, and brought to resolution in 5.11: "And we boast in God through our Lord Jesus Christ." At this point the motif is dropped, occurring again only incidentally in 15.17.

As an introductory segment, 5.12–21 has several functions, and serves as a concise prospectus of the central themes (sin/grace, death/life, condemnation/acquittal, etc.) to be discussed in chapters 6–8. Dunn's commentary is careful to highlight the transition here from the universal to the particular,[8] which he correctly applies to the whole of 6.1–8.39.[9] 5.12–21 places what follows in its salvation-historical context: the reign of death ushered in by the sin of Adam is superseded by the reign of life inaugurated by the righteous act of Christ, the second Adam.[10] The abstract imagery of two opposing kingdoms ("sin *reigned* in death," 5.21) is made concrete in 6.1 ("shall *we* continue in sin?") as Paul sets the individual (and community) within this panorama of redemptive history. This narrowing of thought finds its clearest expression in 6.6 where Paul speaks of the crucifixion of the παλαιὸς ἄνθρωπος, defined by Käsemann as "Adam individualized and represented in us."[11]

Structure

Since Günther Bornkamm's essay, "Taufe und neues Leben bei Paulus,"[12] Romans 6.1–11 has usually been analyzed in terms of the parallel structure of verses 5–7 and verses 8–10.[13] This analysis is essentially correct, but

---

(1991: 363–66). The presuppositions and implications of the various divisions are discussed by Beker (1980: 64–69).

[6] So Nygren (1952: 209–11), Wilckens (1980: 314), Dunn (1988: 272–73), Wright (1991: 35).

[7] With, e.g., Denney (1900: 627), Vollenwieder (1989: 323). Sanday and Headlam (1914: 131) cite other supporters. Cf. Cranfield (1975: 271), Fitzmyer (1993c: 411).

[8] Dunn (1988: especially 271). So also Wilckens (1980: 16), Moo (1991: 369), Dinkler (1992b: 142–43).

[9] Dunn's title for 6.1–8.39 is apt: "The Outworking of the Gospel in Relation to the Individual."

[10] See especially Kuss (1957: 275–91) and Frankemölle (1970).

[11] Käsemann (1980: 169). Similarly Barrett (1957: 125), Wilckens (1980: 314), L. Morris (1988: 252), Ziesler (1989: 159).

[12] Bornkamm ([1952], ET 1969).

[13] E.g., Stanley (1961: 189), Tannehill (1967: 9), Frankemölle (1970: 24), Wilckens (1980: 7), Dinkler (1992b: 139). But note Moo's objections (1991: 370).

should be modified to include verses 2–4. The thesis to be defended in this passage is encapsulated in Paul's emphatic μὴ γένοιτο (2a).[14] Paul's central concern in 6.1–14 is to dismiss the illegitimate conclusion that some have drawn from his gospel: abundant sin makes abundant grace (cf. 3.8). Paul offers one decisive reason for rejecting this false inference, which he unfolds in three parallel ways (vv. 2–4, 5–7, 8–10),[15] though most concisely in 2b: the believer has died to sin. The indicative of 6.1–10 is balanced by the imperative of 6.12–14, which provides a smooth segue into the slavery analogy of 6.15–23 (ἁμαρτία γὰρ ὑμῶν οὐ κυριεύσει, v. 14). The *Stichwort* χάρις brackets this segment (vv. 1 and 14), holding it together as a literary unit.[16] The following analysis visually displays the structure of 6.1–11.

	Verses 2–4	Verses 5–7	Verses 8–10
Death (condition)–	(2) we died to sin,	(5) united in his death	(8) death with Christ,
Life (consequence)	*how can we live in it?*	*united in his resurrection*	*life with Christ*
Verb of knowing + ὅτι	ἢ ἀγνοεῖτε ὅτι	τοῦτο γινώσκοντες ὅτι	εἰδότες ὅτι
Explanation	(3) baptism = death (analogy clarified, 4a)	(6a) the old man has been crucified	(9a) Christ has died
Result	(4c) newness of life	(6b) slavery to sin ended	(9b) death is conquered
Basis	(4b) the resurrection of Christ	(7) death frees from sin	(10) Christ died to sin and lives to God
Summary	*(11) realize that you too are dead to sin and alive to God in Christ Jesus*		

Displaying the text in this way has the advantage of highlighting the analogous pattern of argument in verses 2–4, 5–7, and 8–10, and also points to a certain degree of reciprocity between the corresponding elements. To be sure, the argument progresses ("for if . . ." [v. 5], "and if . . . " [v. 8]), particularly in the strong Christological orientation of verses 8–10. But it is also recapitulated, and this suggests that the segments can be mutually illuminating.[17] Recognizing this structure, as well as the larger structure of 6.1–7.6 strengthens the hand of those who point to the

---

[14] The structure of this passage would be clearer if, as in the parallel text in 6.15, the verse division came after μὴ γένοιτο rather than before.

[15] Rightly, Käsemann (1980: 165) and Siber (1971: 235), though they do not elaborate. The obvious grammatical-structural parallels between vv. 5–7 and 8–10 have tended to obscure the logical-structural parallels existing between all three units.

[16] Dinkler (1992b: 135).   [17] Correctly, Frankemölle (1970: 24).

subsidiary nature of baptism in 6.1–11.[18] It is one of three object lessons (along with slavery [6.15–23] and marriage [7.1–6]) which Paul uses to illustrate his point, and does not seem to be intrinsically connected with his death–life symbolism. This will become more apparent in the examination of other death–life texts in Paul's epistles, none of which employ baptismal imagery.

Death to sin

The movement from death to life, so prominent in 6.1–11, arises organically from Paul's discussion in 5.12–21, where the entirety of human history is sketched in precisely these terms.[19] Yet the vigor with which these themes are pursued in so short a space – one or both of these ideas is expressed in each verse from 6.2 onward – leaves the reader a bit breathless and is indicative of the fact that we have reached one of Paul's soteriological nerve centers. Indeed, an aerial view of Romans 5.12–8.39 would not be amiss in describing its theological topography as one momentous trek from death to life. Given the fundamental significance of this theme in Romans 6.1–11, a closer examination should probably be made of the individual components which make up these death–life equations.

As the most concise expression of this theme, verse 2 repays close scrutiny: "How can we who died to sin live in it still?" The aorist ἀπεθάνομεν points to a specific, though unspecified, event in the past,[20] while the verb ζήσομεν is certainly a logical future. Yet the operative verbs in this sentence are less important for the moment than the phrases to which they are linked. The significance of the relative pronoun οἵτινες becomes clearer as the thought is completed, and has led many to sense a more classical nuance in its use here, in which "the relative clause expresses the general quality" of its referent.[21] Barrett's bold translation, "we who

[18] E.g., Denney (1900: 232), Bonnard (1956: 104), Tannehill (1967: 7–14), Dunn (1970a: 139–46), Frankemölle (1970: 24), E. F. Harrison (1976: 68), Käsemann (1980: 163–64), Moo (1991: 371), Fitzmyer (1993c: 429). Against, e.g., Leenhardt (1961: 152–53), Dinkler (1992b: 138).
[19] Cf. Kertelge (1967: 263), Dunn (1988: 301–3).
[20] Some (e.g., Barrett [1957: 121], L. Morris [1988: 247–48], Moo [1991: 374]) point to conversion as the time of this death, with baptism symbolizing the burial or interment which completes this event. Others (e.g. Kuss [1957: 296], Käsemann [1980: 165–66]) believe baptism itself is the point of death. It is also possible to identify this past death as occurring at the time of Christ's death (Wedderburn [1987: 65]). Cranfield's ambivalence is justified: "The question . . . is not of vital significance" (1975: 300).
[21] BDF §293. Both Robertson (1934: 278) and Moule (1959: 122) corroborate this distinction and cite Romans 6.2 as an illustrative text. BDF also notes that this distinction is more carefully maintained in Paul than elsewhere in the New Testament. Among the

in our essential nature... died,"[22] captures well the exclamation point standing at the end of this rhetorical question. Paul is working with a perception of Christian existence which excludes *by definition* "living" in sin. The individual "in Christ" (v. 11) is defined by an experience of death, and in Paul's view, it would constitute a violation of the law of non-contradiction to suggest that this person can remain in a sphere from which they have been severed.

This emphasis is continued in that peculiar dative expression, ἀπε-θάνομεν τῇ ἁμαρτίᾳ (repeated in vv. 10 and 11), which Moule regards as a "syntactical novelty... formed by Paul on the analogy of 'to live to.'"[23] The idea of "dying to" something and "living to" something (usually God: 6.10–11; 7.4; 2 Cor. 5.15; Gal. 2.20) is a characteristic element of Paul's life-through-death texts, though we must draw back from labeling it *distinctively* Pauline.[24] While it is possible to describe these constructions as datives of advantage or disadvantage,[25] they are best understood as datives of relation,[26] indicating (in the case of the "dying to" statements) the complete and irrevocable termination of a prior relationship. In choosing to describe this severance with the word *death,* Paul leaves no room for doubt concerning the permanence of this state. Moule's summary of this language is not exaggerated: "all these are datives of relation: *non-existence* as far as law is concerned, or sin, or the world."[27]

The subjects of death

If exegetes can speak with confidence regarding (1) the reality of the believer's death in 6.1–11, and (2) the sphere from which the believer has been separated (sin: 6.2, 6, 7, 10, 12, 13, 14, etc.), there is less certainty when it comes to specifying precisely who has died. The difficulty with

commentaries see Denny (1900: 632), Sanday and Headlam (1914: 156), Cranfield (1975: 293), Dunn (1988: 307), L. Morris (1988: 245), Moo (1991: 373).

[22] Barrett (1957: 121). Cf. Murray (1959: 213): "we who are the sort"; L. Morris (1988: 245): "we who are of such a quality as to"; Moo (1991: 373): "we who are of such a nature that."

[23] Moule (1970: 368–69). This was first suggested to him by his (then) student A. J. M. Wedderburn.

[24] Cf. 4 Macc. 7.19 (πιστεύοντες ὅτι θεῷ οὐκ ἀποθνήσκουσιν... ἀλλὰ ζῶσιν τῷ θεῷ); 1 Pet. 2.24; Ps.-Philo, *Lib. Ant.* 28.10.

[25] So Tannehill (1967: 18), Frankemölle (1970: 34), Moo (1991: 374).

[26] With Denney (1900: 632), Schlatter (1935: 199), Kuss (1957: 296), Moule (1970: 374), Wilckens (1980: 10), Ziesler (1989: 89). Frequently (e.g., Schlatter, Wilckens, Ziesler) this relationship is specified as one of *possession.* This accords well with the idea of sin's lordship in 5.21; 6.6–10, 12–14. See BDF §182 (2).

[27] Moule (1970: 374), my emphasis.

this material, as Dinkler notes, is its *bildhaften* character, which is only partly clarified by the context.[28] The parallel structure of verses 2–4, 5–7, and 8–10, suggests that information might be profitably gleaned from surveying the subjects of this death–life experience in each segment.

"We"

The most frequent designation of the subject of this death–life experience is simply "we." It is "we" who have been buried with Christ, and walk in newness of life (v. 4), who have become united with him in his death (v. 5), who no longer serve sin (v. 6), who have died with Christ (v. 8), and so on. This "we" is delineated more precisely by the οἵτινες clause of verse 2, which has the function of singling out death as the *sine qua non* of Christian experience. This point (indeed, the whole of v. 2) is essentially recapitulated in the maxim of verse 7: ὁ γὰρ ἀποθανὼν δεδικαίωται ἀπὸ τῆς ἁμαρτίας.[29] Hence, the "we" of Romans 6.1–11 (and of Paul's letters generally) is always a "we-who-have-died."

The old person

So far all is clear, but with the introduction of the term ὁ παλαιὸς ἡμῶν ἄνθρωπος (6.6) my exegesis encounters unwanted turbulence. It is sometimes suggested that "the old person" has its antithetical counterpart in "the new creation" of 2 Corinthians 5.17,[30] and if this connection is valid, this phrase requires more than just a passing comment.

In relation to Pauline ethics. The phrase ὁ παλαιὸς ἄνθρωπος is also found in Colossians 3.9 and Ephesians 4.22, where it bears a decidedly ethical connotation: "Do not lie to one another, having taken off *the old person* with its practices" (Col. 3.9); "Take off your former way of life, *the old person,* which is decaying through the lusts of deceit" (Eph. 4.22). Without assuming anything about the authorship of these works, it is interesting to note that the phrase has a similar nuance in Romans 6.6, as the following result clauses indicate: "in order that the body of sin [or, sinful body] might be rendered ineffective, so that we no longer

---

[28] Dinkler (1992b: 137). Similarly Moores (1995: 83–84). Morgan (1995: 41) calls Paul's language here "heavily coded" and offers a helpful analysis of this subject (94–127).

[29] Regardless of the origin of this expression, verse 7 serves to illustrate Paul's theological point "by reference to a general truth" (Moo [1991: 394]). So too Wilckens (1980:17). Against, e.g., Frankemölle (1970: 76) and Wedderburn (1987: 64), verse 7 is not a Christological statement. Cf. Käsemann (1980: 170), Dunn (1988: 321), Fitzmyer (1993c: 437).

[30] E.g., Kuss (1957: 312), Beker (1980: 288), Wilckens (1980: 16), Dinkler (1992b: 140).

serve sin." Whatever else may be said of ὁ παλαιὸς ἄνθρωπος, it is closely associated with a way of life characterized by sinful activity.[31] The expression gains clarity, however, when the effects that are ascribed to its crucifixion are noted: the "body of sin" is made powerless and servitude to sin is ended (6.6bc). As we consider the ensuing argument, it becomes apparent that τὸ σῶμα τῆς ἁμαρτίας denotes what Paul elsewhere calls "the flesh."

In relation to "the flesh." Σῶμα occurs a few verses later (v. 12), in Paul's description of the reign of sin in the "mortal body" (θνητὸν σῶμα) which compels one to obey its desires. This surprisingly corporeal picture is re-enforced by what follows, where "mortal body" appears synonymous with "your members" (6.13). For all the interpretive difficulties of 7.14–25, it is arguably clear that one of its primary concerns is to demonstrate the inability of the "σάρκινος" who is sold in slavery to sin (7.14). It is the law at work in this person's "members" which compels them to do what they hate (7.19–23). The answer to this dilemma is given in 8.1–14, where the weakness of the σάρξ is replaced by the power of the πνεῦμα, "in order that the just requirements of the law might be fulfilled in us" (8.4). The central premise of much of Romans 6–8 is stated in 8.8: "For those ἐν σαρκί *are not able* to please God." In Romans 6.6 release from sin's bondage is described as the negation of the "body of sin" (read "sin-possessed body") while in Romans 7 and 8 it is the σάρξ which is rendered powerless. This equation is confirmed by 8.13: "For if you live κατὰ σάρκα you will die, but if by the Spirit you put to death the πράξεις τοῦ σώματος you will live." In this text the "deeds of the σῶμα" are equated with a life κατὰ σάρκα, both of which are set in antithesis to life in the Spirit. Jewett, then, is on firm ground in asserting that "σῶμα is used in place of σάρξ in [8.13]."[32]

The soft dualism which is found in Romans 6–8 should not be ignored, but neither should it be exaggerated. Paul never suggests that humanity's material substance is intrinsically evil, though it is quite apparent that he sees humanity's somatic existence as the sphere in which sin's dominion is most vividly expressed. Kuss is correct to assert that "the dialectic of indicative and imperative in Paul is a necessary consequence of the fact that Easter brought the resurrection . . . and not the parousia."[33] It is no surprise, then, that the redemption Paul envisions as occurring at

---

[31] So also Gundry (1976: 136), Wilckens (1980: 16).
[32] Jewett (1971: 297). So too Wendland (1952: 462) and Kreitzer (1993b: 73); also Moores (1995: 114), who exposes Paul's logic in 8.13a by paraphrasing it, "The deeds of the body kill (σάρξ is a killer)."
[33] Kuss (1957: 315).

the parousia is specifically designated somatic: τὴν ἀπολύτρωσιν τοῦ σώματος ἡμῶν (Rom. 8.23; cf. Phil. 3.21). While this dialectic may cause some to blush, it is nonetheless real and fully justifies Gundry's exegesis of Romans 6.6: "[The body of sin] therefore does not refer to an abstract mass of sin, to the system of sinful desires, to Sin personified as a sphere of power in the old Aeon, or to the sinful personality, but concretely to the physical body which has been dominated by sin, is doomed to destruction and will receive resurrection."[34]

Implications. This exegesis has significant implications for the interpretation of ὁ παλαιὸς ἡμῶν ἄνθρωπος. Against some, "our old person" cannot simply be equated with "the body of sin" in the following clause.[35] This not only hopelessly blurs the argument of the next two chapters, it also ignores the grammar and logic of the sentence: the annulment of the "body of sin" is a *result* (ἵνα) of the crucifixion of the old person. The relationship between the two clauses is that of cause→ effect, not assertion→ restatement. Neither can we so closely identify ὁ παλαιὸς ἡμῶν ἄνθρωπος with Adam of 5.12–21 that the phrase comes to denote "an inclusive *anthropos*," an abstract "inclusive reality."[36] Without being more precise than the evidence allows, it may be possible to identify "the old person" of Romans 6.6 with the *unenabled* person of 7.14–25 and 8.1–14, the σάρκινος (7.14) who *lives* ἐν σαρκί (7.5; 8.9) and walks κατὰ σάρκα (8.4, 5, 13), and so remains shackled in slavery to ἁμαρτία (6.6, 12–14; 7.14, etc.).[37] This interpretation of the crucified παλαιὸς ἄνθρωπος is confirmed by Galatians 5.24–25 which, alternatively, speaks of the crucified σάρξ (5.24). As in Romans 6, the result is ethical renewal through the Spirit (5.25).

Because the effects of the crucifixion of the παλαιὸς ἄνθρωπος are identical to those ascribed to the entrance of the πνεῦμα τῆς ζωῆς (8.1), it

---

[34] Gundry (1976: 58). For a similar understanding of "body of sin" see Denney (1900: 633), Sanday and Headlam (1914: 158), Schlatter (1935: 206–7), Lagrange (1950: 146–47), Kuss (1957: 304), Murray (1959: 220), Leenhardt (1961: 162), Kertelge (1967: 263), E. F. Harrison (1976: 70), L. Morris (1988: 251–52); see also Moule (1959: 38), who describes σῶμα τῆς ἁμαρτίας as an adjectival genitive and translates it "the sin-possessed body."

[35] E.g., Frankemölle (1970: 76), Cranfield (1975: 309), Dinkler (1992a: 53).

[36] Tannehill (1967: 27). So too Cousar (1990: 72–73).

[37] This interpretation is not substantially altered by one's interpretation of the "I" of Romans 7.7–25. Even if Paul is recounting his present experience in this text, he would be conceding only that the death to sin he has just described is not fully realized in his conduct. On this reading of Romans 7 and 8 the σάρκινος of 7.14 refers to Paul in so far as he must still "put to death the misdeeds of the body through the Spirit" (8.13). But could Paul refer to *himself* as σάρκινος in 7.14, while at the same time insisting that believers are no longer ἐν σαρκί (6.6; 8.9)? This is a difficult proposition to accept.

follows that the ideas are related. If one wished to identify an antithetical counterpart to the παλαιὸς ἄνθρωπος, it would be prudent to look at that constellation of ideas associated with the "life" side of Paul's death–life symbolism. The conceptual–structural parallels between 6.6 and 6.4 suggest that "walking in καινότητι ζωῆς" is the verbal antithesis to the nominal παλαιὸς ἄνθρωπος.[38] This idea has its synonym in 7.6: "serving in καινότητι πνεύματος."[39] It is too early to comment on the relationship between "the old person" and the "new creation," especially as the latter has not yet been defined. But given the association of the "old man" with a sarkic existence, and that Paul's new creation stands in contrast to this realm (2 Cor. 5.16; Gal. 6.12–13), it follows that the pair might be antithetically related.

Newness of life

After asserting unambiguously a past death and crucifixion with Christ, one might expect Paul to proceed to an equally clear assertion of a past resurrection with Christ. This expectation, however, is not met, and Paul's language here has proven puzzling to exegetes. There are a number of interrelated questions: (1) Do the verbs ἐσόμεθα (v. 5) and συζήσομεν (v. 8) indicate a logical or temporal future? That is, could they be construed as a reference to the believer's present resurrected status (as in Eph. 2.6 and Col. 2.12) or must they refer only to an eschatological event?[40] (2) If these verbs are temporal futures, is Paul carefully avoiding resurrection language, or is his terminology incidental? (3) If one decides that Paul's wording is deliberately restrained, a plausible reason should be offered for this.[41] Unfortunately, there is nothing close to a consensus on any

[38] Correctly, G. Schneider (1983: 17); Dunn (1988: 366).
[39] Correctly, Denney (1900: 663), Michel (1955: 143), Cranfield (1975: 339), Schlier (1977: 219), Dunn (1988: 366), Fee (1994: 499).
[40] Those who believe ἐσόμεθα in v. 5 is a logical future include Cranfield, Denney, Fitzmyer, Frankemölle, Harrison, Kuss, Leenhardt, Murray, Stanley, and Wilckens. In the opposing corner stand Barrett, Bornkamm, Dinkler, Dunn, Käsemann, Moo, L. Morris, Schmidt, E. Schweizer, Siber, Tannehill, and Ziesler. Lagrange equivocates. The addition of πιστεύομεν in v. 8 persuades most that συζήσομεν is a temporal future, but Cranfield, Denney, Lagrange, and Murray dissent. On 6.8, compare the strongly worded contrary opinions of Cranfield (1975: 312) and Dunn (1988: 322).
[41] The most common explanation for Paul's allegedly guarded language is that he is battling some type of enthusiasm (Käsemann), perhaps of the sacramental variety found in Corinth (Frankemölle, Roetzel, Tannehill), which emphasized the "already" to the exclusion of the "not yet." Wedderburn (1987: 165–232) has recently argued that Paul's avoidance of resurrection terminology issues solely from the fact that the language itself had intrinsically corporeal connotations and could only be used of a physical resurrection. In his view, the authors of Ephesians and Colossians drew "what so obviously seemed to be the corollary

of these questions. Yet, perhaps surprisingly, this does not materially affect the argument of this chapter. For while there is little agreement on these important details, it is all but universally agreed that Paul in Romans 6 is arguing that the resurrection life, *in some sense at least,* is a crucial part of the believer's experience of dying with Christ.[42] To be sure, Käsemann and Tannehill would balk at Beker's assertion that Romans 6.13 "certainly refers to a 'spiritual' resurrection from the dead,"[43] or Michel's description of the believer in Romans 6 as "der Erhöhte,"[44] but there would be no denial that a presently experienced "newness of life" (v. 4) mediated through death (v. 13) is one of the central points of this passage.[45]

Since the question of Paul's allegedly guarded language surfaces again in 2 Corinthians 5.14–15, several points should be clarified here. As all agree, Paul takes for granted some type of resurrection in Romans 6. This assumption is implicit throughout. Further, with Beker, Moo, and others, it is difficult to read verse 13 ("present yourselves to God ὡσεὶ ἐκ νεκρῶν ζῶντας) without thinking "spiritual" resurrection or something equivalent. Granted, Paul did not use the term ἀνάστασις or ἐγείρω, but he seems to be saying nothing substantially different. This raises the question of whether Paul has *avoided* this language, and if so, why? Against Käsemann and Tannehill, it is simply not possible to argue on the basis of subtle terminological distinctions that Paul is locked in a controversy with enthusiasts who make too much of the resurrection. Wedderburn is correct to argue that if Paul were trying to correct an over-realized eschatology, then his language in Romans 6 would be, "to say the least, unguarded."[46] Can Paul really be battling a primitive δόξα theology in Romans 6–8, as Käsemann thinks,[47] and yet conclude this section with the startling declaration, "those he justified, these he also glorified

---

of Paul's statement that we died with Christ, namely, that we also shared his resurrection" (p. 232).

[42] A short sampling from the secondary literature on Romans 6 should suffice to illustrate this point: "In der Taufe hat sich also ein wirkliches Sterben mit Christus, ein wirkliches Auferstehen mit Christus ereignet" (Kuss [1959: 335]); "Paul has already said that we died to sin, now he adds that we too rise from death to new life" (L. Morris [1988: 249]); "We died with him and were raised up with him in his resurrection" (Cranfield [1975: 316]); "[Paul] admet sans hésiter que le baptême opère une véritable résurrection mystique" (Lagrange [1950: 145]); "There is clearly implied a sharing in some degree in Christ's risen life" (Dunn [1988: 330]).

[43] Beker (1980: 224). Similarly Moo (1991: 398).   [44] Michel (1955: 132).

[45] Note Käsemann's frequent use of "resurrection power" in his comments (1980: 166, 169, 177), and Tannehill's concession that "walking in newness of life presupposes that the believer has already risen from the grave" (1967: 11).

[46] Wedderburn (1987: 46).   [47] Käsemann (1980: 162).

(ἐδοξάσεν, 8.30)"? Wedderburn's thesis is better grounded historically and exegetically, but also fails to satisfy completely. Even if one accepts that Ephesians is deutero-Pauline, the very fact that students of Paul could speak unashamedly of a present resurrection (Eph. 2.6; Col. 2.12) renders dubious the presupposition that this terminology had no antecedent in Pauline Christianity. Further, if, as seems likely, Ephesians 5.14 represents a fragment of an early Christian hymn,[48] it is questionable to argue that resurrection language retained "a certain rather obstinate corporeality and physicality" which protected it from metaphorical use.[49] By the time Ephesians was written, the lines Ἔγειρε, ὁ καθεύδων, καὶ ἀνάστα ἐκ τῶν νεκρῶν, καὶ ἐπιφαύσει σοι ὁ Χριστός could be cited in an almost creedal fashion – note the introductory formula: Διὸ λέγει.

But matters are not yet at an impasse. Close attention to the context of Romans 6 and the purpose of initiatory symbolism makes it abundantly clear why Paul chose the phraseology he did: it suited his point. If one keeps in mind that Paul's purpose in this passage is to refute the rhetorical query of 6.1, "Shall we sin that grace might increase?," the question of the "broken parallelism" of 6.4 is rendered moot.[50] In choosing to complete verse 4 with the words "so that we also *might walk* (περιπατέω) in newness of life," Paul has chosen a verb with a decidedly ethical punch which reinforces his argument rather than detracts from it.[51] To be sure, he could have said – as Dunn suggests would have been more "obvious and most balanced"[52] – "so that we might *be raised* with him in newness of life." In doing so, however, he would have missed an opportunity to reiterate his main concern, namely, that dying with Christ has ethical consequences: *walking* in newness of life. The same is true of 6.13, where Paul enjoins his readers to "present yourselves to God *as living from the dead.*" In Romans 5.12–8.39 (and elsewhere) "life" and "death" are ethical concepts and are associated with the realms of grace and sin, respectively: "Sin reigns in *death*, but grace reigns through righteousness unto eternal *life*" (5.21). Given that Paul has repeatedly emphasized that the believer's death is *to sin* (6.2, 6, 7, 10, 11), and hence they can no longer

---

[48] So Barth (1974: 574–75), Schnackenburg (1982: 233–34), A. T. Lincoln (1990: 331–33), among others.

[49] Citing Wedderburn (1987: 230).

[50] Citing Wedderburn (1987: 83).

[51] The ethical connotations of περιπατέω are not disputed. See Michel (1955: 130), Cranfield (1975: 305), Dunn (1988: 315–16), Fitzmyer (1993c: 434–35), and BAGD, which notes that with ἐν (as in Rom. 6.4) περιπατέω denotes "the state in which one lives or ought to live." Paul is especially fond of this idiom, which he has taken over from the OT notion of walking in God's statutes, ordinances, laws, etc. (so BAGD, Cranfield, Dunn).

[52] Dunn (1988: 330).

"*live* in it" (6.2), Paul's wording in 6.13 provides a concise summary of the moral imperative issuing from the believer's death with Christ. This, not incidentally, is the purpose of verses 12–14 and fits comfortably with the purpose of initiatory symbolism generally.

Of course, it is not possible to determine with certainty why Paul (or any ancient writer) chose one word as opposed to another, or what historical circumstances might have rendered one phrase more suitable than another. While the pursuit of such details in Romans 6 should not be curtailed, it should at least be acknowledged that, as it happens, the wording Paul has chosen makes his point fairly well.

Summary

In Romans 6.1–11 we find a densely wooded forest of death–life symbolism. In cutting a path through this material I have scrupulously avoided many issues not directly germane to the argument of this study (e.g., the significance of baptism, Paul's use of traditional material, the origin and meaning of Paul's with-Christ language, etc.). These questions must be left for others. What has been emphasized, however, is the nature and orientation of this symbolism. In keeping with initiatory symbolism generally (chapter 5), Romans 6.1–11 stresses ritual suffering (death, burial, and crucifixion with Christ), empowerment ("so that we might walk in newness of life," v. 4), and transformation ("alive to God," v. 11). Further, and also at home in this broader symbolic network, Paul's death–life symbolism in Romans 6.1–11 is focused on the individual and provides a basis for the moral imperatives which must result from the believer's identification with Christ. This ethical renewal is best expressed by the word "life" (6.2, 4, 10, 11, 13). It is through the believer's ritual death and resurrection that they are made "dead to sin and alive to God" (v. 11). While Romans 6.1–14 is Paul's most elaborate life-through-death text, its main themes are reiterated and enriched by similar passages, two of which I will consider in detail in the following sections: Romans 7.1–6 and Galatians 2.19–20.

7

NEWNESS OF THE SPIRIT: ROMANS 7.1–6

In Paul's thought, redemption and liberation signified in the final
analysis a reaction against death . . . Yet the connection between
the law and sin meant that salvation was perceived initially in
the form of freedom from the law and sin.

H. J. Holtzmann, *Lehrbuch der neutestamentlichen Theologie*

Context

As noted earlier, the rhetorical question of 6.1, "Shall we remain in
sin . . . ?," casts its shadow at least as far as 7.6, and is probably not fully
answered before the end of chapter 8. In refuting this false inference,
Paul yokes his argument to three analogies, baptism (6.3), slavery (6.16),
and marriage (7.2–3).[1] Each of these is introduced by the formulaic "Do
you not know?" (6.3; 6.15; 7.1), revealing three distinct but closely connected literary segments: 6.1–14, 15–23; and 7.1–6. Like ever-widening
concentric circles, the analogies broaden to address the readers from different perspectives: as Christians (baptism), as Romans (slavery), and as
humans (marriage).

The analogy of 7.2–3 represents a daring step in the argument, though
one which Paul has been maneuvering to make since the opening chapter:
Ὁ δὲ δίκαιος ἐκ πίστεως ζήσεται (1.17). To be sure, the word νόμος is
not absent from chapters 1–6,[2] but Paul has yet to look Moses in the
eye without blinking. He does so here. In describing the law as that
which brings the knowledge of sin (3.21), works wrath (4.15), increases
transgression (5.20), stands opposed to grace (5.20–21; 6.14), and so
on, Paul was preparing the ground for the startling declaration in 7.4:
"My friends, you have been put to death with respect to the law." This

---

[1] Correctly, Gale (1964: 190).
[2] Νόμος occurs seventy-four times in Romans, sixty-seven of which are found in the first
eight chapters.

step, however, could not have been taken prematurely, before Paul had adequately treated the problem of sin.[3] In dealing with the believer's death to sin prior to eliminating the law, Paul effectively preempts those who would accuse him of libertinism (3.8; 6.1). So, as Little notes, Romans 7.1–6 "constitutes an important element in the transition Paul makes from his discussion of sin (chap 6) to his discussion of the law (chap 7)."[4] Indeed, the verbal and thematic parallels between chapter 6 and 7.1–6 indicate that death to sin (chapter 6) and death to the law (7.1–6) are two sides of the same coin,[5] and suggest that the proper heading for chapter 7 is 6.14: "For sin shall not rule over you, for you are not under law, but under grace."[6] And for all the confusion that the marriage analogy and its application has generated, in point of fact, it is particularly well calculated to make Paul's point. Paul required a death–life scenario in which death somehow liberates a person who remains alive.[7] Further, Paul's hand would be mightily strengthened if he could establish a legal precedent for his position – that is, if he could find a case in which the law itself stipulated that it no longer applied.[8] Paul draws only one conclusion from this illustration: death severs the relationship.[9] The scandal of this passage consists in the fact that what was said of sin in chapter 6 is now applied to the law. The theological matrix generating this impropriety is

---

[3] Little (1984: 82–83).   [4] Little (1984: 82).

[5] Cf. Michel (1955: 141), Barrett (1957: 135), Leenhardt (1961: 177), Gale (1964: 191), Tannehill (1967: 43), Little (1984: 82–83), Ziesler (1989: 172), Morgan (1995:43).

[6] See the comments of Sanday and Headlam (1914: 170), Kuss (1959: 434), Murray (1959: 239), Jewett (1971: 145), Schlier (1977:214), Wilckens (1980: 63).

[7] Denney (1900: 637).

[8] Correctly noted by Leenhardt (1961: 176–77), Little (1984: 83), Elliott (1990: 242). For the purpose of this discussion it matters little whether νόμος in 7.1 refers to law in general (Denney, Käsemann, Lagrange, L. Morris, Sanday and Headlam), Roman law (Kühl, Jülicherl, Weiss, cited in Fitzmyer [1993c: 455]), or the Torah (Cranfield, Dunn, Fitzmyer, Kuss, Leenhardt, Michel, Schlier, Wilckens). Paul's point is sufficiently established either way (correctly Bruce [1963: 145], E. F. Harrison [1976: 76], Ziesler [1989: 173]) and, in contexts like this, a double entendre cannot be absolutely excluded. In any event, in vv. 4–6 it is certainly the Mosaic law which Paul has in view.

[9] With most (e.g., Kuss [1959: 436], Schlier [1977: 216], Wilckens [1980: 66], Dunn [1988: 366], Ziesler [1989: 173–74], Fee [1994: 503]). The tendency of some (e.g., Sanday and Headlam [1914: 170–72], Dodd [1959: 100–101], Gale [1964:191–92], even Wright [1991: 196]) to treat 7.1–6 as an allegory has resulted in a "false problem" (Stanley [1961: 187–88]). It may be possible to describe 7.2–3 as "la petite parabole" (Lagrange [1950: 161]; similarly Jewett [1971: 145], and Ziesler [1989: 173–74]), though Lagrange is led astray by the designation. Attempts to force vv. 2–3 to correspond in detail to vv. 4–6 will only lead to frustration, as Dodd's conclusion illustrates: "The analogy is hopelessly confused." As with baptism (6.3–4) and slavery (6.16), the marriage analogy is an illustration employed to make one specific point: "Freiheit durch einen Tod" (Kuss [1959: 436]). See the exegesis of Cranfield (1975: 331–35) and Wilckens (1980: 64–66), noting Little's judicious alternative (1984).

significant enough for this study to warrant (briefly) placing this text in the broader contours of Paul's thought.

Even a cursory reading of Romans 6–8 will detect an intriguing interplay between the concepts of (A) the law, the flesh, sin, and death, and (B) grace, the Spirit, righteousness, and life. There is a certain amount of synonymity among the words within each category, which means they can, on occasions, be used interchangeably. Consider Romans 7.5–6: "You were *in the flesh*... But now, you have been cut off *from the law*." Although Paul never spells out the relationships between categories (A) and (B) as explicitly as below,[10] this synopsis is easily confirmed by Romans 6–8.

grace		Spirit		righteousness		life
	> by means of the <		> produces <		> which leads to <	
law		flesh		sin		death

Each idea has its natural antithesis,[11] and each realm (law and grace) has its representative figure: "*in Adam* all die; *in Christ,* all shall be made alive" (1 Cor. 15.22; cf. Rom. 5.12–21).[12] Adam and Christ are of paradigmatic significance to Paul, such that, to be "in" one or the other means, necessarily, to follow that existential paradigm. Keeping in mind these two spheres, along with the chain of events they inevitably entail, it becomes more apparent why Paul is able to use "the law" interchangeably with "the flesh" (7.5–6) and why he is able to speak unapologetically of "the law-of-sin-and-death" (Rom. 8.2). As if by theological synecdoche, Paul can use one element to denote the entire sequence, and he can attach the entire sequence adjectivally to one element.[13]

---

[10] But he comes very close in v. 5, where sin, the flesh, the law, and death are all connected. See also Rom. 5.21; 8.2; 10b; 1 Cor. 15.56; Gal. 5.4–5.

[11] Grace/law: Rom. 4.16; 5.21; 6.14–15; Gal. 2.21; 3.18; 5.4; Spirit/flesh: Rom. 7.5–6, 14; 8.1–11; Gal. 5.16–26; sin/righteousness: Rom. 5.12–21; 6.15–23; death/life: Rom. 6.1–11; 2 Cor. 4.10–12.

[12] For obvious historical reasons, Adam cannot be as closely connected with the law as Paul might like. But while Moses *gave* the law, it was Adam's transgression which *necessitated* the law (Rom. 5.12ff., Gal. 3.19ff.). Hence, in the only two passages where Adam-Christology is explicit, Paul feels compelled to bring up the law (Rom. 5.20–21; 1 Cor. 15.56)

[13] This, however, is not a complete picture of Paul's view of the law. In Romans 7.7–25 Paul labors to redress the balance in favor of God's law, describing it as "holy, righteous, and good" (7.12; cf. 7.14, 16). Paul's thoughts may not be as jumbled as some have alleged. Judged from the standpoint of its *efficacy*, the law receives poor marks from Paul and is regularly associated with sin (Rom. 4.15; 5.20; 7.4–6; Gal. 3.21–22; 5.16–18). In Romans 7.7–14, however, Paul views the law from the standpoint of its *origin and purpose* (εἰς ζωήν, 7.10) and declares it "spiritual" (7.14). The problem is not with the law, but with the flesh, which prevents the fulfillment of the law's requirements. Paul makes this clear in 8.3–4: when πνεῦμα replaces σάρξ, the result is the fulfillment of the (true) requirement of the law.

These antithetical existential paradigms undergird Paul's death–life statements, and will be taken up again in chapter 11. For the moment it is sufficient to expose clearly the infrastructure of Paul's soteriological symbolism, and to keep in mind the reciprocal nature of the terminology in each category.

Structure

As noted above, Romans 7.1–6 constitutes a bridge between the topoi of sin (chapter 6) and the law (chapter 7). Glancing back, it echoes the themes of chapter 6; looking ahead, it anticipates those of chapters 7–8. Especially striking is the way verses 4, 5, and 6 provide an abridgement of chapters 6, 7, and 8, respectively:

Death through the body of Christ: v. 4 = ch. 6
Life ἐν τῇ σαρκί, sin at work "in our members": v. 5 = ch. 7
Free from the law, newness of [the] Spirit: v. 6 = ch. 8

These correspondences are not inconsequential and suggest that Paul has provided his own commentary on these verses in the chapters which precede and follow.[14] The parallels between 7.1–6 and 6.1–11 have, as noted, occasioned much comment, particularly the equation of "newness of life" (6.4) with "newness of the Spirit" (7.6). Yet the pattern of thought in 7.1–6 closely follows another of Paul's death–life texts and the parallels between the two are instructive:

	Romans 7.4–6	2 Corinthians 5.14–17
Dying with Christ	you have died to law through the body of Christ	one died on behalf of all, therefore, all died
Living for another	so that you belong to another, to the one who was raised from the dead	in order that those living should no longer live for themselves, but for the one who died and rose
Annulment of the flesh	we were ἐν τῇ σαρκί	we consider no one κατὰ σάρκα
Soteriological "now"	νυνὶ δέ	ἀπὸ τοῦ νῦν . . . ἀλλὰ νῦν
Transfer of Lordship	we have been cut off from the law	If anyone is in Christ

---

[14] See the comments of Michel (1955: 142), Schlier (1977: 217), Wilckens (1980: 63), and Dunn (1988: 358–59). Although the Greek is anarthrous (ἐν καινότητι πνεύματος), most (e.g. Barrett, Fee, Fitzmyer, Käsemann, Kuss, Lagrange, etc.) assume the reference is to *the* Spirit. Romans 8 points strongly in this direction, as does the same letter–Spirit antithesis of 2 Corinthians 3.

Result	ὥστε	ὥστε
Newness vs.	καινότητι πνεύματος	καινὴ κτίσις
Oldness	not in the oldness of the letter	the old has passed

These similarities, not previously noted, are best understood as family resemblances. Both Romans 7.1–6 and 2 Corinthians 5.14–17 are members of that group of passages in which the physiomorphic imagery of dying and rising with Christ constitutes the dominant soteriological metaphor. Not surprisingly, both start from the same place and move in a similar direction. This is not to say that Paul is affirming precisely the same thing in both passages, but clearly they are mutually illuminating.

The law, the flesh, sin, and death

The close connection between the law, the flesh, sin, and death in Romans 7.4–6 was mentioned above, but it should be carefully noted here how Paul manages to squeeze this entire deadly sequence into verse 5: "For when we were in the flesh, the lusts of sin were at work in our members through the law producing fruit for death." This verse stands in antithesis to verse 6 (νυνὶ δέ), particularly καινότητι πνεύματος, and the fact that Paul juxtaposes the entire law, flesh, sin, and death sequence with "newness of the Spirit" points to the fundamental significance of this idea for understanding the "life" side of Paul's death–life equations. Before turning to verse 6, several exegetical details of verses 4–5 call for attention.

Ἐθανατώθητε makes Paul's point more forcefully than ἀπεθάνομεν of 6.2, 7, and 8, and the term might recall traditions concerning Jesus' crucifixion.[15] As in chapter 6, the subjects of this violent death are described simply as "you" (v. 4) or "we" (vv. 5–6), though the twice repeated "brothers" (7.1, 4) adds an appropriate note of gravity to Paul's provocative claim.[16] Also in common with Romans 6, this death is associated with Christ's own death: "through the body of Christ." This phrase "surely refers to his crucified body,"[17] and is probably nothing more than a circumlocution for the more concise συν- statements of chapter 6 and

[15] See Matt. 26.59; 27.1; Mark 14.55. Ἐθανατώθητε should be treated as a divine passive (Tannehill [1967: 45], Dunn [1988: 631]), and contains no allusion to baptism (against, e.g., Schlatter [1935: 216], Wilckens [1980: 64–65]).
[16] Wilckens (1980: 64), Dunn (1988: 339). Schlier (1977: 214) thinks the expression points to Paul's own participation in what he is about to argue, while Stuhlmacher (1994: 103), believes it points to the Jewish composition of the church in Rome.
[17] Morgan (1995: 43), with Michel (1955: 142), Kuss (1959: 437), Black (1973: 93), Cranfield (1975: 336), Dunn (1988: 262), and others. The context certainly makes this

Galatians 2.19. As with the crucifixion of the παλαιὸς ἄνθρωπος, death
to the law is described in disturbingly corporeal terms: it brings release
from life ἐν τῇ σαρκί, which is dominated by the passions of sin at work
"in our members."

Newness of the Spirit, oldness of the letter

The movement between verse 5 and verse 6 is of epochal significance:
"but now . . . *newness*." Verse 6 substantially augments the understanding
of Paul's death–life symbolism in that it introduces two new elements into
the equation, both of which occur regularly in this family of passages:
the Spirit, and Paul's New Covenant retrospective. The result of release
from the law may at first surprise: it places the believer in servitude (ὥστε
δουλεύειν ἡμᾶς). But Paul is no libertine and Schlatter's comment on verse
6 bears repeating: "Eine Freiheit, die gesetzlos wäre, begehrt er nicht."[18]
As many have observed, "serve in newness of the Spirit" is parallel to
"walk in newness of life" (6.4; cf. 8.4: "walk according to the Spirit"),
and both underscore the ethical demands of dying with Christ. The logic
of this alteration is clarified by reference to the law versus grace scenarios
sketched above. In discussing *sin* (chapter 6) and its consequence, *death*,
Paul naturally emphasizes *life* (6.4). But in dealing with *the law* (chapter 7)
and its henchman *the flesh*, Paul appropriately counters with *the Spirit*
(7.6). The equation, Spirit = life is a familiar one in Paul's letter and
important enough for this study to require separate treatment (chapter 8).
For the moment I note only that it is thoroughly consistent with Paul's
thought to conjoin these expressions and relate them as synonyms. Paul
makes this connection explicit in the next chapter: τὸ δὲ πνεῦμα ζωὴ διὰ
δικαιοσύνην (Rom. 8.10).

The Spirit in 6b stands in antithesis not only to what follows
(παλαιότητι γράμματος), but also, and more importantly, to what precedes: ἐν τῇ σαρκί.[19] It is no misrepresentation of Paul's thought to edit

preferable to seeing διὰ τοῦ σώματος τοῦ Χριστοῦ as a reference to the church (e.g.
Schweitzer [1931: 188], Robinson [1952: 47], C. H. Dodd [1959: 100–1], or the eucharist
(Käsemann [1980: 189]). Even less intelligible is Tannehill's contention that the phrase
denotes "the collective body of the old aeon, the body of 'sin' or 'flesh'" (1967: 46).

[18] Schlatter (1935: 230).

[19] Against Schlatter (1935: 227) and Dunn (1988: 369), ἐν τῇ σαρκί does not have its
antithetical counterpart in ἐν Χριστῷ, though the relationship between Christ and the Spirit
in Paul makes this distinction more technical than substantive. In placing spirit in opposition
to the flesh, Paul was not without biblical precedent (Gen. 6.3; Isa. 31.3), nor was he unique
among his Jewish contemporaries: John 3.6; 6.63; 1QH 4.29–33; 15.16; 1QS 3–4; Philo,
De Gig. 29–31; *Deus. Imm.* 2; *Quis. Her.* 57. These various strands resist homogenization,

verses 4–6 to make this contrast more apparent, though not necessarily more explicit: "For when we were in the flesh ... we bore fruit for death. But now ... we serve in newness of the Spirit." Ἐν τῇ σαρκί, standing opposite to ἐν πνεύματι denotes not bodily existence as such – Paul was still "in the flesh" in this sense: 2 Cor. 10.3; Gal. 2.20; Phil. 1.22 – but a life controlled and dominated by the σάρξ, a life κατὰ σάρκα (8.4–5, 12, 13, etc.).[20] As in chapter 6 – and confirming my earlier exegesis – Paul is speaking of a life unenabled by the Spirit.[21] Again, Paul provides his own commentary in chapter 8: "Those who are ἐν σαρκί are not able to please God. But you are not ἐν σαρκί but ἐν πνεύματι" (vv. 8–9a).

The Spirit–flesh, letter–Spirit contrasts introduce an aspect of Paul's thought rarely explored, but frequently encountered in his letters: his New Covenant retrospective. As the phrase implies, Paul's New Covenant retrospective refers to Paul's perception of redemptive history, which enabled him to juxtapose the old and the new in an antithetical, dialectical fashion. It is the prominence of this theological motif in 2 Corinthians 2–5 which warrants the designation *New Covenant* retrospective, and this will be explored more fully in the following chapter. Comments here will be confined to the meaning and origin of Paul's letter–Spirit antithesis.

The meaning of the letter–Spirit antithesis

Paul's γράμμα–πνεῦμα antithesis is found in two other texts, Romans 2.29 and 2 Corinthians 3.6, both of which are concerned with the adequacy of the law and the Mosaic dispensation. As we have seen, Romans 7.1–6 is governed by similar concerns. In finishing verse 6 with the assertion that believers no longer serve "in oldness of letter," Paul certainly refers back to what he has just said at the beginning of this verse: "you have been cut off from the law." The law is then further described as "that which confined us (κατέχω)."[22] Γράμμα, then, is a slighting reference to the law when viewed from the vantage point of the Spirit, and on this most are agreed. But the commonly expressed view of 7.6,

particularly in their divergent use of σάρξ/בשׂר, but they do attest to the currency of this language in first-century Judaism. See Barclay (1988: 178–215).

[20] Correctly Kuss (1959: 506), Jewett (1971: 153), Cranfield (1975: 337), Schlier (1977: 218).

[21] Also noted by Denney (1900: 638), Sanday and Headlam (1914: 175), E. F. Harrison (1976: 77).

[22] Against Denney (1900: 638), and Lagrange (1950: 164), who take ἐν ᾧ to be neuter and see it as a reference to the flesh, and Sanday and Headlam, who believe it refers to the old man of 6.6. With Dunn, Kuss, Schlatter, Schlier, Wilckens, and others, ἐν ᾧ must be masculine and refers to νόμος.

which superimposes on it the English idiom, "letter of the law/spirit of the law," and so understands the phrase in reference to a Jewish versus Christian hermeneutic, is undoubtedly mistaken. Paul is not talking about the law's "strait-laced interpretation,"[23] nor about "the perverted way of legalism."[24] Rather, "newness of the Spirit" refers to a life defined and controlled by the πνεῦμα, dead to both sin (chapter 6) and the law (7.4). Again, ἐν καινότητι πνεύματος is poised in antithesis to both ἐν τῇ σαρκί and παλαιότητι γράμματος, and this provides justification for Käsemann's conclusion that letter versus Spirit = flesh versus Spirit.[25] The "letter," then, describes the law in so far as it is devoid of the enabling power of the Spirit, is crippled by the flesh, and ultimately leads to death. It is the one-word equivalent of "the law-of-sin-and-death," which stands opposed to "the law of the Spirit of Life in Christ Jesus" (8.2).[26] Read within this conceptual framework, 2 Corinthians 3.6 is less startling: "For the letter kills, but the Spirit gives life." Indeed, the *heilsgeschichtliche* contrast, "newness of Spirit" and "oldness of letter," stands chiastically over chapters 7 and 8 as titles, and this line of interpretation is confirmed as I consider the origin of Paul's letter–Spirit antithesis.

The origin of the Letter–Spirit antithesis

James Dunn remarks that it is "fairly obvious" that the prophecies of Jeremiah and Ezekiel provide the background to the letter–Spirit antithesis of Romans 2.29; 7.6; and 2 Corinthians 3.6,[27] and this is all but universally agreed.[28] This *traditionsgeschichtliche* link is particularly conspicuous in 2 Corinthians 3, where Paul uses this antithesis to introduce his discussion of the New Covenant. I will have occasion later to discuss Romans 2.29 and 2 Corinthians 3.6, but in reference to Romans 7.6,

[23] Black (1973: 138); cf. Barrett (1957: 138).
[24] Cranfield (1975: 432). So too Kamlah (1954: 277–79), Michel (1955: 143), Käsemann (1971: 146–47). More nuanced is B. Schneider (1953), who offers a concise history of interpretation. Hafemann's exhaustive study (1995) is the definitive treatment.
[25] Käsemann (1980: 191).
[26] Even though Hübner (1984: 144–45), Dunn (1988: 416–18), and Wright (1991: 193–216) argue that both occurrences of νόμος in 8.2 refer to the Torah, this is all but impossible. In Paul's view, does the Torah set one free (ἠλευθέρωσεν)? Rather, the construction is rhetorical, almost ironic. Paul has deliberately formulated the first clause to correspond antithetically to the second. See Lagrange (1950: 191–92), Murray (1959: 275–77), Käsemann (1980: 215–16), Deidun (1981: 194–203).
[27] Dunn (1988: 366).
[28] See, e.g., Windisch (1924: 109–10), Bruce (1963: 149), Käsemann (1971: 140–55), Deidun (1981: 45–50; 203–7), Goppelt (1982: 121–22), Furnish (1984: 184–85), Stockhausen (1989: 31–86), Fitzmyer (1993c: 323), Thrall (1994: 230–37), Hafemann (1995: 156–86), etc.

special note should be made of Ezekiel 11.19 and 36.26, where Yahweh promises his people a πνεῦμα καινόν to enable them to keep his δικαιώματα (see Rom. 8.4). This new Spirit is not a re-energized human πνεῦμα, but Yahweh himself taking up residence within the individual to do what they could not: καὶ τὸ πνεῦμά μου δώσω ἐν ὑμῖν καὶ ποιήσω ἵνα... ποιήσητε (Ezek. 36.27). But Paul's familiarity with Ezekiel is not exhausted with reference to chapter 36. Indeed, in terms of Paul's conception of the Spirit, Ezekiel 37 may be more foundational: καὶ δώσω τὸ πνεῦμά μου εἰς ὑμᾶς, καὶ ζήσεσθε (37.14). This critical nexus of ideas, *Spirit, newness, and life*, dominates the "life" side of Paul's death–life equations and, as such, demands further consideration. Before doing so, however, a summary of the main points of chapter 7 is in order.

Summary

Romans 7.1–6 introduces two crucial themes routinely featured in Paul's death–life symbolism: the Spirit, and Paul's New Covenant retrospective. The two are intrinsically, that is, salvation-historically connected, and the presence of one implies the other. This section has also clearly exposed the substructure of Paul's soteriological imagery, which helps to account for the interconnectedness, even interchangeability, of some of Paul's favorite concepts. The significance of this point was signaled in the above discussion of the structure of Romans 7.1–6, with its striking logical, conceptual, and terminological parallels to 2 Corinthians 5.14–17. When these two passages are set side by side, Klaus Berger's claim that καινὴ κτίσις functions as part of Paul's Spirit–flesh dialectic begins to gain cogency.[29] Finally, this section pointed to Israel's prophetic traditions, particularly Jeremiah and Ezekiel, as the inspiration for Paul's letter–Spirit antithesis. Locating Paul's new-creation statements within his death–life symbolism means that καινὴ κτίσις must bear some relation to the ideas which surface on the "life" side of this symbolism in these other texts. In what follows I sketch, with broad strokes, the relevant Jewish background to the ideas most frequently encountered in these passages: the Spirit, newness, and life.

[29] Berger (1994: 470–71).

8

SPIRIT, NEWNESS, LIFE: THE PAULINE ANTECEDENTS

> Because "spirit" is the most life-giving, and God is the author
> of life.   Philo, *De Opificio Mundi*

The question of the correct starting-point for the examination of the Spirit in Paul's letters was posed several decades ago by Otto Kuss,[1] and again recently by Gordon Fee.[2] It is no small irony that Fee, a (neo-)Pentecostal, begins with eschatology, while Kuss, a Roman Catholic, begins with glossolalia. Few would now doubt the correctness of Fee's approach,[3] without implying any criticism of Gunkel's emphasis on the dynamic and ecstatic element associated with the Spirit in the New Testament. Kuss was correct, however, to insist that the Old Testament was decisive for Paul in that it provided him with an eschatological framework and categories with which to interpret his experience of the Spirit, and at this point Kuss stands with the consensus. In sketching the Pauline antecedents, I will restrict myself to two prominent and easily discernible lines of tradition which were not only picked up and continued by Paul, but were intertwined by him as well: the Spirit as *the sign of the eschaton*, and the Spirit as *the creator of life*.[4]

---

[1] See his extensive excursus, "Der Geist" (1959: 540–95). For an appraisal of Kuss' contribution, see Vos (1973: 15–16).

[2] Fee (1994: 792–801).

[3] See Wendland (1952: 457–59), N. Q. Hamilton (1957), Schweizer et al. (1960), Isaacs (1976: 82–96), Rowland (1985: 115, 205), Wedderburn (1987: 268–78).

[4] A third element prominent in the Old Testament and early Judaism and relevant to the Pauline churches, though not to this discussion, concerns the Spirit as the agent of prophecy and enabler for leadership and witness. On this see Schweizer et al. (1960: 1–6), Aune (1983: 103–52), Stronstadt (1984: 13–32), Menzies (1991: 52–111), Moltmann (1992: 43–47), and Fee (1994: 904–13). There is also evidence that in some strands of early Judaism (e.g., Wisdom of Solomon, 1QH) wisdom traditions have influenced earlier Jewish conceptions of the divine רוח/πνεῦμα. See Hoyle (1927: 213–19), Vos (1973: 64–65), Isaacs (1976: 52–54; 145–46), Wedderburn (1987: 278–87), Menzies (1991: 303–15), but note Fee's caution (1994: 910–13).

The Pauline antecedents

The Spirit and the eschaton

The association of the age to come with an outpouring of God's Spirit is a familiar theme in Israel's prophetic traditions, and did not go unnoticed by the early church as it sought to explain its own experience of the Spirit. Joel's prophecy of a universal outpouring was eagerly appropriated toward this end (Acts 2; cf. Rom. 10.13), and this is but one text in a rich archive of material which must have shaped the self-identity of primitive Christianity.[5] According to Isaiah 32.15–17, the descent of the Spirit from on high leads to the manifestation of God's δικαιοσύνη (3x) among his people (cf. Isa. 32.15 with Rom. 5.1). Ezekiel's new heart and spirit should probably be read along these lines, in that it too stresses righteousness as the chief result of the eschatological Spirit. The renewal envisioned by Ezekiel, and the expanded role of the Spirit described by Joel, are also taken up in Isaiah 44.3–5, though the Isaianic oracle restricts the eschatological Spirit to Israel:

> For I will give water to those journeying in thirst through a barren waste. I will give my Spirit to your offspring and my blessing to your descendants and they will sprout like grass in a meadow, and as poplars by flowing water. And one will say 'I am of God' and another will call to the name of the Lord.   (LXX)

The eschatological Spirit was not only associated with the age to come generally, but also with an individual particularly, who would be the bearer of the Spirit in a unique way. The Spirit-endowed "branch from the root of Jesse" (Isa. 11.1–16) will execute judgment in δικαιοσύνη (v. 5) and become a "banner to the nations" (vv. 10, 12). Likewise, the servant of Isaiah 42.1–9 (interpreted Christologically by the early church: Matt. 12.18–21) is one upon whom the Spirit will rest (v. 2), who has been called in δικαιοσύνη, and who will become a "covenant to the peoples, a light to the nations" (v. 6). Another Christologically appropriated passage which links the Spirit with an eschatological figure is Isaiah 61.1–11: "The Spirit of the Lord is upon me to announce the good news" (εὐαγγελίσασθαι, v. 1; cf. Luke 4.18–19). The beneficiaries of this new era will be called "γενεαὶ δικαιοσύνης" (v. 3) because the Lord will make δικαιοσύνη sprout up "before all the nations" (v. 10).[6]

---

[5] So too, Barclay (1988: 84–85).

[6] Zechariah 12.10 and Isaiah 4.4 may also be relevant, though in these texts it is less clear that the divine Spirit is in view.

Given the importance of the eschatological Spirit in the Old Testament, it remains something of a mystery why this theme was not developed in any significant way in the literature of intertestamental Judaism, Qumran being a possible exception.[7] The clearest examples are found in *Testament of Levi* 18.7, 9 and *Testament of Judah* 24.1–3.[8] The former speaks of a new priest (18.2) who will possess "the Spirit of understanding and sanctification" (18.7; cf. Isa. 11.2), and who will usher in a period in which "the Spirit of holiness" will rest on all the righteous (18.9–11). *Testament of Judah* 24 prophesies the rise of "a Star from Jacob ... the Sun of righteousness" who will "pour out the Spirit" to enable Israel "to walk in his first and final decrees" (24.1–3). This eschatological king is later described as "the Shoot of God[9] ... the rod of righteousness for the nations" (24.6). Weaving together the themes of both of these texts, *Psalms of Solomon* 17 describes the coming of "the son of David" (v. 1), "a righteous king" (v. 32) who will be "powerful in [the?] Holy Spirit" (v. 37).[10]

The evidence from the New Testament, as well as the (albeit scant) references to the eschatological Spirit in the surviving literature of the intertestamental period, indicate that the prophetic hope of an age to come characterized by the Spirit continued to germinate quietly wherever the Jewish Scriptures were studied.[11] There is no disputing that the early church felt itself to be the heir of this promise (cf. Gal. 3.14), even if there is little clear evidence for such a position based on what critical scholarship can confidently trace to the teaching of the historical Jesus. It should be remembered, however, that in one of the few passages where Jesus actually explains his ministry with reference to the Spirit, and which has some claim to authenticity,[12] it is precisely the link between the Spirit and

---

[7] The paucity of material in intertestamental Judaism relating to the eschatological Spirit has often been noted: W. D. Davies (1955: 205), Schweizer et al. (1960: 12), Scroggs (1966: 65), Vos (1973: 51–53), Isaacs (1976: 82), Gowan (1986: 65), Wedderburn (1987: 268–74), Menzies (1991: 54–112), Fee (1994: 910). By way of example, in *1 Enoch*, a composite work longer than the entire Pauline corpus, the divine Spirit is mentioned only three times: 62.2; 91.1; 99.16. Of these, only 62.2 could be construed as a reference to the *eschatological* Spirit.

[8] The question of Christian interpolations in these texts cannot be excluded. See de Jonge (1975).

[9] Cf. Isa. 11.1; Jer. 23.5; 33.15; CD 1.7.

[10] The Greek is anarthrous (ἐν πνεύματι ἁγίῳ), though Isaacs, Schweizer et al., Wedderburn, and Wright (in *OTP*) translate it with the article. The same is true in *Pss. Sol.* 18.7, where the messiah (Χριστός) is said to reign "in wisdom of spirit" (ἐν σοφίᾳ πνεύματος). Again, this ambiguity is not usually reflected in translation, but Wright (*OTP*) leaves it anarthrous. A number of other texts are also unclear: *Sib. Or.* 4.46, 189; *1 Enoch* 49.3; *Jub.* 1.21, 23.

[11] With W. D. Davies (1955: 215–16).   [12] See Vermes (1993: 140).

the eschaton which is made: "But if by the Spirit I cast out demons, then the kingdom of God has come upon you" (Matt. 12.28).[13] In light of this, it might be argued that Jesus' proclamation of the Kingdom and Paul's "ministry of the Spirit" (2 Cor. 3.8) are simply variations on a theme.[14]

The Spirit and life

The connection between "spirit" and "life" is a natural one and may well be as ancient as the concepts themselves.[15] Equally understandable is the relationship between *the* Spirit and life, especially for readers of the Hebrew Bible and the Septuagint. The divine *ruach* is introduced at the beginning of the creation account, though this mysterious "brooding over the waters" (Gen. 1.2) is as close as the biblical writers get to linking the Spirit with the creation of non-animate life.[16]

Both "breath of life" (נשמת חיים/πνοή ζωῆς, Gen. 2.7) and "spirit of life" (רוח חיים/πνεῦμα ζωῆς, Gen. 6.17) are used in the Genesis account for the substance which animates humanity, though in neither text is it clear that the divine Spirit is in view. This semantic overlap is reflected in subsequent literature (e.g., Job 34.14; Isa. 42.5; Wisd. 15.11, *JosAs.* chapters 8–21), as is the ambiguity inherent in the phrase πνεῦμα ζωῆς. Hence, Philo can translate πνοή ζωῆς of Genesis 2.7 with πνεῦμα ζωῆς

---

[13] Luke reads "finger of God" for "Spirit of God." On the probable originality of Matthew over Luke see Dunn (1975: 44–46), Carson (1984: 289), and especially Menzies (1991:185–89), who cites many recent supporters.

[14] See N. Q. Hamilton (1957: 19–23), who writes, "Just as in the Synoptics the future kingdom breaks into the present in the action of Jesus, so in Paul the future age has broken into the present in the action of the Spirit... Paul's doctrine of the Spirit should throw as much light on his eschatology as the study of the kingdom has thrown on the eschatology of the synoptics" (p. 23). Cf. Dunn (1975: 46–49).

[15] See Kleinknecht (1968: 332–59), Wedderburn (1987: 275–78). "Spirit" is regularly linked with "life" in early Judaism as its vivifying substance: 2 Macc. 7.23; 14.46; Wisd. 15.11; *Odes Sol.* 28.7–8; *Sib. Or.* 4.46, 189; *T. Abr.* A 18.11 (πνεῦμα ζωῆς); *T. Reub.* 2.4 (πνεῦμα ζωῆς); *JosAs.* 8.9; Jas. 2.26. Numerous passages in Philo could be cited, though none more to the point than his comments on Gen. 2.7 in *Op. Mund.* 32: "Because 'spirit' is the most life-giving, and God is the author of life" (διότι ζωτικώτατον τὸ πνεῦμα, ζωῆς δὲ θεὸς αἴτιος).

[16] It is a curious fact that only in extra-canonical literature (e.g., Judith 16.14; *Syr. Bar.* 21.4) is the creative work of the divine Spirit extended to the inanimate realm. Ps. 33.6 (32.6, LXX) is no exception: "By the word of Yahweh the heavens were made, by the *breath of his mouth* (ברוח פיו/πνεύματι τοῦ στόματος) their starry hosts." Modern translations, noting the parallelism, are correct to translate "breath" here. The reference is to God's creating by means of the spoken word (cf. *JosAs.* 12.1–2). In *Leg. All.* 1.31–42, Philo appears to offer a rationale for restricting the work of the divine Spirit to the animate realm. See also Werner Schmidt (1984: 172); and W. D. Davies (1955: 188–90) who, citing many others, extends this observation to the rabbinic materials and remarks, "The Spirit is almost entirely devoid of cosmic significance" (189).

(*Leg. All.* 3.161; *Det. Pot. Ins.* 80), and label it "the divine Spirit" (τὸ πνεῦμα θεῖον, *Op. Mund.* 135, 144; *Leg. All.* 1.33, 37). Philo, however, was not inferring more than the biblical writers had already done before him: "For the Spirit of God (אל רוח/πνεῦμα θεῖον) made me, the breath (נשמת/πνοή) of the Almighty gives me life" (Job 33.4; cf. 34.14). The role of the divine Spirit as the creative and generative force behind all animate life is most clearly enunciated by the psalmist: "You send forth your Spirit (רוח/πνεῦμα) and they are created (ברא/κτίζειν)" (104.30; LXX: 103.30).

In Ezekiel, however, "spirit" and "life" are connected in a unique way, and this combination bears a decidedly different nuance. Ezekiel himself encountered the divine *ruach* as a compelling and overwhelming force which carried him from one place to another at will: "Then the Spirit (רוח/πνεῦμα) lifted me up and carried me away, and I went in bitterness and anger of my spirit (רוח/πνεῦμα, 3.14; cf. Jer. 20.7)." It is no exaggeration to say that Yahweh dragged this spokesman around by the hair: "He stretched out what looked like a hand and took me by the hair of my head. The Spirit lifted me up between earth and heaven" (8.3).[17] In stark contrast to this coercive, bullying *ruach* is the *ruach* which the prophet perceived to be guiding the cherubim and the wheels of the fiery chariot: "Wherever the Spirit would go, they would go . . . because the πνεῦμα ζωῆς was in (ἐν) the wheels" (1.12–20).[18] It is this same impelling and enabling Spirit which is promised in 36.26–27: "I will put a new heart and a new spirit in you . . . I will put my Spirit in you and move you to follow my decrees." A reasonable inference from this text is that Ezekiel's "new heart" is precisely God's Spirit working from within. As in Jeremiah 31.33, the novelty of this situation lies in its inwardness.[19] The prophet foresees a time when Yahweh will no longer grab his servants by the hair and drag them to their task. Rather, "Wherever the Spirit goes,

[17] See also 2.2; 3.12, 24; 11.1, 5, 24; 43.5.

[18] This text is repeated in 1.21 and 10.17, which also speak of a πνεῦμα ζωῆς controlling the direction of the chariot. The Hebrew is obscure and perhaps allusive: הרוח החיה, "the spirit of the creature/living one/life." The translators of the LXX rendered חיה "life," as in 7.13 (so too BDB, 312). The context leads one to expect a plural noun, referring to the wheels or cherubim. With BDB (926), Stalker (1968: 47–48), Alexander (1986: 759), Allen (1994: 32, 34), הרוח denotes the divine Spirit.

[19] Although Jeremiah 31.31–34 makes no mention of the Spirit, the similarities between it and Ezek. 36.26–27 indicate that the two are closely related. Indeed, Jeremiah's description of an internal Torah which would antiquate human teachers seems to have been connected by Paul with Ezekiel's description of the giving of the Spirit. As the textual apparatus of UBS[4] suggests, Paul's language concerning the "giving" of the Spirit in 1 Thess. 4.8, followed by his reminder to the Thessalonians that they are "taught by God" (θεοδίδακτοι, 4.9), probably echoes and interrelates the prophecies of Ezekiel and Jeremiah, respectively. See Kuss (1959: 572), Deidun (1981: 19–22). Paul certainly connects the two passages in 2 Cor. 3.1–6 (see chapter 10).

they go... because the πνεῦμα ζωῆς is *in* them" (1.20). This picture accords well with von Rad's summary, cited in chapter 2, of the main contribution of Jeremiah and Ezekiel to the religion of Israel:

> If God's will ceases to confront and judge man from outside themselves, if God puts his will directly into their hearts, then, properly speaking, the rendering of obedience is completely done away with, for the problem of obedience only arises when man's will is confronted by an alien will... What is outlined is the picture of a new man, a man who is able to obey perfectly because of a miraculous change in his nature.[20]

Ezekiel connects the Spirit and life one more time, which closely parallels 36.27: "I will put my Spirit in you *and you will live*" (37.14). Clearly, "life" is not a biological concept here, but an ethical one. The similarities between this verse and 36.27 suggest that "life" in 37.14 denotes a moral (and national) renewal which would allow God's people to keep his statutes.[21]

The material from Qumran on this subject is as tantalizing as it is frustrating. One fully expects, given (1) the eschatological orientation of the community (1QSa, 1QM, 4QM), (2) the prominence of רוח in their writings (esp. 1QH), (3) their "New Covenant" perspective (CD 6.19; 8.21), (4) their fondness for applying biblical material to themselves (e.g., CD, 1QpHab., 4Q166–67, etc.), and (5) their remnant theology (CD 1–8), that Ezekiel's prophecy of an eschatological Spirit revivifying Israel [in the dry valley!] would figure prominently in their writings. This, however, seems not to have been the case. To be sure, A. E. Sekki has recently made a brave effort to link Ezekiel 36 and 37 to Qumran pneumatology,[22] but his vague "associations with biblical concepts and vocabulary"[23] leave the reader considerably underwhelmed. Several points need to be kept in mind: (1) Contrary to what we might expect, the Qumran covenanters do not appear to have applied this material from Ezekiel to themselves, nor to have cited the relevant texts in an allusive way, nor to have spoken of receiving a רוח חדשה, the decisive terminology for Ezekiel's eschatological Spirit (Ezek. 11.19; 18.31; 36.26).[24] (2) In the Pseudo-Ezekiel

---

[20] Von Rad (1965: 213–14). Similarly, W. D. Davies (1955: 225), Vos (1973: 34–47), Weippert (1979: 347).
[21] Moral and national renewal are closely associated in Ezekiel. See 36.24–28; 37.22–33.
[22] Sekki (1989: 77–83).   [23] Sekki (1989: 81).
[24] See the index in Sekki (1989: 225–39). Anticipating the potency of this objection, Sekki suggests that this language is absent from the scrolls because it was necessary

fragments published after Sekki's study (4Q385–89), Ezekiel's "valley of
the dry bones" still lies in the future: "O, YHWH, when will these things
happen?"[25] (3) It is not inconsequential that most of Sekki's evidence is
derived from the hymnic/sapiential material (1QH), which is modelled on
the biblical Psalms.[26] Given that the biblical psalmists also felt moved by
the Spirit (Ps. 51.11; 139.7; 143.10), similar language in the hymns from
Qumran should not be too hastily equated with the eschatological Spirit
of Ezekiel. This is not to deny that 1QH employs רוח in reference to the religious experience, even "renewal," of the sectarian, but as Menzies' work
has recently re-emphasized, the concept of רוח in 1QH – and throughout
the scrolls – is decidedly non-eschatological and probably owes more
to wisdom than prophetic traditions.[27] In this respect, the earlier judgments of W. D. Davies, H. W. Kuhn, and J. S. Vos, all of whom pointed
to the lack of explicit eschatologically oriented Spirit statements in the
scrolls, seem to have weathered the storm of recently published material
rather well: "Zu beachten ist auch, daß die gegenwärtige Gabe des Geistes
nirgendwo ausdrücklich als Erfüllung der prophetischen Verheißungen
verstanden ist. Wie in der Apokalyptik ist auch in Qumran die Anschau-
ung von der Gegenwart des Geistes weniger als vom eschatologischen
als vielmehr vom esoterischen Selbstverständnis der Gemeinshaft zu
verstehen."[28]

This does not entirely gainsay Sekki's conclusions, but underscores the
tentativeness which must accompany reconstructions of Qumran's theology. Like so much else relating to the Dead Sea sect, the chief difficulty is
not the paucity of material, but its ambiguity. Having outlined the crucial
Pauline antecedents, I will now show how Paul picked up these threads
and tied them together.

"to assume a posture of unworthiness in spiritual matters" (128). Not surprisingly,
Wachholder's 1992 article, "Ezekiel and Ezekielism as Progenitors of Essenism," which
attempts to root sectarian movements like the Essenes in Ezekiel, passes over Ezek. 36–37
in less than two lines.

[25] 4Q385 frag 2, line 3 (= 4Q386 1.2); cf. 4Q386 2.3. This observation is also made
by Strugnell and Dimant (1988: 48), who are undecided on whether the documents are
sectarian or not. The fragmentary nature of the texts permits only provisional conclusions.

[26] So Mansoor (1961: 25–26), Ringren (1963: 95), Dimant (1984: 522), Knibb (1987:
157–58); and VanderKam (1994: 62), who points out that more copies of the Psalter have
been discovered in the caves than any other Old Testament book.

[27] Menzies (1991: 77–90). On page 83 he notes that "1QS 4.20–22 represents the only
eschatological use of רוח in all the Qumran literature." W. D. Davies (1957: 173) makes a
similar comment. See also Dimant (1984: 536–44), who does not connect רוח in the hymnic
literature with the sect's eschatology.

[28] Vos (1973: 64). Cf. W. D. Davies (1957: 157–82), H. W. Kuhn (1966: 136–39).

The Pauline connection

The promised Spirit

The "durch und durch eschatologische Charakter des Pneuma" in Paul's writings is not in dispute.[29] It could be inferred easily enough from the Old Testament background and from other New Testament writers, yet Paul himself makes this connection explicit. In discussing how God makes righteous the Gentiles (δικαιοῖ τὰ ἔθνη, Gal. 3.8), Paul explains, "he redeemed us ... in order that we might receive *the promise of the Spirit*" (3.14) – a clear reference to the eschatological expectations outlined above.[30] It is this same Spirit which is "*poured out* (ἐκχέω) into our hearts" (Rom. 5.5), and it is difficult not to hear an echo of Joel 3.1–2 (LXX) here: "And after these things I will *pour out* (ἐκχέω) my Spirit on all flesh ... in those days I will *pour out* (ἐκχέω) my Spirit." The Spirit "in our hearts" is also a downpayment guaranteeing a future redemption: "He has given us (δίδωμι, cf. Ezek. 11.19; 36.26–27; 37.6, 14) the pledge (ἀρραβών) of the Spirit *in our hearts*" (2 Cor. 1.22; cf. 5.5; cf. Eph. 1.13–14). In light of Ezekiel's new heart/spirit and Jeremiah's Torah-written-on-the-heart, it is hardly surprising that Paul concentrates the work of the eschatological Spirit here. Closely related to this idea is Paul's description of the Spirit as the "firstfruits" (ἀπαρχή) in Romans 8.23 (cf. *Barn.* 1.7). Again, the Spirit within *points ahead* to a future, somatic redemption: "for in this hope we were saved" (Rom. 8.24). When viewed from the perspective of Pauline eschatology, Bultmann was fully correct in describing the Spirit as the power of the future operative in the present.[31]

The Spirit of life

Like Ezekiel before him, Paul perceived the chief significance of the eschatological Spirit to lie in its ability to produce *life*. Indeed, "life" is the defining feature of the Spirit for Paul and the adjective he is most fond of attaching to it. R. B. Hoyle's work early in the twentieth century on the Spirit in Paul's letters is no longer crucial reading on the subject, but his

---

[29] Citing Wendland (1952: 457–70). See also Schweitzer (1931: 160–76), Bultmann (1952: 155–64), N. Q. Hamilton (1957), Schweizer et al. (1960: 54–67), Dunn (1975: 308–18), Isaacs (1976: 86–92), Lull (1980: 169–85), Paige (1993: 413), Fee (1994: 803–26), etc.

[30] With, e.g., Burton (1921: 177), Barclay (1988: 84), Dunn (1993a: 180), Fee (1994: 395). Against Gunkel (1979: 99).

[31] Bultmann (1952, §§14 and 38), with many: e.g., Wendland (1952: 458), N. Q. Hamilton (1957), Dunn (1975: 311), Gunkel (1979: 110–11), Fee (1994: 803–95).

judgment on this issue could hardly be surpassed: "[For Paul], 'Life' is the comprehensive expression for all that the Spirit works in humanity."[32] The letter–Spirit contrast of 2 Corinthians 3.6 – and this should inform the same antithesis of Romans 7.6 – wraps up Pauline pneumatology in a nutshell: τὸ δὲ πνεῦμα ζῳοποιεῖ. Having recalled the antithesis of Romans 7.6, it is appropriate that I consider Romans 8.1–11, where Paul picks up and expands the first half of that antithetical pair, "newness of the Spirit."

As Romans 6.1–11 overwhelms with its deluge of death–life language, Romans 8.1–11 does the same with its Spirit–life interplay. Paul prepares his readers for this calculated redundancy by introducing this section as "the law of the πνεῦμα τῆς ζωῆς" (v. 2). If the mind of the flesh is death, the mind of the Spirit is *life* (v. 8). As in Ezekiel, God's δικαίωμα[33] (v. 4) is finally kept through the enabling (δύναμαι, vv. 7–8) power of the Spirit within (vv. 9, 11). Paul makes this point again in verse 10: "The Spirit *is life* though righteousness."

Paul's New Covenant retrospective allowed him to depict the whole of salvation-history in terms of the reigns of death and of life (Rom. 5.12–21), and his explanation of the letter–Spirit antithesis of 2 Corinthians 3.6 puts a pneumatological gloss on this evaluation. Here, Paul contrasts "the ministry of death" (2 Cor. 3.7) not, as we would expect, with "the ministry of life" but with "the ministry of the Spirit" (3.9). In this passage, "life" and "Spirit" are interchangeable. Set within this framework, there is a solid exegetical and *traditionsgeschichtliche* basis for the connection that scholars have intuitively made between Romans 6.4 and 7.6: newness of life = newness of the Spirit. In Galatians 3.21 Paul levels his most trenchant criticism of the law, and in light of the above, his accusation is predictable: it cannot give life (ζῳοποιέω). On the contrary, Paul reminds the Galatians, "we live (ζάω) by the Spirit" (5.25).

Returning to Romans 7.6, Paul's "oldness of letter, newness of Spirit" antithesis is seen to possesses a theological potency issuing directly from the apostle's understanding of the Spirit and its fundamental significance in God's redemptive program. This is the point that Kuss is making when he describes Paul's pneuma statements as evidence of "das mächtige Empfinden des Gänzlich-Neuen."[34] This antithesis is Paul's most sweeping, yet concise summary of his New Covenant retrospective, and as such, is both a synopsis and a portent of the apostle's thought. In terms

[32] Hoyle (1927: 130).
[33] Note the importance of this word in Ezekiel: 5.6, 7; 11.20; 18.9, 21; 20.11, 13, 18, 19, 21, 24–25; 36.27; 43.11; 44.24. Paul, however, significantly redefined what was meant by the δικαίωμα of God: Rom. 13.8–10; Gal. 5.13–15.
[34] Kuss (1959: 587).

of its specific function in Romans 7.6, Schlatter grasps better than most the epistolary and *traditionsgeschichtliche* context: "Durch die Schrift [read 'gramma'] wird von außen ein Wort zu ihm gesprochen, das mit verpflichtender Kraft in ihn hineingehen; durch den Geist wird von innen her sein Denken und Wollen erweckt und gefüllt."[35]

Summary

While there is much about Paul's background and education that we do not know, there is also a fair amount that we do know, and the connections and theological framework outlined above are well within the bounds of what we can confidently trace to *certainly verifiable influences*. Paul himself weaves these various strands together, leaving us with little to do but follow the trail of scriptural citations and allusions to their source. In connecting the Spirit with the new age and life from death, Paul was demonstrating nothing more than that he knew his Hebrew Bible; at least a few of his contemporaries were doing likewise. For Paul, however, Ezekiel's "new Spirit" – "the promised Spirit," the "Spirit of life" – was operative in the present, and the implication of this conviction is well summarized by Vos: "Die in der ἐπαγγελία enthaltene, aber für die Öffentlichkeit noch verborgene Schöpfermacht Gottes ist eschatologisch im Geist offenbar geworden."[36] Again, Spirit, newness, and life dominate the "life" side of Paul's death–life equation and it is within this constellation of ideas that we find καινὴ κτίσις. Equally important is the role of Christ in creating this new life, and one text in particular makes this clear: Galatians 2.19–20.

[35] Schlatter (1935: 230).   [36] Vos (1973: 92).

9

CRUCIFIED WITH CHRIST:
GALATIANS 2.19–20

Is he from heaven or from hell?
And does he know
in granting me my life today,
this man has killed me even so?
Les Misérables

In Galatians 2.19–20 there is yet another *crux interpretum*, recently described as "probably the most important single [text] for understanding Paul's theology."[1] While a number of passages could vie for such an accolade, Galatians 2.19–20 definitely belongs in the competition. Not surprisingly, this passage has its interpretive difficulties, especially its concise, heavily coded language. Barclay speaks for many when he says of it, "Paul's thought is so compressed as to be somewhat obscure."[2] This section (2.15–21) is equally crucial for understanding the argument of Galatians itself, and is often seen as a summary of what precedes and a précis of what follows.[3] As a theological and epistolary nodal point, Galatians 2.19–20 repays close scrutiny and significantly augments the understanding of Paul's death–life symbolism. It underscores again the foundational nature of this soteriological metaphor for Paul, while at the same time illuminating the message of Galatians. Its epistolary significance will be highlighted in a later section (chapter 11), where I consider Paul's summary of his argument, Galatians 6.12–16.

---

[1] Gaston (1987: 72).
[2] Barclay (1988: 81). Similarly Mussner (1974: 180), Betz (1979: 114), Ebeling (1985: 120)
[3] So Betz (1979: 144; 121–22), Brinsmead (1982: 73), Cousar (1982: 69), Gaventa (1986b: 318), Hansen (1989: 63–64; 104–8), Longenecker (1990: 81), M. Bachmann (1992: 110–60). Dunn, while eschewing the rhetorical-critical analysis of Betz, accepts this point (1993a: 132).

Context

The line of thought in Galatians 2.15–21 is notoriously difficult and it is neither necessary nor feasible to enter into the intricacies of this debate here.[4] Galatians 2.19–21 concludes Paul's version of the Antioch incident, and it is generally agreed that, somewhere along the line, the focus of Paul's address shifts from Peter to the Galatians. In verse 17 Paul rejects the false inference (μὴ γένοιτο) that Christ becomes a minister of sin when Jews set aside the law and seek to be made righteous by faith. On the contrary, Paul argues, it is only if he reinstitutes what he had previously abolished that his prior action is shown to be wrong (v. 18). Further, it is *the law itself* which determined Paul's subsequent action: "through the law, I died to the law; I have been crucified with Christ" (v. 19).[5] Like Romans 7.1–6, Galatians 2 speaks of dying to the law (v. 19a), and like Romans 6.1–11, it speaks of dying with Christ (v. 19c). In fact, in Galatians 2.19 the two ideas appear to describe the same event. This curious equivocation is of profound theological significance and provides a natural starting-point for discussion of this passage.

Dying and living

In both Romans 7.4 and Galatians 2.19 Paul states the means through which the believer ("I," see below) has died to the law. In the former it is διὰ τοῦ σώματος τοῦ Χριστοῦ, while in the latter it is διὰ νόμου.[6] Some scholars read Galatians 2.19–20 in light of Romans 7.7–25, and see διὰ νόμου as a reference to the law's ability to reveal and incite sin, which ultimately leads to death (Rom. 7.11).[7] This interpretation, however, is not only difficult to justify from the context, it also conflates and confuses two very different senses of death/dying in Paul. The ἐγώ of Romans 7 is *killed* by the law in that it is unable to fulfill the law's requirements. This person is left languishing under the taskmaster of obligation and can only cry out in desperation "who will rescue me from this body of

---

[4] The most important contributions are those of Klein (1964), Bultmann (1967), Kümmel (1973), Lambrecht (1977/78; 1994a; 1994b), Kieffer (1982), and M. Bachmann (1992).

[5] Although the main lines of this synopsis are well supported in the secondary literature (e.g., Bruce [1982: 141–42], Barclay [1988: 79–81], Rohde [1989: 113–15], Longenecker [1990: 90–91], etc.), there is room for disagreement on the details. None of these variations, however, substantially affect my exegesis of 2.19–20.

[6] Διά here expresses agency, not attendant circumstances. Paul's point is not that he died while "im Gesetz" (Borse [1984: 116–17]), or while "in the full heat of his zeal for the law" (Dunn [1993a: 143]), but that he died *through* the law.

[7] So Lightfoot (1890: 117), Burton (1921: 133–34), Mussner (1974: 180), Rohde (1989: 115–16), M. Bachmann (1992: 43–45).

death?" (7.24). This is not at all the situation of Galatians 2.19, where dying to the law brings *release* from the law and "life to God." In spite of the verbal similarities, Romans 7.7–25 and Galatians 2.19–20 describe entirely different scenarios: dying *under* the law (Rom. 7) versus death *to* the law (Gal. 2.19). The former means enslavement, the latter freedom. It is more likely that διὰ νόμου in Galatians 2.19 alludes to the law's role in the death of Christ (Gal. 3.13).[8] This interpretation is strengthened by the connection with Romans 7.4, as well as the way Paul reformulates his death-to-the-law statement: "I have been crucified with Christ (v. 19c)."[9]

This passage, more than any other, reveals the Christological foundation of Paul's death–life symbolism. The union of the believer with Christ is so complete that what is true of Christ is true of the believer as well. This is especially clear in comparing Romans 6.10 with Galatians 2.19, where "Christ" and "I" seem interchangeable: as Christ's death results in "life to God" (Rom. 6.10), so too with the "I" of Galatians 2.19.[10] Also in line with Romans 6, the accent is on "life" in Galatians 2.19–20, the verb ζῶ being mentioned no fewer than five times in these two verses. If Romans 7.6 defines the new life announced in Romans 6.4 as an experience of the Spirit, Galatians 2.19–20 further defines it as an experience of Christ: "I no longer live, Christ lives in me" (cf. 1.6; 4.6).

While it is more common for Paul to speak of the indwelling Spirit than the indwelling Christ, Christ and the Spirit are closely associated in Paul's letters. In Romans 8 Paul announces his theme as "the law of the Spirit of Life *in Christ Jesus*" (8.2) and by the time Paul reaches verses 9–10, the reader hardly blinks to hear him equate the indwelling πνεῦμα θεοῦ with the πνεῦμα Χριστοῦ. In a similar way, Paul can describe the Spirit "in our hearts" as either the πνεῦμα ἅγιον (Rom. 5.5; cf. 2 Cor. 1.22) or the πνεῦμα τοῦ υἱοῦ αὐτοῦ (Gal. 4.6; cf. Phil. 1.19). That both Christ and the Spirit could be envisioned as the vitalizing power within is understandable in light of 1 Corinthians 15.45: "The last Adam became a life-giving Spirit." All this suggests that "Christ in me" could probably be expanded to "Christ through his Spirit in me,"[11] and that the new life

---

[8] So too, Schlier (1949: 62), Bultmann (1967: 397), Tannehill (1967: 58–59), Bruce (1982: 143), Barclay (1988: 80–81), Lambrecht (1994b: 218–19).

[9] With Bultmann (1967: 397), "through the law" and "through the body of Christ" are interchangeable, rendering vv. 19ab and 19c "identisch." Cf. Schlier (1949: 62), Longenecker (1990: 91).

[10] The two passages are often compared: Michel (1955: 130), Cranfield (1975: 314), Wilckens (1980: 18–19), Weder (1981: 175–79), Dinkler (1992b: 151), Fitzmyer (1993c: 430).

[11] So also Dunn (1970a: 107; 1993a: 145–46), Betz (1979: 124), Bruce (1982: 144), Cosgrove (1988: 173), Fee (1994: 373–74).

described here (ὁ δὲ νῦν ζῶ, v. 20) and elsewhere in Paul's death–life texts is equally an experience of Christ *and* the Spirit. Even though one or both of the modifying ideas appended to τὸ πνεῦμα in Romans 8.2 may be absent from its appearance in any given context, they are always theologically implicit: the Spirit→ *of life* ←in Christ Jesus. Conversely, where "new life" and "in Christ" are present, one can be certain that the Spirit is not far from the apostle's thoughts (e.g., 2 Cor. 5.17).

Paul's emphatic "I"

Up to this point I have kept Paul's pronouns in Galatians 2.19–20 at arm's length, but it is probably time to address them specifically. There is general agreement on the reason why Paul shifts to the first person in verse 18. In saying "If *I* rebuild what *I* destroyed," Paul is speaking rhetorically, typically, even gnomically.[12] He is making a point that would be true of anybody, but seems particularly directed to Peter's conduct at Antioch. Employing the first person allowed him to criticize this "pillar" with some semblance of diplomacy and tact.[13] With verse 19, however, opinions diverge, and this divergence reveals as much about the individual scholars as about the text itself. Some insist that Paul's ἐγώ in verses 19–20 remains literary and typical, with no hint of a "persönliche Aussage des Paulus über sich selbst."[14] Others, however, believe that the emphatic ἐγώ which introduces 2.19 indicates that Paul's gaze is moving away from Peter and the Jewish Christians described in verse 18, though he still speaks representatively in some sense: "Au contraire, Paul développe cette fois-ci son expérience personelle . . . Le "je" paulinien devient ici le prototype de toute conversion authentique d'un Juif au Christ."[15]

It is certainly not necessary to eliminate all typicality from Paul's emphatic "I," but it is equally unnecessary to deny that Paul speaks in some sense personally. Dunn is correct to criticize this position for its excessive reserve: "Whether the 'I' is generalized or not . . . the sentence is certainly

[12] With Burton (1921: 132), Bonnard (1972: 55), Bruce (1982: 142), Kieffer (1982: 67), Borse (1984: 115), M. Bachmann (1992: 43), etc.
[13] Schlier (1949: 59–60), Oepke (1964a: 61), Tannehill (1967: 56–57), Bligh (1969: 210), Mussner (1974: 177–78), Barclay (1988: 80).
[14] Kümmel (1973: 169). Similarly Tannehill (1967: 57–58), Bonnard (1972: 55–57), Betz (1979: 121), M. Bachmann (1992: 43–45).
[15] Kieffer (1982: 67), who speaks for the majority, e.g., Burton (1921: 32), Oepke (1964a: 60), Mussner (1974: 179), Lambrecht (1977/78: 495; 1994a: 214), Weder (1981: 175), Bruce (1982: 143), Borse (1984: 116), Gaston (1987: 68), Rohde (1989: 115), Dunn (1993a: 143).

a personal statement of Paul himself."[16] This attempted depersonalization becomes increasingly difficult to maintain as Paul's line of thought reaches its climax in verse 20: "... who loved me and gave himself up for me." It is hardly accidental that Bachmann, Bonnard, Kümmel, and Tannehill pass over this final clause in absolute silence. Indeed, when Kümmel tries to explain the emphatic position of ἐγώ in verse 19 he can only respond rather limply "[das] ist naturgemäß nicht mit Sicherheit zu sagen."[17]

Yet the embarrassment which dogs so much exegesis of Galatians 2.19–20 is not entirely unwarranted. New Testament scholarship has expended no small effort in recent decades trying to correct an over-individualized interpretation of Paul's gospel which it (allegedly) inherited from Luther and saw perfected by Bultmann. As sometimes happens, however, we are in danger of back-pedaling off a cliff. Whatever Paul is describing here, it was clearly of personal, transforming significance and was marked by an experience of the risen Christ: "*I* have been crucified with Christ; *I* no longer live, but Christ lives in *me*." Paul's emphatic "I" should be given full weight and stands in dramatic antithesis to "das in ihm neugeschaffene Leben, Christus."[18] This crucifying encounter with the risen Lord is portrayed as a completely reorienting confrontation which leaves Paul, mysteriously, both dead and alive (2 Cor. 4.10–11). We will meet Paul's emphatic pronouns again at the close of this letter, "For *I* have been crucified to the world... καινὴ κτίσις" (Gal. 6.14–15), and this text may shed light on Galatians 2.19–20. Before concluding part II and turning my attention to 2 Corinthians, verse 20 deserves special attention, especially in its bearing on 2 Corinthians 5.14.

The love of Christ

The language of Galatians 2.20 is striking in its "radically personalized" tone,[19] the significance of which can be seen only when set beside similar

---

[16] Dunn (1993a: 143). Perhaps Dunn has in mind Tannehill's false antithesis: "What Paul is talking about here is not his own private experience, but something which is valid for every Christian" (1967: 57). Tannehill never explains why Paul, speaking in some sense representatively, could not make a personal statement that would also be valid for every Christian. Presumably, if it is valid for all, as Tannehill argues, it is valid for Paul as well.

[17] Kümmel (1973: 179).

[18] Schlier (1949: 63). Cf. Lightfoot (1890: 119), Borse (1984: 118). Both Oepke (1964a: 63) and Dunn (1993a: 145) accept with hesitation the word "mystical."

[19] Citing Dunn (1993a: 147). Similarly Lightfoot (1890: 119), Bligh (1969: 217), Bruce (1982: 139), Lambrecht (1994b: 214).

Pauline texts. Paul often speaks of the sacrificial death of Christ, but nowhere else is this described as "for *me*." Paul is usually more inclusive:

Galatians 1.3–4	Grace and peace to you from God our father and our Lord Jesus Christ, who gave himself on behalf of (ὑπέρ) *our* sins.
1 Corinthians 15.3	What I received I passed down to you of utmost importance: Christ died on behalf of (ὑπέρ) *our* sins.
1 Thessalonians 5.10	Christ died for (ὑπέρ) *us* so that . . . we might live with him.

Paul's "dying" formulas are often linked with "love" and, again, Paul is normally careful to include his readers as beneficiaries of Christ's sacrifice:[20]

Romans 5.8	But God demonstrates his *love for us* in this: while we were sinners, Christ died for (ὑπέρ) *us*.
Romans 8.32, 35	He did not spare his own son, but delivered him up on behalf of *us all* (ὑπὲρ ἡμῶν πάντων) . . . Who can separate us from the *love of Christ*?
2 Corinthians 5.14	For the *love of Christ* compels us, recognizing this: one died on behalf of (ὑπέρ) *all*.

In light of this more normal usage, the language of Galatians 2.20 is all the more arresting: "The life I now live in the flesh I live by faith in the son of God who loved *me* and gave himself up for *me*" (cf. 1 Cor. 8.11). Paul perceived God's action in Christ not only as the death of the messiah for Israel, and as the reconciliation of the world, but also as an action with a direct bearing on Saul of Tarsus. He understood it as a sacrifice of love "for me" which demanded an appropriate response. It was because Paul saw Christ's death not only in its abstract corporate significance, but also in its concrete personal relevance that he was willing, following the example of his Lord, to "spend and be spent" on behalf of his churches (cf. 2 Cor. 8.9 with 12.15). It was Christ's death "for us all" which focused Paul's attention on the world, but it was Christ's death "for me" that set his feet on the road: "for the love of Christ compels us."

Summary of part II

The primary goal of part II has been to establish the general orientation of Paul's death–life symbolism and to highlight its main themes. In keeping with initiatory symbolism generally, Paul's death–life symbolism is

[20] On this, compare Cousar (1990: 43–45; 55–56) and Theissen (1992: 171–74).

anthropologically oriented and maintains a clear focus on the individual. This is not the whole of Paul's theology, nor is it the only thing that should be said about this soteriological imagery, as we shall see in a moment. It is, however, the accent of these texts and this is impossible to ignore. *Spirit*, *newness*, and *life* are the leitmotifs of this grand metaphor and dominate the "life" side of the death–life drama in Paul. This specific constellation of ideas has an easily discernible prehistory in Judaism, being well rooted in the theology of the later prophets, and leads naturally to the application made by Paul. The Christological foundation that undergirds this imagery is Paul's unique contribution, though again, this is not without some analogy in ritual symbolism elsewhere. Standing in antithesis to *Spirit*, *newness*, and *life* is *the flesh*, which constitutes the defining feature of the old person, the "I" which was crucified with Christ. Most importantly, however, this section has underscored Paul's portrayal of dying with Christ as a generative, life-creating event which conveyed both the gift of new life, and the demand of obedience. This dual emphasis is intrinsic to Paul's *creative dying*, and contributes to its fundamentally bifocal nature, addressing both the individual and the community in a single metaphor.

The discussion of initiatory symbolism in chapter 2 provided a methodological foundation for placing Paul's new-creation statements within his death–life symbolism and allowing this larger theological context to play a role in the interpretation of these passages. This methodological starting-point was confirmed *both* by the examination of the relevant texts, where we saw a small collection of ideas repeatedly surfacing, *and* by the consideration of the theological substructure which connects this symbolism. While clearly supporting the anthropological nature of Paul's death–life symbolism, the survey of the purpose and aims of initiatory rituals in chapter 2 equally stressed the social implications of this symbolism and this renders dubious any disjunction between the two. Transformation, ritual suffering, demarcation, and empowerment are themes that apply as much to Paul's death–life symbolism as to death–life symbolism elsewhere, and are of profound social significance. Indeed, their social relevance issues directly from their personal relevance in that in these rituals the moral expectations of the community – along with the ability to satisfy them – are etched into the very being of the initiate. With this larger interpretive framework in place, I turn now to 2 Corinthians 5.17 and Galatians 6.15 in order to see in what ways these texts augment, modify, or depart from the general pattern outlined here.

PART III

The old and the new: new creation in the context of Paul's letters

2 Corinthians 5.16 and 17 have been ranked among "the most famous verses in the whole of the New Testament,"[1] and there is no reason to dispute this claim. Yet familiarity is both friend and foe of good exegesis. Carol Stockhausen lists 2 Corinthians 5.16–21 as one of a small handful of passages in this letter which have come under intense scholarly scrutiny, yet which are all too often examined, "without regard for their function within 2 Corinthians itself."[2] In a similar way, Jörg Baumgarten laments the fact that so much exegesis of Galatians 6.15 and 2 Corinthians 5.17 has been led astray (*verleiten*) by the history-of-religions parallels to Paul's καινὴ κτίσις motif rather than "in erster Linie dem Kontext die Funktion der Deutung zugestehen."[3]

The point made by these authors is legitimate, and in what follows I will take up their challenge and locate Paul's new-creation statements in the argument of the letters in which they are found. Good exegesis is often a delicate balance between the literary context of an idea and the larger conceptual world of which it is also a part. However, when several historical-conceptual backgrounds are on offer, the determinative vote should be cast by the specific literary-theological context. As we shall see, careful attention to the argument of 2 Corinthians and Galatians – along with the historical circumstances which prompted these letters – provides all the necessary clues to the interpretive riddles of these passages, be it what some have called "cosmic crucifixion" (Gal. 6.15), or knowing Christ κατὰ σάρκα (2 Cor. 5.16).

In placing Paul's new-creation statements in their epistolary context, we immediately face the question of which letter to consider first. If the chronological sequence of Paul's letters is deemed relevant here, one might be inclined to treat Galatians before 2 Corinthians. But Pauline chronology is far from fixed, and advocates of a later date for Galatians are not hard to find. Indeed, many would place Galatians in close

---

[1] Martyn (1967: 269).   [2] Stockhausen (1989: 4).   [3] Baumgarten (1975: 164).

chronological proximity to 2 Corinthians,[4] and this uncertainty means that a decision must be reached on other grounds. The decision to examine 2 Corinthians prior to Galatians is based on the judgment that in 2 Corinthians Paul's new-creation statement is more obviously connected to the argument and themes of the section in which it is found. In Galatians, on the other hand, it is stamped summarily across the epistle at its conclusion. The thematic development of 2 Corinthians 2.14–5.21 provides more interpretive signposts to guide the exegesis and for this reason it seems prudent to begin with the clearer text. I do not assume, however, that καινὴ κτίσις is used in a similar way in both 2 Corinthians and Galatians, nor is this approach intended surreptitiously to bring Galatians 6.15 into conformity with 2 Corinthians 5.17. My procedure is less subtle: 2 Corinthians 5.17 is an easier text to interpret and so I begin here.

[4] See, e.g., Lightfoot (1890: 36–56), Kümmel (1975: 293, 304), Lüdemann (1984: 83–87), Hansen (1993: 328–29).

10

IF ANYONE BE IN CHRIST:
2 CORINTHIANS 5.17

But to find a man who in plain terms and without guile speaks his
mind with frankness . . . is not easy, but rather the good fortune
of every great city, so great is the dearth of noble, independent
souls and such is the abundance of toadies, mountebanks and
sophists.   Dio Chrysostom, *Discourses*

The literary context of 2 Corinthians 5.11–21

The unity of the document we now possess as 2 Corinthians was much
debated in the twentieth century, and even now the question is far from
settled.[5] Yet in spite of the lack of consensus on the composition of
canonical 2 Corinthians, no one doubts the unity of 2.14–7.4 (6.14–7.1
excepted). The argument of this chapter is not dependent on any particular
literary reconstruction of 2 Corinthians, nor can the unity of this letter
be positively excluded.[6] In what follows I will assume that chapters 1–9
belong together,[7] and leave open the question of 6.14–7.1.[8] Chapters
10–13 will be used critically to inform this (probably earlier) material,
but only when specific data in both segments can be correlated in such a
way as to warrant this. Given these general assumptions, the connection
between 2.14ff. and what precedes deserves comment.

[5] R. Bieringer (1994a, b, c) has recently produced a comprehensive survey of the question,
and his table on p. 97 reveals at a glance the current and historic diversity of opinion.

[6] Recent proponents of the unity of 2 Corinthians include Young and Ford (1987: 27–
59), Stockhausen (1989: 6–7, 156–57), Wolff (1989a), Bieringer (1994c: 131–79), and
Witherington (1995).

[7] With, e.g., Barrett (1973), Furnish (1984), Dautzenberg (1986), R. P. Martin (1986),
Sumney (1990), Murphy-O'Connor (1991a), Savage (1996: 191–92).

[8] With Furnish (1984: 383), it is probably best to concede that 2 Corinthians 6.14–7.1
"remains an enigma," though recent scholarship has favored its inclusion within 2.14–7.4
(e.g., Patte [1987], Beale [1989], Belleville [1991], Scott [1992: 215–20], DeSilva [1993],
W. J. Webb [1993], Goulder [1994], Thrall [1994: 25–36]).

The transition from 2.13 to 2.14 is abrupt, though it is not unreasonable to suppose that the thanksgiving period of 2.14–17 was occasioned by the mention of Titus in 2.13. Paul resumes this line of thought in 7.5, where we discover the reason for his sudden outburst of thankfulness: he was overjoyed by the reception Titus had received from the Corinthians (7.5–16).[9] Whether or not this particular manner of linking 2.14–7.4 to the material which surrounds it is accepted, the thanksgiving period which introduces this "great digression"[10] raises the important question of the literary tone of this segment, and this should have some bearing on how to interpret its argument and terminology.

The literary tone of 2 Corinthians 2.14–7.4

2 Corinthians is often described as Paul's most personal letter.[11] Indeed, Gerhard Dautzenberg goes so far as to label chapters 2–7 the apostle's *confessio*.[12] The reflective and meditative tone of this material is signaled in the opening paragraph of the letter, where Paul praises "the Father of compassion and God of all comfort who comforts us in all our affliction" (1.3–4).[13] This mood is further evidenced in Paul's style of argumentation (antithetical and associative), his numerous references to his hardships (1.3–7, 8–11; 2.4, 14; 4.7–12, 16–18; 5.1–8; 6.3–11; 7.5–6, 13–16), and the peculiar expression of otherwise familiar Pauline themes. Elsewhere Paul is content to critique the Mosaic dispensation generally, but in 2 Corinthians 3 it is the lawgiver himself who comes under Paul's scrutiny: "For we are not like Moses . . ." (3.13). Elsewhere Paul speaks of Christ's death as the decisive event of his past, but here it is something he bears daily in his mortal body (4.10–11). Whereas Romans describes the triumphant display of the δικαιοσύνη θεοῦ as the climax of redemptive history, 2 Corinthians depicts the humiliating display of the conquered foe (θριαμβεύω, 2.14), the suffering servant (διάκονος, 3.6; 6.4) who himself – along with the believing community – becomes the δικαιοσύνη θεοῦ ἐν

---

[9] This scenario is supported by, e.g., Plummer (1915: 67), Allo (1937: 45), Prümm (1967: 76), Barrett (1973: 97), Kümmel (1975: 291), and R. P. Martin (1986: 40–41; 136–37), though it is not axiomatic. For a sound alternative, consult Thrall (1982) and Hafemann (1990: 80–81).

[10] So Dean, who entitled his 1938 article "The Great Digression: 2 Cor. 2.14–7.4." Similar evaluations are still made: "a prolonged digression" (Lincoln [1981: 58]), a "lengthy excursus" (R. P. Martin [1986: 41]), an "extensive interruption" (Renwick [1991: 87]).

[11] "Dieser brief is vielleicht das persönlichste Schreiben" (van Unnik [1973a: 144]); "The most personal" of Paul's letters (Stockhausen [1989: 2]); "intense" emotional tone (Young and Ford [1987: 15]); "intensely personal" (Fee [1994: 283]). Similarly Plummer (1915: xii), Hickling (1974/75: 381), Savage (1996: 1).

[12] Dautzenberg (1986: 159–62).   [13] Correctly noted by O'Brien (1977: 238–58).

αὐτῷ (5.21). Paul is not unaware of his candor and toward the end of this section he feels obliged to comment on it: "O Corinthians, we have spoken openly with you and have laid open our heart . . . as a fair exchange – I speak as to my children – open yourselves to us as well" (6.11–13).

The point to be noted is that there is an emotive dynamic to 2 Corinthians which must be reckoned with. It may not be correct to see this epistle as written primarily for Paul rather than the Corinthians,[14] nor to call it a theological monologue,[15] but Paul has placed himself conspicuously "in den Mittelpunkt"[16] of this letter and this is evidenced in the way he personalizes its argument and themes. But this by no means severs these chapters from the situation in Corinth. As Galatians demonstrates, apologetic and autobiography are not mutually exclusive categories, and the correlation of the two is in complete accordance with Paul's paradigmatic conception of his ministry: "Be imitators of me, as I am of Christ" (1 Cor. 11.1; cf. 1 Cor. 4.16; Phil. 3.17). Bultmann's warning against an over-psychologized exegesis of 2 Corinthians certainly needs to be heeded,[17] but so does Vanhoye's warning of the opposite error: sterilizing the biblical text.[18] Before examining in detail the relevant themes of 2.14–7.4, I will step back momentarily and consider the salvation-historical framework of this material.

The salvation-historical context of 2 Corinthians 2.14–7.4

In order to appreciate fully the argument and line of thought leading up to Paul's new-creation statement in 5.17, it is critical to recognize the *heilsgeschichtliche* perspective which undergirds this entire section. Discerning the meaning of troublesome texts often requires the exegete to get behind the words on the page, to step inside the author's mind and to locate the correct frame of reference for the thought in question. Yet little in the way of guesswork is required in determining the theological matrix which generated the heady themes of 2 Corinthians 2.14–7.4: Moses, the New Covenant, the Spirit, Paul's "ministry of reconciliation," and so on. Clearly these themes betray an eschatological framework in which the *promise–fulfillment* schema played a major role.[19] It may be possible, however, to delineate more precisely the specific salvation-historical trajectory which runs through 2 Corinthians 2.14–7.4 and which carries Paul's thought in its wake. To this end, two passages warrant consideration: 2 Corinthians 1.21–22 and 5.5.

[14] So Rebell (1992: 13).   [15] Bieringer (1994e: 431).
[16] Dautzenberg (1986: 159).   [17] Bultmann (1985: 16).   [18] Vanhoye (1986: 10).
[19] The salvation-historical framework of 2 Corinthians 1–9 is frequently noted, but the work of Beale (1989), W. J. Webb (1993), and Hafemann (1995) deserves special mention.

2 Corinthians 1.21–22

Corinthians 1.21–22 concludes what Allo has called one of Paul's "belles digressions."[20] Paul begins by offering a defense of his change of plans (vv. 15–16), which had led to the charge of irresponsibility and vacillation from some in Corinth (v. 17). Paul counters by reminding his detractors of God's (and, by implication, his apostle's[21]) faithfulness (vv. 18–20), and it would appear that Paul "lingers" a bit on this idea and allows it to come to fruition in verses 21–22.[22] The subject of God's faithfulness leads naturally to God's promises and the sweeping declaration of verse 20: "However many God's promises may be, they are 'Yes' in him." In referring to God's ἐπαγγελίαι, Paul may have something more concrete in mind than the entire corpus of Old Testament promises, and it is not inconsequential that he concludes this theological excursus with an explicit reference to the Spirit (v. 22). As noted in the previous chapter, the Spirit in Paul's letters is always *the promised Spirit* (Gal. 3.14; cf. Eph. 1.13), and the language of verses 21–22 is overtly pneumatological.[23] Indeed, this entire train of thought may have been set in motion by the recollection in verse 17 of the charge that Paul made his plans κατὰ σάρκα.[24]

The structure of verses 21–22 is debated,[25] as is an alleged baptismal allusion,[26] though these details are not of concern here. It is important

[20] Allo (1937: 27), with many (e.g., Windisch [1924: 70], Barrett [1973: 76], Furnish [1984: 141]).

[21] Cf. Bultmann (1985: 40), Thrall (1994: 144).

[22] Schlatter (1934: 482) writes, "Dabei verweilt Paulus, weil die Ereignisse, die er mit den Korinthern bespricht, an die verwechselnden menschlichen Pläne und Schicksale erinnert." Similarly Strachan (1935: 55), Barrett (1973: 76), Furnish (1984: 141), Fee (1994: 290).

[23] Paul's use of χρίω here is in line with early Christian usage (Luke 4.18; Acts 10.38), where it is similarly connected with the anointing of the Spirit (cf. Windisch [1924: 72], Allo [1937: 29], Dunn [1970a: 133], Fee [1994: 291–93]). Σφραγίζω, of course, is used in Ephesians 1.13 and 4.30 in reference to the Spirit where, as here, it denotes ownership (Bultmann [1985: 42], Thrall [1994: 156–57]; cf. Romans 8.9). In the same way that physical circumcision was regarded as a seal which demarcated the people of God under the Old Covenant (σφραγίς, Romans 4.11; cf. *Barn.* 9.6), so spiritual circumcision was understood by Paul to demarcate the people of God under the New Covenant (Rom. 2.28–29; cf. Col. 2.11; Eph. 4.30). As here, βεβαιόω is used in reference to the work of the Spirit in 1 Corinthians 1.6–8).

[24] See Dinkler (1962: 173–74), R. P. Martin (1986: 26), Fee (1994: 288 n. 19), Thrall (1994: 140).

[25] Compare the divergent analyses of Windisch (1924: 70), Schlatter (1934: 482), Dinkler (1962), Barrett (1973: 81), and Furnish (1984: 148–49).

[26] The case for a baptismal frame of reference is pressed hard by, e.g., Beasley-Murray (1962: 171–77) and Dinkler (1962), and not a few exegetes follow this line of interpretation: Plummer (1915: 41), Allo (1937: 28–29), Collange (1972: 224), Furnish (1984: 148–49), Bultmann (1985: 42). Many, however, remain unconvinced: e.g., Schlatter (1934: 482), Héring (1967: 12), Dunn (1970a: 131–34), Barrett (1973: 81), Young and Ford (1987: 113–15), Fee (1994: 294–96), Thrall (1994: 152).

to note, however, that the "confirming," "anointing," and "sealing" described in these verses are not three distinct activities, but rather a variety of images employed to illustrate the decisive event of the final clause, *the giving of the downpayment of the Spirit* (22b). Plummer believes that "the three metaphors are perhaps meant to form a climax," which is put more crisply by Chrysostom: "What is anointing and sealing? The giving of the Spirit."[27] The relevance of this exegesis will become more apparent in the examination of 2 Corinthians 5.5 which, as Prümm notes, is closely related to 2 Corinthians 1.21–22.[28]

2 Corinthians 5.5

Like 2 Corinthians 1.21–22, 2 Corinthians 5.5 is usually thought of as part of a larger digression,[29] sometimes of a polemical nature.[30] The context is notoriously difficult, though again, this debate is not important here.[31] Both excursuses culminate with reference to ὁ δοὺς τὸν ἀρραβῶνα τοῦ πνεύματος, and it is instructive to consider the direction Paul's thought takes as it meanders. This pneumatological drift is evident throughout 2 Corinthians 2.14–7.4 and helps to clarify the salvation-historical perspective of this material. The remark of Windisch that the language of 1.22 "klingt wie eine Kombination von Joel 3.1ff... und Jeremiah 38 (31).33"[32] should be connected with Fee's observation that 1.21–22 "anticipates" the argument of chapter 3.[33] 2 Corinthians 5.5, however, delineates more precisely the particular strand of prophetic traditions on which Paul is ruminating, and the proximity of this verse to 5.17 should not be overlooked.

In 5.5 Paul concludes his previous line of thought with the statement "the one who fashioned us (ὁ κατεργασάμενος) for this[34] is God, who

---

[27] Cited approvingly by Héring (1967: 12 n. 46) and Barrett (1973: 82). This interpretation has much in common with Strachan (1935: 60), Bultmann (1985: 41), and R. P. Martin (1986: 28).

[28] Prümm (1967: 288), speaking for many.

[29] E.g., Barrett (1973: 149), R. P. Martin (1986: 116), Perriman (1989: 518), Fee (1994: 325).

[30] Schmithals (1971: 259–75), Bultmann (1985: 130–39).

[31] Comprehensive surveys of the interpretation of this passage are given by F. G. Lang (1973: 9–161) and Pate (1991: 1–31). While the digressionary character of 5.1–5 is difficult to deny, recent scholarship has been more careful to trace Paul's line of thought in 4.7–5.10 and, as a result, is less comfortable with extracting the theology of Paul's opponents from this passage. The digression of 5.1–5 issues from Paul's comments in 4.16–18 and appears to be more didactic than polemical. See Furnish (1984: 299–301), Young and Ford (1987: 127–37), Sumney (1990: 141), W. J. Webb (1993: 106–9), Lambrecht (1994e: 312).

[32] Windisch (1924: 174). Similarly Allo (1937: 28), W. J. Webb (1993: 109).

[33] Fee (1994: 291).

[34] That is, the swallowing up of mortality by life (5.4).

gave (ὁ δούς) us the pledge of the Spirit." As in 1.22, the two aorist
participles denote the same event,[35] and the relationship between the two
clauses (*result→means*) is made explicit by Murphy-O'Connor: "God has
prepared us for eschatological life *by* giving us 'the down-payment of the
Spirit.'"[36] The force of the verb κατεργάζομαι, however, is obscured by
rendering it "prepared." To be sure, the word can bear this nuance, though
this meaning is poorly attested[37] and not in line with Paul's usage.[38] More
appropriate to the context and lexical evidence would be "to fashion"[39]
or "create."[40] The larger context suggests that Paul has in mind the re-
creative work of God's Spirit which effects transformation into the *eikon*
of Christ (2 Cor. 3.18; 4.4–6). This same idea is clothed in metaphor in
3.3, where Paul describes the Corinthians as "epistles of Christ . . . written
by the Spirit."

In 5.5, then, Paul has returned full circle to the thought which trig-
gered this digression (4.16–18), and in so doing has explained more
fully what he meant by "the daily making anew (ἀνακαινόω) of the ἔσω
ἄνθρωπος" (4.16).[41] Commenting on the connection between 4.16 and
5.5, and the significance of the Spirit as an ἀρραβών, Erlemann writes,
"Mit [dem Geist] hat schon jetzt das eschatologische Neuwerden be-
gonnen. Der, der das tägliche Neuwerden bewirkt, verbürgt auch das
vollständige Neuwerden, das für die Zukunft erwartet wird."[42] While

[35] Correctly, Windisch (1924: 164), Furnish (1984: 299), Thrall (1994: 384).

[36] Murphy-O'Connor (1991a: 53), my emphasis. So too Furnish (1984: 299); and
Plummer (1915: 150), who notes that ὁ δούς "explains *how* God prepared us for this
sure hope."

[37] See BAGD, which cites only two instances of this usage, both from the fifth century
BC (Xenophon and Herodotus), together with the comments of Fee (1994: 234) and Thrall
(1994: 382–34).

[38] E.g., Rom. 4.15; 5.3; 7.8–20; 2 Cor. 4.17; 7.10–11; 9.11, etc. The word is a favorite of
Paul's, who accounts for 23 (24, including Ephesians) of its 26 NT appearances. Only here,
however, is it used of persons. According to Collange (1972: 223), this may be the only
instance in all of Greek literature where κατεργάζομαι is used with the accusative of person.

[39] So NAB, Perriman (1989: 518), Fee (1994: 234). Cf. Plummer (1915: 149), "He who
wrought us out for this very thing."

[40] So Moule (1965–66: 118 n. 2), R. P. Martin (1986: 103, though his translation of
this verb varies), Young and Ford (1987: 131), Erlemann ("erschaffen"; 1992: 213), Thrall
(1994: 382–84). The NIV renders the verb "made." See BAGD s.v. 2. Windisch, noting the
cogency of this line of interpretation, concedes, "Dennoch ist der Gedanke an ein mystisches
Schaffen des Geistes in uns nicht auszuschließen" (1924: 164).

[41] Correctly, Plummer (1915: 149), Strachan (1935: 101–2), Lincoln (1981: 67–68),
Findeis (1983: 100), Young and Ford (1987: 131–32), Erlemann (1992: 218–20).

[42] Erlemann (1992: 219). So too Rissi (1969: 67), Lincoln (1981: 67–68), Findeis (1983:
161), and, importantly, Markschies (1994: 3). On the present–future dialectic implicit in
the idea of the Spirit as an ἀρραβών see also N. Q. Hamilton (1957: 19), Dunn (1975: 311),
Isaacs (1976: 86–87), Burge (1993: 300–1). With most (e.g., P. Bachmann [1919: 80], Allo
[1937: 28], Dinkler [1962: 188], Furnish [1984: 271], etc.) the genitive in the phrase τὸν
ἀρραβών τοῦ πνεύματος is explicative or appositional.

looking back to 4.16–17, this verse also looks ahead to 5.16–17 and serves to explicate Paul's καινὴ κτίσις statement found there.[43]

Taken in conjunction with the New Covenant(-Spirit) language and transformation motifs of chapters 3 and 4 (on which, see what follows), 2 Corinthians 1.21–22 and 5.5 add definition and clarity to the Jewish traditions which lurk behind nearly every turn of phrase in this segment. The digressionary character of these texts allows us glimpses of Paul's mind at (somewhat) unguarded moments. From 1.20 we learn that Paul's thoughts are occupied with the fulfillment of God's promises *in Christ* (1.20; cf. 5.17a) and through the Spirit "in our hearts." The language of verses 21–22 is clearly reminiscent of the prophetic promises of Joel, Jeremiah, and Ezekiel, and provides the attentive reader with a cipher for the heavily coded Spirit and heart language of the following chapters. In 5.5, which is linked to 1.21–22 by identical terminology, Paul further delimits these prophetic traditions in terms of the creative, generative work of the Spirit of God. These two passages bracket and summarize the major themes of chapters 3 and 4 and provide access to the theological corridor which leads to 2 Corinthians 5.17.

The programmatic character of the introductory thanksgiving (2.14–17)

Having delimited the literary context of 2 Corinthians 5.11–21, I will begin my analysis of the relevant themes of this section with a consideration of its opening thanksgiving in 2.14–17. Peter O'Brien has provided a helpful examination of Paul's introductory thanksgivings, and one of his conclusions is particularly important:

> Paul's introductory thanksgivings have a varied function: epistolary, didactic, and paranetic, and they provide evidence of his pastoral and/or apostolic concern for the addressees . . . But whatever the particular thrust of any passage, it is clear that Paul's introductory thanksgivings were not meaningless devices. Instead, they were integral parts of their letters, *setting the tone and themes of what was to follow.*[44]

---

[43] So Plummer (1915: 149), Findeis (1983: 98), Young and Ford (1987: 131–32). Cf. Thrall (1994: 383–84), who comes very close to this position.

[44] O'Brien (1977: 263), my emphasis. Unfortunately, O'Brien does not consider 2 Corinthians 2.14–17 in his discussion. Cf. Schubert (1939: 26–27, 180) and Belleville (1991: 112). Peter Artz has recently questioned the appropriateness of the designation "thanksgiving formula," though he concedes that "in Paul, just as in Greek papyrus letters, we often find a thanksgiving *that is motivated by the content*" (1994: 35, my emphasis).

The introductory nature of 2.14–17 has not escaped the notice of exegetes,[45] but the specific insights of O'Brien's work have not been adequately brought to bear on 2 Corinthians 2.14–7.4. Employing the canons of rhetorical criticism, George Kennedy believes it is possible to analyze 2.14–17 in terms of Paul's thesis statement (vv. 14–16) followed by the elements by which Paul will prove this statement (v. 17).[46] The precise scheme elaborated by Kennedy is less important than the fact that he isolates specific data in this introductory segment (the *proem*) and suggests that they can elucidate the themes of chapters 2–7. This highly serviceable method of analysis will be employed here. I modify Kennedy only by extending the limits of this introductory segment to 3.6, thereby allowing the whole of 2.14–3.6 to serve as the précis to the ensuing argument.[47]

Paul's sufficiency and the Corinthian complaint

Identifying Paul's "opponents"

The rhetorical question of 2.16, "And who is sufficient for these things?," sets the agenda for chapters 2–7 and provides an early signal of the defense posture Paul will adopt in this section.[48] Most of the following argument is related in some sense to this initial query and this provides substantiation for the universal appraisal of these chapters as an apostolic defense. This raises the important question of Paul's opponents in Corinth and just what or who Paul was defending himself against.

It is no secret that the *Gegnerfrage* is the most complex and heavily trodden issue in studies relating to 2 Corinthians. The extravagant and conflicting profiles of Paul's opponents produced several decades ago[49] have been largely set aside in favor of a more circumspect evaluation of

[45] See Thrall (1982; 1994: 188–90), Furnish (1984: 188–92), Carrez (1987: 84–85), Hafemann (1990: 7–35), Sumney (1990: 107–8); see also Collange, who notes that 2.14–17 provides "un *sommaire* des chapitres qui suivent" (1972: 21).
[46] G. Kennedy (1984: 88). Cf. also Patte (1987: 38–39).
[47] This point has been sufficiently established by Furnish (1984: 185–86), Dautzenberg (1986: 153–62), Patte (1987: 23–39), and Crafton (1991: 75–76), all of whom connect 3.1–6 with the thanksgiving period and see this entire unit as a brief conspectus of chapters 2–7.
[48] On "sufficiency" as the leitmotif of this section see Lietzmann (1949: 109), Rissi (1969: 17–18), Lang (1973: 173–77), Furnish (1984: 177, 185–86), Dautzenberg (1986: 156–58), Belleville (1991: 143), and especially Provence (1982: 55–57) and Hafemann (1990: 85–97).
[49] Especially Schmithals ([1951], ET 1971), Georgi ([1964], ET 1986), Güttgemanns (1966), and Rissi (1969).

the evidence, yet one which verges on agnosticism in some quarters.[50] The magnitude of the problem becomes clearer when the following points are kept in mind: (1) not everything that Paul opposes can be confidently traced to his opponents; (2) not everything that can be confidently traced to Paul's "opponents" (the disaffected among the Corinthians) can be confidently traced to Paul's "OPPONENTS" (the intruders of 2 Corinthians 10–13). In relation to (1), it must be acknowledged that Paul could critique aspects of Greco-Roman society and the Corinthian church in particular without providing any useful information about his rivals. It is wholly inadequate to imagine that Paul's argument in 2 Corinthians bounces back and forth like a pinball between the claims of his adversaries. In relation to (2), while 2 Corinthians 10–13 provides firm evidence of intruders, we know from 1 Corinthians 1–4 that serious questions had already arisen from within the Corinthian community concerning the adequacy of their founding father, so to suppose that all the polemically oriented statements in 2 Corinthians are directed toward a single front is singularly naive.[51] The sheer variety of portraits of Paul's opponents in 2 Corinthians is a vocal witness to the failure of some scholars to consider this second point. Further complicating the whole discussion is Gerd Theissen's contention that in 2 Corinthians Paul "confronts above all himself, for his relationship to Judaism is always, among other things, a relationship to his own life."[52]

In keeping with the more cautious approach of recent scholarship, though without pleading agnosticism, no attempt will be made here to construct a detailed profile of Paul's opponents. It is possible, however, to identify one central complaint in Corinth – a complaint that permeates Paul's extant correspondence with this church. This issue is introduced in the thanksgiving period/*proem* (2.17), and is taken up specifically in 5.11. In fact, it is the only complaint Paul actually cites: "It is said, 'His letters may be forceful and cogent, but his bodily presence is weak and his speech contemptible'" (10.10). The importance of this issue for understanding Paul's argument in 2.14–7.4, and 5.11–21 in particular, demands that the

---

[50] Stockhausen: "The fact that Paul did deal with some who opposed him is certain, but to decide between the various pictures offered of them is impossible" (1989: 6). Danker: "It is impossible to formulate any satisfactory conclusion beyond a few general assessments" (1989a: 24–25). Bieringer: "Wir wissen letztlich nur sehr wenig über die Gegner" (1994d: 221).

[51] The chief deficiency of Sumney's otherwise level-headed study of Paul's opponents in 2 Corinthians (1990) is that he excludes from consideration 1 Corinthians and then homogenizes Paul's opposition into a unified group.

[52] Theissen (1987: 131). Cf. Morgan on Romans: "Another possibility is that Paul is arguing with the Jewish Christian he knows best, namely himself" (1995: 69).

examination of the programmatic components of the thanksgiving period relevant to this study begin with its final clause: "as from God and before God, *we speak in Christ*" (2.17d).[53]

Paul's spoken message in 2.17d

In the course of delineating the primary concerns of what will follow, Paul specifically contrasts himself with "so many" (οἱ πολλοί) who "peddle for profit" (καπηλεύω) the word of God. In contradistinction to these, Paul contends that *what he speaks* (λαλέω) is (a) from sincere motives (ἐξ εἰλικρινείας), (b) of divine origin (ἐκ θεοῦ), (c) in full view of God (κατέναντι θεοῦ) and (d) "in Christ." Further, as most commentators acknowledge, in describing the οἱ πολλοί who hawk the word of God with the term καπηλεύω, Paul has chosen a word with a rich and unmistakable resonance within the debate that raged between philosophy and rhetoric since the time of Plato.[54] Socrates, for example, depicts the sophists as those who "take their doctrines the round of our cities, hawking them about (καπηλεύω) to any odd purchaser."[55] In discussing the proper means of livelihood for philosophers, Arius Didymus (late first century BC) expresses the view that many of his contemporaries "suspect there is something worthless in sophistry, like peddling words (λόγους καπηλεύειν) . . . as this way of making money falls short of the dignity of philosophy."[56] Numerous texts and passages are cited in the commentaries, and there is no need to repeat the material here. It is important to keep in mind, however, that this debate was not confined to the academies of Athens, but extended to distant parts of the Hellenized world. It is common knowledge that Philo had a low opinion of sophists, and it is this particular aspect of their way of life which he found so distasteful: "For manifest surely and clear is the disgrace of those who say that they are wise, yet barter their wisdom for what they can get, as men say is the way

---

[53] A more thorough treatment of this issue can be found in Hubbard (1998). The following material draws heavily on the argument presented there.

[54] On the sophistic allusion in 2.17 see, e.g., Windisch (1924: 100ff.), Wendland (1964: 177), Barrett (1973: 103), Furnish (1984: 14, 178–79), Bultmann (1985: 69), Talbert (1989: 141), Sandnes (1991: 132), and the extensive discussion in Hafemann (1990: 100–25). On the quarrel between philosophy and rhetoric see G. Kennedy (1963: 321–29), Litfin (1994: 39–40), Bowersock (1969: *passim*). Betz (1972: 55ff.; 66ff.) goes so far as to claim that in 2 Corinthians 10–13 Paul *consciously* places himself in the Socratic tradition with its critique of the sophists, though deliberately avoiding the ancient philosopher's name.

[55] Plato, *Protagoras* 313D.   [56] *Epitome of Stoic Ethics* 11m, edited by Pomeroy.

of the peddlers who hawk their goods in the market."[57] In contrasting true philosophy with its sophistic variety Philo writes: "And the wisdom must not be that of the systems hatched by the word-catchers and sophists who sell their tenets and arguments like any bit of merchandise in the market, men who pit philosophy against philosophy without a blush."[58]

Paul, then, introduces 2.14–7.4 by means of a thoughtful and carefully elaborated statement of his apostolic calling *which focuses on the nature of his spoken message*. In doing so he invokes language and imagery commonly associated with the practice of the sophists, the popular teachers of his day. In particular, Paul distances himself from the sophistic preacher-for-pay paradigm which so often led to charges of avarice and disingenuousness. In the pseudo-Socratic epistles, one of Socrates' first-century disciples defends his mentor against the accusation of being "a retailer of education like the Sophists... who go among the masses and demand money from those who want to listen."[59] When the audience holds the purse strings, flattery rather than frank admonition is the order of the day, which is why Dio ridicules the sophists as those who "can't help adopting the thought of their listeners, saying and thinking such things as fit the nature of those listening, whatever it happens to be."[60] As noted earlier, however, the issue of Paul's spoken message is echoed throughout his turbulent exchanges with this church, and before I trace this issue through chapters 3–4, I will strengthen this subsequent analysis by highlighting the prominence of this subject outside 2 Corinthians 2–7.

Paul's spoken message in 1 Corinthians 1–4

In 1 Corinthians 1–4 we find Paul's clearest and most deliberate statement of his modus operandi as a preacher: "I did not come... with the prestige of rhetoric and philosophy" (2.5).[61] This reading of 1 Corinthians 1–4 has recently been argued by Duane Litfin, though, as Litfin himself emphasizes, he only reasserts and more carefully substantiates the traditional interpretation of this passage.[62] From this earlier correspondence we learn

---

[57] *Gig.* 39. See also *Det.* 1, 35, 38–41, 71–74; *Poster. C.* 101; *Conf.* 39; *Quis Her.* 246; *Congr.* 18, 67.

[58] *Vit. Mos.* 2.212.   [59] *Ps.-Socrates* 1.1–2, edited by Abraham Malherbe.

[60] *Discourse* 35.8.   [61] Héring's translation (1962: 14).

[62] Litfin (1994: 1–27). While Litfin's arguments are compelling, there is room for reading facets of 1 Corinthians 1–4 against the background of Greco-Roman rhetoric even within the alternative interpretations. Charles Talbert (1989: 1–11), for example, emphasizes rhetoric and esoteric wisdom as issues in 1 Corinthians, while Kümmel (1975: 272–75) points to rhetoric and incipient gnostic tendencies.

that the form of Paul's proclamation was as important to the apostle as
its substance: "For Christ did not send me to baptize, but to preach the
gospel; not in words of wisdom, lest the cross of Christ be emptied"
(1 Cor. 1.17). In Paul's view, it was possible to present the gospel in a
form which robbed it of its most potent dynamic, the cross:

> In coming to you, friends, I did not come in eloquent speech
> (ὑπεροχὴν λόγου) or wisdom . . . and my words and my preach-
> ing were not in persuasive words of wisdom (οὐκ ἐν πειθοῖς
> σοφίας λόγοις), but in the demonstration and power (δύναμις)
> of the Spirit, so that your faith might not rest in human wisdom,
> but in the power of God.   (2.1–5)

George Kennedy remarks that Paul in this passage "may be said to
reject the whole of classical philosophy and rhetoric."[63] Kennedy may
exaggerate, but the apostle does insist that he has deliberately spurned
persuasive artistry in order that πίστις might not rest on human σοφία
but on God's δύναμις. In Paul's view, when form dominates over content
the result is misplaced faith.

But the Corinthians, like average citizens of any first-century Greco-
Roman city, relished oratory, having been fed a rich diet of rhetoric from
birth.[64] They erected statues to their favorite sophists,[65] modeled their
bema on the rostra in Rome,[66] and became the beneficiaries of public
buildings from the wealthier practitioners of the art.[67] Dio Chrysostom's
description of Isthmia, some six miles from Corinth, is illuminating. He
speaks of "crowds of wretched sophists around Poseidon's temple shout-
ing and reviling one another."[68] Dio purports to describe the situation in
Diogenes' day, though, as Furnish and Savage presume, it more likely
refers to his own.[69]

---

[63] G. Kennedy (1980: 131–32).

[64] According to G. Kennedy, "Corinth was a prosperous and sophisticated city; it is not
surprising that eloquence should have an appeal there" (1994: 259).

[65] This is the subject of Favorinus' address to the Corinthians (see below).

[66] Dinkler (1967: 118), Furnish (1984: 12).

[67] Herodes Atticus, the famous second-century orator and student of Favorinus, donated
the theatre. See Philostratus, *Vit. Soph.* 551, Bowersock (1969: 27), Murphy-O'Connor
(1983: 170–71).

[68] *Discourses* 8.9. The orations of Dio, a contemporary of Paul, provide a unique window
into Paul's world and will be used liberally in what follows. Like Paul he was born in Asia
Minor (Prusa), traveled extensively in this region, and maintained a peripatetic lifestyle
which involved public discourse on religious, moral, and social themes. His *Discourses*
reveal a familiarity with Corinth and the Corinthians (2.3–4; 8.5–11; 9.1–14; 20.7; 31.104,
121–22; 32.92; 79.2, etc.) and it would appear that he was even acquainted with the Essenes.
On this see Mussies (1972: viii–ix) and Jones (1978: 63–64).

[69] Furnish (1984: 14), Savage (1996: 47).

We can safely assume that the Corinthians were exposed to rhetors and sophists on a regular basis. Further, those from families with means would have received an education in rhetoric and philosophy, which constituted "the two principal parts of higher education"[70] in the Greco-Roman world. We know from 1 Corinthians 1.26–27 that at least some of the Corinthian believers were from the upper strata of Corinthian society, and in Theissen's view it was probably this group that was causing Paul the most difficulty.[71] This conjecture fits comfortably with the situation being outlined here. From 1 Corinthians we easily surmise that Paul was aware that he faced opposition in Corinth from those whose rhetorical tastes were more refined. He takes time to defend his style of proclamation, though, as we will see, he did not succeed in silencing his critics.[72]

Paul's spoken message in 2 Corinthians 10–13

As stated earlier, of the many complaints that must have circulated among the Corinthians, Paul cites only one of them directly: "It is said, 'his letters are weighty and strong, but his bodily presence [read "stage presence"] is unimpressive, and his speech contemptible'" (10.10). The accusation of poor rhetorical ability is clear,[73] and not a few commentators specifically link it with 1 Corinthians 2.1–5.[74] It is repeated in 11.6 ("I may be an amateur in speech, but not in knowledge"), in 12.19, and in 13.3, revealing how this issue permeates this section. Regardless of whether chapters 10–13 constitute a separate letter, they certainly represent a complete unit, the main purpose of which is an apostolic defense.[75] In 12.19 this is explicitly stated, as is one of the chief subjects of that defense: "So far it seems that I am making a defense to you? Before God *we speak in Christ.*" The relationship between these two clauses proposed here is corroborated a few verses later (13.2–3) when we read, "When I come

[70] Bowersock (1969: 11). Cf. G. Kennedy (1963: 7, 269–73; 1972: 318–22; 1980: 31, 163–68).

[71] Theissen (1992: 231–77).

[72] In what follows I offer substantiation for Litfin's assessment of 2 Corinthians: "Paul is addressing here the same principle as in 1 Cor. 1–4 but on a somewhat wider front" (1994: 158–59).

[73] See, e.g., Strachan (1935: 15), Betz (1972: 44–57), Furnish (1984: 479), Bultmann (1985: 190), R. P. Martin (1986: 312–13).

[74] E.g., Heinrici (1887: 329–30), Plummer (1915: 283), Windisch (1924: 306), Strachan (1935: 14), Kümmel (1949: 146), Prümm (1967: 581–82), Barrett (1973: 271), Furnish (1984: 479), Bultmann (1985: 190).

[75] Betz's work (1972) is crucial here. Whether or not his genre classification of apologetic letter is accepted, most accept this as the main point of chapters 10–13. Cf. Furnish (1984), R. P. Martin (1986), Murphy-O'Connor (1991a).

again I will spare no one, *since you seek proof that Christ is speaking in me.*"

Yet Paul's continued insistence that Christ (2.17; 12.19; 13.3) or God (5.20) was speaking through him could only have provided his sceptics with fuel for their fire. There is ample evidence to suggest that those engaged in the sophistic arts believed their eloquence could be ascribed to divine giftedness. Philostratus opens his history of the sophistic movement by comparing its practitioners to divine oracles and mouthpieces of the gods.[76] Favorinus (AD 80–150), in a speech to the Corinthians, states that his wisdom and eloquence are evidence that he has been "equipped by the gods for this express purpose."[77] Cicero's remark that the orator was "a god among men,"[78] and Aristides' assessment of oratory as "a divine thing"[79] were by no means idiosyncratic appraisals.[80] The conceits of the orator were fueled by the adoration of the crowds, who, as Plutarch scornfully relates, would show their approval with shouts of "How divine!" and "Spoken like a god!"[81] Given that persuasion itself was deified and worshiped by the Greeks,[82] anyone claiming to be a divine spokesman would have a fairly large order to fill. Paul's convictions concerning his divine call and mission left him little room for maneuvering, but left a great deal of room for misunderstanding on the part of the Corinthians.

A closer examination of 10.10ff. throws valuable light on the predicament in which Paul found himself. After citing the complaint of his unimpressive speech (10.10) and giving a stern warning to those making this complaint (10.11), Paul offers the following explanation (10.12–13): "For we do not dare to class ourselves or compare ourselves with those who commend themselves. For when they measure themselves by themselves and compare themselves with themselves, they have no understanding. But we do not boast excessively . . ."

In confronting the objection of his poor oratory Paul is compelled to distinguish himself and his colleagues from "some" who engage in self-comparison (συγκρίνω), self-commendation (συνίστημι), and boasting

[76] *Vit. Soph.* 481.
[77] This speech has been passed down to us under Dio Chrysostom's name. See his *Discourses* 37.27.
[78] *De Oratore* 3.53.   [79] *In Defense of Oratory* 113; cf. 391.
[80] For similar comments see Lucian, *A Professor of Public Speaking* 11; Epictetus, *Discourses* 3.1.36; Dio Chrysostom, *Discourses* 32.12–13; 34.4; 35.7. According to the *Pseudo-Socratic Epistles* (c. AD 200), it is the mind and the tongue of the philosopher that are "most favored and most god-like" (*Ep.* 31).
[81] *On Praising Oneself Inoffensively* 543E-F. According to Acts 12.22, one of Herod's public addresses was greeted with acclamation, "This is the voice of a god, not of a man."
[82] Buxton's study of πείθω in Greece devotes an entire chapter to "The Goddess" (1982: 31–48).

(καυχάομαι). This description can refer to only one class of people, a group whose presence was ubiquitous in the first-century Greco-Roman world of Corinth: the rhetors and the sophists.

The art of comparison (σύγκρισις) was taught as a "standard exercise"[83] of rhetorical technique and is defined by Paul's contemporary Quintilian as the determination of "which of two characters is the better or the worse."[84] Forbes' examination of the subject relates σύγκρισις to self-advertisement, which he describes as "a prime characteristic of popular teachers."[85] Indeed, Plutarch virtually defines sophists by their excessive use of comparison: "For it is not like friendship, but sophistry to seek for glory in other men's faults."[86]

The association of sophists with self-praise is well known and accounts for the numerous treatises on the propriety and proper bounds of such activity.[87] In a rare moment of unpartisan candor, Philostratus labels the sophistic vocation "a profession prone to egotism and arrogance."[88] Particularly relevant is the speech of self-commendation that the sophist Favorinus gave to the Corinthians after he discovered that a statue the Corinthians had erected in honor of his eloquence had been removed. Given his superior lineage, athletic prowess, wisdom, and eloquence Favorinus concludes, "Ought [I] not have a bronze statue here in Corinth? Yes, and in every city!"[89]

The audience's role in this theatre was that of judge, determining the success or failure of the oration.[90] Maximus of Tyre (c. AD 125–85), himself a professional rhetorician, laments the fate of the orator as "a slave of vindictive judges."[91] From Paul's description of his predicament in 2 Corinthians 10.10ff., along with what we know about sophists in the first century, it becomes apparent that Paul was being classed with this group and judged accordingly. It is entirely conceivable that Paul's pattern of ministry – peripatetic proclamation – was partly responsible for the judgment the Corinthians imposed on him.[92] Corinth, like any

---

[83] G. Kennedy (1983: 25). Important treatments of this subject from the standpoint of the New Testament include Betz (1972: 20), Forbes (1986), Marshall (1987: 53–55; 348–53), and Talbert (1989: 114–15). The lexical data can be culled from Ernesti (1795: 323) and Lausberg (1960: §1130).

[84] *Inst. Or.* 2.4.21, cited in Marshall (1987: 54).   [85] Forbes (1986: 7).

[86] In "How to Tell a Friend from a Flatterer" (*Moralia* 71).

[87] See, e.g., Plutarch's essay, "On Praising Oneself Inoffensively" (*Moralia* 539), along with Quintilian's counsel in *Inst. Or.* 11.1.17, where we learn that even an orator of the stature of Cicero was not immune from criticism on this score.

[88] *Vit. Soph.* 616.   [89] In Dio Chrysostom, *Discourses* 37.26.

[90] Litfin (1994: 130–33).

[91] *Discourse* 36. This speech is reproduced whole by Malherbe (1986: 73–79).

[92] See Litfin (1994: 160–73).

Greco-Roman city, was familiar with traveling sophists and understood
their role in the game. To be sure, Paul was fulfilling his call, but one
would have to admit the Corinthians were doing likewise.

Paul's spoken message in 2 Corinthians 3–4

Now that I have demonstrated the importance of this central complaint
outside 2 Corinthians 2–7, this section can be read with a greater awareness of the issues at stake. After its introduction in 2.17, the theme of
Paul's spoken proclamation threads its way through chapters 3–4 await-
ing specific treatment. In 4.1–6, a passage with clear echoes of the introductory proem,[93] Paul again contrasts himself with those who practice
cunning and deceit and hence distort (δολόω, 4.2a) God's message, while
he commends himself through his open declaration of the truth (4.2b). In
the writings of Philo, trickery and distorting the truth become cliché in
his depiction of the sophists,[94] which was the prevailing view among cul-
tured despisers of sophistry. Using the same terminology as Paul, Lucian
describes this brand of philosophers as those who "sell their lessons as
wine merchants... most of them adulterating (δολόω) and cheating and
giving false measure."[95] The apostle provides further commentary on
this group in 4.5, where we discover the precise nature of their distorted
message: "For we do not preach (κηρύσσω) ourselves but Christ." The
reader is clearly intended to draw the conclusion that these others preach
themselves, and the allusion would not have been lost on the Corinthians.
Dio, who also struggled to distance himself from the sophists, complains
to the Athenians of "οἱ πολλοί who call themselves philosophers, but
who preach themselves (αὐτοὺς ἀνακηρύττουσιν)."[96]

In 4.13–14 Paul manages to place himself in continuity with his Old
Testament predecessors while at the same time providing a profound theological rationale for his spoken message: "And having the same Spirit
of faith, according to that which is written, 'We believed, therefore we
spoke,' so too we have believed, therefore we speak (λαλέω), knowing that
the one who raised the Lord Jesus will also raise us with Jesus." Paul takes

[93] On the verbal-thematic links between 2.14–3.6 and 4.1–6 see Findeis (1983: 89,
109–10), Heiny (1987: 11), Klauck (1987: 269–70, 273–89), Lambrecht (1994c: 261–62).
[94] *Op. Mund.* 45, 157; *Leg. All.* 3.64, 121, 232; *Cher.* 9–10; *Det. Pot. Ins.* 32–44; *Poster.
C.* 85–88, 101, 150–51; *Agric.* 136, 143–44, 159–64; *Ebr.* 71; *Migr. Abr.* 72–85; *Quis.
Her.* 302–5; *Congr.* 67; *Fug.* 209–11; *Mut. Nom.* 208, 240; *Som.* 1.220; 2.240; *Omn. Prob.
Lib.* 4–5; *Aet. Mund.* 132; *Quaest. in Gen.* 27–33.
[95] *Hermotimus* 59.
[96] *Discourses*, 13.11. Dio often refers to the sophists merely as "οἱ πολλοί" (e.g., 12.13;
17.1).

pains to explain that his speech issues from the same Spirit which inspired the psalmist, is rooted in *pistis* and is motivated by the resurrection of the messiah.[97] Citing more fully the passage which introduced this section, Dio Chrysostom (again) offers an illuminating commentary on Paul's insistence that the Corinthians properly understand this important aspect of his ministry:

> But to find a man who in plain terms and without guile (ἀδόλως) speaks his mind with frankness (παρρησία), and neither for the sake of reputation nor for gain makes false pretensions, but out of good will and concern for his fellow-man stands ready, if need be, to submit to ridicule and to the disorder of the mob – to find such a man is not easy, but rather the good fortune of every great city, so great is the dearth of noble, independent souls and such is the abundance of toadies, mountebanks and sophists.[98]

Having made several preliminary passes over his target, Paul takes up the subject specifically in 5.11: "Knowing the fear of the Lord, *we persuade people*."

Summary

When the argument and terminology of 2 Corinthians 2–7 are read in light of Paul's other communications with this church, it becomes apparent that Paul's "sufficiency" was closely related to his spoken message in the minds of the Corinthians. From the time of Isocrates, who taught that "the power to speak well is the surest index of sound understanding,"[99] to Aristides who contended that "as character is, such is the speech,"[100] wisdom and eloquence were intimately connected by the Greeks, and the Corinthians' expectation that their apostle demonstrate *both* is consonant with their Greco-Roman heritage.[101]

Paul's task in 2 Corinthians 2–7 and 10–13 is to wean this church from their immature, superficial, and fleshly evaluation of his ministry. His strategy is to concede weakness while redefining it. To the Corinthians, weakness is weakness; to Paul, weakness is strength (12.10).[102] Paul

---

[97] This interpretation is strengthened by the illuminating parallel passage, 1 Thess. 2.4–5: "But just as we have been found worthy by God to be entrusted with the Gospel, *thus we speak* (λαλέω), not as people pleasers, but before God who tests our hearts. For we did not come with flattering words . . . or seeking glory from people."

[98] *Discourses* 32.11.   [99] *Nicoles* 7.   [100] *In Defense of Oratory* 392.

[101] See Litfin (1994: 119–24) for a more complete presentation of this subject.

[102] On this theme see Savage (1996: 103–92).

understood, as the Corinthians did not, that *the medium is the message*, so he strove to exemplify the crucified messiah he preached (4.7–12). It is conceivable that the primary heresy of the intruders in chapters 10–13 was not one of doctrine but one of demeanor, and this helps to explain why the hunt for heresy in 2 Corinthians so often comes up empty. It should be remembered that it is not the christology of this group that so irritates Paul in chapters 10–13 but their boasting (10.5; 11.12, 18; 12.1–2, 11–12).[103] Because the medium and the message are not fully separable, presenting a crucified, self-sacrificing messiah in an arrogant, self-promoting way constitutes a fundamental distortion of the message itself. It is, in fact, preaching another Jesus and proclaiming another gospel (11.4–6; 4.2, 5).

Paul, on the other hand, was determined that his entire life be lived in the shadow of the cross and this meant that the form of his message had to conform to its content.[104] In contrast to these others, Paul portrays himself as a conquered enemy led about in triumph by his Lord (2.14). Paradoxically, it is precisely by means of this crushed and vanquished existence that Paul becomes the aroma of the crucified Christ to the world (2.15; cf. 4.11–12).

Chapters 2–7, then, constitute a brave attempt by Paul to redefine for the Corinthians the nature of his apostolic work. In an effort to convince this church that the earthen vessel of his ministry concealed the very δύναμις of God (4.7), Paul directs their attention back to the inner dynamic of the Spirit. From this pneumatological basis Paul articulates his perception of his New Covenant ministry and the transformation which it entails. These two closely related items, Paul's New Covenant retrospective and the motif of transformation must be explored in order to grasp adequately 2 Corinthians 5.11–21.

Paul's New Covenant retrospective

The theological antecedents of Paul's argument:
Jeremiah and Ezekiel

In his discussion of the letter–Spirit antithesis in 2 Corinthians 3, Richard Hays remarks that καταργουμένην in 3.7 constitutes "a retrospective

---

[103] Correctly, Savage (1996: 54–62).
[104] See Schrage (1991: 225) on 1 Cor. 2.1–5: "Vom Gekreuzigten kann man nicht mit brillierender rhetorischer Eleganz sprechen, nichts nur aus Geschmacksgründen, sondern weil alle Konzentration dem Verkündigten, nicht dem Verkündiger zu gelten hat."

theological judgement,"[105] and this observation could be extended to much of the material in chapters 3–5. As described earlier, Paul's New Covenant retrospective refers to his critical appraisal of the old dispensation in light of the new. I have already observed a clear pneumatological drift to Paul's thought which betrays a salvation-historical framework issuing from the theology of the later prophets – particularly Jeremiah and Ezekiel. That Paul returns to this theme in chapter 3, making his theological antecedents explicit (3.3, 6), confirms my earlier analysis and demonstrates the strength of the prophetic undercurrents which are directing the apostle's thought. We can, in fact, take for granted the pivotal role of the prophecies of Jeremiah and Ezekiel in the development of Paul's argument in chapter 3. In prefacing this material with reference to the Spirit, tablets of stone versus hearts of flesh, and, most importantly, the New Covenant, Paul leaves no room for speculation concerning the scriptural reservoir which is nourishing his argument. The concentration of New Covenant motifs in the introductory segment foreshadows the theological perspective of the ensuing material, and this literary and history-of-traditions connection is all but universally agreed.[106]

But Paul's overt allusions are less important for this study than other theological emphases derived from these same prophetic exemplars which shape his argument. Paul leaves behind any explicit reference to Jeremiah and Ezekiel in chapter 3, but he takes with him their religious ideal of the interiority of the covenant. This motif lies at the heart of Paul's New Covenant retrospective and helps to explain the recurring antitheses of this segment of 2 Corinthians. Both interiority and antithesis play a vital role in 2 Corinthians 5.11–21, and in order to allow the epistolary context full weight in the exegesis of this passage, these crucial literary motifs will be briefly explored.

The New Covenant antitheses of 2 Corinthians 2–7

Perhaps the most striking stylistic feature of 2 Corinthians 2–7 is the contrasts and antitheses which saturate the argument. Writing in reference

[105] Hays (1989: 134).

[106] In addition to the commentaries, the following monographs and articles are particularly important: Vos (1973: 132–40), Hickling (1974/75), Richard (1981), Hays (1989: 127–29), Stockhausen (1989), Hafemann (1990, 1995), W. J. Webb (1993: 85–92), Lambrecht (1994c: 257–94). Strangely, both Wolff (1976: 131–37; 1989a:) and Belleville (1991: 146–49) deny Paul's obvious dependence on Jeremiah and Ezekiel in 2 Corinthians 3.

to 3.4–4.6, Gerd Theissen notes that "the train of thought is antithetical throughout,"[107] and similar evaluations can be found of every paragraph of this prolonged digression.[108] The thanksgiving period, with its contrasts of life/death, salvation/destruction, and sincerity/huckstering, suitably introduces the antithetical tone of the discourse.

But alongside these oppositions – many of which are mere rhetorical flourish – stands a series of antitheses with a similar focus (internal vs. external) and a common theological ancestry (Paul's New Covenant retrospective). The letter–Spirit contrast of 3.6 provides the theological rubric under which these diverse but related antitheses may be organized,[109] and the evidence of Romans supports Hickling's view that this antithesis "had deep roots in Paul's thoughts" and constituted "a continuing interior dialogue in his mind."[110] Romans also illustrates the dual nature of the letter–Spirit antithesis, focusing both on the *enablement* of the Spirit (7.4–6; see chapter 7) and on the *interiority* of the Spirit (2.28–29; see chapter 11). It is this second emphasis that Paul develops in 2 Corinthians 2.14–5.21, and I highlight here the more prominent texts:

3.1–3	ink on tablets of stone *versus* the Spirit on tablets of human hearts
3.6	letter *versus* Spirit
4.6–7	internal treasure *versus* external vessel of clay
4.7–12	visible affliction *versus* invisible life
4.16	outer person *versus* inner person
4.18	seen *versus* unseen
5.7	walking by faith *versus* walking by outward appearance (εἶδος)[111]
5.12	boasting in appearances *versus* boasting in the heart

All this is covenant language, or more precisely, *New* Covenant language, as Stockhausen explains: "It is entirely typical of the new covenant which Paul ministered, the new covenant of Jeremiah 38.31–34 (LXX) to be interior, to be in the heart."[112]

---

[107] Theissen (1987: 119).

[108] On 2.14–4.6: Heiny (1987: 2, 22); on 3.1–3 and 7–11: Stockhausen (1989: 73–82), Lambrecht (1994c: 264–67); on 2.14–3.18: Provence (1982: 57–58); on 3.1–18: Wolter (1978: 81); on 4.1–6: Klauck (1989: 271–72); on 4.7–5.21: Lincoln (1981: 103–8), Pate (1991: 78), Lambrecht (1994e: 313); on 6.3–10: Findeis (1983: 115–20).

[109] Correctly, Theissen (1987: 143).   [110] Hickling (1974/75: 386).

[111] On this translation of εἶδος over against "sight" see Furnish (1984: 273) and BAGD s.v. 1. Cf. Collange: "forme, objet vu" (1972: 232), Barrett: "the appearance of things" (1973: 158), Thrall: "visible form" (1994: 357, 387–89).

[112] Stockhausen (1989: 174). So too W. J. Webb (1993: 114–15), and especially Vos (1973: 132–43).

Interiority and Covenant

Given the prophetic traditions on which Paul is relying, his "multiplication of interiorized conceptions [with reference to the heart]"[113] is easily comprehensible. As we have already seen (chapters 2 and 8), both Jeremiah and Ezekiel analyzed Israel's dilemma in terms of the heart (Jer. 3.10; 4.4; 5.23; 12.2–3; 17.1, 9, etc.; Ezek. 6.9; 11.19–21; 14.3–7, etc.) and both presented the solution in terms of God's new work in the heart (esp. Jer. 31.33 and Ezek. 36.26). 2 Corinthians provides incontrovertible evidence of Paul's conviction that the cleavage between inner and outer – a central concern of the prophets – had been overcome by his New Covenant "ministry of the Spirit" (3.8). With Jeremiah and Ezekiel as his mentors, Paul sets his ministry "into the framework of the eschatological and pneumatological restoration"[114] foretold by them and boldly portrays it as the fulfillment of this prophetic hope: "Paulus trifft hier genau die Intention der jeremianischen Verheißung: In dem neuen Bund ist die Spaltung von Innen und Außen dadurch aufgehoben, daß Gott seine Willensverfügung statt auf steinerne Tafeln jetzt in die Herzen schreibt."[115]

The motif of interiority is given its most dramatic expression in 4.6, a verse to be considered in more detail later: "The same God who said, 'Let light shine from darkness,' made his light shine *in our hearts* (ἐν ταῖς καρδίαις ἡμῶν)." Paul argues that, unlike his Jewish contemporaries with a veil upon their hearts (ἐπὶ τὴν καρδίαν αὐτῶν, 3.16), turning to Christ initiates a process of inner transformation (cf. 3.18). Equally noteworthy is that the light of Genesis 1 shines not on the cosmos, or humanity in general, but on the center of the individual, the human heart.[116] Connecting 4.6 with 3.18, 4.16–18, 5.12 and 5.17, Carol Stockhausen believes that these texts "bear witness to the interiority of the transformation of the Christian,"[117] which introduces the final crucial motif preparatory to the exegesis of 5.14–17.

From life to life: the motif of transformation

As we might expect, Paul introduces the theme of transformation in his opening remarks (ἐκ ζωῆς εἰς ζωήν 2.16), and this refrain resonates throughout the argument of chapters 2–7. Without placing undue weight

---

[113] Theissen (1987: 143). Note the prominence of καρδία in Paul's argument: 1.22; 3.2, 3, 15; 4.6; 5.12; 6.11; 7.3.

[114] Sandnes (1991: 134–35).   [115] Vos (1973: 140).

[116] Cf. the comments of Klauck (1987: 291–94) under the heading "Die Erleuchtung der Herzen."

[117] Stockhausen (1989: 175).

on Paul's terminology, this motif is particularly evident in his frequent use of ζωή, πνεῦμα, δόξα, and εἰκών.

Spirit and life

Given the intimate connection between "Spirit" and "life" in Paul (chapter 8), it is scarcely surprising that, having inscribed "life to life" at the head of this passage, we soon find Paul talking about the Spirit. The meaning of the phrase ἐκ ζωῆς εἰς ζωήν (2.16) is easier to sense than define; its rhetorical force is blunted rather than sharpened by grammatical analysis. Paul intends his readers to understand that his New Covenant ministry of the Spirit produces life in its fullest form. He unfolds the phrase gradually.

Because Paul's ministry dispensed the life-giving Spirit (3.6, 8), Paul could describe the previous dispensation as a ministry of death (3.7). As 3.9–10 make clear, this is a retrospective theological judgment. As I noted earlier (chapter 8), that Paul contrasts ἡ διακονία τοῦ θανάτου with ἡ διακονία τοῦ πνεύματος demonstrates the interchangeability of "Spirit" and "life" for Paul and indicates that Paul could have just as easily employed the phrase ἡ διακονία τῆς ζωῆς. The "life" motif is eclipsed in 3.7–4.6 by the (related) δόξα motif, but it is picked up again in 4.7–5.10 and amplified.[118] Hence, in 4.10–11 Paul's apostolic suffering reveals ἡ ζωή τοῦ Ἰησοῦ while at the same time benefiting the Corinthians: "So, death works in us, *but life in you* (4.12). Moreover, in describing believers with phrases like "we who are alive" (ἡμεῖς οἱ ζῶντες, 4.11) and "those who live" (οἱ ζῶντες, 5.15), Paul makes "life" the quintessential feature of Christian existence, and it follows from this that the consummation of this state could be thought of as mortality being swallowed by *life* (5.4). While 4.16 does not employ any cognate of ζωή, it is probably correct to see the continual making anew (ἀνακαινόω) of the inner person as a further development of the "life to life" theme as announced in 2.16. This analysis lends credibility to Dinkler's assertion that 5.11–6.10 concerns "die Offenbarung der Ζωή in der Verkündigung."[119]

Image and glory

Chapters 3 and 4 of 2 Corinthians contain the highest concentration of δόξα language in the New Testament, which underlines its importance in Paul's argument.[120] Paul introduces the concept in 3.7 as he begins

---

[118] Cf. Thrall (1982: 114).   [119] Dinkler (1992c: 178); so too Bultmann (1985: 109).

[120] With, e.g., Renwick (1991: 99–109) and Collange (1972: 73–74), though, against both, it is unnecessary to conclude that δόξα must have been a central theme of Paul's opponents.

to explain the phrase καινὴ διαθήκη (3.6), and it is very possible that Paul is drawn to the Exodus story not because it was used against him by his opponents but because it provided him with a clear reference to the glory of the παλαιὰ διαθήκη (3.14; cf. Exod. 34.29–30).[121] Arguing from the lesser to the greater (3.8–11), Paul is then able to demonstrate the surpassing glory of his ministry of the Spirit.

The motif of transformation reaches its climax in 3.18 and 4.6, verses which have received more than their share of scholarly attention. Transformation, of course, is a regular theme in religious literature and Paul was certainly not alone among his contemporaries in making use of it. It is possible to identify two varieties of transformative events in Paul,[122] and this bifocality should be kept in mind in any pursuit of history-of-religions parallels. Paul speaks both of a present process of inner transformation (Rom. 12.2; 2 Cor. 3.18; 4.6; 4.16–17; Gal. 4.19; Phil. 3.10), and of a future, instantaneous, bodily transformation which serves to bring the outer person in conformity to the (already renewed) inner person (Rom. 8.23; 1 Cor. 15.42–44; 2 Cor. 5.1–4; Phil. 3.21). This bifurcation undoubtedly arises from Paul's already–not yet dialectic and helps to explain the curious expression in 5.4 about mortality being swallowed up by "life."

2 Corinthians 3.18

While most studies relating to transformation in 2 Corinthians 3.18 focus on the origin of its imagery,[123] my concern is not from where Paul derived this symbolism, but how he uses it. Three components in the development of Paul's thought are especially important, both here and in 4.4–6: (1) his explicit reference to conversion, (2) his application of an Old Testament text to the Corinthians' present experience, and (3) his reliance on Genesis imagery. My treatment of this complex and disputed passage will be ruthlessly concise.

In 3.13 Paul contrasts his ministry with that of Moses by recalling the story in Exodus 34 concerning the lawgiver's practice of veiling himself before emerging from the tent of meeting (Exod. 34.33–35). In applying the story, Paul places the veil over the hearts of his unbelieving kinsmen, with its removal occurring only "in Christ" (3.14–15). Verse 16 is crucial for two reasons. First, Paul has deliberately altered the verb in Exodus 34.34 from εἰσεπορεύετο to ἐπιστρέψῃ. As nearly all agree, this change

---

[121] Similarly Theissen (1987: 128), Stockhausen (1989: 111), Savage (1996: 105).

[122] See Koenig (1971).

[123] E.g., Theissen (1987: 135–38), Belleville (1991), Fitzmyer (1993a), and the literature cited by Thrall (1994: 290–97).

introduces the idea of conversion[124] and enables Paul unobtrusively to merge his interpretation with his application.[125] Second, Paul leaves the subject of the verb undefined, which allows for a maximum degree of applicability. The implicit subject is Moses (v. 15), who becomes paradigmatic for New Covenant conversion.[126] But the intentionally ambiguous referent, combined with both the vague temporal clause ἡνίκα ἐάν ("whenever") and the aorist subjunctive, leaves the reader with the distinct impression that Paul's point is broader: "Whenever *anyone* turns to the Lord the veil is removed."[127] Paul concludes his appropriation of Exodus 34 in precisely the manner we would expect given the dominant theme of chapter 3, the New Covenant: "Now, 'the Lord' here, means the Spirit" (v. 17).[128] The transformative process which Paul describes in verse 18 – itself a commentary on τὸ πνεῦμα ζῳοποεῖ (3.6) – is thoroughly pneumatological, being both initiated (v. 17) and sustained (v. 18) by the Spirit.[129] Its goal, however, is Christological, and concerns the εἰκών (τοῦ θεοῦ) (3.18 and 4.4).

[124]   The evidence for seeing ἐπιστρέφω as a technical term for conversion is substantial: e.g., Isa. 6.9–10; 19.22; 29.1–4; Jer. 3.10–14, 22; 4.1; 5.3 (and throughout Jeremiah); Ps. 21.27; Hos. 5.11; Joel 2.13; Judith 5.19; Tobit 13.6; Sir. 5.7; 17.25–29; *Ep. Bar.* 2.33[A]; Luke 1.16; Acts 9.35; 11.21; 14.15; 15.19; 26.18, 20; 1 Thess. 1.9; Gal. 4.9. See Windisch (1924: 123); Dunn (1970b: 313); Collange (1972: 101–4); Furnish (1984: 211); Kim (1984: 12); Bultmann (1985: 89); Thrall (1987: 205); Sandnes (1991: 136), etc. Belleville demurs (1991: 252–53).

[125]   Thrall (1994: 269).

[126]   With, e.g., Theissen (1987: 122–23), Thrall (1994: 271), Hafemann (1995: 393). Although καρδία can function as the subject of "turning" verbs (1 Kings 8.58; 11.2, 4; 18.37; Ps. 43.19 [LXX]; 104.25 [LXX]; Mal. 3.23 [LXX]; Luke 1.17) it is probably not the subject of ἐπιστρέψῃ in 3.16 (against Allo [1937: 92–93], Rissi [1969: 35–36], Barrett [1973: 122], Richard [1981: 356–57]).

[127]   See, e.g., van Unnik (1973b: 207), Hays (1989: 140–49), Stockhausen (1989: 89), Fee (1994: 310), Hafemann (1995: 390). Similarly, Heinrici (1887: 132), Collange (1972: 103), and Kim (1984:12) argue that the subject of ἐπιστρέψῃ is an unexpressed τις.

[128]   Although dissenters can be found (e.g., Kim [1984: 12–13], Fitzmyer [1993: 73], Lambrecht [1994d]), this interpretation assumes that Dunn's influential article (1970b) is substantially correct. Κύριος in 3.16 and 17 refers to Yahweh of Exod. 34. As in Galatians 4.25, 1 Corinthians 10.4, and 15.27, δέ introduces Paul's comment on the OT text under consideration. This exegesis is rapidly becoming the consensus view: e.g., Collange (1972: 101–25), Furnish (1984: 210–13), R. P. Martin (1986: 70–71), Stockhausen (1989), Belleville (1991), Fee (1994: 311), Thrall (1994: 272–74), Hafemann (1995). But this should not exclude the possibility that Paul uses κύριος allusively in 3.16: "Ici le nom κύριος, pour les uns, représente Dieu, le Dieu qui parlait sur le Sinaï... mais pour la généralité, le Christ" (Allo [1937: 97]).

[129]   The phrase καθάπερ ἀπὸ κυρίου πνεύματος is difficult. Καθάπερ ἀπό denotes agency (Schlatter [1935: 521], Héring [1967: 28], Belleville [1991: 292], Thrall [1994: 286]). Κυρίου πνεύματος is best rendered "the Lord, the Spirit" (Barrett [1973: 125], Furnish [1984: 202]), or perhaps "the Lord who is the Spirit" (R. P. Martin [1986: 57], JB, NIV, RSV).

The phrase τὴν αὐτὴν εἰκόνα (3.18) has an elliptical quality which is not always perceived by those following the line of interpretation advanced above.[130] While εἰκών makes its debut in 2 Corinthians in this verse, we know that the Corinthians had some familiarity with this important theme of Paul's gospel from his previous ministry among them (1 Cor. 15.49). If there were any questions, Paul answers them in 4.4, where Christ is specifically identified as the εἰκών. Transformation into the εἰκών of Christ occurs elsewhere in Paul (Rom. 8.29; 1 Cor. 15.49; cf. Phil. 3.21; Col. 1.15), which strengthens the hand of those who see a Christological allusion in 3.18. In 1 Corinthians 15.42–49 Paul employs this concept in relation to his Adam–Christ typology, clearly demonstrating the roots of this imagery in Paul's reading of Genesis (cf. Gen. 1.26–27; 5.1, 3; 9.6). The literature of the Second Temple period reveals an increased interest in Adam and the eschatological restoration of his pre-fall glory,[131] and Paul's Adam–Christ typology bears some resemblance to this peculiar variety of Urzeit and Endzeit speculation. Paul, however, allows no room for the veneration of Adam. The thesis statement of Paul's Adam-Christology is 1 Corinthians 15.22: "In Adam all die, in Christ all will be made alive" (cf. Rom. 5.12–21). Christ had supplanted Adam in the apostle's eschatology; Paul didn't look back to the garden, but ahead to the parousia (Phil. 3.21).

Εἰκών, then, functions as part of Paul's theology of creation/consummation and, due to its protological-Christological orientation, is regularly associated with restoration of glory: ἀπὸ δόξης εἰς δόξαν (3.18; cf. 1 Cor. 15.43 and 49; Rom. 8.29–30; Phil. 3.21).[132] This is not to deny the importance of wisdom traditions in relation to Paul's Christology, and 2 Corinthians 3.18 in particular.[133] Certainly Wisdom 7.26, which speaks of σοφία as "the untarnished mirror of God's active power, the εἰκών of his goodness," is relevant to any discussion of 2 Corinthians 3.18. Yet even in this document, εἰκών cannot be separated completely from the Genesis narrative, as the author has already made clear: "For God created humanity for immortality, as the εἰκών of his own nature" (Wisd. 2.23).

---

[130] It is readily acknowledged, however, by those who read vv. 16–17 differently. Murphy-O'Connor (1991: 39), for example, labels this phrase as a "discrete allusion to Christ," and then refers to 4.4. See also Eltester (1958: 165–66), Kim (1984: 5–13; 195–205), Klauck (1987: 271), Lambrecht (1994d: 300).

[131] See 1QS 4.22–23; CD 3.18–20; 1QH 17.15; 4Q504; 4Q171; *1 Enoch* 62.15–16; 69.11; 85.3 with 90.37–38; *2 Enoch* 30.10–12; 4 Ezra 7.88–92; *3 Baruch* 6.16; *The Life of Adam and Eve* 12–16; *Apoc. Mos.* 20.1–5, and the recent works of Kim (1984: 162–93), Levinson (1988), and Pate (1991: 33–65).

[132] Cf. Scroggs (1966: 96–99), Rissi (1969: 38–39), Kim (1984: 260–68), Pate (1991:22; 80–85).

[133] On which see Eltester (1958: 131), Kim (1984: 137–268), Pate (1991).

2 Corinthians 4.4, 6

The relationship between 2 Corinthians 3.18, 4.4, and 4.6 is especially close, and many see the three texts as parallel.[134] The antithetical symmetry of 4.4 and 4.6 is striking:[135]

4.4	4.6
The god of this age	The God who said "Light from darkness"
has blinded the minds of the unbelieving	has shone in our hearts
so they cannot see the light	to bring about the enlightenment
of the gospel of the glory of Christ	of the knowledge of the glory of God
who is the image of God.	in the face of Christ.

Once again Paul's εἰκών-Christology moves into the foreground, and there is general agreement that the figure of Adam is lurking in the background.[136] Indeed, this passage stands at the center of Seyoon Kim's thesis that it was the revelation of Christ as the true εἰκών τοῦ θεοῦ in the Damascus Christophany which led to Paul's use of Adam, and not his prior understanding of Adam as the image of God.[137] In any event, with very few exceptions,[138] most believe that Paul's description of a shining light which revealed the glory of God in the face of Christ (4.6) betrays the apostle's vivid memory of his encounter with the risen Christ on the road to Damascus.[139] The consensus in this direction is strong enough to warrant taking this position as established.[140]

We have, then, a further reference to conversion, and one in which the apostle offers his own experience as somehow typical of believers

[134] E.g., Collange (1972: 141), Furnish (1984: 248, 251–52), Dietzfelbinger (1985: 50; 62–64), Theissen (1987: 150–52), Stockhausen (1989: 101), Fee (1994: 321), Hafemann (1995: 424).

[135] See also Elteser (1958: 132), Klauck (1987: 271–72), Sandnes (1991: 137), Newman (1992: 220–22), Savage (1996: 127).

[136] See Scroggs (1966: 97–98), Baumbauch (1979: 200–2), Findeis (1983: 158–59), Bultmann (1985: 106), Dietzfelbinger (1985: 73–75), Dunn (1987: 262), Hooker (1990: 18–23), Murphy-O'Connor (1991a: 43), Pate (1991: 82–85), Kreitzer (1993a: 13–15), Thrall (1994: 310–11), Hafemann (1995: 424).

[137] Kim (1984: 136–238).

[138] Notably, Rissi (1969: 38–39), Collange (1972: 140), Furnish (1984: 250–52).

[139] Compare the language and imagery of Acts 9.3–6; 22.6–18; 26.12–18; 1 Cor 1.9; 15.8.

[140] Detailed arguments for this position can be found in Kim (1984: *passim*), Dietzfelbinger (1985: 49–75), and Newman (1992: 184–212). Other proponents include Plummer (1915: 121), P. Bachmann (1919: 192), Windisch (1924: 140–41), Allo (1937: 103), Prümm (1967: 222–23), Bornkamm (1971: 21–23), Barrett (1973: 135), Berger (1976: 556), Bultmann (1985: 108–9), R. P. Martin (1986: 80), Dunn (1987), Klauck (1987: 293–94), Hengel (1991: 79–80), Sandnes (1991: 137), Fitzmyer (1993b: 8–9), Lambrecht (1994d: 301), Thrall (1994: 314–20).

generally (ἐν ταῖς καρδίαις ἡμῶν).[141] Paul, however, strips his story of its
non-paradigmatic elements (external light, a voice from heaven, blind-
ness) in order to highlight its most crucial feature: ὁ θεὸς . . . ἔλαμψεν ἐν
ταῖς καρδίαις ἡμῶν. Entirely in keeping with the dominant themes of 2
Corinthians 2–7, Paul presents the significance of this momentous apocalypse not in terms of what happened *around* him but in terms of what
happened *within* him (cf. Gal. 1.16).

Yet the Damascus Christophany was a revelation in the fullest sense
of the word and served to "transform Paul's convictional world."[142] Paul
himself accentuates the cognitive aspect of this event when he describes
it as πρὸς φωτισμὸν τῆς γνώσεως τῆς δόξης τοῦ θεοῦ ἐν προσώπῳ
Χριστοῦ (4.6). Indeed, Christian Dietzfelbinger has argued persuasively
that each of the generally agreed allusions to the Damascus Christophany in Paul's letters is associated with a significant Christological
designation,[143] which points to this event as the primary impetus for
Paul's radical reappraisal of the man from Galilee: "Es ist kein Zufall,
daß [Paulus], wenn er an den vier besprochenen Stellen jenes Erlebnisses
gedenkt, dies in Verbindung mit zentralen christologischen Hoheitsaus-
sagen tut. Damit gibt er zu verstehen, daß mit dem Berufungserlebnis der
große Wandel in der christologischen Erkenntnis verbunden war."[144]

Paul's conversion on the Damascus road involved a complete reversal
of his prior judgments concerning Jesus. Paul was compelled not only to
abandon his mission against the fledgling Jesus movement (Gal. 1.15–17),
but to admit that his previous perception of Christ was woefully inadequate (1 Cor. 15.9–11). It was, in fact, judging Christ κατὰ σάρκα, and
Paul reflects more than once on the error of his former convictions
(1 Cor. 15.8–11; Gal. 1.13–17; 5.11; Phil. 3.2–11; *2 Cor. 5.16*).

Paul's allusion to his conversion in 4.4–6 is hard to miss, and the same
can be said of both his reliance on Genesis imagery and his application
of an Old Testament text to the present experience of the Corinthians. As
in 3.16, these final two threads are neatly intertwined: ὁ θεὸς ὁ εἰπών, Ἐκ
σκότους φῶς λάμψει, ὃς ἔλαμψεν ἐν ταῖς καρδίαις ἡμῶν. As was noted
earlier (chapter 4), the movement from darkness to light is typical transfer

[141] So too Dietzfelbinger (1985: 63), Klauck (1987: 294), Sandnes (1991: 137), Thrall
(1994: 317).
[142] Newman (1992: 183). Seyoon Kim's study is the most comprehensive statement of
this position, though it has been criticized (e.g. Dunn [1987]) for perhaps reading too
much into the Damascus Christophany. Even so, Dunn accepts the foundational nature of
this event for Paul's subsequent Christology (Dunn [1987: 265]).
[143] 1 Cor. 9.1: κύριος; 1 Cor. 15.3–8: Χριστός; Gal. 1.16: υἱὸς (τοῦ Θεοῦ); 2 Cor. 4.4–6:
εἰκὼν τοῦ θεοῦ.
[144] Dietzfelbinger (1985: 64–75; here, 74).

symbolism, as is the analogy of creation. Indeed, Klaus Berger's summary of the history-of-religions material deserves reiteration: "Die Erschaffung des Lichts als des ersten Schöpfungswerkes Gottes (Gen. 1.3) wird zum ätiologischen Mythos für den Vorgang jeglicher Bekehrung (2 Cor. 4.6). Es ist der Schöpfergott, der erleuchtet."[145]

But as obvious as the creation language appears to most – and a full page of authors could be cited to this effect – it has not gone unchallenged.[146] The alternative is to see Isaiah 9.1 (LXX) as the principal text in view: "The people walking in darkness – behold a great light! Those dwelling in the land of the shadow of death – light will shine on you." Like Genesis 1.2–3, Isaiah 9.1 mentions both φῶς and σκότος, but it also contains the identical phrase λάμψει φῶς, where Genesis 1.3 reads γενηθήτω φῶς.[147] Isaiah 9.1, however, is not introduced as an oracle of Yahweh.[148] While it is impossible to deny an allusion to Genesis 1.3 in 2 Corinthians 4.6, it seems likely that Isaiah has influenced Paul's wording. Indeed, Carol Stockhausen maintains that 2 Corinthians 4.6 is a composite of both texts, arguing convincingly that for Paul, "Genesis 1 and these prophecies of Isaiah stand together. They are mutually interpreting."[149] She explains further: "It is extremely likely that Paul has amplified and altered his reference to Genesis 1.3 with the vocabulary of Isaiah 9.2 . . . In their exegetical association, the creation of light is viewed as salvific, or re-demptive, while the salvation promised by Isaiah is cast as creative or re-creative."[150]

What is significant about 4.6 is that Paul views conversion through the lens of Genesis and deems the initial creation to be a fitting analogy to God's New Covenant work in the hearts of believers. Moreover, as 3.16–18 suffuses Deuteronomy 34 with the prophetic hopes of Jeremiah and Ezekiel, 4.6 merges the primordial events of Genesis with the eschatological vision of Isaiah and considers both to be realized Christologically (ἐν προσώπῳ Χριστοῦ) in conversion. This same confluence of themes (creation, conversion, Christology, and Isaiah) will surface again in 5.17, and the almost symbiotic relationship between these two texts prompts Reumann to ask, "Is this a clue to how [Paul] will understand the phrase 'new creation'?"[151] Before turning to 2 Corinthians 5.14–17, I will summarize the most salient aspects of the discussion thus far.

[145] Berger (1994: 269).
[146] Most notably by Collange (1972: 138–40), who is followed by Richard (1981: 359–61), R. P. Martin (1986: 80–81), W. J. Webb (1993: 95–97), and Savage (1996: 111–27).
[147] Cf. Stockhausen (1989: 161).   [148] Thrall (1994: 315).
[149] Stockhausen (1989: 162). Similarly Hays (1989: 152–53). Cf. Klauck (1987: 289) who, while emphasizing Genesis 1, admits Isaiah 9.1 (and other texts) may be in view.
[150] Stockhausen (1989: 161).   [151] Reumann (1973: 91).

Summary

The foregoing material has emphasized the salvation-historical framework of 2 Corinthians 2–7. Paul's frequent references to the Spirit, along
with his explicit reliance on Jeremiah and Ezekiel as the scriptural foun-
dations of his argument, reveal a promise–fulfillment schema focusing
on the hopes of these prophets. Central to these Jewish traditions was
the expectation that God would perform a new work in the hearts of his
people, by which his Spirit would transform them from the inside out. The
antitheses which permeate this section of 2 Corinthians issue from the
hopeful imagination of these same prophetic exemplars and are sharpened
by the intense tone of the letter.

Yet the argument of 2 Corinthians 2–7 is hardly an introspective Pauline
soliloquy with no clear relevance to the situation in Corinth. Paul's presentation of his New Covenant ministry as life concealed in death, inner
renewal in the midst of outer decay, a glorious treasure in an earthen
vessel, and so on, is carefully calculated to undermine the complaint of
his detractors while at the same time exposing the larger issue as Paul
saw it. On the surface, the Corinthians were embarrassed by the oratory and demeanor of their apostle – especially in comparison with the
crowd pleasers they were accustomed to – and this became a running
joke among some of them. But under the surface was the much larger
issue of a superficial, status-conscious community who had yet to grasp
the message of the cross and the power of a cruciform life.[152] Indeed, a
consideration of this broader context is perhaps the best reason for reading βλέπετε in 10.7 as an indicative: "O Corinthians, you see only on the
surface (Τὰ κατὰ πρόσωπον βλέπετε)."[153] In 5.11–21, Paul addresses
their complaint specifically.[154]

Persuasion, madness, and the ambassador for Christ

Paul's ministry of πείθω

In Kennedy's analysis, 5.11 begins to elaborate the heading "we speak
in Christ," first announced 2.17, but not yet given specific treatment.[155]

[152] Cf. Belleville's statement of the thesis of of 3.4–4.18: "The proper criteria for as-
certaining credibility are ones that focus on the inward, spiritual dimension as opposed to
some outward material dimension" (1991:146).
[153] Note especially Savage's defense of this reading (1996: 184).
[154] Much of the following material is adapted from Hubbard (1998).
[155] Kennedy (1984: 90). A reference to Paul's spoken message is often included in
headings for 5.11–21, quite apart from any consideration of the thematic development of

162   *The old and the new: Paul's letters*

O'Brien's work, as well as the explicit (though undeveloped) references to Paul's spoken proclamation in 4.2–5 and 4.13 corroborate this conclusion. The striking feature of 5.11 is Paul's surprising use of πείθω to characterize his work. The word itself was "synonymous with rhetoric"[156] and enjoyed a literary and cultural heritage in the Greco-Roman world which few other words could rival.[157] Paul's choice of this term is especially peculiar when one recalls his adamant disavowal of persuasive artistry in 1 Corinthians 2.1–5: οὐκ ἐν πειθοῖς σοφίας λόγοις! This fact has not escaped the notice of exegetes and many believe that πείθω reflects Paul's opponents' terminology: he is either taking up a slogan of his rivals and appropriating it for his own purposes,[158] or he is echoing a charge leveled against him of unscrupulous persuasion.[159] Identifying the vocabulary of Paul's opponents is an uncertain business. The tone of 5.11–13 is polemical, yet this is not sufficient evidence for either of these interpretations of πείθω.[160] It may be that commentators have not paid sufficient attention to the preceding verse (5.10), where Paul speaks of standing before the bema of Christ. The bema had two distinct functions in the civic life of the polis: it served as the seat for judicial pronouncements and, more commonly, as the platform for public oration.[161] Corinth's bema was located in the center of the agora, where access to large audiences was assured.[162] In 5.10 it is the judicial aspect of the bema that Paul is emphasizing, though the imagery may well have shaped his vocabulary in 5.11. If we made an attempt to hear 5.10–11 with Corinthian ears, the close link between the bema and Paul's πείθω, would probably seem natural. In a speech in Tarsus, Dio Chrysostom reminds his audience that it is through the power of πείθω that one gains victory in the ἀγορά and on the βῆμα.[163]

2 Corinthians 2–7 as proposed here. See Heinrici (1887: 195), Güttgemanns (1966: 282), Bultmann (1985: 109), R. P. Martin (1986: 116), Dinkler (1992c: 178).

[156] Marshall (1987: 331).

[157] See Buxton (1982) and Litfin (1994: 21–134). More general in nature are G. Kennedy's standard works (1963, 1972).

[158] Wendland (1964: 176), Murphy-O'Connor (1991: 56).

[159] Plummer (1915: 169), Schlatter (1934: 556), Strachan (1935: 106), Bultmann (1947: 13; 1985: 147), Lietzmann (1949: 123–24), Héring (1962: 41), Schmithals (1971: 189), Furnish (1984: 306, 323), F. Lang (1986: 294), Thrall (1994: 402). Güttgemanns (1966: 310) adds the twist that the accusation is that Paul can only persuade through sober instruction and not through ecstatic displays.

[160] A number of commentators reject both positions: Windisch (1924: 176), Prümm (1967: 311), Barrett (1973: 164), and Litfin (1994: 195) see in πείθω nothing more than an innocent reference to Paul's missionary task. Hughes (1962: 187), Collange (1972: 245), and Wolff (1989a: 119), on the other hand, believe that Paul seeks to "persuade" his critics of his own personal integrity and apostolic qualifications. R. P. Martin (1986: 121) combines both.

[161] Dinkler (1967: 118–23). Further details of Corinth's bema are discussed by Murphy-O'Connor (1984: 147–59).

[162] Dinkler (1967: 118), Furnish (1984: 12).   [163] *Discourses* 33.1.

Yet this does not diminish the arresting nature of Paul's vocabulary. Paul utilizes a variety of words to describe his ministry of proclamation (εὐαγγελίζομαι, κηρύσσω, καταγγέλλω, λαλέω, παρακαλέω, μαρτυρέω, νουθετέω) and they are all, without exception, decidedly non-rhetorical.[164] Commentators are right to stumble over this expression and grope about for an explanation. While it cannot be demonstrated decisively that πείθω was the vocabulary of Paul's opponents, it was undoubtedly the quintessential expression of the goal of rhetoric,[165] and the very feature of the art which Paul decried. And Paul is not unaware of the import of his language in 5.11, so offers two important provisos with respect to his ministry of πείθω, both of which echo 2.17: as for his motivation, it is the fear of the Lord; as for his conduct, it is with complete openness – to God and to the Corinthians. In brief, Paul's provocative affirmation "We persuade people" (duly qualified) is stationed like a signpost at the head of this passage and should serve to guide the exegesis of this text – especially the troublesome verses which follow. Because 5.14–17 was penned partly as an explanation (γάρ, 5.14) for 5.12–13, it will be necessary to spend some time unraveling this *crux interpretum* before offering an exegesis of 5.14–17.

The complaint of Paul's ἐξίστημι

Major interpretations. The interpretive enigma of 2 Corinthians 5.13 is summed up by Ralph Martin as "the mystery of what [Paul] means by ἐξίστασθαι, 'to be out of one's mind.'"[166] While Paul's point in this verse is straightforward enough – he is affirming that his actions are free of selfish ambition and entirely "other" directed[167] – the same cannot be said for the way in which he makes it. The history of interpretation of

---

[164] Litfin (1994: 195), citing many of these verbs, notes that they "play no significant role in the rhetorical literature." This conclusion receives tacit confirmation from the rhetorical lexicons of both Lausberg and Ernesti, neither of which cites any of these terms. Cf. Bultmann (1985: 148), Thrall (1994: 402).

[165] The opening section of Aristotle's *Rhetoric* (1355b8 ff.) defines the art as "the discovery of the available means of persuasion," and it is not without reason that G. Kennedy entitled his standard reference work on rhetoric in Greece, *The Art of Persuasion*. Note also Buxton (1982: 5–66), and Litfin (1994:110–15).

[166] R. P. Martin (1986: 126). The word is found only here in the Pauline corpus. In biblical literature, ἐξίστημι (used intransitively) means to be amazed or confounded (Gen. 44.33; Ruth 3.8; Matt. 12.23; Luke 8.56). It occurs in a different sense in Mark 3.21, where Jesus' family attempt to restrain him, reasoning, "He must be beside himself." This text is often used by those who see 5.13 as an accusation concerning Paul's outrageous way of life.

[167] See, e.g., Plummer (1915: 173), Schlatter (1934: 557–8), Hughes (1962: 189), Wendland (1964: 176), Barrett (1973: 166), Harris (1976: 351).

2 Corinthians 5.13 reveals two distinct groups: those who read verse 13a as a complaint against Paul, and those who do not. The former, older, interpretation sees behind ἐξίστημι an accusation of abnormal or eccentric behavior on Paul's part, be it his religious fanaticism,[168] an excessive estimation of his apostolic authority,[169] or even his penchant for self-recommendation.[170] The latter interpretation, which has become the consensus view, believes that Paul's ἐξίστημι–σωφρονέω contrast is equivalent to the more common ἐξίστημι–μαίνομαι antithesis, so refers to his religious ecstasy (cf. 1 Cor. 14.2, 14). Bultmann's paraphrase of 5.13 is echoed throughout the literature: "Paul's thought is, 'As far as my ecstatic experiences are concerned, they are not your affair, but are between me and God.'" Rather, the Corinthians should boast only in Paul's σωφρονεῖν, that is, "the conscious, sober execution of my office."[171]

Critiquing the consensus. The equation of ἐξίστημι with μαίνομαι, along with the connections made with 1 Corinthians 14 are plausible, but only just. Difficult texts often require such stretches, though the resulting exegesis is usually less than satisfying for it. More serious objections issue from a consideration of the grammar and the line of thought in 5.13, as Windisch pointed out long ago: "Paul cannot intend to compare or contrast himself to his opponents, for in that case he would have had to begin with ἡμεῖς γάρ... In addition, the clause is not understandable as an ἀφορμὴ καυχήματος."[172] Windisch's observation on the word order of 5.13 is illustrated by scores of texts where Paul contrasts his belief or behaviour with that of others, and simply cannot be ignored.[173] These passages demonstrate a very clear pattern: the presence of the (otherwise unnecessary) personal pronoun in the emphatic position followed by the post-positive conjunction. In other words, Paul does not say, "For if *we* were ἐξίστημι (in contrast to our opponents)"; he says, "For if we *were* ἐξίστημι (as some of you are saying)."

Equally troublesome for the consensus view is the connection between verse 12 and verse 13 and the explanatory γάρ in 13a.[174] Consider the line

---

[168] Schlatter (1935: 557).   [169] See Strachan (1935: 106) and Oepke (1964b: 459–60).
[170] Plummer (1915: 171–73), who mentions other possibilities.
[171] Bultmann (1947: 15). See also Käsemann (1942: 67), Barrett (1973: 166–67), Furnish (1984: 324–25), Bultmann (1985: 149–50), F. Lang (1986: 294–95), R. P. Martin (1986: 126–27), Wolff (1989a: 120–21), Murphy-O'Connor (1991a: 156).
[172] Windisch (1924: 179). Thrall (1994: 405, 407) is the only recent commentator to recognize the force of Windisch's remarks.
[173] See for instance, 1 Cor. 1.22–23; 2.12; 2.16; 4.10; 9.25; 2 Cor. 3.13, 18; 6.16; 10.12–13; 13.7; Phil. 3.2–3; Gal. 5.5; 1 Thess. 2.17; 5.8.
[174] A problem noted by Strachan (1935: 106), Bultmann (1947: 14), Fee (1994: 327), Thrall (1994: 405).

of thought suggested by Bultmann: "We are giving you a reason to boast on our behalf, *for* our ecstasies are none of your affair, only the sober execution of our duties concerns you." The logic is not impossible, but neither is it obvious. Moreover, as the older expositions of this passage recognized, 13a, following as it does on the heels of the polemical verse 12, reads quite naturally as an accusation against Paul: "Rather, we are giving you incentive to boast on our behalf, so that you might have something to say to those boasting in appearances and not in the heart. For if we *were* ἐξίστημι, that was for God; if we *are* σωφρονεῖν, that is for you."

The chief deficiency of both views, however, is their inability to account for this verse in the context of 2 Corinthians 1–9 and the focus of 5.11–21.[175] If Paul is bringing up the issue of abnormal behavior or ecstatic phenomena, it is an abrupt intrusion into his argument and is not taken up elsewhere in chapters 1–9.[176]

Reassessing the complaint. But these scholars may have decided too quickly on the nature of the complaint in 5.13. As noted earlier, 2 Corinthians 5.11–13 picks up the theme of Paul's spoken proclamation as introduced in the thanksgiving period/proem. The parallels are unmistakable.[177] As in the proem, so here, it is Paul's spoken message that is at issue (λαλέω/πείθω). As in the proem, so here, this aspect of Paul's ministry is carried out in complete openness before God (κατέναντι θεοῦ/πεφανερώμεθα θεῷ). As in the proem, so here, Paul disavows self-commendation (ἀρχόμεθα πάλιν ἑαυτοὺς συνιστάνειν/οὐ πάλιν ἑαυτοὺς συνιστάνομεν). Further, in both passages Paul's concern is to contrast his work and demeanor with that of others. If this reading is correct, there is good reason to equate "those hawking the word of God" in 2.17, with "those boasting in appearances" in 5.12.

The sophistic allusion in 2.17 was pointed out earlier and, again, is widely acknowledged in the secondary literature. The extremely close parallels between 2.14–3.6 and 5.11–13 provide substantiation for the suggestion of Windisch that 5.12 might also reflect the polemic between philosophers and sophists,[178] and offers an elucidating frame of reference for Paul's concern to give the Corinthians a reason to be proud of him (5.12c). D. A. Russell points out that in the typical Greek city the sophist/rhetor was "something of a hero."[179] Philostratus, the historian

---

[175] A difficulty acknowledged by Fee (1994: 327).   [176] Rightly, Sumney (1990: 145).

[177] Correctly Wolter (1978: 80), Findeis (1983: 102), Bultmann (1985: 145), Breytenbach (1989: 122), Bieringer (1994e: 430).

[178] Windisch (1924: 178).

[179] Russell (1983: 22). The distinction between sophists and rhetors is subtle, though Bowersock notes that sophists were extremely polished, professional rhetors with "a big public reputation" (1969: 13).

of the second sophistic,[180] goes to great lengths to recount the various exploits and entrepreneurial acts of the sophists, all in service of one essential point: "For not only does a city give a man renown, but a city itself acquires it from a man."[181] As Bowersock puts it, "sophists were a cause of boasting [to the local citizenry] as were buildings, canals, or coinage."[182] This, of course, was the reason why the Corinthians erected statues to eloquent sophists, and the reason why Favorinus was so bothered when his was removed.

Keeping in mind the central complaint in Corinth (Paul's unimpressive oratory), the development of thought in 2.14–5.21, and the specific thrust of this passage ("We *persuade* people," 5.11), it seems reasonable to try to locate the complaint of 2 Corinthians 5.13 within this framework. Given that Paul faced opposition from those whose rhetorical tastes were more refined, we are justified in allowing them to explain their complaint, and in using their lexicons to define their terminology.

Σωφρονέω *in 5.13b.* Looking first at 5.13b, Helen North's important lexical study of σωφροσύνη (and cognates) has demonstrated the importance of this word group for understanding the Greek demand "for fitness and propriety in speech and action." Citing rhetorical theorists from just prior to the turn of the era (Dionysius, Demetrius), and from the first and second centuries AD (Maximus of Tyre, Aristides, Dio Chrysostom, Philostratus), North's work concludes that the σώφρων style was an essential quality of a good orator and refers to "moderation, good taste, and avoidance of excess."[183]

Ἐξίστημι *in 5.13a.* We are now in a position to look at ἐξίστημι in 5.13a and the complaint made against Paul. Ἐξίστημι (used intransitively) has a wide variety of meanings in the rhetorical literature, and these are in keeping with the general semantic range of the word elsewhere.[184] However, in Aristotle's handbook on the subject, *Rhetoric*, the word is used in specific reference to the orator's style of delivery. In cautioning against a style of speech which is too metrical and rhythmic in its delivery, Aristotle warns his students that this would not only fail to persuade (ἀπίθανον), but be confusing (ἐξίστημι) as well.[185] Aristotle uses

---

[180] G. Kennedy (1994: 239) defines the second sophistic as "a cultural and literary movement in Greek society that began in the first century and greatly flourished in the second."

[181] *Vit. Soph.* 532.   [182] Bowersock (1969: 90).

[183] H. North (1948: 317). Ernesti (1795: 346–47) also relates σωφρονεῖν to moderation in style.

[184] Cf. Ernesti (1795: 114), Lausberg (1960: §257).

[185] *Rhetoric* 1408b. Cope (1877: 83–84) defines ἐξίστημι here as an action which "diverts the hearer's attention from the main subject." A similar rendering is offered by Freese, *LCL.*

ἐξίστημι here in reference to a style which is deemed to be excessive and, taking Helen North's definition of σωφρονέω as "fitness and propriety in speech and action," would seem to make a suitable antithesis to this verb. Again, this deficiency of style is evidenced in its *inability to persuade.* A bit later, in discussing deliberative rhetoric, Aristotle uses ἐξίστημι to describe the orator who "wanders from his subject."[186] In both instances the verb denotes an activity on the part of the speaker which is detrimental to his or her delivery.

Aristotle's influence on rhetorical theory can be overestimated,[187] though it is precisely here, in his discussion of style, where his impact was most keenly felt. Summarizing the influential work of Friederich Solmsen on this subject, Litfin lists as one of the central contributions of Aristotle to subsequent generations, "the emphasis upon certain stylistic virtues a speech must possess (clarity, appropriateness, Ἑλληνισμός, etc.). Wherever we discover these emphases . . . we are hearing an echo of Aristotle."[188] Helen North's study emphasizes the importance of Aristotle's *Rhetoric* in the *vocabulary* of subsequent discussions of style. Of the four virtues of style venerated by ancient rhetoricians, three were introduced by Aristotle.[189] It was Aristotle, North argues, who supplied the precedent for the transfer of the term σώφρων from ethics to rhetoric. Cicero, writing in reference to a work of Aristotle on rhetoric which has not survived, said,

> [Aristotle] so surpassed the original authorities in charm and brevity that no one becomes acquainted with their ideas from their own books, but everyone who seeks to know what their doctrines are, turns to Aristotle, believing him to give a much more convenient exposition. He then published his own works and those of his predecessors, and as a result we became acquainted with him and the others as well through his work.[190]

If it is admissible to allow Paul's detractors to explain their complaint and define their terminology, an alternative reading of 2 Corinthians 5.13 is possible: "If, as some of you complain, my speech was unpolished and excessive, credit that to God's account; if I am presently reasonable and lucid, credit that to yours. For the love of Christ compels us . . ."[191]

---

[186] *Rhetoric* 1418a, translation by Freese, *LCL.* Cope (1887: 203) equates ἐξίστημι here with ἐκτοπίση in 1414b, which he defines as "absence from one's proper or ordinary place" (p. 164).
[187] Cf. G. Kennedy (1980: 81), Litfin (1994: 78).   [188] Litfin (1994: 78).
[189] North (1948: 2).   [190] *De Inv.* 2.6, cited in Litfin (1994: 28–29).
[191] This interpretation should be compared with Marshall (1987: 230–32). Surprisingly, Marshall and I arrive at a similar interpretation from entirely different angles.

For those trained in rhetoric and accustomed to elocutionary excellence, this was a common complaint against the amateur: "[The philosopher's] speech, like his life, should be composed; and nothing that rushes headlong and is hurried is well ordered . . . The rapid style, which sweeps down without a break like a snow-squall, is assigned to the younger speaker."[192]

The datives of 5.13. Paul's compressed datives are notoriously difficult, and 2 Corinthians 5.13 is representative of many. The critical point to note concerning the datives of 5.13 (θεῷ/ὑμῖν) is that Paul is offering some type of theological justification for his ἐξίστημι, his unadorned style. When we recall – as the Corinthians surely would have – Paul's extensive defense of his style of proclamation in 1 Corinthians 1–4, the idea that Paul, with these datives, "is dividing into categories his behaviour toward God, namely ecstatic; and toward the Corinthians, namely rational and controlled,"[193] loses all appeal. In fact, Paul can afford to be concise with his datives in 2 Corinthians 5.13 because he has spent fully four chapters in a previous letter explaining them. Far from discrediting him as a divine spokesman, Paul's determination to shun manipulative rhetorical techniques in deference to the persuasive work of the Spirit issued from his self-perceived task as a herald (κηρύσσω, Rom. 10.8–15; 1 Cor. 1.23; 2 Cor. 1.19; 4.5; Gal. 2.2, etc.) and should have been a source of pride to the Corinthians.

Paul as a πρεσβευτής. Having explicitly introduced this passage as an explanation of his apostolic πείθω, it is reasonable to expect that Paul would carry this theme to completion. Recent work on the background of the καταλάσσω terminology which dominates 5.18–21 has demonstrated that the Greco-Roman political arena is the primary and determinative context for this word group.[194] Breytenbach's study concludes, "Es zeigt sich, daß die Versöhnungsterminologie des Paulus aus der zeitgenössischen nicht-religiösen diplomatischen Terminologie entliehen ist."[195] Yet this need not exclude clear resonances with prophetic

---

[192] Seneca, *Ep.* 40.2

[193] R. P. Martin (1986: 127). Similar comments are made by Käsemann (1942: 67), Hughes (1962: 192), Barrett (1973: 166), and Furnish (1984: 324), among others.

[194] See Breytenbach (1989), Porter (1993: 695–99), and most recently Bash (1997). Cf. also Büchsel (1964), Beale (1989: 550), and Thrall (1994: 429–30). This language is all but absent in the Old Testament (only Jer. 31.39, LXX) and only rarely encountered in Hellenistic Judaism (2 Macc. 1.5; 5.20; 7.33; 8.29), where it is used quite differently than in Paul. See R. P. Martin (1986: 147–48), Thrall (1994: 429–30).

[195] Breytenbach (1989: 4). So too Porter (1993: 695), summarizing his forthcoming monograph on the subject: "The fact that the almost exclusive provenance of *katallage* and *katallasso* is Greek secular literature, or literature heavily influenced by the Hellenistic world, makes the Greek milieu foundational."

traditions,[196] nor with the ministry of Jesus.[197] Indeed, in appropriating the terminology of Greek diplomacy and employing it as a vehicle for communicating the gospel, we see Paul the missionary at his best, as Hahn explains: "Entscheidend ist, daß für Urchristentum hiermit gerade die Bedeutung des Sühnestodes Jesu für die nichtjüdische Welt artikuliert werden kann."[198]

Given the Hellenistic background to the imagery of 5.18–21, as well as Paul's perceptive use of this background, his claim in 5.20 to serve as an ambassador (ὑπὲρ Χριστοῦ οὖν πρεσβεύομεν) is considerably illuminated. The task of an ambassador in ancient Greece fell, naturally, to the educated and eloquent, "the literati" who could best represent the interests of the polis.[199] By the first and second centuries AD these prestigious assignments had become so monopolized by rhetors and sophists that modern scholarship "regularly identifies"[200] the second sophistic with ambassadorial service. According to Philostratus, the crowning achievement of a sophist's career was to be chosen as an ambassador, especially in making a petition to the emperor.[201] The ancient historian recounts famous embassies by sophists to Domitian (AD 81–96),[202] Trajan (AD 98–117),[203] and Hadrian (AD 117–38),[204] revealing the influence and power of these individuals in Greco-Roman society. On a monument from Roman Corinth we find one such person extolled as a "philosopher and ambassador (πρεσβευτήν)" in the service of the emperor Hadrian.[205] Corinth's strategic position near the narrow strip of land that separated the Corinthian and Saronic Gulfs rendered it a necessary layover for couriers, diplomats, and others who wished to shorten their journey from Asia Minor to Rome. According to Favorinus, Corinth served as the "the promenade of Hellas" in that "every year crowds of travelers,

---

[196] With Beale (1989: 550–81), and W. J. Webb (1993: 114–20).

[197] As emphasized by Goppelt (1968: 152–53) and Hofius (1989: 1–14).

[198] Hahn (1973: 247).

[199] Citing Bowersock (1969: 42). More detailed support for this assertion is offered by Bash (1997: 55–80).

[200] Bowersock (1969: 42). Cf. G. Kennedy (1972: 561–63; 1994: 230–33). The πρεσβ-word group is exclusively employed in the rhetorical literature.

[201] In Dio's version of the legendary meeting of Alexander and Diogenes, he notes that the great emperor first "received all the Greek πρεσβείας," who had gathered in Corinth to meet him (4.12).

[202] *Vit. Soph.* 520.

[203] *Vit. Soph.* 533. Dio Chrysostom also boasted of his ambassadorial exploits (*Discourses* 51.8), which according to Philostratus, won him the admiration and friendship of Trajan (*Vit. Soph.* 488).

[204] *Vit. Soph.* 489, 530.

[205] This translation is based on Kent's plausible reconstruction of the surviving fragments (1966: 55–56). The name of the person honored cannot be determined.

pilgrims, merchants, and *ambassadors* (πρεσβευτής)" passed through
its gates.[206] So important were the ambassadorial achievements of the
sophists that Bowersock concludes his chapter, "Sophists and Emperors,"
with the words, "It could be argued without apology that the Second
Sophistic has more importance in Roman History than it does in Greek
literature."[207]

Heard within this context – as it would have been in Corinth – the
argument of 5.18–21 is significantly sharpened, revealing a polemical edge hitherto unrecognized. Unlike so many who would have as-
pired to represent the Corinthian community as its spokesman before
the emperor, Paul turns this venerated tradition upside down and claims
to represent the Great Emperor to the Corinthians: ὑπὲρ Χριστοῦ οὖν
πρεσβεύομεν ὡς τοῦ θεοῦ παρακαλοῦντος δι' ἡμῶν. Paul's λόγος τῆς
καταλλαγῆς (5.19) certainly refers to the message he preached,[208] his
"foolish" λόγος τοῦ σταυροῦ (1 Cor. 1.18) which he defended in an
earlier correspondence. Moreover, Michael Wolter has shown that Paul's
language in 5.18–19 (λόγον τιθέναι ἐν) is deliberately reminiscent of the
Old Testament description of prophetic commissioning, where it refers
to "die Sendung von Boten mit einem bestimmten, ihnen aufgegebe-
nen Redenauftrag."[209] Once again Paul employs imagery drawn from the
Greco-Roman political sphere – easily intelligible to the Corinthians – in
order to correct their own misunderstanding of his apostolate.[210] Paul,
then, concludes this passage in the same way as he began it, adopting the
common parlance of Greco-Roman Corinth while carefully redefining
it. He "persuades" – but only with integrity before God (5.11–13). He
is "an ambassador" – but in the service of Christ, not the Corinthians
(5.18–21). Situated between these mild rebukes is 2 Corinthians 5.14–
17, a passage which reveals both the driving force behind Paul's missionary activity, and the fundamental deficiency of Paul's detractors in
Corinth.

---

[206] Transmitted under the name of Dio Chrysostom, *Discourses* 37.7–8.

[207] Bowersock (1969: 58).

[208] Correctly Schlatter (1935: 567), Collange (1972: 273), Barrett (1973: 178), Wolter
(1978: 82–83), F. Lang (1986: 302), Breytenbach (1989: 113), Rebell (1992: 73), Thrall
(1994: 435–36).

[209] Wolter (1978: 83), who is followed by Wolff (1989a: 130–32), and Thrall (1994:
435–36). See Ps. 104.27; 2 Kings 14.3, 19; 2 Esdr. 8.17. This connection is disputed by
Furnish and Hofius, though Thrall and Wolff have countered adequately.

[210] On this reading of 5.18–21, 19b–21 is not an appeal to the Corinthians, but a concise
enunciation of Paul's proclamation. Cf. Windisch (1924: 196). While written independently
of Bash, this interpetation complements his emphasis on "the scandal of the metaphor"
(1997: 109–10).

New creation

Given the foregoing contextual analysis, the exegesis of 2 Corinthians 5.14–17 can proceed at a more lively pace. The argument and themes of the preceding chapters have been clarified, and these, in turn, will illuminate 5.14–17. Each section will be introduced by a translation of the verse or verse-segment under consideration, and will contain an analysis of the relevant material in that segment. The intent is not to offer a commentary on these verses, that is, a detailed grammatical, syntactical, lexical, and theological analysis. Rather, my concern is to locate 2 Corinthians 5.14–17 in its literary context and demonstrate the importance of this context for understanding this "epitome"[211] of Paul's gospel. Secondarily, I will ask how this passage informs and is informed by the larger theological context of Paul's death–life symbolism.

For the love of Christ impels us ... (14a)

The explanatory γάρ which begins 5.14 introduces the "Grundmotiv des Apostel-Dienst,"[212] the love of Christ.[213] We have already encountered Paul's perception of the death of Christ as a sacrifice of love which moved him to service (chapter 9), and Paul expects his readers to be motivated likewise (2 Cor. 8.8–9). The verb συνέχω is usually translated "compel," "constrain," "beherrschen," and so on, though the word *impel* seems most appropriate here.[214] Paul elsewhere describes God's love evidenced in the death of Christ as something poured out "in our hearts" (Rom. 5.5–8), and the idea of compulsion *from within* fits the context precisely. Paul contrasts his labor among the Corinthians with those who are motivated by financial gain (2.17), who vaunt themselves as "lords" (4.5), who are driven by the outward and visible (5.6; 4.18), and who glory in externals (5.12). Paul, on the other hand, speaks with open sincerity (2.17; 5.11–12), is driven by πίστις (4.13; 5.7), and concentrates on what is unseen (4.18) and ἐν καρδίᾳ (5.12; cf. 1 Sam. 16.7). Indeed, Paul modeled his ministry in Corinth on the servant-like example of his Lord: δοῦλοι ὑμῶν διὰ Ἰησοῦν (4.5; cf. 8.9; 1 Cor. 4.1; Phil. 2.7).

---

[211] Sanders (1977: 460).
[212] Findeis (1983: 128). Similarly Schlatter (1934: 558), Collange (1972: 253), Furnish (1984: 326–27), Breytenbach (1989: 128–29), and most.
[213] The genitive (ἀγάπη τοῦ Χριστοῦ) is subjective: Christ's self-sacrificing love on our behalf. An objective genitive (Héring [1967: 41–42]) is ruled out by the Pauline parallels (Rom. 5.8; 8.32–35; Gal. 2.20), as well as by Paul's explanation in 14b–15. See Furnish (1984: 309).
[214] So BAGD s.v. συνέχω 7; cf. Allo (1937: 165).

. . . recognizing this: one died for all, therefore all died (14bc)

Paul now supports 14a by providing the reason why Christ's love so moved him: a conviction formed in the past (κρίναντας) regarding the significance of Christ's death. Bypassing for the moment the import of the aorist participle, it is the death of *one* for *all* which stands out in bold relief.[215] There is considerable debate over whether the term *substitution* or *representation* best captures Paul's thought here,[216] and an equal amount of confusion over how to interpret 14c: ἄρα οἱ πάντες ἀπέθανον. The questions are interrelated. That Paul follows 14b with the conclusion, "therefore, *all* died," clearly indicates that Christ's death is being viewed in terms of its representative significance. A substitute dies so that others *do not*, whereas a representative embodies the community as its delegate and so includes others in his/her sacrificial act (cf. Heb. 7.9–10). This reading is strengthened by 15bc, where ὑπέρ certainly carries the more general sense of "for the benefit of." Substitution may be an appropriate category elsewhere in Paul (e.g., 5.21) and, as the discussion of 1 Corinthians 5.7–8 will demonstrate, the two images cannot be neatly separated.

In describing Christ as a representative whose story somehow affects the whole of humanity,[217] the submerged analogy of Adam–Christ again becomes visible.[218] This connection is confirmed by 1 Corinthians 15.22 where, as here, Paul's πάντες–πάντες interplay proves an exegetical snare: "In Adam *all* die; in Christ *all* will be made alive."[219] For the present discussion, the critical point to note is the re-emergence of the *Urbild* and *Abbild* schema, that grand salvation-historical metaphor which will later

---

[215] Correctly Hahn (1973: 248), and Findeis (1983: 131).

[216] *Substitution* is supported by, e.g., Strachan (1935: 107–8), Hughes (1962: 193–95), Bultmann (1985: 151), F. Lang (1986: 293), R. P. Martin (1986: 129–33), Cousar (1990: 77), while *representation* is prefered by Plummer (1915: 174), Wolff (1989a: 122), Rebell (1992: 22–24), Lambrecht (1994f: 378), Thrall (1994: 409–10). Barrett (1973: 168) and Furnish (1984: 310) equivocate.

[217] Giving full weight to the πάντων–πάντες interplay. See also Windisch (1924: 182–83), Schlatter (1934: 158–59), Allo (1937: 166), Bruce (1971: 207), Furnish (1984: 327), Breytenbach (1989: 125–27), Beasley-Murray (1993: 220), Lambrecht (1994f: 377–78), Thrall (1994: 409–11).

[218] Most agree on this, even those who argue for substitution in 14a. See, e.g., Kümmel (1949: 204), Hughes (1962: 195), Prümm (1967: 323), Findeis (1983: 133), F. Lang (1986: 295–96), R. P. Martin (1986: 131), Pate (1991: 139), Thrall (1994: 411).

[219] Because it is not germane to the present argument, I will not pause to iron out this wrinkle in Paul's thought. Thrall's remarks (1994: 411) repay close scrutiny, and I add only one further consideration. The nature of the analogy demands that a symmetry exist between the effects of the two representatives. Paul's language is formed rhetorically rather than theologically. Cf. Romans 5.15–19, where πολλοί–πολλοί and πάντες–πάντες are used interchangeably.

be important in the argument of Romans 5–8. In this pattern of thought, the failings of the first Adam are rectified by the second (Rom. 5.12–21), who restores the εἰκών (Rom. 8.29) and δόξα (Rom. 8.30) lost by the former (cf. Rom. 3.23). This conception contributes to the theological substructure of 2 Corinthians 5.14–17, and this should be kept in mind as Paul's thought unfolds.

And he died on behalf of all (15a)
in order that those living should no longer live for themselves, (15b)
but for the one who died and was raised on their behalf. (15c)

The opening clause of verse 15 recapitulates the main thought of the previous verse, while 15b introduces the intended result *(ἵνα)* of Christ's sacrificial death: living for another. If verse 14 portrays Christ's death as beneficial to all (πάντες), verse 15 describes it as specifically applicable to some: οἱ ζῶντες.[220] Given the larger context, it is extremely unlikely that οἱ ζῶντες is coterminous with the preceding πάντες – as if "the whole of humankind is in a sense redeemed on the cross"[221] – or that it refers to all those living at that time.[222] As we have already seen, Paul introduced these chapters as an elaboration of the phrase ἐκ ζωῆς εἰς ζωήν, and this in contrast to "those who are perishing" (2.15–16). "Life" in 2 Corinthians 2–7 is restricted to the believing community, and the thematic development of this motif cannot simply be ignored. Particularly important is 4.11, where Paul defines οἱ ζῶντες as "we who are ever being handed over to death for Jesus' sake." When we add to this the orientation of "life" in Paul's other death–life equations, no other reading is allowable. The movement of thought between verse 14 and verse 15 is from the universal (πάντες) to the ecclesiological (οἱ ζῶντες),[223] as Paul spells out the behavioral consequences of dying with Christ.

So, from now on . . .

Ὥστε draws a further consequence of verses 14–15, which is qualified temporally, ἀπὸ τοῦ νῦν. The point of reference behind this vague temporal clause has been variously identified as (1) "die große einscheidende Wende der Bekehrung,"[224] (2) "the turn of the ages in the death and

---

[220] With, e.g., Windisch (1924: 183), Furnish (1984: 311, 328), Bultmann (1985: 152–53), Mead (1989: 148), Wolff (1989b: 86), Dinkler (1992: 179).

[221] Lambrecht (1994f: 376). Similarly Barrett (1973: 169), Mell (1989: 360).

[222] Against Plummer (1915: 175) and Thrall (1994: 412).

[223] Breytenbach (1989: 128).

[224] Windisch (1924: 184), who speaks for most: Bachmann (1919: 255–56), Schlatter (1934: 559), Lietzmann (1949: 126), Stuhlmacher (1967: 5–6), Barrett (1973: 170),

resurrection of Jesus,"[225] or (3) a combination of (1) and (2).[226] The strength of (3) is its refusal to separate sharply Paul's eschatological "now" (cf. Rom. 3.21; 16.26) from his soteriological "now" (Rom. 5.9, 11; 7.6; 8.1; Gal. 2.20), especially in light of the way they are interwoven in 6.2. Yet even with this important qualification in place, the emphasis in 5.16 is on soteriology, making (1) the best alternative. Four considerations support this interpretation: (1) I have already noted the prominence of conversion in the argument of chapters 2–7 (3.16, 4.4–6; 5.5), and 5.14–17 would constitute only one more link in this chain.[227] (2) The immediate context points decisively to this interpretation. As Hughes explains, "ἀπὸ τοῦ νῦν explicates the aorist κρίναντας of v. 14: 'Henceforth' doubtless means from the time when he formed the judgment or conclusion in the preceding verses, that is, the time of his conversion."[228] (3) Soteriology dominates Paul's other death–life equations, though this is certainly from an eschatological point of view. Finally (4), the parallel structure of 16a and 17a (ὥστε... ἀπὸ τοῦ νῦν; ὥστε... ἐν Χριστῷ) strengthens this conclusion, which is rendered beyond dispute by Paul's parenthetical comment in 16b concerning his pre-conversion perception of Christ (see below). In line with the main theme of verses 14–15, soteriology – specifically, conversion – forms the basis of the transformation which Paul describes in verses 16–17.

. . . we evaluate no one from a merely human point of view (16a)

The emphatic ἡμεῖς which opens 16a refers ostensibly to Paul and his companions, though it is equally paradigmatic,[229] and renders the clause more of an appeal than a simple affirmation. The *crux interpretum* of 2 Corinthians 5.16ab is whether κατὰ σάρκα should be read adjectivally, modifying οὐδένα and Χριστόν, or adverbially, modifying οἴδαμεν and ἐγνώκαμεν. For the sake of convenience, I will include this aspect of 16b in the discussion here.

Furnish (1984: 312), Wolff (1989a: 123), Dinkler (1992c: 190), Lambrecht (1994f: 379), Thrall (1994: 415).
[225] Martyn (1967: 274). So also Bultmann (1947: 17; 1985: 154), Kümmel (1949: 205), Tannehill (1967: 67), R. P. Martin (1986: 151), Danker (1989b: 114–16), Mell (1989: 366–67), Pate (1991: 148).
[226] So Prümm (1967: 338), Collange (1972: 258), Findeis (1983: 128, 141). Heinrici (1887: 207) remains uncommitted.
[227] Indeed, many cite 5.16–17 as another allusion to the Damascus Christophany: Prümm (1967: 338), Kim (1984: 14–15), Beale (1989: 556), Newman (1992: 166).
[228] Hughes (1962: 197); so too Plummer (1915: 176), Schlatter (1934: 559), Barrett (1973: 170), Wolff (1989a: 123), Thrall (1994: 409, 415). Cf. Heinrici (1887: 207) and R. P. Martin (1986: 129), who also see a reference to conversion in κρίναντας.
[229] Correctly Michel (1954: 22).

The prevailing skepticism concerning an alleged "false Christology" of Paul's opponents has hastened the demise of an adjectival reading of κατὰ σάρκα, and virtually every recent discussion of this passage interprets κατὰ σάρκα adverbially.[230] The older interpretation of 2 Corinthians 5.16 seems to have been more the *product* of a historical-theological agenda than its *impetus*, and as the one has fallen, so has the other. But it is the exegetical considerations that are decisive. Of the remaining sixteen occurrences of κατὰ σάρκα in the undisputed letters of Paul, six are adjectival, and in these κατὰ σάρκα always follows the substantive (Rom. 1.3; 4.1; 9.3, 5; 1 Cor. 1.26; 10.18); never does it follow the verb as here. Further, where Paul does attach κατὰ σάρκα to Christ (Rom. 9.5), it both follows the proper noun and includes a "'substantiving' neuter article."[231]

In dismissing a κατὰ σάρκα knowledge of people (16a) and Christ (16b) Paul is "rejecting the judgment of Jesus or any other person according to fleshly human standards."[232] In relation to 16a, one cannot help but hear an echo of Paul's stinging criticism in 1 Corinthians 3.3: ἔτι γὰρ σαρκικοί ἐστε... καὶ κατὰ ἄνθρωπον περιπατεῖτε. Paul would like to address the Corinthians as "spiritual" (πνευματικοί), as "mature" (τέλεοι), but in fact they are "unspiritual" (ψυχικός) and "infants" (νήπιοι). Their perspective is "sarkic" (3.1–3) and "this worldly" (1 Cor. 1.18–20; 2.6–8; 3.18–19), and is preeminently displayed in their practice of pitting Christ's servants against each other as rivals and then boasting in their hero: "For when one says 'I am of Paul,' and another, 'I am of Apollos,' are you not behaving as mere ἄνθρωποι?" (3.4; cf. 1.10–13). Paul adjures them, "Stop boasting in men" (3.21) and "boast in the Lord" (1.31). Indeed, it would appear that it is the Corinthians' infatuation with the eloquent Alexandrian that is coming under Paul's scrutiny: "These things, friends, I have applied to Apollos and myself" (1 Cor. 4.6; cf. Acts 18.24–28). Paul was aware that the Corinthians had turned a critical eye on him, and it is precisely their judgment which he rejects as irrelevant: "It is of little concern to me that I am judged by you... it is the Lord who judges me" (1 Cor. 4.3–4).

If this analysis is correct, 2 Corinthians 5.16a appears as a thinly veiled exhortation to the Corinthians to put behind them their worldly, sarkic judgments – especially of their apostle – and to reject once and for all

[230] Ulrich Mell is a notable exception to the consensus, which includes Barrett, Breytenbach, Collange, Findeis, Furnish, F. Lang, R. P. Martin, Prümm, Rebell, Thrall, Wendland, Wolff, etc.

[231] Furnish (1984: 313). Cf. Rebell (1992: 34). The phrase ὁ Χριστὸς τὸ κατὰ σάρκα (Rom. 9.5) might be rendered, "Christ, in so far as his human lineage is concerned."

[232] Jewett (1971: 126), speaking for most. Cf. Thrall, "using wordly criteria in assessing other people" (1994: 420); Furnish, "judging other people on the basis of externals" (1984: 329); Collange "'hier' on jugeait sur l'apparence" (1972: 259).

those who boast ἐν προσώπῳ and not ἐν καρδίᾳ (5.12). In light of this discussion, Murphy-O'Connor's appraisal of 2 Corinthians 5.16a is hard to improve: "Paul is thinking of those who assessed his performance as a minister by the standards applied to pagan orators."[233]

even though we once evaluated Christ from a merely human point of view, we see him thus no longer (16bc)

The most important exegetical issue in 5.16b has already been resolved, but at least two more questions merit discussion. (1) How should this εἰ καί clause be analyzed grammatically? (2) What has prompted this observation about Paul's previous misperception of Christ?[234] In regard to (1), there are two main exegetical options: (a) εἰ καί introduces a concession which acknowledges a past misapprehension of Christ;[235] or (b) εἰ καί introduces a "hypothetically real condition" which does not admit an *actual* misconstrual of Christ.[236] As the notes indicate, the vast majority of commentators prefer (a), and this is surely the soundest alternative. Εἰ καί normally introduces a concessive clause[237] ("even though..."), *and is used by Paul to concede a fact.*[238] The implications of this exegesis can be summarized by Hengel: "Paulus räumt ein: Gewiß hatte er früher als er noch ein Verfolger der Gemeinde war (vgl. 1 Cor. 15.9; Phil. 3.6; Gal. 1.13, 23), ein völlig verkehrtes oder, wie er selbst sagt 'fleischliches' Bild von Jesus."[239] This interpretation is strongly supported by my previous analysis of 4.4–6 – where Paul recalls his transformed perception of Christ at the Damascus Christophany – and confirms the exegesis of 5.16a: conversion is the leitmotif of this section. It is impossible to specify precisely how Paul's pre-conversion estimation of Christ was deficient, though we can safely assume that the conflict between his Jewish messianic ideas – whatever they may have been – and the reality of Jesus as a condemned and crucified heretic (cf. Deut. 21.23 and Gal. 3.13) must have

233 Murphy-O'Connor (1991a: 59).
234 With most (see below), Paul's "we" in 16b is best taken as a literary plural which, while applicable to others, refers primarily to Paul himself. Cf. the plurals in vv. 11–15.
235 So Plummer (1915: 177–79), Windisch (1924: 186–87), Schlatter (1934: 562), Hughes (1962: 199), Prümm (1967: 326), Bruce (1971: 208), Barrett (1973: 171–72), Lincoln (1981: 57), Findeis (1983: 141), Kim (1984: 14), F. Lang (1986: 293, 297), R. P. Martin (1986: 151), Breytenbach (1989: 130), Wolff (1989a: 126–27), Murphy-O'Connor (1991a: 58), Rebell (1992: 37), Lambrecht (1994f: 383), Thrall (1994: 415–20).
236 So Furnish (1984: 313), Bultmann (1985: 156), and Lietzmann (1949: 125–26), who concedes it is grammatically less likely.
237 See BDF §§ 374 and 457; BAGD s.v. εἰ, IV.4
238 See 2 Cor. 4.16; 7.8 (3x), 12; 11.15; 12.11; Phil. 2.17. The only possible exception is 1 Cor. 7.21, but see Breytenbach (1989: 116). Phil. 3.12 is disputed textually.
239 Hengel (1967: 60–89).

been great. A corollary to this line of interpretation is that 5.16b represents a parenthetical "Einschub,"[240] an "autobiographische Bemerkung"[241] in which the person of Paul is again placed "in den Mittelpunkt"[242] of this letter. And as I have already shown, this is entirely in keeping with the tone of this correspondence.

Given this analysis, and keeping in mind the broader context of Paul's difficulties with the Corinthians, Paul's recollection of his previous misperception of Christ (number [2] above) is perhaps not so "schwer zu verstehen."[243] In fact, it is impossible to avoid the conclusion that as Paul once misunderstood the person and mission of Jesus, so now the Corinthians have misunderstood the person and mission of his apostle. It is just conceivable that Paul's reflective glance at his past in 5.16b issues from the fact that he sees a bit of himself in the Corinthians and, here at least, the word *confessio* might not be inappropriate.[244]

So, if anyone be in Christ – new creation; (17a)

The logical connection between 5.16 and 5.17 is unclear, particularly the force of the introductory ὥστε.[245] Syntactically, 5.17 and 5.16 are parallel, both being introduced by ὥστε and drawing a conclusion from 5.14–15.[246] Yet 5.17 also supports 5.16 by providing the grounds for Paul's repudiation of sarkic evaluations, as Kümmel explains: "Weil so beim Christen eine Neuschöpfung stattgefunden hat ... kann man den Paulus auch nicht mehr κατὰ σάρκα beurteilen."[247]

Stylistically, 2 Corinthians 5.17 is compact, lacking a main verb in 17a, and resembles that kind of elevated prose which borders on the poetic.[248] Formulated as a condition, εἴ τις picks up the ἡμεῖς of 16a[249] and expresses it gnomically: "If *anyone* ..." Yet granted this gnomic generalization, there can be no disputing that the ἡμεῖς–τις interplay leads one to expect a personal referent in the next clause,[250] and this point will

---

[240] Prümm (1967: 326). [241] Findeis (1983: 141).
[242] Dautzenberg (1986: 159) on the tone of chapters 2–7. [243] Windisch (1924: 186).
[244] Dautzenberg's description of chapters 2–7 (1986: 159–62).
[245] See the comments of Plummer (1915: 176), Furnish (1984: 314), Thrall (1994: 424).
[246] This is generally agreed: Plummer (1915: 179), Allo (1937: 167), Wolter (1978: 75), Findeis (1983: 128), Thrall (1994: 424), and others.
[247] Kümmel (1949: 205). So too Furnish (1984: 33) and Breytenbach (1989: 131).
[248] The verb "to be" should be supplied in the first clause (BAGD s.v. εἰ, I.1) and perhaps the second as well, though this would diminish its rhetorically intended starkness. On the alternative punctuation see, e.g., Allo (1937: 167), Thrall (1994: 424).
[249] With Tannehill (1967: 68) and Dinkler (1992c: 183).
[250] Against Stuhlmacher (1967: 4), who seems to think that a gnomic maxim excludes a personal referent. Note the counter-arguments of Baumgarten (1975: 166–67), Findeis (1983: 150–52, 162), Liebers (1989: 216), Rebell (1992: 55), Thrall (1994: 427–28).

be made more forcefully in my evaluation of the apodosis. Because καινὴ κτίσις is conditioned upon being ἐν Χριστῷ, this important concept must be briefly explored. Given the variety of meanings of this flexible idiom (ἐν Χριστῷ, ἐν αὐτῷ, ἐν κυρίῳ, εἰς Χριστόν), the context of 2 Corinthians 5.17 must play a determinative role in its interpretation.

Particularly noteworthy in the argument of 2 Corinthians 3–5 is Paul's portrayal of ἐν Χριστῷ as the sphere of transformation. It is ἐν Χριστῷ that the veil is removed from the heart: ὅτι ἐν Χριστῷ καταργεῖται (3.14). Paul goes on to explain that this unveiling *in Christ* is the condition for transformation: "And we all, with unveiled faces . . . are being transformed from glory unto glory as from the Lord, the Spirit" (3.18). Indeed, 3.16, also introduced gnomically, provides an interesting parallel to 5.17:

| Whenever anyone turns to the Lord | If anyone be in Christ, |
| the veil is removed . . . the Spirit transforms | new creation |

This idea is brought to a crescendo in 5.21, where Paul declares that "in him" (ἐν αὐτῷ) believers (ἡμεῖς) become the δικαιοσύνη θεοῦ.[251] 2 Corinthians 5.21b and 5.17a are sometimes related by commentators in their discussion of 5.21,[252] and occasionally Paul's new-creation motif is employed to elucidate the enigmatic δικαιοσύνη θεοῦ.[253] Never, however, has this hermeneutical circle been reversed. While it may be putting it too strongly to say that "Neuschöpfung = Gerechtwerdung,"[254] the proximity and correspondences between the two statements indicate they are mutually illuminating. Following the word order of 5.17, the parallel elements might be arranged thus:

| ὥστε | εἴ τις | ἐν Χριστῷ, | – | καινὴ κτίσις |
| ἵνα | ἡμεῖς | ἐν αὐτῷ | γενώμεθα | δικαιοσύνη θεοῦ |

Two conclusions may be drawn at this point. (1) Against some,[255] ecclesiology is not the dominant chord in Paul's ἐν Χριστῷ-statement in 2 Corinthians 5.17; soteriology is. To be sure, the two ideas cannot be fully separated, but it is certainly the latter which Paul is emphasizing

---

[251] The mutually illuminating character of the "in Christ" formulas in 3.14–16, 5.17, and 5.21 was noted long ago by Deissmann (1892: 108–11).

[252] Barrett (1973: 181), Furnish (1984: 165), R. P. Martin (1986: 153), Wolff (1989b: 97), Rebell (1992: 89).

[253] Kümmel (1949: 205), Wendland (1964: 183), Bultmann (1985: 165), F. Lang (1986: 303) Wolff (1989a: 133).

[254] Kümmel (1949: 205). So also Souza (1977: 173) and Breytenbach (1989: 141): "Der δικαιοσύνη θεοῦ von Gott her erschuf uns neu, uns, die wir ἐν Χριστῳ/ἐν αὐτῷ (v17a, 21b) sind."

[255] Especially Neugebauer (1961: 111–12).

here.[256] (2) The motif of transformation – so important in the argument of chapters 3 and 4 – surfaces again in 5.17 and, as elsewhere in this letter, it is an anthropological-soteriological motif (τις).

Turning now to the apodosis, καινὴ κτίσις, the essential question is this: do we have here a statement of Paul's (soterio-)cosmology, or his anthropology? Understood cosmologically, Cousar's translation is representative: "If anyone is in Christ, there is a new creation . . . a brand new world." If understood anthropologically, Thrall's rendering is typical: "Consequently, if anyone is in Christ, there is a newly-created being." The history-of-religions material provides evidence for either reading, as does a lexical survey of κτίσις,[257] the context being the decisive factor. The same should hold true here, and we have yet to find any evidence for a cosmological interpretation of this passage. Indeed, just the opposite is true, as the following summary indicates:

(1) *The governing* τις. As noted above, the singular τις of the protasis governs the apodosis and speaks for a "streng anthropologische, gleichsam personalisierende Deutung" of καινὴ κτίσις.[258] This much has been argued by others,[259] but what has not been observed is that εἴ (δέ) τις constructions are common in Paul and *in every other parallel text the* τις *of the protasis is picked up in the apodosis.* Two examples from the Corinthian correspondence should suffice to illustrate this:

Εἰ δέ **τις** ἀγαπᾷ τὸν θεόν, **οὗτος** ἔγνωσται ὑπ᾽ αὐτοῦ (1 Cor. 8.3).

Εἴ **τις** πέποιθεν ἑαυτῷ Χριστοῦ εἶναι, τοῦτο **λογιζέσθω** . . . (2 Cor. 10.7).

Unless 2 Corinthians 5.17 is wholly exceptional, we can assume that καινὴ κτίσις is related to the preceding τις.

(2) *The force of the conditional construction.* The weight of (1) is significantly increased as one attempts to fathom the logic of the if–then construction if the alternative "cosmic" reading is correct: "If someone is in Christ, then the creation 'has been totally refashioned.'"[260] It is difficult to see how "the eschatological

---

[256] Similarly Collange (1972: 164) and Thrall (1994: 425–26).

[257] See BAGD, s.v. κτίσις, Baumgarten (1975: 162–63), Petzke (1990) in *EDNT*, s.v. κτίζω. Statistically, "creation" is more common in Paul than "creature," but the latter also occurs: Rom. 1.25, 8.39; cf. Col. 1.15, 23.

[258] Findeis (1983: 150).

[259] See note 250, along with Tannehill (1967: 68) and Wolff (1989a: 127).

[260] Citing Furnish (1984: 321).

macrocosm of the new heavens and the new earth"[261] *is contin-gent upon* any person (τις) being in Christ.[262] This incongruity becomes an absurdity if, as Martin argues, the new creation is an objective reality, not a subjective one, "as if it were merely the individual's viewpoint which had changed."[263]

(3) *The theological and literary context.* The primary theological context for Paul's new creation motif is his death–life symbol-ism and, as commonly agreed, this imagery is not cosmological but soteriological and anthropological. "Spirit," "newness," and "life" dominate the "life" side of this symbolism and it is within this matrix of thought that καινή κτίσις should be interpreted. Looking at the literary context of 2 Corinthians 5.17, Paul's ar-gument is introduced under the heading ἐκ ζωῆς εἰς ζωήν, and this idea is unfolded via the anthropologically oriented motif of transformation. 2 Corinthians 5.17 epitomizes this line of thought (transformation by the Spirit, 3.18; conversion = cre-ation *ex nihilo*, 4.6; the making anew of the inner person, 4.16, etc.) in a climactic *Jubelruf* of thanksgiving.[264]

(4) Ἐν Χριστῷ. Finally, new creation is said to occur "in Christ," and this is easier to relate to Paul's anthropology than to his cosmology.[265] Particularly important in this connection is Galatians 2.19–20, where the "life" side of the death–life equa-tion is also explained Christologically: "Christ lives in me."

Taken together, these arguments create a strong prejudice in favor of an anthropological reading of καινή κτίσις. I will suspend judgment on the question until the rest of Paul's argument has been considered, though this exegetically derived bias should inform the evaluation of what follows.

. . . the old things have passed, behold, the new has come (17b)

2 Corinthians 5.17b comprises Paul's only commentary on καινή κτίσις, and as such it warrants special consideration. Following a cos-mological interpretation of καινή κτίσις, Victor Furnish believes that the "old things" (τὰ ἀρχαῖα) which have passed refer to "the totality of

---

[261] Citing Hughes (1962: 201–2).

[262] Correctly Baumgarten (1975: 166), Murphy-O'Connor (1991a: 60 n. 46), Thrall (1994: 427).

[263] R. P. Martin (1986: 152), with reference to Tannehill (1967: 68–69).

[264] Von Harnack's term (1918: 101). On καινή κτίσις and the motif of transformation, cf. Sanders (1977: 468–69).

[265] Correctly, Baumgarten (1975: 166). Cf. Thrall (1994: 427).

creation."[266] This interpretation is typically advanced along three lines: (1) a cosmological reading of καινὴ κτίσις; (2) a cosmological understanding of reconciliation in verses 18–21; (3) a cosmological interpretation of the Isaianic material on which Paul is relying. If, as I have argued, καινὴ κτίσις does not appear to be a cosmological motif, argument (1) loses all validity. It may, however, be supported by (2) and (3), if these can endure close scrutiny.

On the surface, (2) seems beyond dispute in that Paul certainly speaks of the reconciliation of the κόσμος. Yet the Greek word κόσμος can be translated in a variety of ways and does not always denote what the English word "cosmos" does. Indeed, the standard Greek lexicon for the New Testament, BAGD, lists κόσμος in 2 Corinthians 5.19 under the heading "*the world* as mankind," and this reading is confirmed by the context. In 5.18 Paul speaks of God reconciling *us* (ἡμᾶς), which is then described as God reconciling the κόσμος (5.19a). Moreover, Paul then defines this "reconciliation of the κόσμος" as "not counting against *them* (αὐτοῖς) *their* (αὐτῶν) transgressions" (5.19b). That Paul uses "us" and "them" interchangeably with κόσμος in 5.18–19 renders only one conclusion tenable: the κόσμος in 5.19 denotes the world of humanity.[267] Paul's "reconciliation of the world" is a soteriological-anthropological idea rhetorically framed in universalistic terms. Jörg Baumgarten's appraisal could hardly be surpassed:

> Will man die Intention des Apostels unter Berücksichtigung des Gesamtzusammenhanges der V. 14–21 nicht verzerren, so erscheint es sachgemäß, zur Präzisierung eine "kosmische-universale" Tendenz von einer "anthropologisch-universalen" begrifflich zu unterscheiden. Demgemäß liegt hier nur eine "anthropologisch-universale" Tendenz vor, wenngleich die Grenze zwischen Kirche und gesamter Menschenwelt nicht reflektiert wird.[268]

In reference to (3), given the previous analysis of the Isaianic "former things/new things" (chapter 2) – an analysis widely supported in the

---

[266] Furnish (1984: 315). Cf. Wendland (1964: 181), "der alte Kosmos, die alte Weltzeit"; Héring (1967: 43), "old world"; Stuhlmacher (1967: 8), "der alte Äon."

[267] As elsewhere in the New Testament (John 3.16; 17.6; Jas. 2.5, etc.) and Paul (Rom. 3.6, 19; 1 Cor. 1.27–28, etc.). Most exegetes interpret κόσμος in 2 Corinthians 5.19 anthropologically. See, e.g., Plummer (1915: 183), Schlatter (1934: 566), Allo (1937: 171), Wolter (1978: 78–79), F. Lang (1986: 302), Breytenbach (1989: 132–33), Hofius (1989: 2–7), Wolff (1989a: 133), Lambrecht (1994f: 385–87), Thrall (1994: 434–35). However, Collange (1972: 272), Barrett (1973: 177), and Furnish (1984: 321) dissent.

[268] Baumgarten (1975: 168–69).

secondary literature – a cosmological interpretation of this motif here is rendered dubious at the outset. Paul does not directly cite any specific prophetic text, but his language is closest to Isaiah 43.18:

Isaiah 43.18	2 Corinthians 5.17b
τὰ ἀρχαῖα μὴ συλλογίζεσθε	τὰ ἀρχαῖα παρῆλθεν,
ἰδοὺ ποιῶ καινά	ἰδοὺ γέγονεν καινά

There is little controversy over the interpretation of the Isaianic motif, and von Rad can summarize the earlier discussion:

> By the former things Deutero-Isaiah means the act of deliverance at the Red Sea on which the saving history was based, and the exodus from Egypt . . .

> By the 'new' event he means the saving act about to come after a long pause in the saving history.[269]

In other words, the Isaianic motif is soteriological and depicts God's impending action on Israel's behalf as a kind of second exodus.[270] Moreover, the Isaianic oracles contain important and memorable cosmologically framed statements relating to the "new heavens" and the "new earth," and it is arguably clear that Paul could have cited these texts had they been conducive to his argument. Liebers makes this point well: "Der Apostel knüpft an dieser Stelle eben nicht an die denkbare kosmologische Vorstellung an, wie sie sich in der Apokalyptik findet, sondern greift mit seiner Anspielung auf Jes 43.18f bewußt auf einen Text zurück bei dem die anthropologisch-heilsgeschichtliche Ausrichtung im Vordergrund steht."[271]

At this juncture we should recall 4.6, where God's first creative act is offered as an analogy to conversion, and then amplified by means of Isaiah. Is it possible that Paul is doing the same thing here? As in 4.6, creation, conversion, Christology, and Isaiah coalesce in 2 Corinthians 5.17 to form an intriguing soteriological nexus, and it may be that Carol Stockhausen's assessment of 4.6 is equally relevant here: "In their exegetical association, the creation of light [read, 'new creation'] is viewed as salvific, or redemptive, while the salvation promised by Isaiah is cast as creative or re-creative."[272] This analysis supports Baumgarten's conclusion that Paul employs Isaiah 43.18 as kind of "gnomische Sentenz,"[273] that is, an

---

[269] Von Rad (1965: 247).
[270] With Beale (1989: 552–59) and W. J. Webb (1993: 121–28), whose works contain the only extensive discussions of the Isaianic motif and its bearing on 2 Corinthians 5.17.
[271] Liebers (1986: 216).   [272] Stockhausen (1989: 161).
[273] Citing Baumgarten (1975: 166).

allusive and pithy summary of 5.14–17. The Isaianic context is certainly suggestive, but Paul fills the idea with a content all his own. What then are the "old things" which have passed in 2 Corinthians 5.17? We need look no further than the context: boasting in appearances (5.12), living for self (5.14–15), and judging others κατὰ σάρκα (5.16).

Conclusions and corollaries

I conclude, then, that there is no compelling evidence for interpreting καινὴ κτίσις in 2 Corinthians 5.17 cosmologically. Quite the opposite is true. As the context makes clear, in 2 Corinthians 5.17 καινὴ κτίσις is an anthropological motif relating to the new situation of the individual "in Christ." As long as the term "individual" is not misconstrued *individualistically*, this interpretation should pose no difficulty for modern interpreters of Paul. The question of what label most adequately relates the concept of new creation to the person in Christ – ontological, functional, baptismal, forensic, and so on – can be deferred until after the examination of Galatians 6.15. For the moment, I will draw several corollaries to the foregoing argument. These both support the main conclusion of the exegesis, while also informing the question just raised.

New creation and the Spirit

Many commentators have sensed a connection between Paul's new-creation statement in 2 Corinthians 5.17 and his Spirit language, though no serious attempt has been made to correlate the two. Much of the preceding argument has been preparing the ground for such a correlation, and I can sketch the main lines of evidence briefly.

(1) Κατὰ σάρκα–καινὴ κτίσις. The most obvious indication that new creation in 5.17 is related to Pauline pneumatology is the fact that it is poised in antithesis to κατὰ σάρκα. Πνεῦμα cognates are so often related antithetically to σάρξ cognates in Paul's letters that it is difficult for the serious reader of Paul to hear κατὰ σάρκα without also hearing κατὰ πνεῦμα. It is for this reason that many have suggested, albeit wrongly in my view (see below), that "knowing κατὰ σάρκα" implies a "knowing κατὰ πνεῦμα."[274]

[274] E.g., Plummer (1915: 176), Windisch (1924: 189), Michel (1954: 25), Martyn (1967: 278–84), Collange (1972: 259), Findeis (1983: 147 n. 262), Young and Ford (1987: 181), Wolff (1989a: 127–28).

(2) *The pneumatological drift of chapters 3–5.* If the aforementioned antithesis were situated within an argument with no clear pneumatological framework, it probably could not be advanced with full conviction. But this is certainly not the case with 2 Corinthians 3–5. References to the creative, life-giving work of the Spirit punctuate Paul's argument and provide decisive evidence of its pneumatological orientation. In reminding the Corinthians that they are "written by the Spirit" (3.3), "transformed by the Spirit" (3.18), and "fashioned by the Spirit" (5.5), Paul is only teasing out the implications of his central Spirit affirmation: τὸ δὲ πνεῦμα ζῳοποιεῖ (3.6). This line of thought is brought to a fitting consummation in καινὴ κτίσις.

(3) *Death–life symbolism in Paul.* I have been grinding this axe for several chapters and by now its edge should be sharp enough. To reiterate, 2 Corinthians 5.14–17 belongs to that family of passages in which the biological analogy of death and life constitutes the foundational soteriological metaphor. The "life" side of this symbolism is dominated by the concepts of "Spirit," "newness," and "life," and one would be hard pressed to find a better synopsis of these ideas than the phrase καινὴ κτίσις. Particularly relevant is the line of thought in Romans 7.1–6. This passage is developed in the same way as in 2 Corinthians 5.14–17, but in place of the phrase καινὴ κτίσις, we read ἐν καινότητι πνεύματος (see chapter 7).

(4) Ἐν Χριστῷ. Finally, a pneumatological interpretation of καινὴ κτίσις accords perfectly with the pre-condition of being "in Christ." Indeed, the fluidity of expression involved in this aspect of Paul's thought ("in Christ" and "Christ in you"; "in the Spirit" and "the Spirit in you") allows me to advance Romans 8.10 as a possible parallel to 2 Corinthians 5.17: εἰ δὲ Χριστὸς ἐν ὑμῖν ... τὸ πνεῦμα ζωή.

Yet while some have intuitively connected new creation and the Spirit, the suggestion that "knowing κατὰ σάρκα" implies a "knowing κατὰ πνεῦμα" fails to grasp what Paul is doing in 2 Corinthians 5.17. Paul is not answering the question *how* we now evaluate people, but *why* we no longer evaluate them κατὰ σάρκα. As argued above, 5.17 provides the basis for 5.16 and constitutes an appeal to this errant community to bring their actions into conformity with who they now are in Christ: a new creation. This intermingling of indicative and imperative is best illustrated by the parallel passage in 1 Corinthians 5.7 (see below): "Throw out the old yeast, in order that you might be a *new* lump of dough – *as you really are*."

Interiority, Covenant, and new creation

Building on this pneumatological interpretation of καινὴ κτίσις in 2 Corinthians 5.17, it is quite reasonable to suggest that Paul's κατὰ σάρκα–καινὴ κτίσις antithesis should be added to that long list of internal–external antitheses noted earlier and seen as a further elaboration of Paul's New Covenant retrospective. As such, καινὴ κτίσις relates to the internal work of the Spirit and should be closely associated with the "making anew of the inner person" (4.16). As outlined earlier (chapter 2, chapter 8, and above), this kind of eschatological renewal figured prominently in the prophetic hopes of Jeremiah and Ezekiel, and it is precisely these prophets on whom Paul relies to introduce his argument.[275] This is not to say that a history-of-traditions link with the apocalyptic notion of new heavens and a new earth is inconceivable for Paul, but there is simply no evidence for it in relation to 2 Corinthians 5.17.[276]

Adam, image, and new creation

If the arguments presented above are sound, there is ample justification for connecting καινὴ κτίσις with Paul's Adam–Christ typology and relating it to the idea of transformation into the εἰκών of Christ (3.18; 4.4–6). The prominence of this typology in relation to Paul's death–life symbolism in Romans, as well as its emergence in 2 Corinthians 3–4 and 5.14–15, warrant placing 2 Corinthians 5.17 within this broad collection of ideas. This confirms the earlier suggestion (chapter 6) that the antithetical counterpart to the παλαιὸς ἄνθρωπος of Romans 6.6 is the καινὴ κτίσις of 2 Corinthians 5.17. Against much recent exegesis,[277] 2 Corinthians 5.17 is not essentially about the presence of the new age, but the presence of a renewed image and a new humanity. There is nothing novel in this proposal,[278] and the work of Robin Scroggs and Morna Hooker on this

[275] Cf. G. Schneider (1959: 249–53; 1992: 357–72).
[276] Against many, e.g., Windisch (1924: 189), Michel (1954: 27), Stuhlmacher (1967: 1, 8), Beker (1980: 101, 151–52), Furnish (1984: 314–15), Petzke (1992: 326).
[277] E.g., Strachan (1935: 113), Hughes (1962: 203–4), Héring (1967: 43), Martyn (1967: 269–87), Stuhlmacher (1967), Tannehill (1967: 65–69), Bruce (1971: 209), Barrett (1973: 173–74), Furnish (1984), R. P. Martin (1986: 152–53), Mell (1989: 386–87), Cousar (1990).
[278] See, e.g., Scroggs (1966: 59–74), Kim (1984: 137), Newman (1992: 222), Berger (1994: 470–74).

theme should, in particular, be singled out.[279] It does, however, reinforce an anthropological interpretation of καινὴ κτίσις in 2 Corinthians 5.17, so is underscored as I conclude.

The social function of new creation in 2 Corinthians 5.17

The primary purpose of Paul's stark καινὴ κτίσις statement in 2 Corinthians 5.17 is to portray conversion as a complete and irrevocable break with one's former way of life. We have seen this symbolism employed for the same purpose by the author of *Joseph and Aseneth* and, as the survey of initiatory symbolism demonstrated (chapter 5), this is precisely the intent of death–life imagery. The categories associated with life-crisis rituals by anthropologists (empowerment, transformation, demarcation, etc.) apply to 2 Corinthians 5.14–17 as well, and suggest that Paul is similarly concerned with "the transformation of raw human material into socially responsible persons."[280] Specifically, Paul's objective in 2 Corinthians 5.14–17 is to undermine the practice of some who judge him according to the "wisdom of this world" (1 Cor. 1.20; 3.18–19), and expect him to perform like a showman in the agora. Paul, however, does not argue that the world has changed since the Christ event, but that the Corinthians have been changed by Christ: "no longer κατὰ σάρκα... καινὴ κτίσις."

While it cannot be denied that the person in Christ is the focus of "new creation" in 2 Corinthians 5.17, the ultimate aim of this symbolism is to create a distinctive *community*, and the relationship between the two is best illustrated by comparing 1 Corinthians 5.7–8 with 2 Corinthians 5.14–17. The two passages are conceptually parallel, though 1 Corinthians 5.7–8 has the community in view:

	1 Corinthians 5.7–8	2 Corinthians 5.14–17
Imperative *and*	Throw out the old leaven (7a)	no longer κατὰ σάρκα
Indicative	so that you might be a new batch of dough – as indeed you are! (7b)	new creation!
grounded in		
The sacrificial death of Christ	For our Passover lamb, Christ, has been sacrificed. (7c)	one died for all

---

[279] Scroggs (1966), Hooker (1990).   [280] La Fontaine (1985: 115).

leading to		
The passing of the old	So let us feast not with the old leaven of malice and wickedness (8a)	the old has passed
and		
The coming of the new	but with unleavened bread of sincerity and truth. (8b)	the new has come

As often noted, the logic of 1 Corinthians 5.7–8 is unclear and angular, and the analogy appears strained as a result.[281] Yet once we see that Paul has superimposed Passover imagery on top of his death–life symbolism, the peculiar movement of thought in 1 Corinthians 5.7–8 becomes intelligible. The common denominator between the two metaphors is the idea of a sacrificial death, though Passover symbolism excludes any notion of rising to new life. Yet the fact that Paul could jump from the idea of throwing out old leaven (7a) to the bizarre notion of becoming "a new lump of dough" (7b), and then explain this on the basis of the death of Christ (7c) renders only one conclusion allowable: he is expressing one idea (dying and rising with Christ) through the symbolism of another (the Passover) and the result is a less than elegant piece of reasoning.[282] What is clear, however, is that new creation applies to the community as well as to the individual. In keeping with initiatory symbolism generally, its social relevance is grounded in its personal significance and this dual focus cannot be obscured if Paul is to be understood correctly.[283]

2 Corinthians 5.17, however, is not the only occurrence of Paul's new-creation motif. I have been arguing that the context is the decisive factor for the interpretation of this symbolism, and Galatians is very different from 2 Corinthians 2–7. If the context so dictates, one should be prepared to interpret καινὴ κτίσις differently in Galatians 6.15. One need not however, be committed *a priori* to such a resolve.

[281] Barrett (1968: 128), Conzelmann (1975: 98–99).

[282] Several commentaries on 1 Corinthians actually refer to 2 Corinthians 5.17 in their discussion of 1 Corinthians 5.7: Robertson and Plummer (1914: 102), Bruce (1971: 57), Mare (1976: 218), Schrage (1991: 380).

[283] This interplay between personal and communal is also evident in Paul's "temple of the Spirit" motif (1 Cor. 3.16 and 6.19). Compare also the "new person" of Eph. 2.15 and 4.24.

11

NEITHER CIRCUMCISION NOR
UNCIRCUMCISION: GALATIANS 6.15

But the Lord said to Samuel, "Do not look at his appearance, or at the height of his stature, because I have rejected him."

1 Samuel 16.7

Galatians: recent issues in interpretation

Pauline studies have undergone something of a Copernican revolution in recent years, and the epistle to the Galatians has figured prominently in every reconfiguration of the Pauline solar system. The critical issues raised by the "new perspective" on Paul concern, among other things, the nature of first-century "Judaism" – a controversial term in itself – and the reason(s) behind Paul's rejection of his "former way of life in Judaism" (Gal. 1.13). Because Galatians is one of our primary sources in this debate, scholarly writing on this letter has been (rightly) preoccupied with this subject, and this is reflected in the "ever-burgeoning literature" on the theme.[1] Indeed, the "new perspective" has generated a whole body of material devoted solely to keeping up with the debate.[2]

A second important issue in the interpretation of Galatians, though perhaps not of Copernican magnitude, gained prominence with the publication of Hans Dieter Betz's Hermeneia commentary, which analyzed the argument of Galatians in terms of classical rhetorical theory. Betz's work has been challenged and modified in a number of ways,[3] though most would accept that the relationship between *structure* and *meaning* so ably illustrated by Betz's exegesis had not been fully appreciated prior to his detailed rhetorical analysis.[4]

---

[1] Citing Hagner (1993: 127 n. 67).

[2] See, e.g., Fung (1981), Barclay (1986), Moo (1987), Bruce (1988), Bandstra (1990), O'Brien (1992), Hagner (1993), etc.

[3] For the most important criticisms and modifications see Aune (1981: 323–28), Brinsmead (1982), G. Kennedy (1984: 144–42), Lyons (1985), Hansen (1989), Smitt (1989: 1–26), Longenecker (1990), and now R. D. Anderson (1996: 106–8).

[4] Note the comments of Dunn (1993a: 20) to this effect, who himself is skeptical of the rhetorical approach.

Given the all-encompassing nature of these two issues, it may come as a surprise to discover that Paul's new-creation motif in Galatians may be pursued largely independently of these interpretive maelstroms.[5] Two of the most prominent figures within the "new perspective," E. P. Sanders and James Dunn, offer completely different readings of καινὴ κτίσις in Galatians 6.15 and 2 Corinthians 5.17,[6] and this suggests that any marriage between "new creation" and the "new perspective" is one of convenience rather than necessity. In a similar way, while rhetorical analyses have sharpened our understanding of the significance of Paul's closing comments, they have added little to our understanding of καινὴ κτίσις specifically. And as important as this insight is, it has to be said that the import of Paul's concluding remarks in Galatians 6.11–18 was noted long ago by Lightfoot, Sieffert, and Zahn (see below). Indeed, Galatians 6.11–18 belongs to that unfortunate group of texts recently designated by Jeffrey Weima as Paul's "neglected endings."[7] Unlike the memorable 2 Corinthians 5.17, Galatians 6.15 is usually cited only because of its opening clause: "neither circumcision nor uncircumcision."[8]

But if these issues do not impinge significantly on Paul's new-creation motif in Galatians 6.15, others may, particularly the current enthusiasm with all things "apocalyptic" – another controversial term.[9] Again however, Paul's new-creation motif is capable of a variety of interpretations, even within an "apocalyptic" framework. Ernst Käsemann, for instance, could apply this motif anthropologically ("a transformation of our human existence . . . effected in baptism"),[10] ecclesiologically ("the church as the company of the obedient who . . . stand in the succession of the obedient Adam"),[11] soterio-cosmologically ("the beginning of the new aeon")[12] or theologically (a "parallel" expression to καινὴ διαθήκη).[13] Granted, Käsemann is employing this phrase as a heuristic theological construct with little reference to its epistolary-exegetical significance, yet even so, there remains a fair amount of latitude in the way καινὴ κτίσις is interpreted, and this from the father of the modern "apocalyptic" Paul.

These opening comments are intended to preface the ensuing discussion in a number of ways. First, because Paul's new-creation motif has received scant attention in the secondary literature on Galatians, the evaluation of this idea in Galatians 6.15 can be more succinct than the

[5] See, e.g., Mell (1989).
[6] Compare Sanders (1977: 468–69) and Dunn (1993a: 342–43).
[7] This is the title of Weima's 1994 monograph on the Pauline postscripts.
[8] E.g., Sanders (1983: 20, 100, 143, 149, 159, etc.), Thielmann (1989: 59, 63, 90), T. Schreiner (1993a: 136, 142, 166), etc.
[9] See especially Matlock (1996: 247–340).   [10] Käsemann (1969: 176).
[11] Käsemann (1969: 134).   [12] Käsemann (1964:161).   [13] Käsemann (1969: 178).

examination of 2 Corinthians 5.17. Second, it should be clear from even these brief remarks that new creation should not be seen as intrinsically connected with a larger interpretive agenda, be it that of a post-Käsemann or a post-Sanders interpretation of Paul. Third, I have deliberately highlighted one aspect of rhetorical-critical analysis of Galatians which, while not entirely novel, provides the most fruitful starting-point for an analysis of καινὴ κτίσις in this letter: Galatians 6.12–18 as the *recapitulatio*.

Galatians 6.12–18 in epistolary and rhetorical perspective

It is rare to find an issue on which there is complete agreement among interpreters of Paul's letters, but the significance of Paul's concluding comments in Galatians may be one of them. As a literary document, Galatians has been scrutinized along both rhetorical[14] and epistolary lines,[15] and the unanimous conclusion of these studies is that Galatians 6.12–18 functions as a "hermeneutical key,"[16] "carefully adapted and reshaped by Paul to echo better the major tensions and essential concerns expressed throughout the letter."[17] As in the above examination of the thanksgiving period/*proem* of 2 Corinthians 2.14–3.6, rhetorical and epistolary analyses dovetail perfectly, and this surely attests to the universal principles which undergird argumentative, persuasive discourse.[18] Intrinsic to good argumentation are periodic summations[19] and a final recapitulation, so we have every reason to expect that the central concerns of Galatians will be crystallized in its postscript/*conclusio*. In fact, Paul himself makes this clear by introducing his closing comments with the words, "See with what large letters I now write with my own hand" (6.11).[20] More than merely drawing attention to his idiosyncratic penmanship, most see this peculiar statement as the ancient equivalent of placing what follows in boldface type.[21] According to Lightfoot, "The boldness of the handwriting answers

---

[14] E.g., Betz (1979), Brinsmead (1982), G. Kennedy (1984: 144–42), Lyons (1985), Smit (1989: 1–26), R. D. Anderson (1996).

[15] E.g., Bahr (1968), Hansen (1989), Longenecker (1990), Weima (1994).

[16] Betz (1979: 313), Weima (1993: 90–107).

[17] Weima (1993: 91). Similar comments could be cited from *all* the major commentaries on Galatians: Becker, Betz, Bonnard, Borse, Burton, Dunn, Lagrange, Lightfoot, Mussner, Sieffert, Zahn, etc.

[18] See Boers (1994: 50–51), who displays in parallel fashion both epistolary and rhetorical outlines of Galatians.

[19] See chapter 9 and the literature cited there on the function of Gal. 2.15–21 as an encapsulation of the argument as a whole.

[20] With most, the aorist ἔγραψα is epistolary, and does not indicate that Paul had penned the whole letter.

[21] Lightfoot (1890: 221), Burton (1921: 348), Lagrange (1926: 162), Schlier (1949: 280), Oepke (1964a: 158), Mussner (1974: 410), Lührmann (1978: 100), Longenecker (1990: 290), etc.

to the force of the Apostle's own conviction,"[22], and this means that Paul's concluding remarks are the last thing interpreters can afford to neglect. Moreover, 6.14–15, Paul's final death–life statement (cf. 2.19–20; 5.24–25), is particularly crucial and is often regarded as "nichts anderes als die zentrale These der paulinischen Argumentation im Galaterbrief."[23] Functioning as the "life" side of this death–life equation, καινὴ κτίσις resonates back through the entire epistle and may well "epitomiz[e] the major thesis of the letter."[24]

If Galatians 6.12–18 represents a concise restatement of the main themes of Galatians, it follows that the body of the letter should be particularly helpful in unpacking these terse, abbreviated salvos which bring the argument to a close. In approaching this passage, then, I will look first at the major sections of the letter in order to highlight the most prominent themes *relevant to Paul's new-creation motif.* Obviously I will have to pass over some important issues in the interpretation of Galatians in silence, but this should serve only to focus attention on the task at hand.

Paul as paradigm (Galatians 1 and 2)

Paul's detailed and somewhat laborious rehearsal of his apostolic calling (1.11–17), early ministry (1.18–2.10), and confrontation with Peter at Antioch (2.11–21) is sometimes regarded as less than crucial for understanding the argument that follows, though such an approach, I contend, fails to apprehend adequately Paul's argumentative strategy.[25] As Dunn observes, the very fact that Paul both introduces and concludes his argument in "the highly personal language" of autobiography "is indication in itself of the degree to which Paul saw his own experience as an epitome of the Gospel."[26] In summarizing his argument in Galatians 6.12–18, Paul not only picks up central themes of chapters 1–2, he also returns to the paradigmatic first-person singular, clearly underscoring the importance of the autobiographical narrative. In what follows I highlight the

[22] Lightfoot (1890: 221).

[23] Harnisch (1987: 282). So too Betz (1979: 319 n. 15), Longenecker (1990: 295), Hong (1993: 88).

[24] Cousar, in an unpublished paper cited approvingly by Weima (1994: 170).

[25] Although the identity of Paul's opponents in Galatians is debated (cf. Barclay [1988: 36–73]), with the majority of commentators I assume that they were Jewish-Christians. The importance of circumcision and the law in Galatians render this conclusion a near certainty. Beyond this, the argument of this chapter is compatible with a variety of specific profiles.

[26] Dunn (1993b: 5). This thesis has received detailed exposition by, e.g., Schütz (1975: 114–58), Lyons (1985: 123–86), Gaventa (1986b), and Cosgrove (1988: 119–46). Beker's brief comments on this point are also worthy of note. He speaks of "the correlation of the apostle and gospel which dominates Gal 1.12–2.21," arguing that here, as in 2 Corinthians, "the gospel and its bearer are interlocked" (1980: 47).

paradigmatic rather than the apologetic function of Galatians 1–2, though without denying the importance of the latter. As noted earlier, autobiography and apologetic are closely related in Paul's letters, and here they prepare the ground for the frank appeal of 4.12: "Friends, become like me!"[27]

Paul's "biography of reversal"

The sharp contrasts which characterize the postscript,[28] particularly 6.14–15, serving to distinguish Paul from his opponents, offer a convenient point of departure for a survey of Galatians 1–2. It is through just such a contrast that Paul begins his letter: "Paul, an apostle [appointed] neither by human beings, nor through any human agency, but through Jesus Christ and God the Father who raised him from the dead" (1.1). John Schütz has argued that the "patterns of contrast" which permeate the autobiographical narrative constitute a "biography of reversal" and illustrate "Paul's ruthlessly personal way of perceiving and narrating the story."[29] Expanding Shütz's insight, George Lyons has analyzed Galatians 1–2 in terms of a series of antithetically related pairs, principally the "formerly–now" and "God–man" contrasts.[30] The God–man contrast, evident in 1.1, 1.11–12, 1.15–17, and 2.9–10, is intended to substantiate the apostle's claim to divine authority. The formerly–now contrast is interpreted by Lyons as "a contrast of redemptive history personalized in Paul's self-description and made paradigmatic for the experience of every Christian."[31] Because Paul's new-creation statement is also set within a formerly–now antithesis ("neither circumcision nor uncircumcision, but new creation"), I will concentrate attention here. Three closely related texts warrant special comment: 1.10; 1.13–17; and 2.19–20.

Galatians 1.10. Paul's first formerly–now contrast occurs early in the narrative, where he scandalously labels his former way of life "people pleasing" (ἀνθρώποις ἀρέσκειν, 1.10b). That Paul reflects – *in retrospect* – on his pre-conversion orientation in the statement, "If I were *still* seeking to please *people* . . . ," is evident from the conclusion he draws: " . . . then I would not be a servant of Christ." Paul sets his former way of life as

---

[27] This plea "really amounts to a call for decisive resistance against the trouble makers" (Hansen 1989: 107), and refers to Paul's exemplary pattern of resolute adherence to "the truth of the Gospel" in the face of pressure from certain elements within the Jewish wing of the early church. See also Lagrange (1926: 110–11), Schlier (1949: 209), Bonnard (1972: 91–92), Mussner (1974: 305–6), Betz (1979: 222–23), Lyons (1985: 164–68), Gaventa (1986b: 320), Longenecker (1990: 189–90), Castelli (1991: 115–16).

[28] On which see Weima (1993; 1994: 156–74).   [29] Schütz (1975: 133–44).

[30] Lyons (1985: 146–64).   [31] Lyons (1985: 152).

a "people pleaser" in deliberate contrast to his present way of life as a "servant of Christ" (cf. 5.11).[32] Paul's words here are strongly reminiscent of the "Dialogue with the People Pleasers" in *Psalms of Solomon* 4. This Jewish work (first century BC) heaps contempt upon the "hypocrite" (4.6, 20, 22) and "people pleaser" (ἀνθρωπαρέσκος, 4.1, 7, 8) who sits in "the ruling council of the devout" (ἐν συνεδρίῳ ὁσίων), yet who lives only "to impress people" (4.7). The decisive turning point for Paul was his conversion/call, to which the following verses bear witness.[33]

Galatians 1.13–17. Elaborating on this formerly–now theme – and in support of my interpretation of 1.10 – Paul goes on to describe the "revelation of Christ" given to him (1.12; cf. 1.16) and explicitly comments on what he calls "my former way of life in Judaism" (1.13). As in 1.10, Paul's evaluation is surprisingly negative. From his post-Damascus vantage point he views his previous life in terms of his violent enforcement of the Jewish faith (1.13), professional "ladder-climbing" (προέκοπτον ἐν τῷ Ἰουδαϊσμῷ, 14a), competition with his peers (ὑπὲρ πολλοὺς συνηλικιώτας ἐν τῷ γένει μου, 14b), and zeal for ancestral traditions (14c). John Barclay astutely remarks that in this passage "Judaism . . . appears to be merely κατὰ ἄνθρωπον and thus κατὰ σάρκα,"[34] and this is an impression Paul is purposefully cultivating. We need not suppose that Paul's Jewish contemporaries would have concurred with this (retrospective) judgment, nor should we draw far-reaching implications about the religious atmosphere of first-century "Judaism." Still, this was *Paul's* perspective and hence the *epistolary* perspective, so should play a leading role in the present interpretation of the letter.[35]

Paul's point should not be missed. His intention is to align Torah-advocacy (hence, his opponents) with misguided zeal, "people pleasing," and *merely* human religiosity.[36] This perspective undergirds much

---

[32] This interpretation of 1.10 is supported by Sieffert (1899: 51), Burton (1921:33–34), Schlier (1949: 42), Cole (1965: 83), Bligh (1969: 92–93), Lietzmann (1971: 6), Bonnard (1972: 26 n. 2), Mussner (1974: 64), Betz (1979: 56), Ebeling (1985: 64–65), Lyons (1985: 147–48), and Gaventa (1986b: 314). Whether Paul was accused of "people pleasing" by his opponents (so Bruce [1982: 84–86], Longenecker [1990: 18–19], Dunn [1993a: 50–51]) is uncertain (correctly, Betz [1979: 56], Howard [1990: 8–9], B. J. Dodd (1996: 90–92)].

[33] I posit no sharp distinction between "conversion" and "call." Both terms apply in discussing Paul's biography. See Gaventa (1986a: 17–51), Everts (1993: 156–63); also Segal (1990: *passim*, here 6): "From the viewpoint of mission Paul is commissioned, but from the viewpoint of religious experience Paul is a Convert."

[34] Barclay (1988: 207 n. 80).

[35] On this point see Cosgrove (1988: 5–38, here 16): "Not what the agitators or Galatians regard as the center of dispute but what Paul sees as the real issue must form the *presupposition* of exegesis."

[36] See Barclay (1988: 206–7).

of Galatians, not least Paul's account of Peter's conduct at Antioch (2.11–15).[37] For Paul, this "former way of life" was brought to an abrupt end by the revelation of Christ *in him* (ἐν ἐμοί, 1.16). While never depreciating the objective nature of the Damascus Christophany (cf. 1 Cor. 9.1; 15.8), here, as in 2 Corinthians 4.6, Paul consciously underscores the subjective element involved in this apocalypse. His purpose is to accentuate "the personal transformation effected by the revelation from heaven."[38] Indeed, in Galatians Paul regularly emphasizes this (inner) dimension of conversion, and in each case it is the convert's relationship to (external) nomistic observance that is at issue:

	Formerly	Now
Galatians 1.13–16	ancestral traditions	"his son *in me*"
Galatians 2.18–20	the law	"Christ lives *in me*"
Galatians 4.4–6	under law	"the Spirit of his son *in our hearts*"
Galatians 4. 8–10	observance of "days, months, seasons and year"	"until Christ is formed *in you*"
(Galatians 6.15	circumcision and uncircumcision	"new creation,")

The appropriateness of placing Galatians 6.15 within this specific pattern of thought will be demonstrated more fully in what follows, though given "the antithetical formulation of Paul's autobiographical statements" throughout Galatians,[39] its prima facie coherence should at least be noted here.

Galatians 2.19–20. Paul's stunning announcement, "I no longer live" (2.20; see chapter 9), brings his biography of reversal to a climax. The one who *formerly* persecuted followers of Christ *now* confesses, "Christ lives in me." Paul's previous existence in Judaism was terminated by his confrontation with Christ, and any reversion to nomism would, in his view, constitute a rejection of God's χάρις (2.21a; cf. 1.6) and a repudiation

---

[37] See B. J. Dodd (1996: 100–4).

[38] Dunn (1993a: 65). Dunn adds, "when Paul wanted to use a [simple] dative with the verb 'reveal' he did so (1 Cor. 2.10; 14.30; Phil. 3.15)." Most interpret ἐν ἐμοί in terms of Paul's inner experience of this revelation: Sieffert (1899: 62), Burton (1921: 50–51), Lagrange (1926: 14), Betz (1979: 71), Bruce (1982: 93), Kim (1984: 5–7), Longenecker (1990: 32l), Segal (1990: 64), Dunn (1993a: 64). Dissenters include Lightfoot (1890), Moule (1959: 76, with reservation), Mussner (1974), Gaventa (1986a: 27).

[39] Citing Lyons (1985: 171). Cf. Schütz (1975: 133–50), Hansen (1989: 84–85), Weima (1994: 161–74). The antithetical nature of Paul's argument is also discussed by Watson (1986: 46–47).

of Christ's sacrifice (2.21b). The Galatians are clearly intended "to hear their own story in Paul's description of God at work in his mission"[40] and to see their apostle as the exemplary paradigm of Christocentric transformation. As Dunn observes, Paul employs "his own personal testimony as prolegomena to his main argument,"[41] expecting his readers to draw the conclusion that Christ *in them* (see 4.19) is the only necessary and sufficient answer to those advocating circumcision. Indeed, Paul's refusal to yield to the pressure of "those from James" (2.12) is explained on precisely the same basis as his rejection of his "former way of life in Judaism," his transformative encounter with Jesus: "his Son/Christ in me" (1.15–16 and 2.19–20).[42]

Working in tandem with the formerly–now contrast – perhaps even supporting it – is another, more foundational antithesis, which is brought to the surface in Paul's discussion of "the seemingly important" (οἱ δοκοῦν-τες: 2.2, 6, 9): "Whatever they *once* were, matters little to me. *God does not look at [mere] appearances*" (2.6). Paul specifically correlates his formerly–now contrast with an "appearance versus reality" antithesis, and the prominence of this motif in the postscript (εὐπροσωπῆσαι ἐν σαρκί, 6.12) cannot be adequately grasped without considering its prior epistolary development.

Appearance versus reality

As a religio-philosophical topos, the appearance versus reality (δοκεῖν/ εἶναι) motif had roots deep in Greek culture, being widely attested in philosophical literature from as early as Aeschylus (fifth century BC).[43] The notion was also current in early Jewish and Christian writings,[44] and the specific phrase "appearance versus reality" is sometimes applied to Galatians 2.6.[45] Because the underlying principle is larger than any one particular religio-philosophical background, Paul's own perspective must govern the interpretation of this motif in Galatians 2. Before exploring

---

[40] Cosgrove (1988: 122).   [41] Dunn (1993b: 66).

[42] The word "transformation" (cf. Romans 12.2) often receives special emphasis in discussions of Paul's conversion. See, e.g., Kim (1984: esp. 315–29), Gaventa (1986a: 17–51), Segal (1990: 3–183).

[43] See, e.g., Aeschylus, *Seven* 592; Plato, *Gorgias* 472A; *Euthydemus* 303C; *Republic* 2.361B/262A; Plutarch, *Moralia* 212B, along with the texts and literature cited by Hay (1969) and Kittel (1964: 232–33).

[44] 2 Macc. 1.13; 9.8–10; Philo, *Ebr.* 37; *Migr. Abr.* 12, 40; *Fug.* 156; Mark 10.42; 1 Cor. 3.18; 8.2; *1 Clem.* 48.6; 57.2; *2 Clem.* 2.3; 17.3; 20.4; Ignatius, *Pol.* 3.1; *Trall.* 10.1; *Smyrn.* 2.1; 4.2; *Diogn.* 8.10; 10.7; *Barn.* 10.10–11.

[45] See Hay (1969), Schütz (1975: 140–50). Cf. Hansen (1989: 84–85), who applies the phrase more broadly to Paul's style of argumentation in Galatians.

relevant material from Paul's letters, a brief summary of the salient points of Galatians 2.1–10 is offered.

Galatians 2.1–10. Continuing his autobiographical narrative, Paul's chief concern in 2.1–10 is to demonstrate that both he and his message – particularly its circumcision-free character (2.1–5) – had the full approval of the "pillars" in Jerusalem, and this without any modification or reservation (2.6–10). The outstanding feature of Paul's narration is his designation of the Jerusalem apostles with the phrase οἱ δοκοῦντες, "those who seem to be something,"[46] While some argue that the phrase is completely neutral, bearing no dismissive undertone,[47] three considerations tell against this. (1) In 2.6 Paul interrupts his thought to offer his own commentary on the individuals standing behind this phrase, and his words are hardly complimentary: "whatever they *once* were means nothing to me, God does not look at appearances."[48] Paul's deliberate correlation οἱ δοκοῦντες with the notion of *mere* externals can be missed only by those refusing to see it. (2) Δοκέω in Paul often implies a negative judgment, which is exactly how Paul uses it later in this epistle: "If any consider themselves to be something when they are nothing (δοκεῖ τις εἶναί τι μηδὲν ὤν), they deceive themselves" (6.2).[49] (3) Another concern of Paul's in 2.1–10 is to provide the theological rationale for his rejection of the position of Peter (and James?) in Antioch, and the appellation οἱ δοκοῦντες is perfectly suited to this purpose. Dunn's description of οἱ δοκοῦντες as a "distancing formula" which, while acknowledging a perceived authority, "includes a certain degree of personal questioning of that authority" commends itself.[50]

As noted above, Paul's parenthetical comment in 2.6 provides the theological principle for his subsequent stance in Antioch.[51] Paul claims a

[46] With most, I understand οἱ δοκοῦντες principally in reference to James, Peter, and John, as 2.9 makes clear: "those seeming to be pillars, James, Cephas and John . . ." So too Zahn (1910: 96), Foerster (1937: 286), Barrett (1953: 1–2), Bonnard (1972: 144), Longenecker (1990: 42), Dunn (1993a: 92), and others. Cf. Schlier (1949: 35–36), Oepke (1964b: 44), and Mussner (1974: 104), who add the qualification that "the pillars" (2.9) are a sub-group of οἱ δοκοῦντες.

[47] E.g., Lightfoot (1890: 103), Burton (1921: 71), Lietzmann (1971: 9–10), Bonnard (1972: 40), Mussner (1974: 104–5).

[48] The most likely explanation of the phrase ὁποῖοί ποτε ἦσαν is that Paul has in mind the apostles' association with the earthly Jesus. So too Lightfoot (1890: 108), Burton (1921: 87), Barrett (1953: 19), Cole (1965: 108), Bruce (1982: 118), Longenecker (1990: 87), Dunn (1993a: 102).

[49] See also 1 Cor. 3.18; 8.2; 10.12; 11.16; 14.37; Phil. 3.4.

[50] Citing Dunn (1993a: 93). Similarly, Foerster (1937: 287), Käsemann (1942: 42), Oepke (1964b: 78), Cole (1965: 107–8), Hay (1969: 37–44), Schütz (1975: 142), Betz (1979: 92), Borse (1984: 78), Longenecker (1990: 48), and now Heitsch (1995: 175–76).

[51] So too Hay (1969: 42–44), Schütz (1975: 143), Betz (1979: 94–95).

divine mandate for his criterion of evaluation and this he explains with
the maxim, πρόσωπον ὁ θεὸς ἀνθρώπου οὐ λαμβάνει. More than a
momentary digression or anacoluthon, Paul enunciates here one of the
guiding principles of his thought. Not surprisingly, this theological dictum
figures prominently elsewhere in Paul's writings.

"*Receiving a face.*" Galatians 2.6c, "God does not receive a face," represents one of several Old Testament idioms (λαμβάνειν πρόσωπον, ἰδεῖν
πρόσωπον, θαυμάζειν πρόσωπον, [ἐπι]γινώκειν πρόσωπον) relating
to favoritism and impartiality.[52] In Paul's letters the πρόσωπον motif is
closely associated with his internal–external antithesis – an unavoidable
connection given the terminology involved (cf. 2 Cor. 10.7). I have already discussed the complex καρδία–πρόσωπον interplay of 2 Corinthians 3.12–4.6, as well as that of 2 Corinthians 5.12 (chapter 10). This latter
passage, where Paul speaks of those who boast ἐν προσώπῳ and not ἐν
καρδίᾳ, is often cited to illuminate Galatians 2.6c.[53] In Romans 2.11 Paul
applies this motif to God's impartial judgment of both Jew and Gentile (οὐ
γάρ ἐστιν προσωπολημψία παρὰ τῷ θεῷ), a position he rewords and
justifies more fully at the close of the chapter: "For true Jewishness is not
a matter of outward appearance (ἐν τῷ φανερῷ), neither is circumcision
external, in the flesh. Rather, true Jewishness is inward (ἐν τῷ κρυπτῷ),
and circumcision is of the heart, by the Spirit" (2.28–29; cf. 2.14–16).
In this passage, which sounds very much like a programmatic announcement, Paul redefines the people of God by means of the Spirit and his
internal–external antithesis, thus elevating this idea to the level of a theological canon (cf. Rom. 9.6–7; 1 Cor. 10.10–13; 2 Cor. 4.18; 5.7; 10.7;
Phil. 3.3).

Given Paul's elaboration of the πρόσωπον motif elsewhere, exegetes
are correct in emphasizing the notion of externality/internality in relation
to Galatians 2.6.[54] The specific "external" Paul has in mind relates to the
status and position of the "pillar" apostles. He implicitly contrasts this
with "intrinsic character"[55] and its concomitant adherence to the "truth
of the Gospel" (see 2.11–21). Often cited in relation to 2 Corinthians

---

[52] Lev. 19.15; Deut. 1.17; 10.12, 17; 16.19; 2 Chron. 19.7; Job 34.19; Ps. 81.2; Wisd.
6.7; Sir. 4.22, 27; 35.12–13; 44.1; 1 Esdr. 4.39. Cf. *Jub.* 5.6; 30.16; 21.4.

[53] See Burton (1921: 88), Hay (1969: 42), Lietzmann (1971: 12), Bonnard (1972: 40),
Schütz (1975: 144). Cf. 1 Thessalonians 2.17.

[54] "Gott sieht nicht auf das Äußere" (Foerster [1937: 288]). Similarly, Lightfoot (1890:
107), Burton (1921: 88), Oepke (1964b: 48), Hay (1969: 40), Lietzmann (1971: 11), Schütz
(1975: 155–56), Borse (1984: 89), Rohde (1989: 83).

[55] Lightfoot (1890: 108). Cf. Zahn (1910: 96–7): "Die Außenseite des Menschen ... im
Gegensatz zu dem oft verborgenen inneren Wert."

5.12, and occasionally in reference to Galatians 2.6,[56] the most likely antecedent for this crucial, but largely ignored antithesis in Paul is 1 Samuel 16.7: "For humans look at externals (ὄψεται εἰς πρόσωπον), but God looks at the heart (ὄψεται εἰς καρδίαν)." Given the close connection between Galatians 2.6 and 2 Corinthians 5.12, it is tempting to read Paul's cynical commentary on οἱ δοκοῦντες in light of 2 Corinthians 5.16: "We no longer judge anyone κατὰ σάρκα."[57]

Summary

The importance of Galatians 1–2 for Paul's subsequent argument should be apparent. Paul's autobiographical narrative "implicitly form[s] the basis of Paul's later exhortation"[58] and this in some very specific ways. Paul presents himself as a "paradigm,"[59] "an 'incarnation' of the Gospel of Jesus Christ,"[60] and expects his readers to hear their own story as he narrates his. Indeed, as Paul superimposed the experience of Jesus onto his own life ("I have been crucified with Christ"), so too he hopes the Galatians will allow his biography to interpret their own. The apostolic paradigm which Paul advances consists of the rejection of all competitive religious systems, and this on the basis of an inwardly transforming experience of the crucified and risen Christ (1.15–16; 2.19–20). Paul deliberately portrays his own Jewish religious past as "people pleasing" and *merely* human religiosity in order to render his circumcising opponents in Galatia guilty by association.

At the same time, this portrayal is also aimed at undermining the position of Peter at Antioch, so compels Paul to make explicit his theological rationale for daring to oppose the Jerusalem "pillars." In essence, Paul argues that both he and they are subject to God's criterion of judgment, and this takes no regard of external factors such as social status or prior religious advantages (Gal. 2.6c). Paul's insistence on the priority of intrinsic factors over extrinsic considerations undergirds much of the ensuing argument (e.g., Spirit versus flesh), *especially his rejection of nomistic observance*, and this foundational religious axiom is echoed throughout Paul's letters. Its epistolary significance is best grasped by John Schütz in his summary of Paul's "biography of reversal" and the appearance versus reality motif in 2.6: "The central agency is the gospel and its power to

---

[56] Zahn (1910: 97), Hay (1969: 39).
[57] With Lightfoot (1890: 108), Burton (1921: 87), and Longenecker (1990: 54).
[58] Gaventa (1986b: 310). So too Lyons (1985: 147), Dunn (1993b: 66–72).
[59] So Schütz (1975: 134), Beker (1980: 47), Gaventa (1986b: 319), Hansen (1989: 107).
[60] Lyons (1985: 225).

both subordinate and to re-create, to make sufficient what was deficient, to make new what is wanting – to shape a new creation."[61]

As the argument continues, Paul leaves behind his paradigmatic "I" and turns to address the Galatians directly. Approaching the issue from a slightly different angle he asks, "This one thing I wish to know: did you receive the Spirit from works of the law or the message of faith? . . . Having begun with the Spirit are you now going to finish in the flesh?" (3.2–3).

Faith and the Spirit: redefining the people of God (Gal. 3.1–5.12)

The decisive question: πίστις or νόμος?

Paul begins his explicit theological argumentation in Galatians with terminology which epitomizes the issues as he sees them and which will dominate the remainder of the letter: faith, the Spirit, the law, and the flesh (3.2–3). Having made a new beginning in the Spirit (ἐναρξάμενοι πνεύματι), Paul warns the Galatians that turning to the law is actually reverting to the unaided realm of the flesh (3.3). This parity of law and flesh (cf. 5.17–18; 6.12–13; Rom. 7.5–6) was implicit in his autobiographical comments (1.10–16), and constitutes a further assault on the position of "the troublemakers" (1.7; 5.10).

In calling attention to the starting-point of the Galatians' Christian experience, receiving the Spirit, and asking how this was attained, Paul posits two antithetical alternatives, ἐξ ἔργων νόμου or ἐξ ἀκοῆς πίστεως. The meaning of the phrase ἐξ ἀκοῆς πίστεως in 3.2–5 is disputed,[62] but by all accounts the emphasis falls on πίστις, as evidenced by Paul's programmatic summary which immediately follows: "Just as Abraham *believed* God and it was credited to him as righteousness, realize, then, that *those of faith* (οἱ ἐκ πίστεως), these are children of Abraham" (3.6–7). Regardless of how ἐκ πίστεως Χριστοῦ is read in 2.16, in drawing an inference (ἄρα) from καθὼς Ἀβραὰμ ἐπίστευσεν (3.6), Paul surely intends οἱ ἐκ πίστεως (3.7) to mean something like, "those who (likewise) believe," or "those of a similar kind of faith."[63]

---

[61] Schütz (1975: 143).

[62] Both πίστις and ἀκοή are capable of a number of translations, and the genitival relationship is also open to question. The alternatives are adequately covered in the exchange between Hays (1983: 143–49) and Williams (1989: 82–93). I prefer "the message which concerns faith," or "the faith-message" (Hays [1983: 149]). See Schlier (1949: 78), Oepke (1964b: 68), Mussner (1974: 204).

[63] With most, e.g., Lightfoot (1890: 136–37), Schlier (1949: 87), Bligh (1969: 246), Bonnard (1972: 65–6), Mussner (1974: 216–18), Bruce (1982: 155), Borse (1984: 126–27),

Paul's insistence that it is "those of faith" who are Abraham's children clearly exposes the primary question of 3.1–5.12: *what now demarcates the people of God?* The salvation-historical antithesis νόμος/πίστις (cf. 3.23–24) figured prominently in 2.15–21, the *propositio* of Galatians, where Paul applies it to Jewish believers generally (2.15–18), and to himself paradigmatically: "I died to νόμος . . . I live now by πίστις" (2.19–20). In the main body of the letter Paul intends to apply this principle to the Galatians, and even a cursory reading of Galatians 3.1–5.12 will reveal that most of Paul's energy is devoted to redefining the people of God in terms of *faith* and *the Spirit* and away from the law and nomistic observance. E. P. Sanders is perfectly correct to argue that "the subject of Galatians . . . is the condition on which Gentiles [or anyone] enter the people of God," and that "the topic is in effect soteriology."[64] Cousar's judgment is similar: "The issue under debate, raised by the agitators, demand for circumcision, was basically soteriological, how God saves people."[65] A closely related issue, though of secondary importance in Galatians, has to do with the unity of God's people as Jew and Gentile.

Paul, of course, was well aware of the ecclesiological and sociological dimension of the situation in Galatia (cf. 3.28; 6.16), but he never allows it to overshadow the more pressing theological-soteriological principle he is addressing. Even Peter's withdrawal from community meals at Antioch, which afforded Paul a splendid opportunity to channel the ensuing discussion in the direction of Jew–Gentile unity, is taken in an entirely different direction and used to illustrate the soteriological principle of nomistic observance (ἐξ ἔργων νόμου, 2.16 [3x!]) versus faith/faithfulness (2.15–18). Indeed, it could be argued that Paul's confrontation with Peter found a place in this epistle solely because of its usefulness as an illustration of faithfulness under nomistic pressure and as a springboard into the central issue of Galatians: the place of Torah in the Christian community.[66] This is, arguably, how it functions in the argument.[67]

Longenecker (1990: 114), Dunn (1993a: 162), Eckstein (1996: 103–4). Against Hays, who would expand the phrase to read "those who are given life on the basis of [Christ's] faith" (1983: 201).

[64] Sanders (1983: 18 and 46, respectively).   [65] Cousar (1982: 61).

[66] The careful reader of Galatians will notice that Peter's action in Antioch is deliberately described in the same language as Paul's circumcising opponents (ἀναγκάζειν, 2.3; 2.14; 6.12). This makes the correspondence between the illustration and the application a bit tighter while also revealing the analogous relationship in Paul's mind between Peter's action and the circumcising campaign of his opponents.

[67] Recognizing the force of this observation, Wolfgang Kraus must deny that Gal. 2.15–21 functions as a kind of *propositio* within Galatians because the *Gottesvolkthematik* is conspicuously absent. Hence, against most, 2.15–21 cannot be an epitome of the argument

While in no way determinative for the interpretation of καινὴ κτίσις, failure to acknowledge the clear priority of the soteriological issue in Galatians could potentially affect one's understanding of Paul's new-creation motif, as the recent work of Wolfgang Kraus illustrates.[68] However, *unless Paul's argument misleads*, the question of who constitutes the people of God is an important but subsidiary corollary issuing from the more crucial question, the "truth of the gospel" question: *what now demarcates the people of God – νόμος or πίστις?*

The decisive evidence: the Spirit

The "argument décisif,"[69] the "knock-down proof"[70] which Paul adduces in favor of not rebuilding what he has already torn down (the law, 2.18–19) is the work of the Spirit.[71] Whether the entirety of Galatians should be conceived of as a "defense of the Spirit"[72] is debatable, but Paul's dramatic, "This one thing I wish to know . . . " (3.2) is certainly intended to focus attention on this theme. Paul's appeal to the Spirit as the incontrovertible proof of πίστις over νόμος constitutes a transition from his own biography to that of his readers, and in both cases Paul unashamedly sets forth personal experience as "exhibit A."[73] In 3.1–5 Paul's rejection of the law is substantiated on the basis of the Spirit's work within (3.2–3; cf. 4.6) and among the Galatians (3.5), and this pattern of thought (Spirit obviates law) is replicated in every allusion to the Spirit in 3.1–5.12. Moreover, while explicit references to the Spirit are less numerous in 3.6–5.12 than might be expected on the basis of 3.1–5, all the major themes that follow – the blessing, the promise(s), the covenant(s), heirship, adoption – are related in some way to the Spirit. This indicates that Paul's Spirit statements in 3.1–5 are seminal to the ensuing argument and that the neat division of Galatians 3–5 into arguments from experience and arguments from Scripture is somewhat artificial.[74] The following survey of these interrelated themes will demonstrate that most of 3.6–5.12 should be understood as an elaboration of the essential crux of 3.1–5: *the Spirit renders the law obsolete.*[75]

---

of Galatians (1996: 213–15). Alternatively, it might be that Kraus is mistaken about the centrality of this theme in Galatians.

[68] Kraus (1996: 203–54).   [69] Lagrange (1926: 58).   [70] Barclay (1988: 83).

[71] On the importance of the Spirit in the argument of Galatians see Lull (1980), Barclay (1988), Cosgrove (1988), and Fee (1994: 367–471). Note also the significant treatment of the Spirit in Galatians by Betz (1976: 99–14), Williams (1987, 1988), and Dunn (1993b: 59–63).

[72] So Betz (1976: 99–114).   [73] On this see Eckstein (1996: 82–93).

[74] Correctly, Byrne (1979: 147).   [75] See Byrne (1979: 147–49), Lull (1980: 39).

The blessing, the inheritance, the promise, and the Spirit

Galatians 3.7–14. In keeping with the "thematic statement"[76] of 3.7, "Realize then, that *those of faith* are Abraham's children," Paul proceeds to redefine many of the treasured terms of his – and presumably his opponents' – Jewish vocabulary. In 3.7–12 Paul argues that the blessing of Abraham is not achieved through the law, for this actually pronounces a curse. Release from this curse is brought about by Christ (3.13) who allows "the blessing of Abraham, that is, the promise of the Spirit" to come to all "in Christ" and "by faith" (3.14).[77] In this verse, Paul not only identifies the Abrahamic blessing with the Spirit, he specifies this as *"the promised* Spirit." This certainly echoes the prophetic hopes outlined earlier (chapter 8),[78] and has the effect of circumventing the Mosaic dispensation. Paul's claim is that "the blessing" belongs to believers in the form of the Spirit, whose reception was actually obstructed by the law and its curse. Having appropriated Abraham's blessing, Paul turns his attention to the law and its relation to "the promise."

Galatians 3.15–22. Paul's tacit bypassing of the Mosaic dispensation in 3.7–14 becomes the main topic in 3.15–22, where Paul asserts that "the promises" were not spoken to Israel but to Abraham and to his singular seed, Christ (3.16). This assertion is placed within a more cogent line of reasoning based on the temporal priority of the promise (3.15, 17). The premise (and goal) of this argument is expressed in 3.18, where Paul states that if "the inheritance" could be gained by law, it would lose its promissory, χάρις character.[79] In Jewish Scripture and tradition, "the inheritance" of Abraham was usually associated with the land,[80] though here it is equivalent to "the blessing of Abraham," which Paul has just described

---

[76] Dunn (1993a: 162).

[77] Most see the two ἵνα clauses of 3.14 as parallel and emphasize the resulting identification of the blessing with the Spirit: Sieffert (1899: 188), Schlier (1949: 96), Oepke (1964b: 76), Lietzmann (1971: 19), Byrne (1979: 156), Bruce (1982: 167), Borse (1984: 130), Williams (1987: 95), Barclay (1988: 84–85), Dunn (1993a: 179).

[78] Correctly, Mussner (1974: 235), Barclay (1988: 84), Cosgrove (1988: 96–105), Dunn (1993a: 180), Fee (1994: 395).

[79] In light of the emphasis in Galatians on χάρις as the principle at stake in accepting the law (1.6, 15; 2.9, 21; 5.4; see Schütz [1975: 116–58]), Paul's choice of the verb χαρίζομαι here is not incidental. See Schlier (1949: 103–4), Bonnard (1972: 72), Longenecker (1990: 134) and especially Betz (1979: 160 n. 62).

[80] E.g., Josh. 12.7–8; Ps. 78.55; Jer. 12.14–15; Ezek. 47.13–23; Sir. 44.22; 2 Macc. 2.16–18; *Jub.* 17.3; 32.19; *Pss. Sol.* 9.1; Philo, *Vit. Mos.* 1.155. The promise to inherit the land could also be interpreted figuratively: 4QpPs37 2.4–15; *1 Enoch* 39.8; 71.6; 4 Ezra 7.96. See Foerster and Hermann (1965: 758–85), Kraus (1996: 227–28).

as "the promised Spirit" (3.14).[81] This interpretation is confirmed by the chain of reasoning that follows. (1) Those in Christ are the true children and seed of Abraham, hence "heirs of the promise" (3.26–29). (2) All who are true children of Abraham are given the Spirit (4.6). (3) Therefore, "Since you are children, you are also heirs" (4.7). Mussner speaks for many: "Worin das durch Segen Abrahams seinen Nachkommen ('Söhnen', 3.7) solidarisch vermittelte 'Erbe' für den Apostel besteht, war schon in v.14 angedeutet worden: es ist das Pneuma."[82]

In light of this, and given the virtual identification of the Spirit with "life" in Paul's letters (chapter 8), Paul's reformulation of this point in verse 21b is predictable: "For if a law had been given *that was able to impart life* (ζωοποιέω), then righteousness would have actually come about through law." Because the Spirit not the law produces life (Gal. 5.25; Rom. 7.6; 8.1–11; 2 Cor. 3.6), the law can neither lead to righteousness nor supplant the promises (3.21a). Paul again associates the Spirit with the promise made to Abraham, and again posits a mutually exclusive relationship between the law and work of the Spirit (ζωοποιέω, 3.21). The identification of the Spirit with the promise is so complete that in the following verse Paul can speak simply of "the promise" being given to those who believe (3.22; cf. 3.14). The difficulty with this line of thought is summarized by Williams: "But where does God give the promise of the Spirit to Abraham? . . . Nowhere!"[83]

Children, heirs, the Spirit and the covenants

Galatians 3.26–4.6. The curious connection made by Paul between the Spirit and the Abrahamic covenant has been partially clarified above, and issues from the apostle's conviction that the Spirit begets true children of Abraham.[84] This point is important enough to require an initial statement (3.29), a supporting illustration (4.1–6), and a final reiteration (4.7). Although discussion of this passage often focuses on the phrase τὰ στοιχεῖα τοῦ κόσμου, recently described as "one of the great riddles in Pauline studies,"[85] the crux of the argument is contained in the three parallel statements which bracket the illustration.[86] In each case Paul's

[81] So also Burton (1921: 185), Cole (1965: 147), Byrne (1979: 157), Hays (1983: 210–12), Cosgrove (1988: 32, 50–51), Hansen (1989: 128), Dunn (1993a: 186), Hong (1993: 131–32), Fee (1994: 396–97).
[82] Mussner (1974: 242).   [83] Williams (1988: 714).
[84] On this see Williams (1988: 709–20).
[85] Scott (1992: 157). See also Martyn (1997: 394).
[86] See Bonnard's description of 3.29: "l'idée centrale du contexte" (1972: 79).

pattern of argumentation is *assertion→inference*. The phrase included in brackets makes the logical connection common to each explicit.

	Assertion			Inference
3.29	Since you are of Christ	[this means that]	→	you are the seed of Abraham, heirs of the promise.
4.6	Because you are sons	[this means that]	→	God has sent the Spirit of his son in our hearts crying "Abba, Father."
4.7	Since you are of sons	[this means that]	→	you are also heirs through God.

Galatians 3.29 and 4.7 are conditional constructions, though given the certainty of the assertion, the introductory particle εἰ is best translated "since."[87] 4.6 is introduced by ὅτι which, grammatically, could be either declarative (as above) or causal: "God sent his Spirit *because* you are sons." The wider context favors a declarative use, in that Paul has been arguing that the Spirit *is the evidence and starting-point* of their new status. When 4.6 is placed alongside its immediate parallels, each of which draws a certain conclusion from an assumed fact, this choice is confirmed.[88] This line of reasoning (the Spirit proves "sonship"[89]) is crucial in Romans 8 ("all who are led by the Spirit of God are children of God," 8.14; "the Spirit bears witness . . . that we are children of God," 8.16), and is especially evident in the phrase "the Spirit of 'sonship'" (Rom. 8.15). Because the Spirit and "sonship" are inseparable for Paul, it would be misleading to read any chronological order or logical priority into Paul's wording in 4.6. "Sonship" *assumes* the presence of the Spirit, as verse 7 makes clear: "Since you are 'sons,' this means you are heirs [of the promise/blessing/Spirit]."

These tight parallels (3.29; 4.5; 4.6) decisively clarify Paul's alternating use of the terms blessing/promise/inheritance and children/heirs/seed-of-Abraham throughout Galatians. Even a glance at the "inference" column above demonstrates the interchangeability of this terminology, quite apart from my earlier comments. The unifying term is the Spirit, which forms the content of the blessing/promise/inheritance and so creates children/heirs/seed-of-Abraham. Once again the work of the

---

[87] Cf. BAGD s.v. εἰ, III.

[88] With Zahn (1910: 202–3), Lagrange (1926: 103–4), Moule (1959: 147), Zerwick (1963: 143), Lietzmann (1971: 27), Byrne (1979: 184 n. 177), Rohde (1989: 173), Dunn (1993a: 219).

[89] For lack of an acceptable alternative, the gender-specific language of the original is retained in inverted commas.

eschatological Spirit is set in antithesis to the law. More specifically, the external constraint of the law (ὑπὸ νόμον, 4.4–5) is contrasted with the inner dynamic of the Spirit (εἰς τὰς καρδίας ἡμῶν, 4.6). This emphasis, as we have seen, has clear epistolary antecedents in the autobiographical narrative.

Paul's conclusion, "So then, you are no longer slaves, but sons" (4.7), picks up the slavery imagery of 4.1–3, which requires brief comment. As mentioned earlier, Paul's description of slavery under the στοιχεῖα τοῦ κόσμου has generated no small debate. The unsolved riddle of this passage involves finding a definition of this phrase which both fits the context and is contemporary with Paul. Is Paul describing the basic principles of religion,[90] the essential components of the universe,[91] or personal, supernatural beings of some kind?[92] The phrase "remains a mystery,"[93] but this need not sidetrack the present discussion, for in every estimation the στοιχεῖα τοῦ κόσμου are closely associated with the law and nomistic observance. Enslavement ὑπὸ τὰ στοιχεῖα (4.3) is equivalent to slavery ὑπὸ νόμον (4.5). Similarly, submission to the "weak and miserable στοιχεῖα" (4.9) is described in terms of "observing days, months, and years" (4.10). In other words, Paul is bending over backwards to paint Judaism and paganism with the same brush and so minimize the allure of a Torah-oriented religiosity: "Beide sind Erscheinungsformen jener den Menschen versklavenden (4.3, 5, 8–9), im Vergleich zur (v. 5) ärmlichen (v. 9) Macht, die die Grundlage rel[igiöser] Existenz des Menschen vor Christus darstellte."[94]

Whatever root idea underlies τὰ στοιχεῖα (τοῦ κόσμου), Paul harnesses it to his soteriology and uses it to illustrate the common plight of both Jew and Gentile before the coming of πίστις (3.29). Paul has just described this state as one of bondage and tutelage under (ὑπό) a παιδαγωγός (3.24–25), a point which is certainly being recapitulated in

---

[90] So Burton (1921: 510–18), Delling (1971: 670–87), Carr (1981: 75–76), Belleville (1986: 64–69), Fung (1988: 181), Longenecker (1990: 165–66), Plümacher (1992: 664–66).

[91] Vielhauer (1976: 543–55), Cosgrove (1988: 75–77), Schweizer (1988: 455–68), Thielmann (1989: 80–83), Rusam (1992: 119–25), and now Martyn (1997: 395–406). This interpretation bears close affinities with the "principles of religion" interpretation, often describing the στοιχεῖα as "the law, sin, and death" (Vielhauer [1976: 553]).

[92] Schlier (1949: 133–37), Sanders (1977: 554–55), Betz (1979: 204), Bruce (1982: 204), Cousar (1982: 92–23), Rohde (1989: 131), Howard (1990: 66–82), Hong (1993: 165), Reid (1993: 229–33), Arnold (1996: 55–76). Dunn (1993a: 212–13) incorporates all three views into his interpretation.

[93] Byrne (1979: 176).

[94] Plümacher (1992: 665). Similarly Vielhauer (1976: 553), Byrne (1979: 182), Sanders (1983: 68–69), etc.

the analogy of the heir being under guardians until coming of age (4.1–3). This much is clear: Paul's elusive τὰ στοιχεῖα τοῦ κόσμου is used to illustrate the soteriological principle concerning the antiquated status of the law and affords no immediate entrée into Paul's "cosmology." Indeed, Richard Longenecker would translate τοῦ κόσμου here "worldly" or " 'fleshly' as opposed to 'spiritual.' "[95] Following the development of Paul's argument, the νήπιοι languishing under the στοιχεῖα (4.3) are set in antithesis to the υἱοί who possess the πνεῦμα τοῦ υἱοῦ αὐτοῦ (4.6), and Paul's point, as throughout Galatians, is fundamentally soteriological: the Spirit renders the law obsolete.

Galatians 4.21–5.12. The allegory of Hagar and Sarah (4.21–5.1) constitutes Paul's final major argument against "those who wish to be ὑπὸ νόμον" (4.21).[96] Paul's aim is to associate *again* the Mosaic covenant with the notion of slavery (cf. 3.21–4.11), while at the same time linking the motifs of freedom, "sonship," the promise, and the Spirit to believers as the true descendants of Abraham. As such, no one would dispute the observation of Kraus that "die Vorstellung der zwei διαθῆκαι [steht] im Mittelpunkt der paulinischen Ausführungen."[97] There is, however, some question as to which two covenants Paul has in mind. One, no doubt, is the covenant made with Moses on Mount Sinai: μία μὲν ἀπὸ ὄρους Σινᾶ (4.24). The other, it is sometimes argued, is the New Covenant – at least implicitly.[98] Against this view however, is the obvious fact that Paul does not use the phrase καινὴ διαθήκη here or elsewhere in Galatians. Moreover, Paul has already referred to God's promise to Abraham as a διαθήκη (3.15–17), and in light of the Abraham and Sinai contrast which introduces this allegory, it seems best to understand "the two covenants" of 4.24 as the Abrahamic and Sinaitic/Mosaic covenants.

But the issue is not yet fully clarified. According to 4.23, the child of the slave woman was born κατὰ σάρκα, while the child of the free was born δι' ἐπαγγελίας. In applying the narrative to his readers, Paul alters his terminology slightly and speaks of the one born κατὰ σάρκα versus the one born κατὰ πνεῦμα. This further illustrates the synonymity involved in Paul's promise/Spirit language in Galatians and again raises the question of the relationship between God's promise to Abraham and God's promise of the Spirit.

---

[95] Longenecker (1990: 166).
[96] Paul may be using the argument of his opponents against them. See Barrett (1976: 1–16), Longenecker (1990: 197–219), Kraus (1996: 234–46).
[97] Kraus (1996: 238).
[98] See Luz (1967: 319–21), Betz (1979: 242–44), Koch (1986: 205–10), Hübner (1990: 90–92).

In the analysis of 2 Corinthians 3.18, 4.6, and 5.17 (chapter 10) we observed a tendency in Paul to interpret the Genesis narrative by means of prophetic themes, and it would appear that something similar is happening in Galatians. Paul's ability to fill out the Abrahamic covenant with New Covenant motifs was not the product of an exegetical method but a salvation-historical perspective. As Paul looked back over the landscape of redemptive history, the twin peaks of the New Covenant and the Abrahamic covenant were not fully distinguishable, but what was completely obscured was the great valley of the Mosaic dispensation which lay between. Paul could conflate the Abrahamic covenant and the New Covenant because the promise of innumerable descendants (Gen. 15.5) was being achieved through the universal outpouring of God's Spirit (Ezek. 36–37; Joel 2).

As elsewhere in Galatians, it is the work of the Spirit that makes superfluous the works of the law, but here Paul specifically describes the Spirit in terms of its creative, life-giving function of making anew those who experience its presence. I noted earlier Paul's fondness for birth metaphors (chapter 5), and this same imagery has already occurred in 4.19. In this rather tortured metaphor, Paul depicts the conversion of the Galatians as a painful experience of new birth which effects the formation of Christ within them. That Paul could envision coming to faith as both an inner experience of Christ and the Spirit is explained by his description of conversion in 4.6: "God sent forth *the Spirit of his son* into our hearts."

Paul's insistence that the Galatians' Spirit-generated new existence rendered moot a nomistic lifestyle is continued in 5.2–12, as is the correlation of life in Christ with life in the Spirit. After asserting that righteousness ἐν νόμῳ severs one from Christ (5.4), Paul reminds his readers in two parallel explanatory statements that life through the Spirit (ἡμεῖς γὰρ πνεύματι, 5.5) and in Christ (ἐν Χριστῷ, 5.6) made such external boundary markers as "circumcision" and "uncircumcision" irrelevant. The Christological and pneumatological basis for the exclusion of "circumcision" and "uncircumcision" encapsulates much of the preceding argument and, as I will argue, is reiterated at the close of the letter when this same antithetical pair is again rejected by Paul (6.15).

The Spirit and the flesh (Gal. 5.13–6.10)

Given the heavy pneumatological emphasis of 3.1–5.12, it is hardly surprising that Paul's moral exhortations (5.13–6.10) are predicated upon the same basis. After a transitional segment (5.13–15) that reintroduces the category of σάρξ (v. 13) and redefines what is meant by fulfilling the law (i.e., loving one's neighbor, v. 14), Paul returns to that crucial antithesis with which he began his assault: the Spirit and the flesh.

I have addressed Paul's Spirit–flesh dialectic on several occasions (chapters 6–8), and in Galatians 5.17 we see it expressed in terms of general theological principle: "For these two are opposed to one another." This antithesis is not entirely without analogy in Jewish literature of the period,[99] though in 5.16–18 it is Paul's equation of the law with the σάρξ which calls for comment. Having just posited a sharp Spirit–flesh antithesis (vv. 16–17), the reader naturally expects Paul to conclude, "But if you are led by the Spirit you are not controlled by the flesh," in reiteration of verse 16. Instead Paul reasons, "But if you are led by the Spirit you are not *under law*," thus repeating exactly the thought of 3.3: submission to the law is tantamount to continuing in the flesh.[100] This recalls the schema outlined in the discussion of Romans 6–8, and the importance of this pattern of thought in the argument of Galatians warrants its repetition here:

grace		Spirit		righteousness		life
	> by means of the <		> produces <		> which leads to <	
law		flesh		sin		death

As demonstrated earlier (chapter 7), Paul sometimes condenses the entire law, flesh, sin, and death scenario into a single term, and this goes some way toward explicating his use of law and flesh as synonyms. To be ὑπὸ νόμον (5.18) is to live in the unaided realm of the flesh, which inevitably results in the "works of the flesh" (5.19). To be led by the Spirit is to be enabled to produce its fruit (5.23), which Paul earlier sums up with the word "righteousness" (3.21). Keeping in mind the semantic-soteriological congruity among the terms in each category, it follows that "death to the law" (2.19) could also be described as "crucifying the flesh" (5.24), the result of which could be described either as "Christ lives in me" (2.20) or "living by the Spirit" (5.25).

In 5.24–25 we meet the final death–life text relevant to this investigation, and by now its emphases should be familiar. As in all these passages, the focus is anthropological ("*those* of Christ," "*we* live," "let *us* walk") and, as elsewhere, the "life" side of the equation is interpreted as an experience of the Spirit: "We live by the Spirit" (5.24). Once again, the newness of Christian existence is summarized by the terms "Spirit"

---

[99] See chapter 8, along with W. D. Davies (1955: 17–35), Jewett (1971: 82–95), Barclay (1988: 178–215).

[100] See Romans 7.5–6; 4.21–29, and chapter 7.

and "life," which, as throughout Galatians, constitutes Paul's response to those pressing for a Torah-centered piety (5.23).

Summary

In John Barclay's view, the final Spirit–flesh antithesis of 6.8 "sums up . . . the message of the whole letter,"[101] and much of the preceding argument could be marshaled in support of this assessment. Paul began his case against yielding to nomistic pressure with "his most important argument . . . his indisputable evidence,"[102] and almost all of what follows relates in some way to the essential crux of 3.1–5: *the Spirit renders the law obsolete.* Against those who would define God's people by means of the law and the external boundary marker of circumcision, Paul argues that faith and the inner presence of the Spirit now demarcate God's people. Paul accomplishes this task by (deliberately?) conflating the prophetic and Abrahamic promises, so redefining pneumatologically the crucial terminology of the letter: the blessing, the inheritance, the promise, "sonship," heirs, and seed of Abraham. In what might be called an argument by double entendre, Paul incorporates this language into his vocabulary of the Spirit and posits a mutually exclusive relationship between these and Torah observance, particularly circumcision. In keeping with the dominant emphasis of 3.1–5.12, the parenetic material (5.13–6.10) continues to argue Paul's case on the basis of the Galatians' experience of new life by the Spirit, which is contrasted with the way of the flesh/law.

Paul's basic approach to the central issue in Galatians – the place of Torah in the believing community – was anticipated in his "biography of reversal" where he deliberately aligned the law and "his former way of life in Judaism" with a merely human, sarkic, perspective. Paul's experience of Christ *in* him (1.16; 2.20) brought an end to his externally oriented piety, and Paul expects the Galatians' experience of "the Spirit of his son in [y]our hearts" to do the same.

New creation

The procedure in this section will be similar to the approach to 2 Corinthians 5.14–17 in chapter 10. A translation of the segment under consideration will be followed by an exegesis particularly concerned to locate the text within its epistolary context. This is all the more crucial

---

[101] Barclay (1988: 164). Similarly Brinsmead (1982: 81).   [102] Betz (1976: 109).

in relation to Galatians 6.12–18, the epistolary postscript/*recapitulatio*, which "epitomizes the heart of the letter."[103] Consonant with this interest, and issuing directly from the foregoing analysis, two questions arise as a preface to the exegesis: (1) in a letter which lacks any reference to καινὴ κτίσις, why does this phrase suddenly appear in Paul's summation of the central themes of the letter?; (2) having dealt extensively and painstakingly with life in the Spirit, why does Paul fail to mention the Spirit as the crucial points of the letter are reiterated? The two questions are inextricably connected.

All those who wish to make a good appearance outwardly, (12a)
these compel you to be circumcised ... (12b)

The correlative pronoun introducing 12a (ὅσοι: "as many as," "whoever") adds a gnomic, generalizing tone to the opening clause, which is immediately focused on Paul's opponents: those "compelling" circumcision are portrayed as a specific manifestation of the universal concern for "making a good impression outwardly." The phrase εὐπροσωπῆσαι ἐν σαρκί is allusive, but not unequivocally so.[104] The importance of circumcision in Galatians, and particularly the following verse, where the opponents are said to boast "in the flesh" of their converts, has persuaded some that ἐν σαρκί in 12a refers literally to the circumcised flesh of the Galatians.[105] Without denying a certain polyvalence in Paul's σάρξ language, the emphasis in 12a lies elsewhere. It is true that σάρξ in 13b includes an allusion to the circumcised flesh of the Galatians, but there this is made explicit by the use of the personal pronoun ("*your* flesh"). This sense of σάρξ can be easily related to the verb καυχᾶσθαι in 13b ("to boast in circumcision"), which cannot be said of the verb εὐπροσωπέω in 12a: "to make a good appearance in circumcision" (?).

The anarthrous ἐν σαρκί of 12a (note the articular use in 13b), taken in conjunction with the maxim-like character of this introductory clause suggests that Paul has in mind a *sphere* which he designates σάρξ. Indeed, the phrase εὐπροσωπῆσαι ἐν σαρκί resonates back through the argument of Galatians, and the attentive reader would no doubt be reminded of Paul's "biography of reversal." There Paul portrayed his own Jewish past in

---

[103] Cousar (1982: 149).

[104] Prior to the fourth century, the verb εὐπροσωπέω occurs only in a letter from P. Tebt. 1.19.12, dated at 114 BC (see Moulton and Milligan 1930). The corresponding noun, however, is well attested. See Gen. 12.11; Aristophanes, *Plut.* 976; Lucian, *Merced. Con.* 711.

[105] So Sieffert (1899: 251), Lightfoot (1890: 222), Burton (1921: 350–51), Longenecker (1990: 291), Dunn (1993a: 336).

terms of "people pleasing" (1.10), religious ladder-climbing (1.14), and violent enforcement of the Jewish faith (1.13), and the correlation of his own past with the present activity of his rivals is hardly discreet. Paul's autobiographical comments also associated his opponents (prefigured in Peter, "those from James," and οἱ δοκοῦντες) with an inappropriate concern for mere appearances, which was specifically articulated by means of the πρόσωπον motif. Paul's refusal to allow prior religious advantages to be determinative of one's present standing reflects his own spiritual biography, as Philippians 3.2–10 also illustrates. In this passage Paul explains that he has good reason "to take confidence ἐν σαρκί" (3.3–4 [3x]), which he defines as "what I once considered my advantage" (3.7): "circumcised on the eighth day, of the people of Israel, of the tribe of Benjamin, a Hebrew of Hebrews, a pharisee in regard to the law, a zealous persecutor of the church," and so on (3.5–6). All this indicates that ἐν σαρκί in 12a refers to the sarkic realm of "humanity's value systems as they stand in opposition to God's"[106] and that Paul sees his Torah-oriented opponents as focusing on only "the external or outward side of life."[107]

But regardless of one's interpretation of ἐν σαρκί in 12a, virtually all agree that the notion of *mere* externals is implicit in this language,[108] and this is strongly reminiscent of the way Paul introduces his new-creation statement in 2 Corinthians 5. Be it "making a good appearance ἐν σαρκί" (Gal. 6:12), or "boasting ἐν προσώπῳ" (2 Cor. 5.12), both new-creation statements are introduced by means of an internal–external antithesis, and this may not be coincidental. The πρόσωπον–καρδία contrast of 2 Corinthians 5.12 suggests a σαρκί–πνεύματι contrast here, which is explicit in the parallel text, Philippians 3.3, as well as Galatians 3.3, 5.16, and 5.24–25.[109] This extended comment on the opening clause of the postscript may have belabored the obvious, but it is a point that needs to be pressed: the categories of Spirit versus flesh, and internal versus external are as prominent in the closing of the letter as they were

[106] Erickson (1993: 304). So too Zahn (1910: 278): "auf fleischlichem Gebiete"; Bonnard (1972: 129): "dans l'ordre de la chair, de l'humaine"; Balz (1992: 206): "vor Menschen *einen guten Eindruck machen* (wollen)," and others: Lagrange (1926: 163), Oepke (1964b: 159), Mussner (1974: 411), Borse (1984: 219), Eckstein (1996: 251).
[107] BAGD s.v. σάρξ, n. 6, which lists Gal. 6.12 under this heading.
[108] E.g., Sieffert (1899: 251), Lightfoot (1890: 222), Burton (1921: 349), Rohde (1989: 273), Cousar (1990: 139–40), Longenecker (1990: 291), and those cited in note 106 above. Only Dunn takes exception to this interpretation.
[109] Many see an implicit Spirit–flesh antithesis here: Zahn (1910: 281), Lagrange (1926: 163), Schlier (1949: 207), Lietzmann (1971: 44), Mussner (1974: 411), Bruce (1982: 268), Borse (1984: 219), Longenecker (1990: 291), Finsterbusch (1996: 59).

in its body, and Paul's abbreviated manner of expression does little to conceal this.

... these compel you to be circumcised (12b)
only in order to avoid persecution for the cross of Christ (12c)

In 12b Paul equates the circumcising campaign of the trouble makers with the sarkic perspective of 12a, which is but a variant of the law and flesh parity noted earlier. Paul also says that these people are "compelling" circumcision (οὗτοι ἀναγκάζουσιν ὑμᾶς περιτέμνεσθαι), which raises questions concerning the nature of this coercion and the authority of those behind it. Before reading too much into this phrase however, it is worth recalling that Peter's withdrawal from table-fellowship in Antioch is similarly described as *"compelling* to Judaize" (ἀναγκάζεις 'Ιουδαΐζειν, 2.14), so the verb may denote nothing more than an activity which exerts an unwanted influence on others.[110]

12c provides the second of three motives Paul ascribes to the agitators: the avoidance of persecution.[111] It can be reasonably postulated that those within the Jewish wing of the early church, wishing to maintain diplomatic relations with their fellow-Jews, would have recommended circumcision for Christian converts, and this to avoid the charge of apostasy.[112] Whether Paul has in mind the kind of persecution he carried out (1.13, 23) and experienced (2 Cor. 11.24; Gal. 5.11; 1 Thess. 2.14–16), or merely a cold shoulder from fellow-Jews, there is no reason to doubt that those Jewish-Christians whose "gospel" entailed close adherence to prevailing Jewish customs and beliefs would have experienced less difficulty from their peers than did Paul with his law-free version.[113] In

---

[110] See Lagrange (1926: 163), Betz (1979: 315–17), Barclay (1988: 46 n. 27).

[111] The others are found in 12a (to make a good appearance outwardly) and 13b (to boast "in the flesh" of the Galatians). Paul's ascription of motives to his opponents is problematic. Compare the divergent evaluations of Borse (1984: 220), Longenecker (1990: 290–91), and Dunn (1993a: 336).

[112] Although there is some evidence for a softening of the requirement of circumcision for Jewish converts in segments of Diaspora Judaism (e.g., Josephus, *Ant.* 20.2.4; Philo, *Quaest. Gen.* 3.46–52; cf. McEleney [1973–74: 319–41]), it was generally regarded as necessary: Esth. 8.17 (LXX); Judith 14.10; Josephus, *Vita* 23; *Ant.* 13.9.1; 13.11.3; 20.2.4; *JW* 2.17.10; Philo, *Migr. Abr.* 89–93. In the Maccabean period circumcision became an important sign of fidelity to the the covenant: 1 Macc. 1.60–61; 2.46; 2 Macc. 6–7. See Nolland (1981: 173–94), Millar in Schürer (1986: 168), Barclay (1988: 45–60), T. Schreiner (1993b: 138).

[113] See Rowland (1985: 26): "It is essential to grasp the central importance of this rite [circumcision] as a sign of membership of the covenant people to understand the strength of feeling generated by Paul's decision not to insist on circumcision for his Gentile converts to Christianity."

linking this "persecution" with the cross of Christ Paul probably has in mind "the scandal of the cross" (5.11), that is, a crucified messiah (2.19; 3.1; 3.13).

For not even those who are circumcised keep the law (13a)

The identity of the referents behind the present participle οἱ περιτεμνόμενοι is disputed, though most believe the vague expression "those who are circumcised" – while not without wider implications – is directed primarily at Paul's Judaizing opponents.[114] The accusation of failure to keep the law has been understood by some as an indication that the Judaizers were selective in observance of the Torah,[115] though there is little in the argument of Galatians to support such a view.[116] The charge itself was commonplace in intrasectarian Jewish rhetoric[117] and is echoed elsewhere in Paul's letters.[118] It has also been conjectured that, in Paul's view, his opponents were less scrupulous in their performance of the law than he was in his days as a pharisee.[119] Equally likely, however, is that this verse reflects Paul's skepticism concerning human ability to fulfill the requirements of the law.[120]

---

[114] E.g., Lagrange (1926: 163), Schlier (1949: 207), Bonnard (1972: 129), Mussner (1974: 412–13), Betz (1979: 316–17), Bruce (1982: 269–70), Rohde (1989: 274–45), Howard (1990: 17–19), Longenecker (1990: 292–93). The position of Burton that οἱ περιτεμνόμενοι refers to Gentiles who accept circumcision entails the insurmountable difficulty of supposing that the subjects of the verbs θέλουσιν, ἀναγκάζουσιν, and διώκωνται in verse 12 and θέλουσιν and καυχήσωνται in 13b are the Judaizers, while the subject of φυλάσσουσιν 13a is their converts. See also Dunn (1993a: 338–39). Munck argues that the present participle indicates that Paul's own Gentile converts are the Judaizers (1959: 87–90). This proposal has convinced few and two points are commonly made: (1) Munck has pressed the contemporaneous aspect of the present participle beyond all reasonable bounds; (2) had this been Paul's meaning, he probably would have written οἱ ἐν ὑμῖν περιτμηθέντες.

[115] See Jewett (1971: 207–8), Schmithals (1972: 32–34).

[116] With, e.g., Barclay (1988: 60–65), Howard (1990: 14–17), Hong (1993: 107–10), Finsterbusch (1996: 57–60). Paul's sustained polemic against "works of the law," his repeated attempts to subordinate the law to the promise (chapters 3–4), and his appeal in 4.21 to "you who want to be under the law" count against this view. Indeed, 6.13 would not be an accusation unless the Galatians expected the opposing missionaries to be keeping the law in its entirety.

[117] Matt. 23.3; John 5.45–48; 8.31–59; Acts 7.53; *Pss. Sol.* 4.1–8; *1 Enoch* 99.2; *Jub.* 6.33–38; 1QH 4.7–12; CD 1.10–21; 4Q267; 1QpHab; 4Q171, etc.

[118] Romans 1.8–3.20; 3.23; 7.7–25.

[119] See Barclay (1988: 65), Longenecker (1990: 293).

[120] So too Sieffert (1899: 355), Oepke (1964b: 159), Liebers (1989: 80–82), Rohde (1989: 274), Howard (1990: 15–16), Longenecker (1990: 293), Dunn (1993a: 338–39), Hong (1993: 108), T. Schreiner (1993a: 64–65). Although provision was made for transgression, the obligation of complete obedience was still in place (Gal. 3.10; 5.3), which no one satisfactorily discharged: Gal 3.22; Rom. 1.18–2.29; 3.9–26; 7.7–25; 11.32.

. . . but they wish you to be circumcised in order that they might boast in your flesh (13b)

Echoing the charge of 12a ("making a good appearance outwardly"), 13b narrows this generalization and applies it to the agitators: they wish only to "boast in your flesh." Paul's wording may involve a pun based on the description in Genesis of circumcision as "the covenant in your flesh,"[121] though his opponents would have hotly contested the way Paul construes it, and them. Given the tight connection in verse 13 between keeping the law, circumcision, and "boasting in the flesh," Liebers is on firm ground in arguing that Paul's criticism of his opponents is that "die *Tora* die Instanz ist, auf die sie sich verlassen."[122] Philippians 3.3–6 supports this judgment where, in a similar warning against Judaizers, Paul speaks of his former "confidence ἐν σαρκί," defined in part as "blamelessness in the law." This may not warrant a direct correlation between "boasting in circumcision/your flesh" and "boasting in the law" (Rom. 2.23), but the two are clearly related (see below).

Here, the apostle equates zeal for the law with a sarkic perspective so external in its orientation it could be described as delighting merely in the foreskin of the convert. This caustic appraisal echoes Paul's earlier evaluation of his own "former way of life in Judaism" (1.10–14), and further illustrates Paul's determination to align Torah-advocacy with misguided zeal, people pleasing, and a *merely* human religiosity. His biting, even crass polemic brings to a climax the apostle's parity of law and flesh, and does so in crudely physical terms (cf. 5.12). This language heightens the ensuing contrast, which begins with the familiar Pauline motif of proper boasting.

But as for me, may I never boast, save in the cross of our lord Jesus Christ (14a)

The emphatically positioned first-person pronouns that characterize verse 14 (ἐμοί . . . ἐμοί . . . κἀγώ) signal a return to autobiography, and allow Paul to place himself in dramatic antithesis to "them" of the preceding verses. This contrast is strengthened through a forceful μὴ γένοιτο, which rejects any possibility of a sarkic boast (13b) from Paul.[123] Yet centuries of Christian veneration of the cross has had the effect of stifling the irony

---

[121] Gen. 17.11–14. The phrase is also found in Sir. 44.20; *Jub.* 15.13–34; *Lib. Ant.* 9.15; cf. Barclay (1988: 180).

[122] Liebers (1989: 74). Cf. Oepke (1964b: 160).

[123] In all of its fourteen occurrences in Paul's letters μὴ γένοιτο rejects a possible, but incorrect, inference from Paul's teaching. Cf. Rom. 3.4, 6, 31; 6.2, 15; 7.7, 13; 9.14; 11.1, 11; 1 Cor. 6.15; Gal. 2.17; 3.21.

of Paul's boast. For Paul the cross was the supreme example of God's foolishness that mocked human wisdom:

> For the word of the cross is folly to those who are perishing, but to us who are being saved it is the power of God ... For since, in the wisdom of God, the world through its wisdom did not know God, God was pleased to save those who believe, through the foolishness of what was preached.   (1 Cor. 1.18, 21)

Paul's point in 1 Corinthians is that "no flesh may boast before God" (1.29), so he closes, appropriately, with the Jeremianic dictum, "Let the one who boasts, boast in the Lord" (1.31; cf. 3.21; 2 Cor. 10.17). The influence of Jeremiah 9.22–23 on the motif of boasting in Paul is widely acknowledged,[124] and the passage itself is often cited in relation to Galatians 6.14.[125] Its pertinence, however, is not limited to verse 14, as the later analysis will demonstrate.

... through which the world has been crucified to me, and I to the world (14b)

"To assert that the world has been crucified," writes Paul Minear, "is surely an enigma."[126] C. F. D. Moule makes a similar comment in his discussion of Paul's "death to" expressions, remarking that in Galatians 6.14b Paul is "stretching this curious phrase to the breaking point."[127] The interpretive crux for both writers involves finding a suitable definition for κόσμος here.[128] There is, in fact, widespread confusion on this question, as the following survey illustrates:

Κόσμος as soterio-cosmology
  (1) The old aeon with its cosmic powers of sin, death, the law, and the
      flesh.[129]

---

[124] See J. Schreiner (1974: 530–42), Barrett (1986: 363–67), Rusche (1987: 116–19), Liebers (1989: 61–62).

[125] See Lührmann (1978: 101), Ebeling (1985: 264), Harnisch (1987: 282). Those commentators who do not cite Jer. 9.22–23 in their comments on Gal. 6.14 usually refer to the Corinthians passages (1 Cor. 1.31; 3.21; 2 Cor. 10.17) where Jeremiah is quoted: Oepke (1964b: 161), Bonnard (1972: 130), Betz (1979: 317–19), Borse (1984: 221), Dunn (1993a: 349), Longenecker (1990: 294), etc.

[126] Minear (1979: 395).   [127] Moule (1970: 373).

[128] The phrase "crucified to" is a Christologically intensified form of the Pauline "dying to" formula. The dative is one of relation: "non-existence as far as law is concerned, or sin, or the world" (Moule [1970: 374]).

[129] Tannehill (1967: 64–65), Brinsmead (1982: 65–67), Bruce (1982: 272), Dunn (1993a: 340), Hong (1993: 88–89).

Κόσμος as ecclesiology

(2) "Κόσμος . . . ist weder 'streng anthropologisch noch kosmologisch' zu verstehen. Es handelt sich vielmehr um einen ekklesiologischen Gebrauch."[130]

Κόσμος as soterio-anthropology

(3) The flesh as physical passions and "worldly" aspirations.[131]
(4) The law as an antiquated salvation-historical principle.[132]
(5) The world as a system of values: its sarkic standards and perspectives, particularly in reference to Paul's former way of life in Judaism and his previous orientation as a pharisee.[133]

Some of these suggestions can be dismissed more easily than others. The primary support offered for an ecclesiological definition of κόσμος (2) is an ecclesiological definition of καινή κτίσις, which will be disputed below. If we exclude the notion of physical passions, which is not involved in Paul's use of σάρξ in 6.12–13, (3) ("worldly aspirations") can be combined with (5). Deciding between (1), (4), and (5) is difficult, not least because each can claim support elsewhere in Paul's letters, and represents a different aspect of Paul's soteriology, broadly understood. *If* κόσμος stands in antithesis to καινή κτίσις, and *if* καινή κτίσις is equivalent to "the new age," (1) is certainly the best choice. I will argue against both of these conditions, yet (1) is still a viable option. Paul speaks of deliverance from "the present evil age" in 1.4, and also describes the law as one of the στοιχεῖα τοῦ κόσμου (4.3, 9). Unfortunately for this interpretation, 1.4 is rather remote from the present context, and the phrase στοιχεῖα τοῦ κόσμου is not only widely disputed, it can also be read in support of (4) as illustrating the salvation-historical principle of the obsolescence of the law, which is the main thrust of 3.1–5.1. The specific context points toward a composite of (4) and (5).

---

[130] Kraus (1996: 250), including a citation of Mussner.
[131] Sieffert (1899: 358), Lagrange (1926: 165), Bultmann (1952: 235; 256–57), Lull (1980: 115).
[132] Zahn (1910: 283), Lietzmann (1971: 45), Bonnard (1972: 130 n. 1), Mussner (1974: 414–416), Weder (1981: 207), Liebers (1989: 74), Cf. Borse (1984: 221).
[133] Lightfoot (1890: 223), Burton (1921: 354), G. Schneider (1959: 155–56), Oepke (1964b: 261), Moule (1970: 373), Bonnard (1972: 130), Beker (1980: 206), Harnisch (1987: 283), Longenecker (1990: 295). See Gaventa (1986a: 28). J. L. Martyn (1997) might be cited here, in that in his comments on this verse he asserts, "Paul suffered the loss of the nomistic cosmos in which he had been living . . . The crucifixion of Christ . . . was now the crucifixion of Paul's cosmos, everything he had held sacred or dependable" (p. 564). Yet later he expands this to mean, "The world that is now passé is not Judaism as such, but rather the world of *all* religious differentiation" (p. 565; similarly, p. 571). Unfortunately, Martyn never explains what he means by "*all* religious differentiation." Given that so much of Paul's theology and mission is predicated on the basis of some kind of religious differentiation (error/truth, salvation/destruction, believers/unbelievers, and so on), Martyn's proposal is difficult to accept.

The first point to note is that Paul defines the term κόσμος by means of the phrases which bracket it: "boasting in your flesh" (13b), and "circumcision and uncircumcision" (15a). In contrast to those who boast in the flesh/circumcision (13b), Paul boasts in the cross, through which the κόσμος has been crucified.[134] The implicit identification of κόσμος with the preceding σάρξ (circumcision) is hard to miss, so many commentators feel obliged to mention "the flesh" in their definition of κόσμος.[135] The crucifixion of the κόσμος is then immediately and explicitly identified as the negation of "circumcision and uncircumcision" (15a), as Klaiber explains: "Περιτομή und ἀκροβυστία repräsentieren zusammen den Kosmos, dem Paulus gekreuzigt ist."[136] So, the "cosmos" which no longer exists for Paul is defined *on either side* in terms of the requirement of circumcision and this must be an essential component of any definition of this word.

The rejection of circumcision, of course, is one of the main themes of Galatians, and cannot be separated from Paul's dismissal of the law. Because Paul has already flatly equated his "crucifixion" with his "death to the law" (2.19; cf. Rom. 7.4–6), many believe the term κόσμος in 6.14 is merely a clever circumlocution for the word νόμος.[137] Yet the very choice of the word κόσμος suggests a larger principle, so it would be a mistake to reduce the term simply to "the law." The autobiographical character of these closing verses invites us to look back at Paul's "biography of reversal" with its formerly–now antithesis. In these opening chapters Paul describes not only his severance from the law, but also the rejection of his "former way of life in Judaism" as one of people pleasing, religious ambition, and violent enforcement of a distinctively Jewish lifestyle (1.10–14). This picture is corroborated by Philippians 3.2–11, where Paul similarly depicts his former "confidence in the flesh" in terms of his Jewish descent, his status as a pharisee, his blamelessness in the law, and his persecution of the church. All of this, moreover, is offered by way of contrast to Paul's present orientation as one who "boasts in Christ" (Phil. 3.3). We have good reason then, for seeing Paul's severance from law, along with the rejection of his privileged religious position as a pharisee, crystallized

---

[134] With most, the antecedent of δι' οὗ is probably "the cross," not "our Lord Jesus Christ," but this decision has little effect on one's exegesis. Cf. the contrasting views of Mussner (1974: 414) and Dunn (1993a: 334).

[135] See Sieffert (1899: 359), G. Schneider (1959: 155–56), Mussner (1974: 414), Bruce (1982: 271), Longenecker (1990: 294–95).

[136] Klaiber (1982: 98). So too Lightfoot (1890: 224), Lagrange (1926: 165), Cole (1965: 234), Mussner (1974: 415), Betz (1979: 320), Minear (1979: 397), Rohde (1989: 276). I assume here, with the majority, that περιτομή and ἀκροβυστία refer to the requirement of circumcision, and not to ethnic groups. This position will be defended below.

[137] E.g., Lietzmann (1971: 45), Weder (1981: 207), Liebers (1986: 74 n. 78).

in the phrase "the world has been crucified to me," in that Paul viewed his former Jewish world of "circumcision and uncircumcision" as a world of "making a good appearance outwardly" (12a). In other words, the "world" which ended for Paul was the only "world" he had ever known: his "former way of life in Judaism" (1.13). Keeping in mind the paradigmatic function of his autobiographical remarks, Paul's phraseology in 14b is not as enigmatic as some have alleged. The inclusive, even generic word κόσμος allows the Galatians to hear their own story as Paul narrates his, and contains an implicit plea for them to reject the nomistic world which the opposing missionaries offered. Having already equated Torah-observance with the Galatians' former pagan practices, explaining *both* as slavery under the στοιχεῖα τοῦ κόσμου (4.1–11), the Galatians could hardly have missed Paul's point.

Yet Paul speaks not only of a crucified world, but also of a crucified "I." Indeed, if the emphatically placed pronouns are to be given due weight, it is here where the emphasis lies (cf. 2.19–20).[138] This language of dual crucifixion highlights the idea of a complete and irrevocable severance, and is particularly important if, as Dunn believes, the main thought of verse 14 is "rephrased" in the verse that follows.[139]

For neither circumcision, nor uncircumcision count for anything; (15a)

Introduced as an explanation (γάρ) of the crucifixion of 14b, verse 15 defines this crucifixion as the abrogation of περιτομή and ἀκροβυστία. This language, however, admits of two interpretations, both of which occur elsewhere in Galatians. In 2.7–9 Paul speaks of "the circumcision" and "the uncircumcision" (note the articular nouns) in reference to Jews and Gentiles, and some attempt to read Galatians 6.15a in light of these.[140] The more usual interpretation, however, relates this language to the rite of circumcision or the state of being circumcised or uncircumcised,[141] and this is undoubtedly the better alternative. Twice in verses 12 and 13

---

[138] Against Tannehill (1967: 64), the significance of these emphatic pronouns cannot be reduced simply to a matter of Paul distinguishing himself from his rivals *and nothing more*. See Betz (1979: 318), Weima (1994: 156–63); also Barclay (1988: 102), "Paul's statement that the cosmos was crucified *to me* (ἐμοί 6.15) demonstrates that this event is primarily conceived in anthropological rather than physical terms."

[139] Citing Dunn (1993a: 342). Similarly G. Schneider (1992: 360).

[140] E.g., Zahn (1910: 282), Stuhlmacher (1967: 3), Baumgarten (1975: 169), Cousar (1982: 156; 1990: 146), Klaiber (1982: 98), G. Schneider (1992: 360).

[141] E.g., Sieffert (1899: 358), Burton (1921: 355), Lagrange (1926: 165), Bonnard (1972: 130), Betz (1979: 230), Bruce (1982: 273), Rohde (1989: 276), Longenecker (1990: 297), Dunn (1993a: 342); BAGD, s.v. ἀκροβυστία, 2 and περιτομή, 2.

Paul speaks of *the rite* of circumcision which is being forced upon the Galatians, and this with direct reference to the foreskin of the convert (13b). Given the forceful and unambiguous language of the immediate context, it is extremely unlikely that, without any indication, Paul's focus would suddenly shift in verse 15. Moreover, apart from in 2.7–9, Paul's circumcision/uncircumcision terminology in Galatians refers either to the *rite* of circumcision or to the *state* of being circumcised or uncircumcised (2.12; 5.2–11; 6.11–13), as do the important parallel texts, Galatians 5.6 and 1 Corinthians 7.19. In both of these passages Paul employs the formula "neither circumcision nor uncircumcision, but...," and in neither is there any doubt that Paul has in mind the rite or state of circumcision/uncircumcision. Finally, had Paul intended a contrast between Jew and Gentile, he could have easily made this apparent by using the terms Ἰουδαῖος and Ἕλλην, as he does when contrasting these two in 3.28, Romans 10.12, 1 Corinthians 1.20–22, and 1 Corinthians 12.13.

Because the phrase "neither circumcision nor uncircumcision" is poised in antithesis to "new creation" it is crucial that this idea be defined as closely as possible. The parallel passages, which contrast this pair with "faith working through love" (Gal. 5.6), and "keeping God's commands" (1 Cor. 7.19), offer some help, and indicate that this formulaic antithesis highlights what Paul believes to be of more fundamental significance. Paul's choice of verbs in these texts makes this especially clear: ἡ περιτομὴ οὐδέν ἐστιν... (1 Cor. 7.19); οὔτε περιτομή τι ἰσχύει... (Gal. 5.6); οὔτε γὰρ περιτομή τί ἐστιν... (Gal. 6.15). The context of the Galatian postscript, with its accusations of "making a good appearance outwardly" (v. 12), and "boasting in the flesh/circumcision" (v. 13), suggests that the "appearance versus reality" motif is receiving one final airing in verse 15, and that Paul's dismissal of "circumcision" and "uncircumcision" as irrelevant relates to his insistence on the priority of internal versus external considerations.[142] These same themes (proper/improper boasting, circumcision/uncircumcision, internal over external) converge elsewhere in Paul's letters (Rom. 2.17–29; Phil. 3.2–11), and this pattern of thought has its clearest theological antecedent in the prophecies of Jeremiah. A brief discussion of Jeremiah 9.22–25 and its application by Paul will shed valuable light on Galatians 6.12–16.

---

[142] So also Lightfoot (1890: 224) "external distinctions"; Oepke (1964b: 162) "Äußerlichkeiten"; Cole (1965: 234), "outward states"; Longenecker (1990: 297) "external expressions".

Excursus: boasting in Paul and Jeremiah

I noted earlier the influence of Jeremiah 9.22–23 on the motif of boasting in Paul, and this is nowhere disputed. What has not been recognized, however, is that Paul read Jeremiah 9.22–23 in conjunction with the verses that follow, 9.24–25, and so linked "boasting in the flesh/boasting in the Lord" with the rejection of external boundary markers such as "circumcision" and "uncircumcision." The text from the LXX is important enough to cite in full:

[22] Let not the wise boast in their wisdom
    nor the strong in their strength
    nor the wealthy in their wealth.

[23] Rather, the one who boasts should boast in this:
    that they know and understand that I am the Lord
    who practices mercy and judgment and righteousness
        upon the earth.

[24] Behold, the days are coming, says the Lord,
    when I will visit [destruction] upon all those
        circumcised, but really uncircumcised:[143]
25   upon Egypt, Judah [!], Edom, and the sons of Ammon, upon Moab ...

    For all the nations are uncircumcised in σαρκί,
    and the whole house of Israel is uncircumcised in καρδία.

Jeremiah 9.22–23 sum up what Paul calls "boasting in the flesh" (2 Cor. 11.18; Phil. 3.3), and "boasting in the Lord" (Rom. 15.17; 1 Cor. 3.21; 15.31; 2 Cor. 10.17; Gal. 6.14; Phil. 2.16; 3.3), respectively. The distinction made in verses 24–25 between circumcision of the flesh versus circumcision of the heart, while not unique,[144] is taken one step further by Jeremiah in that it is employed not only to stress the primacy of inner religion over its outer expression, but also to impugn the significance of the external rite and so eliminate the special status of Israel: *Judah is placed second in the list of pagan nations.* The line of thought in Jeremiah 9.22–25 (improper confidence → proper confidence → spiritual circumcision) is replicated in Paul (e.g., Rom. 2.17–29; Gal. 6.12–15; Phil. 3.2–11), and as the textual apparatus of Nestle–Aland[26] and UBS[4] indicates, Romans 2

---

[143] The LXX reads περιτετμημένος ἀκροβυστίας αὐτῶν for MT's מול בערלה, "circumcised in their foreskin." The sense of both seems to be "circumcised *only* in their flesh" (so Bright [1965: 77–78], R. K. Harrison [1973: 92], Carroll [1986: 249–50], Feinberg [1986: 445], Craigie, Kelley, and Drinkard [1991: 153–54]; RSV, NIV, JB).

[144] See Lev. 26.11; Deut. 10.16; 30.6; Jer. 4.4; 6.10; Ezek. 44.7, 9; 1QS 5.5; 1QpHab 11.13; 4Q434 1.4; *Jub.* 4.23; *Odes Sol.* 7.2; Philo, *Spec. Leg.* 1.6; *Quaest. Gen.* 3.45, 48; *Quaest. Ex.* 2.2.

even echoes the phraseology of Jeremiah 9.25 at crucial points.[145] It
can be inferred that Paul perceived an effect–cause relationship between
Jeremiah 9.22–23 and Jeremiah 9.24–25 such that, *improper boasting was
the result of an uncircumcised heart.* A comparison of Romans 2.23–29
and Galatians 6.13–15 makes this chain of reasoning apparent:

	Romans 2.23–29	Galatians 6.13–15
Improper confidence	boasting in the law, while breaking it (23–25)	boasting in "circumcision" while breaking the law (13)
⇓		
Proper confidence	keeping the [true] requirements of the law (26–27)	the cross of Christ (14)
⇓	οὐ γάρ…	οὔτε γάρ…
Outer	for "Jewishness" is not about an outer mark	for neither circumcision
	οὐδε…	οὔτε…
	nor is circumcision something external, in the flesh (28)	nor uncircumcision
versus	ἀλλ'	ἀλλα
Inner	true Jewishness is an inner reality and circumcision is done by Spirit on the heart (29)	new creation (15)

Throughout this study I have made a point of allowing Paul to interpret
Paul wherever possible, and we can take for granted a special relationship between Romans and Galatians.[146] Without downplaying the differences between these two letters, the similarity of themes, illustrations, Old
Testament material, and so on, often makes Romans the best commentary on Galatians, and this is particularly evident in the passages above,
which share the same structure, pattern of thought, phraseology, themes,
and aim. This comparison has obvious relevance to Paul's new-creation
motif, and supports Segal's interpretation of Paul's "neither circumcision
nor uncircumcision" antithesis: "His point is that circumcision without
transformation is contradictory to Christian faith."[147]

[145] Compare Rom. 2.25 and 29 with Jer. 9.25.

[146] This is a common assumption among interpreters of Paul's letters, though it is explained in a number of ways. For three recent, but different interpretations of the connection between Romans and Galatians, compare Hübner (1984), Boers (1994), and Morgan
(1995: 60–77).

[147] Segal (1990: 209).

What matters is new creation! (15b)

In relation to Galatians 6.15, Paul's new-creation motif has been interpreted along three lines, roughly parallel to the interpretation of the preceding κόσμος:

(1) Καινὴ κτίσις as ecclesiology
   "Versteht man nämlich καινὴ κτίσις im Gesamtzusammenhang des Gal, und d.h. im Rahmen der zentralen Aussage 3.26–29, so ist er als Ausdruck zu verstehen, der die durch Christus gesetzte *Gemeindewirklichkeit* beschreibt."[148]

(2) Καινὴ κτίσις as soterio-cosmology
   "As the antithetical opposite [to κόσμος], the new-creation must therefore mean the age to come (cf. Rom. 8.19–22 and 2 Cor. 5.17). . . . the old world [is] replaced through the apocalyptic shift of the cross by the new creation."[149]

(3) Καινὴ κτίσις as soterio-anthropology
   "The concept is not merely exaggerated imagery, but it interprets Paul's anthropology . . . Through the Christ-event the Christian is enabled to participate in the new human existence 'in Christ' which in Galatians is described as 'the fruit of the Spirit' in all its manifestations."[150]

I noted at the close of chapter 10 that an anthropological reading of καινὴ κτίσις in 2 Corinthians 5.17 should not be determinative for Galatians 6.15, and this point is illustrated by several studies which interpret the phrase anthropologically in 2 Corinthians 5, while soteriocosmologically in Galatians 6.[151] Yet there are some remarkable similarities between the two passages, and these deserve consideration: death–life symbolism, boasting in appearances, "the flesh," and "cosmic" imagery.[152] Moreover, the two new-creation statements are syntactically identical, being formulated absolutely without subject, verb, or article: new creation! This initial list of correspondences will be augmented later, and demands that options (1) and (2) be subjected to close scrutiny.

---

[148] Kraus (1996: 250–51). So too, Baumbach (1979: 198), Cousar (1982: 154–56), Klaiber (1982: 97–101), Hong (1993: 148).

[149] Dunn (1993b: 49). So too G. Schneider (1959: 146–48), Tannehill (1967: 65), Minear (1979: 71–73), Brinsmead (1982: 65–67), Bruce (1982: 273), Barclay (1988: 101–4), Cosgrove (1988: 77, 180–83), Fung (1988: 308), Mell (1989: 316–18), Cousar (1990: 143–45), Weima (1994: 169–71). Martyn (1997: 570–74) combines elements of (1) and (2).

[150] Betz (1979: 319–20). Though variously nuanced, see also Sieffert (1899: 359), Lightfoot (1890: 223–24), Burton (1921: 355), Lagrange (1926: 165–66), Bonnard (1972: 130–31), Reumann (1973: 97), Mussner (1974: 414), Chilton (1977/78: 312), Weder (1981: 207), Borse (1984: 222), Rohde (1989: 277), Longenecker (1990: 296), Segal (1990: 147, 263), Friederich (1996: 2732), etc.

[151] See G. Schneider (1959, 1992), H.-W. Kuhn (1966: 50), Tannehill (1967: 62–69), Mell (1989), Kraus (1996: 256–61).

[152] See Baumgarten (1975: 169), Klaiber (1982: 95–97).

Option (1) rests on a twofold foundation: (a) a reading of Galatians which emphasizes ecclesiology (the Jew–Gentile question) to the virtual exclusion of soteriology (the faith versus law question), and (b) a close correlation of Galatians 3.28 with 6.15. In line with the history of interpretation of Galatians, I have argued against (a), though without denying the importance of the Jew–Gentile issue (see further below). In relation to (b), it must be emphasized that the content, aim, and symbolism of 3.28 is very different from 6.15, so the commonplace speech structure, "neither . . . nor," proves an inadequate bridge between the two. The symbolism of 6.14–15 is death/life, whereas the foundational metaphor of Galatians 3.28 is that of baptism, *which in this passage is not related to the death–life scenario.* The baptismal metaphor is capable of numerous applications by Paul (cf. 1 Cor. 10.2; 12.13) and is not intrinsically connected to the motif of dying and rising with Christ. The logic and aim of Galatians 6:14–15 is *death → life → newness,* whereas the logic and aim of Galatians 3.28 is *baptism → reclothing → oneness.* These two texts are making entirely different points, and whatever similarities may exist between them are more superficial than substantive.

In relation to (2), all the essential components of a soterio-cosmological definition of καινὴ κτίσις are included in Dunn's enunciation above: (a) a "cosmos" and new-creation antithesis, (b) an equation of the "new age" with "new creation," (c) an opaque reference to "apocalyptic." Regarding (a), one important question needs to be asked: why should καινὴ κτίσις correspond to κόσμος in verse 14 and not to ἐγώ? In verse 14 Paul's personal pronouns are placed in the emphatic position (ἐμοί . . . ἐμοί . . . κἀγώ), while in verse 15 new creation receives the emphasis, and it seems only reasonable to relate the two.[153] This reading corresponds to Paul's other death–life texts, where the new life of the believer follows from death, and is strongly reminiscent of Paul's previous autobiographical crucifixion statement in 2.19–20: "*I* through the law died to the law in order that *I* might live to God. *I* have been crucified with Christ . . . and now *I* live by faith." It is not surprising that *none* of the interpreters cited in support of (2) offer any significant comment on the emphatic personal pronouns of 6.14.

The correlation of "the new age" with καινὴ κτίσις (b) is a more complex issue, but again, one crucial question should be addressed: did Paul really believe "the new age" had dawned *extra nos* in the way that these interpreters insist? Consider the following statements: "The old world passes away as the new creation comes."[154] "The New Creation

---

[153] See Thrall (1994: 423).   [154] Tannehill (1967: 65).

has dawned."[155] Christ's death "has inaugurated ... a new creation."[156] "Paul now lives in the freedom of the new creation."[157] In the course of their exegesis, all these interpreters (and many more could be cited) not only equate "the new age/aeon" with "new creation," but they also add the definite article as if Paul had actually written "*the* new creation." Three specific points need to be made.

First, no one doubts that "new creation" describes a positive, even exuberant, *present* reality, yet Paul often speaks of the present age (ὁ αἰὼν οὗτος, ὁ νῦν καιρός, οὗτος κόσμος) and *nowhere* does he describe it in anything other than negative terms. According to Paul, "this present age" has its own god (2 Cor. 4.4), its own (false) wisdom (1 Cor. 1.20; 2.6; 3.18), its own rulers (1 Cor. 2.8), and its own ephemeral perspectives (Rom. 12.2). It is, in fact, "the present *evil* age" (Gal. 1.4). To be sure, believers experience deliverance (ἐξέληται ἡμᾶς ἐκ τοῦ αἰῶνος τοῦ ἐνεστῶτος, Gal. 1.4), though all agree that the force of the verb ἐξαιρέω here is not "to take out of" this age, but "to deliver from within" this age.[158] Paul makes this point quite explicit in Romans 12.2: "Do not be conformed *to this age*, but be transformed by the making anew (ἀνακαίνωσις) of your mind" (cf. 2 Cor. 4.16). From Paul's perspective, the newness of Christian experience was the Spirit's work *within* (Rom. 5.5; 7.6; 8.1–17; 1 Cor. 6.19; 2 Cor. 1.22; 3.6, 18; 5.5; Gal. 3.2–4; 4.6, 29; 5.25), so it is less accurate to speak of the believer entering the new age *than it is to speak of the new age entering the believer.*

Second, had Paul intended a reference to the well-defined Jewish expectation of the new heaven and the new earth, he surely would have made this apparent by including the definite article: ἡ καινὴ κτίσις. Paul, however, deliberately leaves this phrase anarthrous and this is certainly an embarrassing omission for advocates of position (2), who must resort to rewriting Paul's sentence for him.

Third, there is no use in appealing to Romans 8.18–22, for according to this passage the present age (ὁ νῦν καιρός) is one of suffering (8.18), with the whole created order (πᾶσα ἡ κτίσις, 8.22) groaning in bondage to decay and futility *in anticipation of the age to come*. The groaning of the believer – though not in bondage and futility – is related to the presence of the Spirit within while they await the redemption of their bodies (8.23).

[155] Martyn (1985: 420). Similarly Martyn (1997: 570–74).
[156] Fung (1988: 308).   [157] Weima (1994: 171).
[158] Citing Burton (1921: 13). So too, e.g., Bruce (1982: 76), Longenecker (1990: 8), Dunn (1993a: 35–36); also Betz (1979: 42) who notes, "It does not say that the coming aeon has already begun. Rather, while the present evil aeon continues, Christ's coming and the gift of the Spirit ... have granted freedom to the believers in Christ." Cf. BAGD s.v. ἐξαιρέω 2.

In other words, the Christian groans because of the "already," while the creation groans because of the "not yet."

Regarding (c), "the apocalyptic shift of the cross," two points should be noted. First, applying the word "apocalyptic" to Galatians 6.15 is extremely dubious, if for no other reason than that there are no "shifting crosses" in any Jewish apocalypse. Indeed, this use of the adjective "apocalyptic" is not easily related to the apocalypses themselves, and seems intended only to connect Paul, however vaguely, to "apocalyptic" rather than to clarify substantively Galatians 6.15.[159] This whole enterprise has recently come under sustained criticism by Barry Matlock,[160] whose work may prove to be the thin end of a large wedge. More importantly however, we have already seen that new creation has both an anthropological and a cosmological dimension in the apocalypses (chapter 3), so that simply to invoke the word "apocalyptic" and then assume a cosmological interpretation of καινὴ κτίσις is wholly inadequate.

Despite these serious deficiencies, were there no convincing alternative, option (1) or (2) might still hold some appeal. In what follows I outline the case for option (3), which more than tips the balance in its favor.

Καινὴ κτίσις in the argument of Galatians

The primary support for an anthropological reading of καινὴ κτίσις in Galatians 6.15 is its coherence within the argument of Galatians itself. Even recalling the significance of the Galatian letter closing as a *recapitulatio*, it is nonetheless remarkable how every phrase of 6.12–16 dovetails with major themes of the body of the letter. Paul introduces his closing comments with reference to "those who wish to make a good appearance outwardly" (v. 12), and this clearly picks up the "appearance versus reality" motif of chapter 2, with its emphasis on the priority of internal over external considerations. It is this evaluative framework (internal vs. external) which provides the dominant chord of the postscript, entirely in keeping with the body of the letter and the perspective of Paul elsewhere.

---

[159] The work of J. L. Martyn is the supreme example of this unbridled enthusiasm for all things apocalyptic. Martyn defines "apocalyptic" so broadly that the mere presence of argumentative contrasts in Galatians is sufficient to render this letter "fully apocalyptic" (1997: 570). Yet the difficulty with such an unrestricted definition is that when "apocalyptic" means virtually *everything*, it also means virtually *nothing*, and the very term becomes meaningless as a result. Barry Matlock's assessment of Martyn's ingenuity is entirely on target: "it seems almost as if this matter of 'apocalyptic' is something that we are stuck with, and whatever we want to do with Paul, we had better work it so that we can call it 'apocalyptic'" (1996: 311).

[160] Matlock (1996).

Closely related to this is the formerly–now antithesis, by which Paul portrayed his own Jewish past as one of people pleasing and *merely* human religiosity. Paul's rejection of his Torah-oriented way of life was the result of his transforming encounter with Jesus Christ (1.15–16; 2.19–20), and it is difficult not to see these crucial themes (formerly/now, external vs. internal) crystallized in the words "neither circumcision nor uncircumcision, but *new creation!*"

In applying these principles to the Galatians, the antithesis "Christ in me" versus Torah becomes "the Spirit in you" versus Torah, and this modification allows Paul to depict the choice facing the Galatians as one between the *Spirit* and the *flesh.* Throughout Paul's argument the agitators' demand for circumcision is contrasted with the presence of the "life generating" Spirit (3.21; 4.29; 5.25), and this in such a way as to render these mutually exclusive alternatives. Indeed, the fundamental (and nearly ubiquitous) antithesis of Galatians is that of the law/flesh/circumcision versus the Spirit, and it is more than reasonable to view this final antithesis, "neither circumcision nor uncircumcision, but new creation" within this same crucial antithetical framework.

Καινὴ κτίσις and the Spirit

While never receiving more than a line or two of comment, a pneumatological reading of καινὴ κτίσις in Galatians 6.15 has been suggested before,[161] and strongly supports the anthropological reading of this phrase. In defence of this interpretation, it should be noted that the preceding verses (6.12–15a) virtually itemize the Spirit-contrasted ideas of the law, the flesh, and circumcision, to which καινὴ κτίσις is antithetically juxtaposed. The prominence of σάρξ in this reiteration is redolent of 2 Corinthians 5.16–17 and suggests that here, as there, καινὴ κτίσις occupies a position typically reserved for πνεῦμα. Moreover, given the importance of the Spirit in the argument of Galatians *it is utterly inconceivable that Paul could summarize this letter's central themes and entirely omit any reference to the Spirit.* Writing in reference to an alleged proto-rabbinic background to καινὴ κτίσις, Hans Lietzmann spoke most clearly on this point: "aber jedenfalls hat er ihm [καινὴ κτίσις] einen eigenen Inhalt gegeben der von der Pneumalehre aus begriffen werden will."[162] In other words, Paul is only reiterating his previous crucifixion–new life statement: "We have crucified the flesh, *we live by the Spirit*" (5.24–25).

[161] Cf. Sieffert (1899: 223–24), Lietzmann (1971: 45), Betz (1979: 319–20), Longenecker (1990: 295–96), and now Eckstein (1996: 72).
[162] Lietzmann (1971: 45).

Καινὴ κτίσις and interiority

Several lines of the preceding argument converge and are supported in considering new creation and the motif of interiority. Contrasted with the outward state of circumcision or uncircumcision, new creation should be related to the inner dynamic of the Christian life, which is precisely where Paul locates the work of the Spirit (Rom. 2.28–29; 5.5; 8.9–11, 23; 1 Cor. 6.19; 2 Cor. 1.22; 3.3; Gal. 4.6). In Romans 2.28–29, which read like a commentary on Galatians 6.15, Paul again rejects the outer state of circumcision, allowing validity only to the inner state of circumcision of the heart by the Spirit. This imagery and line of thought has its theological ancestry in the prophecies of Jeremiah, and this suggests that Paul's new-creation/circumcision of the heart language should be related to that inner renewal promised by the later prophets. We have already seen how the perspective of these prophets influenced the argument of Galatians, and the prominence of the motif of interiority in their writings (chapters 2 and 8) makes its appearance in Galatians 6.15 and Romans 2.28–29 almost predictable.

Καινὴ κτίσις and new birth

Given the synonymity of new-creation and new-birth imagery in religious literature and initiatory symbolism, it is somewhat surprising that the pronounced new-birth imagery of 4.21–31 has not previously been brought to bear on Paul's new-creation language in Galatians 6.15. In keeping with the pattern of argument throughout chapters 3–5, the nomistic framework advocated by Paul's opponents (4.21) is rejected on the basis of the Galatians' birth κατὰ πνεῦμα (4.29), and this corresponds precisely to the fundamental contrast of this letter (law/flesh/circumcision versus Spirit) and the culminating antithesis of 6.15: "neither circumcision nor uncircumcision, but new creation."

Καινὴ κτίσις and death–life symbolism

The fact that καινὴ κτίσις expresses the "life" side of one of Paul's death–life equations should be regarded as more than merely prima facie evidence for an anthropological interpretation – all the more given the autobiographical nature of 6.14–15 (cf. 2.19–20). Again, Paul's death–life symbolism consistently depicts new life granted to the individual, and it is arguably more prudent to relate Galatians 6.15 to these passages than to construe this text in an entirely different manner.

But as clear as this emphasis is, the soteriological issue in Galatia (νόμος or πίστις) had ecclesiogical implications as well, and these are reiterated, albeit cryptically, in the verse that follows.

And to all who are guided by this principle, (16a)
peace and mercy be upon them, (16b)
even upon the Israel of God. (16c)

The phrase "the Israel of God" has been much debated, and I add nothing new to the discussion here. It is also possible to translate 16b, "peace upon them, and mercy also upon the Israel of God," thus distinguishing between "those who are guided by this principle" (Gentile believers in Galatia) and "the Israel of God" (ethnic Jews in some sense).[163] Most, however, reject this interpretation for the simple reason that it threatens to undo much of what Paul has been doing in Galatians.[164] The "principle" (κανών) that Paul wishes to be applied relates primarily to the rejection of such external criteria as "circumcision" and "uncircumcision." Consonant with the function of the postscript, this nicely summarizes much of 3.6–5.12, which argues that *"those of faith"* are Abraham's descendants" (3.7), not those of the law/circumcision. Rather than rejecting his earlier argument that *"you are all* sons of God *through faith in Christ Jesus"* (3.26), Galatians 6.15–16 reaffirm Paul's previous redefinition of the people of God: "You are all one in Christ Jesus" (3.26). The phrase "Israel of God," then, includes all believers, Jew and Gentile, who through faith and the Spirit are born κατὰ πνεῦμα (4.29) and so become "children of the promise" (4.28).

The importance of this ecclesiological addendum in 6.16b lies in its emphasis in the postscript being in proportion to its emphasis in the body of the letter. Most of the postscript has been occupied with rejecting the way of the law, circumcision, the flesh, and all related external criteria, and this is a fair reflection of the dominant themes of Galatians. Yet an important corollary to the main point that faith and the Spirit now demarcate the people of God, not the law and circumcision, is that it is possible to speak of an "Israel τοῦ θεοῦ" as well as an "Israel κατὰ σάρκα" (1 Cor. 10.18; cf. Rom. 2.28–29; 9.3, 6). In the former, labels such as "Jew and Gentile," "male and female," or "slave and free" count for little, "for you are all one in Christ Jesus" (3.26–29). This issue does

---

[163] Perhaps Jewish believers (so Schrenk [1949, 1950]), or the eschatological πᾶς Ἰσραήλ of Romans 11.26 (Mussner [1974: 417], Bruce [1982: 275]), or the sincere Jew "who had not seen the truth as Paul saw it" (Burton [1921: 358]); cf. Dunn (1993a: 345).

[164] So Sanders (1983: 174), Barclay (1988: 98 n. 54), Longenecker (1990: 298–99), and now Harvey (1996: 225–26).

not dominate the postscript, nor was it uppermost in Paul's thoughts in the main body of the letter. It was, however, an obvious implication of the Christocentric soteriology of Galatians, so is appropriately, if subtly, underscored before he concludes.

Conclusions and corollaries

The most important conclusions of this chapter were stated above in my defence of an anthropological reading of καινὴ κτίσις in Galatians 6.15, and these relate to the function of Galatians 6.15 as an epitome of the argument of Galatians. I will not repeat these conclusions here, but will allow the following corollaries to summarize the crucial points.

Galatians 6.15 and the motif of transformation

As a literary theme, the motif of transformation is not often discussed in relation to Galatians, though it has been recently highlighted by James Dunn,[165] and should be extended to include Paul's καινὴ κτίσις motif. In his "biography of reversal" (chapters 1–2), Paul described his severance from the law and Judaism as the direct result of the revelation of Christ *in him*, and it is this crucifying, transformative experience which serves "as prolegomena to his main argument."[166] Given the paradigmatic function of Paul's conversion narrative, it is appropriate to call this an "argument by example."[167] Paul's rejection of "circumcision" and "uncircumcision" on the basis of his own Christocentric re-creation (2.20) provides the apostolic model which the Galatians are expected to embrace as their own.

In applying this principle to the experience of the Galatians, Paul speaks in terms of their "new beginning with the Spirit" (3.3), and it is primarily a *pneumatic* (as opposed to Christological) transformation which is emphasized in chapters 3–5. Since the Galatians have received the Spirit (3.3, 14; 4.6), have been "made alive" by the Spirit (3.21–22 with 3.14 and 5.25), have been "begotten" by the Spirit (4.29), "live" by the Spirit (5.25), "walk" by the Spirit (5.16, 18, 25), and have become "children" and "heirs" through the Spirit in their hearts (4.6–7), Paul argues that the law and circumcision are no longer relevant. This entire chain of reasoning is perfectly summarized under the heading "the motif of transformation," and succinctly recapitulated in the phrase, "neither circumcision nor uncircumcision, but *new creation!*"

[165] Dunn (1993b: 118–20).   [166] Dunn (1993b: 66).
[167] Hansen (1989: 89–90). Gaventa (1986b: 313) speaks of "the motif of the imitation of Paul."

Καινὴ κτίσις and the crucified cosmos

The juxtaposition of "new creation" with "the crucified cosmos" expresses Paul's already–not yet dialectic in the boldest language possible. Yet Galatians 6.14–15 is not without analogy, and bears witness to Paul's conviction that the power of the future was operative in the "present evil age" (Gal. 1.4). For Paul, Christian experience was one of inner renewal in the midst of outer decay (2 Cor. 4.16; Rom. 12.2), and this tension is directly related to the presence of the Spirit within (2 Cor. 5.5; Rom. 8.23). In keeping with this already–not yet dialectic, in Romans 13 Paul describes the present age (τὸν καιρόν, v. 11) as one of "deepest night" characterized by "deeds of darkness," in which believers wield "weapons of light" (v. 12). More forceful is Philippians 2.15: "Be blameless and pure, unblemished children of God in the midst of a crooked and perverse generation in which you shine as stars in a [dark] cosmos." Galatians 6.14–15 fits perfectly within this pattern of thought in that it depicts, not a new world, but a new humanity living in a crucified and dying κόσμος (cf. 1 Cor. 7.31).

Καινὴ κτίσις and the Gentile mission

I noted in the introductory comments that Galatians 6.15 is often cited because of the phrase "neither circumcision nor uncircumcision," an axiom that is obviously relevant to Paul's work among the Gentiles (cf. 1 Cor. 7.19; Gal. 5.6). Indeed, Klaus Berger has recently argued that "das Phänomen der beschneidungsfreien Heidenmission für Paulus der historische Anlaß gewesen ist, die Konzeption der neuen Schöpfung zu begründen."[168] Without diminishing the importance of such historical-sociological considerations, it should also be observed that much of the argument of Galatians runs counter to this analysis.

Paul builds his case against nomistic observance, in the first instance, on the basis of his own transformative encounter with Christ which forced him to abandon his "former way of life in Judaism": "Through the law I died to the law; *I have been crucified with Christ*" (Gal. 2.19). According to 1.16, the purpose of this apocalypse of Christ "in him" was to commission him to "preach the gospel to the Gentiles." In appealing to the Galatians Paul argues in a similar fashion, though now he speaks primarily of their experience of the Spirit (but see 4.6 and 4.19). The argument that

[168] Berger (1994: 472).

the Spirit begets true children of Abraham (Gal. 3–4) is of a piece with the programmatic affirmation of Romans 2.28–29 that true circumcision is done by the Spirit on the heart, and further illustrates Paul's radical application of the prophetic notion of the interiority of the covenant. In other words, if Paul's argument can be trusted, his redefinition of the people of God in terms of Christ and the Spirit was not a *function* of the Gentile mission but its *impetus*. If, as I have argued, Paul's new-creation motif is related to these, the same can be said of καινὴ κτίσις.

Of course, if one suspects Paul of being truly disingenuous in relating his motives for preaching Christ among the Gentiles, then the line of argument sketched above will probably fail to persuade. Be that as it may, any serious defense of the alternative view is surely obliged to acknowledge that Paul himself explains the matter differently.

Galatians 6.15 and 2 Cor. 5.17

In relating Galatians 6.15 to Paul's motif of transformation, the obvious question arises as to the relationship between καινὴ κτίσις in Galatians 6.15 and 2 Corinthians 5.17. I noted earlier that some would differentiate between the two uses of the phrase, arguing for a cosmological nuance in Galatians, while acknowledging an anthropological use in 2 Corinthians. I have been mounting a case against such a distinction, and the principal evidence for this view is the striking similarities between the two passages. Repeating and expanding the earlier list on p. 222, I now offer a complete summary of these correspondences.

(1) Both passages are introduced by the appearance versus reality motif.
(2) Both passages employ an internal–external antithesis, relying particularly on the concept of σάρξ.
(3) Both passages make use of a formerly–now antithesis.
(4) In both passages καινὴ κτίσις stands in antithesis to σάρξ and occupies a place normally reserved for πνεῦμα.
(5) Both passages summarize a heavily pneumatological argument and are related to Paul's motif of transformation.
(6) Both passages have as their foundational soteriological symbolism the physiomorphic transformation symbolism of death/life
(7) The new creation statements are syntactically identical, being formulated absolutely without subject, verb, or article: new creation!

(8) Both new-creation texts are expanded either ecclesiologically (Gal. 6.16), or anthropologically-universally (2 Cor. 5.18–20) so as to preclude a narrowly individualistic perspective.

(9) Both new-creation statements contain a clear autobiographical element, and it is no surprise that they are found in the two letters which exhibit "a greater display of his own feelings than in any other portion of his writings."[169]

The striking parallels between the clearly anthropological 2 Corinthians 5.17 and the (slightly) less clear Galatians 6.15 may be taken as support for an anthropological interpretation of Galatians 6.15, yet we need not conclude that the two statements are identical in every respect. At least two discussions of these passages conclude that, while both uses of καινὴ κτίσις are anthropological, they are differently nuanced,[170] and it is this position which will be modified and defended here. In 2 Corinthians 5.17, καινὴ κτίσις explicates the preceding τις, so this verse can be legitimately translated "If anyone is in Christ, [that person is] a new creation." This stands in the same line of thought as Paul's earlier description of the "making anew of the inner person" (4.16). In Galatians 6.15, however, καινὴ κτίσις is contrasted with the external rite of circumcision (6.12, 15) performed on "the flesh" (6.13; cf. Rom. 2.28–29), and this suggests that here Paul has in mind God's new creative work within the individual which renders the outer state irrelevant: "God does not look on mere externals" (2.6).

Whether or not the distinction between inner *person* (2 Cor. 5.17) and inner *activity* (Gal. 6.15) fully persuades, one essential point remains: Paul's new creation expresses a reality *intra nos* not a reality *extra nos*, and functions as an alternative formulation of his central Spirit affirmation – *the Spirit creates life* (2 Cor. 3.6; cf. 2 Cor. 5.6; Rom. 7.6; 8.2, 10–11; 1 Cor. 15.45; Gal. 3.22–23; 5.25).

---

[169] Jowett (1859: 120) on the relationship between Galatians and 2 Corinthians, cited approvingly by Bruce (1982: 47).

[170] See BAGD s.v. κτίσις, 1.b.a, and Reumann (1973: 98).

12

SUMMARY AND CONCLUSIONS

New creation in the context of Paul's letters and the contours of his thought

From death to life

Beginning with the broader theological context, the first point to be reiterated is that Paul's new-creation motif belongs to that family of passages whose foundational metaphor is the movement from death to life, and 2 Corinthians 5.17 and Galatians 6.15 should not be treated in isolation from this crucial soteriological matrix. The examination of initiatory symbolism in chapter 5 emphasized the interconnectedness of such physiomorphic transformation symbolism, while also locating the Pauline material within a larger, universal pattern of symbolic expression. Death–life symbolism is hardly unique to Paul, and a consideration of this wider context adds definition and clarity to the same imagery in Paul's letters.

The primary purpose of initiatory rituals is to mark the initiate's transition from one status to another. While the symbolism varies from culture to culture, the common emphases of the death–life drama are *transformation* (a change of identity and status), *demarcation* (separation from uninitiated), and *empowerment* (enablement for service within a new social structure). While the focus of these life-crisis rituals is on the individual, their ultimate aim is "the transformation of raw human material into socially responsible persons."[1] The new individual is the building-block of the new community, and the perspective of the apostle Paul fits comfortably within this broader religious framework.

The discussion of death–life symbolism inevitably raised the issue of new-birth imagery, the two being intimately connected in religious symbolism from antiquity. Indeed, "resurrection," "new birth," and "new creation" are merely alternative formulations of the "life" side of the

---

[1] La Fontaine (1985: 115).

death–life equation, and the argument of this monograph is that Paul's letters provide further evidence of this common association. Although this interpretation is currently out of vogue, Paul's new-creation motif was regularly connected with the idea of new birth in earlier discussions of these passages,[2] so much so that Paul Billerbeck could simply refer his readers to his comments on John 3 rather than treat Galatians 6.15, 2 Corinthians 5.17, and John 3.3 separately.[3] The fact that the sixth-century Greek commentator Oecumenius could make this equation without argument is good evidence that he was not the first to do so: "Whether circumcision or uncircumcision, all who believe have become a new creation (καινὴ κτίσις), having buried the old man and having been born anew (ἀναγεννηθέντων) in the bath [of baptism]."[4]

We have good reason, then, to be suspicious of Ulrich Mell's peculiar methodological *presupposition* of separating new-birth and new-creation imagery.[5] Not only does this fail to appreciate the dominant soteriological metaphor of Galatians 6.15 and 2 Corinthians 5.17, the movement from death to life, it also betrays a complete lack of understanding of the interconnectedness of religious symbolism. To be sure, the simple phrase "new creation" is capable of denoting something entirely different from spiritual new birth. However, given the soteriological context (death–life symbolism), along with the prominence of new-birth imagery in Paul's letters (chapter 5), and Galatians in particular (chapter 11), Mell's *a priori* dichotomization is rash, to say the least.

The Spirit and the flesh

Without repeating *in extenso* the argument of the preceding sections, my exegesis of Galatians, 2 Corinthians, and the relevant texts in Romans demonstrates that new creation in Galatians 6.15 and 2 Corinthians 5.17 functions as an aspect of Paul's *pneumatology*. Both Galatians and 2 Corinthians 2–5 are heavily pneumatological in orientation and argument, and in both of its occurrences καινὴ κτίσις stands in antithesis to σάρξ, a position Paul typically reserves for πνεῦμα and cognates. Moreover, unless this connection is correct, the entire Spirit-driven argument of Galatians is simply left dangling as Paul reiterates his main concerns in the summation of the letter (6.12–16). However, given that "Spirit," "newness," and "life" dominate the "life" side of Paul's death–life

---

[2] E.g., Weiss (1882: 463–64), Deissmann (1892: 108), von Harnack (1918).
[3] Strack and Billerbeck (1926: 519).
[4] Translated from Karl Staab (1933: 448); cf. Titus 3.5.   [5] Mell (1989: 13).

equations, it is more than reasonable to see this constellation of ideas encapsulated in the pithy epigram, καινὴ κτίσις, and so to recognize the thoroughly pneumatological emphasis of the *recapitulatio* of Galatians. The motif of new creation, then, is one of several ways in which Paul articulates the triumph of the Spirit over the flesh, and announces the decisive demise of the unenabled "old person" (Rom. 6.6). It stands as an abbreviated form of the apostle's central Spirit affirmation: "*The Spirit gives life*" (2 Cor. 3.6; cf. 1 Cor. 15.45; Rom. 8.2, 6, 10; Gal. 5.25).

A pneumatological interpretation of Paul's new-creation motif also helps us navigate a course through Paul's indicative–imperative dialectic without running aground on either shoal. In introducing this study, I outlined the background to the current debate and made special note of Adolf von Harnack's forensic interpretation of Paul's new-creation motif. Von Harnack's analysis stood in marked contrast to the ontological interpretation of his contemporaries and established the main lines of argument for subsequent exegesis. Paul's dramatic announcement of the believer's new creation expresses his soteriological *indicative* in its sharpest possible form, and comes dangerously close to obviating the soteriological *imperatives* which permeate the very letters in which the phrase is found. Yet a strictly forensic interpretation of καινὴ κτίσις runs the risk of taming Paul's language to the point of docility, and this kind of solution is no solution at all.

It is probably better, however, to describe καινὴ κτίσις in Galatians 6.15 and 2 Corinthians 5.17 not in terms of an *ontological transformation*, but in terms of a *pneumatological restoration*, and there is more than mere subtlety involved in this distinction. For Paul, the Spirit is not an impersonal force whose irresistible will compels obedience, but a personal being (cf. 2 Cor. 3.17–18), *the Spirit of his son* (Gal. 4.6; Rom. 8.9), who guides (Rom. 8.14; Gal. 5.18), teaches (1 Cor. 2.13), groans in intercession for God's children (Rom. 8.26–27), mediates to them the love of God (Rom. 5.5; 15.5) and, most importantly, *whose promptings can be resisted* (Gal. 5.16–17, 25; 6.8; 1 Thess. 4.8; cf. Eph. 4.30). Paul's admonition to the Galatians that they "keep in step with the Spirit" (Gal. 5.25b) emphasizes the importance of personal resolve in the spiritual life, and does so while also stressing the new "indicative" of the Spirit: "Since we live by the Spirit . . . " (5.25a). On this reading, new creation refers to the new inner dynamic of the Spirit which has begun the process of restoring the *imago dei* marred by Adam's sin, and which enables those who rely on its power to fulfill the (true) requirement of the law (Rom. 8.4). Reflecting the familiar Pauline tension between the already and the not yet, the problem is solved where the problem began, in the human heart, while the created order waits in eager expectation of the full consummation of God's redemptive plan (Rom. 8.18–25).

Interiority and covenant

Continuing this line of thought, Paul's new-creation motif should be interpreted in light of the internal–external antithesis so prominent in the argument of Galatians and 2 Corinthians, and equally important in the broader religious perspective of the apostle Paul. In Romans 2.28–29 Paul makes this antithesis foundational to his perception of the Christian life and the Christian era, which is strongly reminiscent of the ethic and eschatology of Jeremiah and Ezekiel. These prophets spoke of a day when God's law and God's Spirit would indwell his people, and it is hardly surprising that Paul echoes their terminology as he elaborates his theology of the New Covenant. Moreover, Paul's "newness" vocabulary is regularly associated with inner renewal (Rom. 6.4; 7.6; 12.2; 1 Cor. 5.6–8; 2 Cor. 3.3–6), and in the argument leading up to "new creation" in 2 Corinthians 5.17, the apostle makes specific reference to "the making anew (ἀνακαινόω) of the inner person" (2 Cor. 4.16). All this suggests that new creation in Paul was essentially a reality *intra nos*, not *extra nos*, though Paul never severs personal experience from social responsibility and participation in the larger community of faith.

New creation: antecedents and analogies

An analogical versus a history-of-traditions methodology

Throughout this study I have stressed the primacy of the literary and theological context of Paul's letters for the interpretation of his new-creation motif, and it is appropriate that this cardinal rule of exegesis be reiterated as I conclude. In critical dialogue with the history-of-traditions approach to this subject, my contention is that given (1) the complete lack of relevant *traditionsgeschichtliche* data in Paul's letters themselves, and (2) the diverse use of new-creation imagery in the literature of the period and religious symbolism generally, it is more sound methodologically first to locate this motif within the context of Paul's letters and thought, and then to look for *analogies* in contemporary literature. In fact, while this monograph followed the conventional format of treating relevant Jewish background material prior to analyzing the New Testament texts, this order could have been reversed with no substantive effect on the argument.

Seen from the perspective of the history-of-traditions approach, the new-creation texts of Second Temple Judaism resemble a large connect-the-dots image lacking any numbers telling one where to begin and where to end. On the basis of this evidence alone, one can, quite plausibly, connect the dots in any number of ways, with a different picture emerging at each attempt.[6] Even more problematic, however, is the very assumption that a complex set of lines ever existed which now must be sketched-in in order to make sense of the Pauline material. These comments should not be construed as a rejection of the *traditionsgeschichtliche* methodology *per se*, but simply as a warning against employing it prematurely, circumventing the context, and effectively turning a primary source (in this case, Paul's letters) into a secondary source.

Jubilees and *Joseph and Aseneth*

In reference to the two Jewish works examined in part I of this study, my conclusion is that *Joseph and Aseneth* offers a far more fruitful comparison to the Pauline motif of new creation than does the book of *Jubilees*. Aseneth's conversion is depicted as a movement from death to life, and is unfolded through the vocabulary of "Spirit," "newness," and "life." *Joseph and Aseneth*'s use of cosmic imagery to describe conversion, along with its emphasis on transformation and new birth can all be related to the soteriological symbolism of Paul's death–life/new-creation imagery, and provide a solid foundation for comparative analysis.[7] Moreover, as the most radical transfer-symbolism available, new creation is used by the author of *Joseph and Aseneth* to emphasize Aseneth's complete and irrevocable break with her pagan past, which is precisely the context of this symbolism in Paul's letters. One might argue that because the controversy in Galatia involved the Galatian church adopting *Jewish* distinctives, new creation could not possibly refer to the rejection of *pagan* practices. It should be remembered, however, that Paul's boldest and most controversial argument in Galatians occurs in chapter 4, where he shamelessly equates life ὑπὸ νόμον (4.5) with slavery ὑπὸ τὰ στοιχεῖα τοῦ κόσμου (4.3), and so makes the Galatians' contemplated turn to Judaism a *de facto* return to paganism: "How can you again return to those weak and miserable στοιχεῖα?" (4.9).

---

[6] As illustrated in chapter 1.

[7] The chief deficiency of J. L. Martyn's interpretation of new creation in Galatians 6.15 is that he focuses exclusively on apocalyptic "parallels" and refuses to consider relevant texts from other strands of first-century literature, like *Joseph and Aseneth*.

The book of *Jubilees*, on the other hand, employs new creation in ways which contrast sharply with Galatians 6.15 and 2 Corinthians 5.17, and any analysis of this motif must be prepared to reckon with both continuity *and* discontinuity. In *Jubilees*, and throughout apocalyptic literature, "the new creation" has a concrete cosmological point of reference, and denotes God's remaking of heaven and earth. Galatians 6.15 and 2 Corinthians 5.17 cannot possibly refer to the physical cosmos, so the current consensus interprets καινὴ κτίσις figuratively as the advent of the new age. For Paul, however, new creation takes place *in Christ*, not *since Christ*, and the simplest solution is to interpret this motif soterio-anthropologically, not soterio-cosmologically. Moreover, Paul's new creation is a *present* reality, whereas the apocalyptic vision is focused on the future.

Paul and apocalyptic

But while these observations highlight discontinuity, they also allow us to speak of continuity between Paul and apocalyptic. In line with the perspective of the apocalypses, Paul believed the created order would experience renewal *in the eschaton* (Rom. 8.18–25), and the interpretation of Paul's new-creation motif advanced in this study actually brings Paul closer to the "apocalyptic" perspective than does the current consensus view. Further continuity is revealed as we juxtapose the Pauline and the apocalyptic paradigm, and note the function of the new-creation motif in each. New creation, in fact, functions similarly in each paradigm: *as the answer to the human dilemma*. But whereas the writers of the apocalypses analyzed that dilemma primarily in terms of *extrinsic* factors (Satan and the Gentiles), Paul analyzed that dilemma primarily in terms of *intrinsic* factors (sin and the flesh), which underscores again the importance of locating this motif within the broader theological framework of the writer. Pessimism, for instance, is a word used in reference to *both* Paul *and* the apocalyptic writers, but in Pauline studies it surfaces in discussions of the apostle's *anthropology*. Unlike the apocalypses of, for example, *1 Enoch* and *Jubilees*, which viewed the present historical circumstances through lenses of despair, for Paul, the events of history were moving along quite nicely: "*But now*, apart from law, a righteousness from God has been revealed *which was witnessed to by the law and the prophets*" (Rom. 3.21; cf. Rom. 16.25–26; 1 Cor. 15.4). Rather than inciting his churches against their (sometimes oppressive) Roman overlords, Paul described them as "servants of God for your good" (Rom. 13.4).

The anthropological situation, however, is differently perceived by Paul. In crossing this portal we enter the darkest cavern of the apostle's thought. It is the realm of sin, bondage, depravity, and wickedness. Its rulers are *sarx* and *hamartia*. From deep within this abyss comes the agonizing cry of Adamic humanity: "O wretched man that I am! Who will rescue me from this body of death?" (Rom. 7.24). It is true, of course, that Satan and the demonic realm represent an ever-present threat according to Paul (2 Cor. 4.4). Yet it is equally true that the apostle's most poignant, gripping analysis of the human predicament is reserved for his discussion of *the flesh*, and E. P. Sanders' comments on this topic repay close scrutiny:

> It is this analysis which is one of the main reasons why Paul can be called a *theologian*; his analysis of the human predicament (anthropology) is his principal contribution to theological thought... His penetrating observations have to do with how it is that the man who does not have faith in Christ is not only lost in a formal sense – handed over to destruction – but is even lost to himself, being unable to achieve the goal which he so ardently desires. For that which is desired – life – can be received only as a gift, so that the effort to attain it is self-defeating.[8]

The argument presented in this work supports Sanders' interpretation, and it is impossible not to hear echoes of Jeremiah and Ezekiel at this point. Their analysis of the human predicament was remarkably similar to Paul's, and it is hardly surprising that the inner renewal foretold by them is often summarized with the phrase "new creation."[9] With respect to his anthropology, Paul's theological ancestry can be traced directly to these prophets, and it is this conceptual framework which best informs Paul's understanding of the *plight* and the *solution*.

Nearly thirty years ago Klaus Koch complained that when New Testament specialists made use of the apocalyptic writings, "Questions about the context, general trend, or the author's way of thinking are not raised,"[10] and this objection is truer today than when Koch penned it. When these questions *are* raised in relation to the subject of this study, it becomes clear that new creation functions similarly within the plight and solution pattern of both Paul and apocalyptic. But because their analysis of the plight was very different, so too was their perception of the solution. Pitted against earthly and heavenly powers, the apocalyptic writers envisioned a totally refashioned cosmos. Reflecting on the dilemma of sin and inability, Paul spoke of an inwardly transformed person. Both solutions

---

[8] Sanders (1977: 509).   [9] See chapter 2.   [10] K. Koch (1972: 92).

are appropriate to the plight, and both could be adequately summarized with the phrase *new creation.*

New creation and conversion

I have argued that the Jewish romance *Joseph and Aseneth* provides a very close parallel to Paul's new-creation motif, yet it would be difficult to imagine two literary works more dissimilar than *Joseph and Aseneth* and the Pauline epistles. While there is no evidence that *Joseph and Aseneth* was a literary influence on any New Testament writer, it is true, as Burchard observes, that it provides "a witness to that Jewish heritage which helped early Christians to govern their lives, form their thought, and communicate it to others."[11] The similarities between Paul's new-creation motif and that found in *Joseph and Aseneth*, however, are not rooted simply in a shared historical-cultural milieu, but issue from the fact that both make use of a common repertoire of religious symbols to describe *conversion.* These "natural symbols," as Mary Douglas has called them, are found in countless settings and cultures throughout the globe, and are typical transfer symbols used to illustrate the neophyte's passage from one state or status, to another.

Both 2 Corinthians and Galatians, as we have seen, provide ample evidence of Paul's reflection upon his own conversion, and in 2 Corinthians 4.6 he virtually defines this as an experience of *new creation:* "The same God who said 'Let light shine from darkness' has shone in our hearts." The evidence of Paul's letters suggests that his understanding of the person in Christ as a new creation issued from his own experience in the Damascus Christophany, and if this connection is valid, a rigid commitment to the history-of-traditions methodology will almost certainly lead the exegete astray. Is it true, as Margaret Thrall supposes, that "the general idea of a 'new creation' *must* have come to Paul from the OT and contemporary Judaism"?[12] To her credit, Thrall allows her keen exegetical sense to prevail over the dictates of her methodology, so argues for an anthropological interpretation of καινὴ κτίσις in 2 Corinthians 5.17. She is aware, however, that her methodological presuppositions leave this reading somewhat stranded, so she is forced to conjecture that Paul modified the original cosmological dimensions of new creation as he inherited it from the tradition. Herein lies the danger of an exclusivistic history-of-traditions approach to Paul's new-creation motif. This methodology allows Paul to adopt, adapt, transform, and reapply the terminology of

[11] Burchard (1987: 104).   [12] Thrall (1994: 428), my emphasis.

the "tradition," but it virtually excludes the possibility that this imagery is rooted in *the single most important event of Paul's biography:* his crucifying, life-giving encounter with Jesus Christ.

This interpretation of Paul's new-creation motif is not without precedent, and was advanced one hundred years ago by H. J. Holtzmann. As I write in the centenary year of the initial publication of his *Lehrbuch der Neutestamentlichen Theologie*, Holtzmann's description of Paul's Damascus road confrontation provides a fitting conclusion to this study:

> Standing victorious on the battlefield, ruling all further thoughts, emotions, and desires with absolute sovereignty, was the newly acquired image of the glory of God shining on the face of Jesus. For Paul, this was a new light of creation, corresponding to the first light of creation (2 Cor. 4.6); a personally experienced new creation: "Behold, all things have become new" (2 Cor. 5.17) – new perspectives, new objectives, new motives, new values, a new basis for relationships, a new criterion of self-appraisal, new courage, and a new rushing current of ethical power. And as the negative counterpart to all this: a real and palpable experience of the destruction of "the law of sin in my members."[13]

[13] Holtzmann, translated from the second edition (1911: 66, vol. II; first edition, 1897). Note also the more recent work of Kim (1984).

REFERENCES

Adams, Edward. 2000. *Constructing the World: A Study in Paul's Cosmological Language.* Edinburgh: T. & T. Clark.

Alexander, Ralph H. 1986. *Ezekiel.* In *The Expositor's Bible Commentary*, vol. VI. Grand Rapids: Zondervan.

Allen, Leslie C. 1994. *Ezekiel 1–19.* WBC 28. Waco: Word.

Allo, E.-B. 1937. *Saint Paul: Seconde épître aux Corinthiens.* EBib 45. Paris: J. Gabalda.

Anderson, Bernhard W. 1987. *Creation Versus Chaos: The Reinterpretation of Mythical Symbolism in the Bible.* Philadelphia: Fortress.

1994. *From Creation to New Creation: Old Testament Perspectives.* Philadelphia: Fortress.

Anderson, R. Dean Jr. 1996. *Ancient Rhetorical Theory in Paul.* Kampen: Kok Pharos.

Antweiler, A. 1965. "Religion als Einweihung." In *Initiation*, 232–60. Edited by C. J. Bleeker. Supplements to *Numen*, SHR 10. Leiden: E. J. Brill.

Arnold, Clinton. 1996. "Returning to the Domain of the Powers: *Stoicheia* as Evil Spirits in Galatians 4.3–9." *NovT* 38: 55–76.

Artz, Peter. 1994. "The 'Epistolary Introductory Thanksgiving' in the Papyri and in Paul." *NovT* 36: 29–46.

Aune, David. 1981. Review of *Galatians*, by Hans Dieter Betz. *RSR* 7: 323–28.

1983. *Prophecy in the Early Church and the Ancient Mediterranean World.* Grand Rapids: Eerdmans.

1993. "Apocalypticism." In *Dictionary of Paul and His Letters*, 25–35. Edited by Gerald F. Hawthorne et al. Downers Grove, IL. and Leicester: InterVarsity Press.

Aymer, Albert Joseph Dani. 1983. *Paul's Understanding of "KAINE KTISIS": Continuity and Discontinuity in Pauline Eschatology.* Ann Arbor: UMI Dissertation Services.

Bachmann, Michael. 1992. *Sünder oder Übertreter: Studien zur Argumentation in Gal 2.15ff.* Tübingen: J. C. B. Mohr.

Bachmann, Phillip. 1919. *Der zweite Brief des Paulus an die Korinther.* ZKNT. Leipzig: Verlagsbuchhandlung Werner Scholl.

Bahr, G. J. 1968. "The Subscriptions of the Pauline Letters." *JBL* 87: 27–41.

Balz, Horst R. 1992. "εὐπροσωπέω." In *EWNT* I, 206. Second edition. Edited by Horst Balz and Gerhard Schneider. Stuttgart, Berlin and Cologne: W. Kohlhammer.

Bandstra, A. J. 1990. "Paul and the Law: Some Recent Developments and an Extraordinary Book." *CJT* 25: 249–61.

Barclay, John. 1986. "Paul and the Law: Observations on Some Recent Debates." *Themelios* 12: 5–15.

1988. *Obeying the Truth: A Study of Paul's Ethics in Galatians.* Philadelphia: Fortress.

1996. *Jews in the Mediterranean Diaspora.* Edinburgh: T. & T. Clark.

Barker, Margaret. 1978. "Slippery Words III: Apocalyptic." *ExpTim* 89: 324–29.

Barnard, L. W. 1993. "The Epistle of Barnabas in Its Contemporary Setting." In *ANRW* 2.27.1, 159–207.

Barnett, Paul. 1997. *The Second Epistle to the Corinthians.* NICNT. Grand Rapids: Eerdmans.

Barrett, C. K. 1953. "Paul and the 'Pillar' Apostles." In *Studia Paulina*, 1–19. Edited by J. N. Sevenster and W. C. van Unnik. Haarlem: Bohn.

1957. *The Epistle to the Romans.* BNTC. London: Black.

1968. *The First Epistle to the Corinthians.* BNTC. London: Black.

1973. *The Second Epistle to the Corinthians.* BNTC. London: Black.

1976. "The Allegory of Abraham, Sarah and Hagar in the Argument of Galatians." In *Rechtfertigung*, 1–16. Edited by J. Friederich et al. Tübingen: J. C. B. Mohr.

1986. "Boasting (καυχᾶσθαι κτλ) in the Pauline Epistles." In *L'apôtre Paul: Personnalité, style et conception du ministère*, 363–67. Edited by A. Vanhoye. BETL 73. Leuven: Leuven University Press.

Barstad, Hans M. 1989. *A Way in the Wilderness: The "Second Exodus" in the Message of Second Isaiah.* JSSM 12. Manchester: University of Manchester Press.

Barth, Markus. 1974. *Ephesians: Translation and Commentary on Chapters 4–6.* AB 36. Garden City, NY: Doubleday.

Bash, Anthony. 1997. *Ambassadors for Christ: An Exploration of Ambassadorial Language in the New Testament.* WUNT 2.92. Tübingen: J. C. B. Mohr.

Bauckham, Richard. 2000. Review of *When Aseneth Met Joseph: A Late Antique Tale of the Biblical Patriarch and His Egyptian Wife, Reconsidered*, by Ross Shephard Kraemer. *JTS* 51/1: 226–28.

Baudry, G. H. 1992. "Le péché originel dans les pseudépigraphes de l'Ancien Testament." *MScRel* 49: 163–92.

Baumbauch, Günther. 1979. "Die Schöpfung in der Theologie des Paulus." *Kairos* 21: 196–209.

Baumgarten, Jörg. 1975. *Paulus und die Apokalyptik: Die Auslegung apokalyptischer Überlieferungen in den echten Paulusbriefen.* WMANT 44. Neukirchen-Vluyn: Neukirchener.

Beale, G. K. 1989. "The Old Testament Background of Reconciliation in 2 Corinthians 5–7 and Its Bearing on the Literary Problem of 2 Corinthians 6.14–7.1." *NTS* 35: 550–81.

Beasley-Murray, G. R. 1962. *Baptism in the New Testament.* Grand Rapids: Eerdmans.

1993. "Dying and Rising with Christ." In *Dictionary of Paul and His Letters*, 218–22. Edited by Gerald F. Hawthorne et al. Downers Grove, IL and Leicester: InterVarsity Press.

Beker, J. Christiaan. 1980. *Paul the Apostle: The Triumph of God in Life and Thought*. Philadelphia: Fortress.

Belleville, Linda. 1986. "'Under Law': Structural Analysis and the Pauline Concept of Law in Galatians 3.21–4.11." *JSNT* 26: 64–69.

1991. *Reflections of Glory: Paul's Polemical Use of the Moses-Doxa Tradition in 2 Corinthians 3.1–18*. JSNTSup 52. Sheffield: JSOT Press.

Berger, Klaus. 1975. "Jüdisch-hellenistische Missionsliteratur und apokryphe Apostelakten," *Kairos* 17: 232–48.

1976. *Die Auferstehung der Propheten und die Erhörung des Menschensohnes: Traditionsgeschichtliche Untersuchungen zur Deutung des Geschickes Jesu in frühchristlichen Texten*. SUNT 13. Göttingen: Vandenhoeck & Ruprecht.

1981. *Das Buch der Jubiläen*. JSHRZ 2.3. Gütersloh: Gerd Mohn.

1994. *Theologiegeschichte des Urchristentums*. Tübingen: Franke.

Bernardi, Berardo. 1986. "Initiation and Post-Pubertal Transition." In *Transition Rites: Cosmic, Social and Individual Order*, 81–99. Edited by Ugo Bianchi. Rome: "L'Erma" di Bretschneider.

Bettelheim, Bruno. 1955. *Symbolic Wounds*. London: Thames and Hudson.

Betz, H. D. 1972. *Der Apostel Paulus und die sokratische Tradition*. Tübingen: J. C. B. Mohr.

1976. "In Defense of the Spirit: Paul's Letter to the Galatians as a Document of Early Christian Apologetics." In *Aspects of Religious Propaganda in Judaism and Early Christianity*, 99–114. Edited by E. Schüssler Fiorenza. Notre Dame, IN: University of Notre Dame Press.

1979. *Galatians: A Commentary on Paul's Letter to the Churches in Galatia*. Hermeneia. Philadelphia: Fortress.

Bianchi, Ugo. 1986. "Some Observations on the Typology of 'Passage.'" In *Transition Rites: Cosmic, Social and Individual Order*, 45–61. Edited by Ugo Bianchi. Rome: "L'Erma" di Bretschneider.

Bieringer, R. 1994a. "Teilungshypothesen zum 2. Korintherbrief. Ein Forschungsüberblick." In *Studies on 2 Corinthians*, by R. Bieringer and J. Lambrecht, 67–105. Leuven: Leuven University Press.

1994b. "Der 2. Korintherbrief als ursprüngliche Einheit." In *Studies on 2 Corinthians*, by R. Bieringer and J. Lambrecht, 107–30. Leuven: Leuven University Press.

1994c. "Plädoyer für die Einheitlichkeit des 2. Korintherbriefes. Literarkritische und inhaltliche Argumente." In *Studies on 2 Corinthians*, by R. Bieringer and J. Lambrecht, 131–79. Leuven: Leuven University Press.

1994d. "Die Gegner des Paulus im 2. Korintherbrief." In *Studies on 2 Corinthians*, by R. Bieringer and J. Lambrecht, 181–221. Leuven: Leuven University Press.

1994e. "2 Korinther 5.19a und die Versöhnung der Welt." In *Studies on 2 Corinthians*, by R. Bieringer and J. Lambrecht, 429–451. Leuven: Leuven University Press.

Black, Matthew. 1973. *Romans*. NCB. London: Oliphants.

1976. "The New Creation in 1 Enoch." In *Creation, Christ and Culture*, 13–21. Edited by R. W. A. McKinney. Edinburgh: T. & T. Clark.

Bleeker, C. J. 1965a. "Some Introductory Remarks on the Significance of Initiation." In *Initiation*, 15–20. Edited by C. J. Bleeker. Supplements to *Numen*, SHR 10. Leiden: E. J. Brill.

1965b. "Initiation in Ancient Egypt." In *Initiation*, 49–58. Edited by C. J. Bleeker. Supplements to *Numen*, SHR 10. Leiden: E. J. Brill.

Bligh, John. 1969. *Galatians: A Discussion of St. Paul's Epistle*. Householder Commentaries 1. London: St. Paul Publication.

Boers, Hendrikus. 1994. *The Justification of the Gentiles: Paul's Letters to the Galatians and the Romans*. Peabody, MA: Hendrickson.

Bohak, Gideon. 1996. *Joseph and Aseneth and the Jewish Temple in Heliopolis*. SBLEJC 10. Atlanta: Scholars.

2000. Review of *When Aseneth Met Joseph: A Late Antique Tale of the Biblical Patriarch and His Egyptian Wife, Reconsidered*, by Ross Shephard Kraemer. *Review of Biblical Literature* (http://www.bookreviews.org).

Bonnard, Pierre. 1956. "Mourir et vivre avec Jésus Christus selon saint Paul." *RHPR* 36: 101–12.

1972. *L'épître de saint Paul aux Galates*. Second edition. CNT 9. Paris: Delachaux et Niestlé.

Bornkamm, Gunther. 1971. *Paul*. London: Hodder & Stoughton.

1969. "Baptism and the New Life in Paul (Romans 6)." In *Early Christian Experience*, 71–86. London: SCM Press.

Borse, Udo. 1984. *Der Brief an die Galater*. RNT. Regensburg: Pustet.

Bousset, Wilhelm. 1970. *Kyrios Christos: A History of the Belief in Christ from the Beginnings of Christianity to Irenaeus*. Nashville: Abingdon.

Bowersock, G. W. 1969. *Greek Sophists in the Roman Empire*. Oxford: Oxford University Press.

Braun, Herbert. 1963. "Das 'Stirb und Werde' in der Antike und im Neuen Testament." In *Gesammelte Studien*, 136–58. Tübingen: J. C. B. Mohr.

Breytenbach, Cilliers. 1989. *Versöhnung: Eine Studie zur paulinischen Soteriologie*. WMANT 60. Neukirchen-Vluyn: Neukirchener.

Bright, John. 1965. *Jeremiah: A New Translation with Introduction and Commentary*. AB 21. New York: Doubleday.

Brinsmead, B. H. 1982. *Galatians: A Dialogical Response to Opponents*. SBLDS 65. Chico: Scholars.

Bruce, F. F. 1963. *The Epistle to the Romans*. Grand Rapids: Eerdmans.

1971. *1 and 2 Corinthians*. NCB. London: Oliphants.

1982. *Commentary on Galatians*. NIGTC. Grand Rapids: Eerdmans.

1988. "Paul and the Law in Recent Research." In *Law and Religion: Essays on the Place of the Law in Israel and Early Christianity*, 115–25. Edited by B. Lindars. Cambridge: James Clark.

Brueggemann, W. 1986. *Hopeful Imagination: Prophetic Voices in Exile*. Philadelphia: Fortress.

Büchsel, Friederich. 1964. "καταλλάσσω." In *TDNT* I, 254–58.

Buis, Pierre. 1968. "La nouvelle alliance." *VT* 18: 1–15.

Bultmann, Rudolf. 1947. *Exegetische Probleme des zweiten Korintherbriefes*. Uppsala: Wretmans.

1952. *Theology of the New Testament*. Vol. I. London: SCM Press.

1967. "Zur Auslegung von Gal. 2. 15–18." In *Exegetica: Aufsätze zur Erforschung des Neuen Testaments*, 394–99. Edited by Erich Dinkler. Tübingen: J. C. B. Mohr.

1985. *The Second Letter to the Corinthians*. Minneapolis: Augsburg.

Burchard, Christoph. 1965. *Untersuchungen zu Joseph und Aseneth: Überlieferung- und Ortsbestimmungen*. WUNT 8. Tübingen: J. C. B. Mohr.

1970. *Der dreizehnte Zeuge: Traditions- und kompositionsgeschichtliche Untersuchungen zur Lukas Darstellung der Frühzeit des Paulus.* FRLANT 103. Göttingen: Vandenhoeck & Ruprecht.

1983. *Unterweisung in erzählender Form: Joseph und Aseneth.* JSHRZ 2.4. Gütersloh: Mohn.

1985. "Joseph and Aseneth." In *The Old Testament Pseudepigrapha*, vol. II, 177–247. Edited by J. H. Charlesworth. Garden City, NY: Doubleday.

1987. "The Importance of Joseph and Aseneth for the Study of the New Testament: A General Survey and a Fresh Look at the Lord's Supper." *NTS* 33: 102–34.

1996. *Gesammelte Studien zu Joseph und Aseneth.* SVTP 13. Leiden: E. J. Brill.

Burge, G. M. 1993. "First Fruits, Down Payment." In *Dictionary of Paul and His Letters*, 300–1. Edited by Gerald F. Hawthorne et al. Downers Grove, IL and Leicester: InterVarsity Press.

Burton, Ernest De Witt. 1921. *A Critical and Exegetical Commentary on the Epistle to the Galatians.* ICC. Edinburgh: T. & T. Clark.

Buxton, R. G. A. 1982. *Persuasion in Greek Tragedy: A Study of Peitho.* Cambridge: Cambridge University Press.

Byrne, SJ, Brendan. 1979. *"Sons of God" – "Seed of Abraham": A Study of the Idea of the Sonship of God of All Christians in Paul against the Jewish Background.* AB 83. Rome: Biblical Institute Press.

Caird, G. B., with L. D. Hurst. 1994. *New Testament Theology.* Oxford: Clarendon Press.

Carmignac, J. 1979. "Qu'est-ce que l'apocalyptique? Son emploi à Qumrãn." *RQ* 10: 3–33.

Carr, W. 1981. *Angels and Principalities. The Background, Meaning and Development of the Pauline Phrase "hai archai kai hai exousiai."* SNTSMS 42. Cambridge: Cambridge University Press.

Carrez, M. 1987. "ΊΚΑΝΟΤΗΣ: 2 Co 2.14–17." In *Paolo. Ministro del Nuovo Testamento (2 Co 2.14–4.6)*, 79–95. Edited by L. de Lorenzi. Benedictina 9: Rome.

Carroll, Robert P. 1986. *Jeremiah: A Commentary.* Philadelphia: Westminster.

Carson, D. A. 1984. *Matthew.* In *The Expositor's Bible Commentary*, vol. VIII. Grand Rapids: Zondervan.

Castelli, Elizabeth A. 1991. *Imitating Paul: A Discourse of Power.* Louisville, KY: Westminster/John Knox.

Charles, R. H. 1902. *The Book of Jubilees or The Little Genesis.* London: Adam and Charles Black.

Charlesworth, James H. 1976. *The Pseudepigrapha and the New Testament.* Chico, CA: Scholars.

1981. *The Pseudepigrapha and Modern Research, with a Supplement.* Chico, CA: Scholars.

1985. *The Old Testament Pseudepigrapha and the New Testament: Prolegomena for the Study of Christian Origins.* SNTSMS 54. Cambridge: Cambridge University Press.

Chesnutt, Randall D. 1988. "The Social Setting and Purpose of Joseph and Aseneth." *JSP* 2: 21–48.

1995. *From Death to Life: Conversion in Joseph and Aseneth.* JSPSup 16. Sheffield: Sheffield Academic Press.

1996. "From Text to Context: The Social Matrix of *Joseph and Aseneth.*" In *The Society of Biblical Literature 1996 Seminar Papers*, 285–302. Atlanta: Scholars.

2000. Review of *When Aseneth Met Joseph: A Late Antique Tale of the Biblical Patriarch and His Egyptian Wife, Reconsidered*, by Ross Shephard Kraemer. *Review of Biblical Literature* (http://www.bookreviews.org).

Chilton, Bruce. 1977/78. "Gal 6.15: A Call to Freedom before God." *ExpT* 89: 311–13.

Clements, R. E. 1988. *Jeremiah.* Interpretation. Atlanta: John Knox.

Cody, Aelred. 1984. *Ezekiel (with an Excursus on Old Testament Priesthood).* OTM 11. Wilmington, DE: Michael Glazier.

Cohen, Shaye J. D. 1987. *From the Maccabees to the Mishnah.* Philadelphia: Westminster.

Cole, R. A. 1965. *The Epistle of Paul to the Galatians.* Grand Rapids: Eerdmans.

Collange, J.-F. 1972. *Enigmes de la deuxième épître de Paul aux Corinthiens.* SNTSMS 18. Cambridge: Cambridge University Press.

Collins, J. J. 1983. *Between Athens and Jerusalem: Jewish Identity in the Hellenistic Diaspora.* New York: Crossroads.

1984. *The Apocalyptic Imagination.* New York: Crossroads.

Conzelmann, Hans. 1975. *1 Corinthians.* Hermeneia. Philadelphia: Fortress.

Cope, E. M. 1877. *The Rhetoric of Aristotle, with a Commentary by the Late Edward Meredith Cope.* Cambridge: Cambridge University Press.

Cosgrove, Charles. 1988. *The Cross and the Spirit: A Study in the Argument and Theology of Galatians.* Macon, GA: Mercer University Press.

Cousar, Charles B. 1982. *Galatians: A Bible Commentary for Teaching and Preaching.* Louisville, KY: John Knox Press.

1990. *A Theology of the Cross. The Death of Jesus in the Pauline Letters.* Minneapolis: Fortress.

Crafton, J. A. 1991. *The Agency of the Apostle. A Dramatic Analysis of Paul's Responses to Conflict in 2 Corinthians.* JSNTSup 51. Sheffield: JSOT Press.

Craigie, Peter, Kelley Page, and Joel F. Drinkard. 1991. *Jeremiah 1–25.* WBC 26. Dallas: Word.

Cranfield, C. E. B. 1975. *The Epistle to the Romans.* Vol. I. ICC. Edinburgh: T. & T. Clark.

Crum, Walter E. 1913. *Theological Texts from Coptic Papyri.* Oxford.

Danker, F. W. 1989a. *II Corinthians.* Minneapolis: Augsburg.

1989b. "Exegesis of 2 Corinthians 5.14–21." In *Interpreting 2 Corinthians 5.14–21*, 105–28. Edited by J. P. Lewis. Lewiston, NY and Queenston: Edwin Mellen.

Dautzenberg, Gerhard. 1986. "Motive der Selbstdarstellung des Paulus in 2 Kor 2.14–7.4." In *L'apôtre Paul. Personnalité, style et conception du ministère*, 150–62. Edited by A. Vanhoye. Leuven: Leuven University Press.

Davenport, Gene L. 1971. *The Eschatology of the Book of Jubilees.* Leiden: E. J. Brill.

Davies, G. I. 1978. "Apocalyptic and Historiography." *JSOT* 5: 15–28.

Davies, W. D. 1955. *Paul and Rabbinic Judaism.* Second Edition. London: SPCK.

1957. "Paul and the Dead Sea Scrolls: Flesh and Spirit." In *The Scrolls and the New Testament*, 157–82. Edited by Krister Stendahl. New York: Harper.

Dean, J. T. 1938. "The Great Digression: 2 Cor 2.14–7.4." *ExpT* 50: 86–89.

Deidun, T. J. 1981. *New Covenant Morality in Paul.* AnBib 89. Rome: Biblical Institute Press.

Deissmann, Adolf. 1892. *Die neutestamentliche Formel "in Christo Jesu."* Marburg: Elwert.

Delling, Gerhard. 1963. "Partizipiale Gottesprädikationen in den Briefen des Neuen Testaments." *StTh* 17: 1–59.

———. 1971. "στοιχεῖον." In *TDNT* VII, 670–87.

———. 1978. "Einwirkungen der Sprache der Septuaginta in 'Joseph und Aseneth.'" *JSJ* 9: 29–56.

Denis, A.-M. 1970. *Introduction aux pseudépigraphes grecs d'Ancien Testament.* SVTP 1. Leiden: E. J. Brill.

Denney, James. 1900. *St. Paul's Epistle to the Romans.* EGT. London: Hodder & Stoughton.

Derrett, J. D. M. 1985. "New Creation: Qumran, Paul, the Church, and Jesus." *RevQ* 29: 597–608.

DeSilva, David A. 1993. "Measuring Penultimate against Ultimate Reality: An Investigation of the Integrity and Argumentation of 2 Corinthians." *JSNT* 52: 41–70.

Dietzfelbinger, Christian. 1985. *Die Berufung des Paulus als Ursprung seiner Theologie.* WMANT 58. Neukirchen-Vluyn: Neukirchener.

Dimant, Devorah. 1984. "Qumran Sectarian Literature." In *Jewish Writings of the Second Temple Period*, 483–550. Edited by Michael E. Stone. Philadelphia: Fortress.

Dinkler, Erich. 1962. "Die Taufterminologie in 2 Kor 1.21f." In *Neotestamentica et Patristica*, 173–91. NovTSup 6. Leiden: E. J. Brill.

———. 1967. "Das Bema zu Korinth." In *Signum Crucis*, 118–33. Tübingen: J. C. B. Mohr.

———. 1992a. "Die Taufaussagen des Neuen Testaments." In *Im Zeichen des Kreuzes: Aufsätze von Erich Dinkler*, 39–132. BZNW 92. Berlin and New York: Walter de Gruyter.

———. 1992b. "Römer 6.1–14 und das Verhältnis von Taufe und Rechtfertigung bei Paulus." In *Im Zeichen des Kreuzes: Aufsätze von Erich Dinkler*, 133–53. BZNW 92. Berlin and New York: Walter de Gruyter.

———. 1992c. "Die Verkündigung als eschatologisch-sakramental Geschehen: Auslegung von 2Cor 5.14–6.2." In *Im Zeichen des Kreuzes: Aufsätze von Erich Dinkler*, 177–97. BZNW 92. Berlin and New York: Walter de Gruyter.

Dodd, Brian J. 1996. "Christ's Slave, People Pleasers, and Galatians 1.10." *NTS* 42: 90–104.

Dodd, C. H. 1959. *The Epistle of Paul to the Romans.* New York: Harper.

Douglas, Mary. 1966. *Purity and Danger.* London: Routledge and Kegan Paul.

———. 1970. *Natural Symbols.* London: Barrie & Rockliff.

Douglas, Rees Conrad. 1988. "Liminality and Conversion in Joseph and Aseneth." *JSP* 3: 31–42.

Dowden, Ken. 1989. *Death and the Maiden: Girls' Initiation Rites in Greek Mythology.* London and New York: Routledge.

Dunn, James D. G. 1970a. *Baptism in the Holy Spirit: A Re-examination of the*

New Testament Teaching on the Gifts of the Spirit in Relation to Pentecostalism Today. London: SCM Press.

1970b. "2 Corininthians 3.17 – 'The Lord is the Spirit.' " *JTS* 21: 309–20.

1975. *Jesus and the Spirit: A Study of the Religious and Charismatic Experience of Jesus and the First Christians as Reflected in the New Testament*. London: SCM Press.

1987. " 'A Light to the Gentiles': The Significance of the Damascus Road Christophany for Paul." In *The Glory of Christ in the New Testament: Studies in Christology in Memory of George Bradford Caird*, 251–66. Edited by L. D. Hurst and N. T. Wright. Oxford: Clarendon Press.

1988. *Romans 1–8*. WBC 38. Dallas: Word.

1993a. *The Epistle to the Galatians*. BNTC. London: A. & C. Black.

1993b. *The Theology of Paul's Letter to the Galatians*. Cambridge: Cambridge University Press.

1998. *The Theology of Paul the Apostle*. Edinburgh: T. & T. Clark.

Ebeling, Gerhard. 1985. *The Truth of the Gospel: An Exposition of Galatians*. Philadelphia: Fortress.

Eckstein, Hans-Joachim. 1996. *Verheissung und Gesetz: Eine exegetische Untersuchung zu Galater 2.15–4.7*. WUNT 86. Tübingen: J. C. B. Mohr.

Efron, Joshua. 1987. *Studies on the Hasmonean Period*. SJLA 39. Leiden: E. J. Brill.

Eichrodt, Walther. 1967. *Theology of the Old Testament*. London: SCM Press.

Eissfeldt, Otto. 1966. *The Old Testament: An Introduction*. Oxford: Basil Blackwell.

Eliade, Mircea. 1961. *Images and Symbols: Studies in Religious Symbolism*. London: Harvill Press.

1965a. *Rites and Symbols of Initiation: The Mysteries of Birth and Rebirth*. New York: Harper & Row.

1965b. "L'initiation et le monde moderne." In *Initiation*, 1–14. Edited by C. J. Bleeker. Supplements to *Numen*, SHR 10. Leiden: E. J. Brill.

Elliott, Neil. 1990. *The Rhetoric of Romans: Argumentative Constraint and Strategy and Paul's Dialogue with Judaism*. JSNTSup 45. Sheffield: JSOT Press.

Eltester, F.-W. 1958. *Eikon im Neuen Testament*. BZNW 23. Berlin: Walter de Gruyter.

Emerson, Grace I. 1996. *Isaiah 55–66*. Sheffield: Sheffield Academic Press.

Endress, John C. 1987. *Biblical Interpretation in the Book of Jubilees*. CBQMS 18. Washington, D.C.: The Catholic Biblical Association of America.

Erickson, R. J. 1993. "Flesh." In *Dictionary of Paul and His Letters*, 303–6. Edited by Gerald F. Hawthorne et al. Downers Grove, IL and Leicester: InterVarsity Press.

Erlemann, Kurt. 1992. "Der Geist als ἀρραβών (2 Kor 5.5) im Kontext der paulinischen Eschatologie." *ZNW* 83: 202–23.

Ernesti, J. C. G. 1795. *Lexicon Technologiae Graecorum Rhetoricae*. Leipzig.

Everts, J. M. 1993. "Conversion and Call of Paul." In *Dictionary of Paul and His Letters*, 156–63. Edited by Gerald F. Hawthorne et al. Downers Grove, IL and Leicester: InterVarsity Press.

Fee, Gordon. 1994. *God's Empowering Presence: The Holy Spirit in the Letters of Paul*. Peabody, MA: Hendrickson.

Feinberg, Charles L. 1986. *Jeremiah*. In *The Expositor's Bible Commentary*, vol. VI. Grand Rapids: Zondervan.

Feldman, Louis H. and Meyer Rheinhold. 1996. *Jewish Life and Thought among Greeks and Romans*. Edinburgh: T. & T. Clark.

Findeis, Hans-Jürgen. 1983. *Versöhnung–Apostolat–Kirche: Eine exegetisch-theologische und rezeptions-geschichtliche Studie zu den Versöhnungsaussagen des Neuen Testaments (2 Kor, Röm, Kol, Eph)*. FzB 40. Würzburg: Echter.

Finsterbusch, Karin. 1996. *Die Thora als Lebensweisung für Heidenchristen: Studien zur Bedeutung der Thora für die paulinische Ethik*. SUNT 20. Göttingen: Vandenhoeck & Ruprecht.

Fischer, Ulrich. 1978. *Eschatologie und Jenseitserwartung im hellenistischen Diasporajudentum*. BZNW 44. Berlin: Walter de Gruyter.

Fitzmyer, Joseph A. 1993a. "Glory Reflected in the Face of Christ (2 Cor 3.7–4.6)." In *According to Paul: Studies in the Theology of the Apostle*, 64–79. New York and Mahwah: Paulist.

1993b. "The Spiritual Journey of the Apostle Paul." In *According to Paul: Studies in the Theology of the Apostle*, 1–17. New York and Mahwah: Paulist.

1993c. *Romans*. AB 33. New York: Doubleday.

Foerster, W. 1937. "Die δοκοῦντες in Gal 2." *ZNW* 36: 286–92.

Foerster, W. and J. Herrmann. 1965. "κληρονόμος." In *TDNT* III, 758–85.

Forbes, C. 1986. "Comparison, Self-Praise and Irony: Paul's Boasting and the Conventions of Hellenistic Rhetoric." *NTS* 32: 1–30.

Frankemölle, Hubert. 1970. *Das Taufverständnis des Paulus: Taufe, Tod und Auferstehung nach Röm 6*. SBS 47. Stuttgart: Katholischer Bibelwerk.

Freese, J. H. 1927. Translator of *The Art of Rhetoric* by Aristotle. Loeb Classical Library. Cambridge, MA: Harvard University Press.

Friederich, Gerhard. 1996. "Der Realismus des biblischen Menschenbildes." In *ANRW* 2. 26.3, 2715–35.

Fung, R. Y. K. 1981. "The Status of Justification by Faith in Paul's Thought: A Brief Survey of a Modern Debate." *Themelios* 6: 4–11.

1988. *The Epistle to the Galatians*. NICNT. Grand Rapids: Eerdmans.

Furnish, Victor Paul. 1984. *II Corinthians*. AB 32A. New York: Doubleday.

Gale, H. M. 1964. *The Use of Analogy in the Letters of Paul*. Philadelphia: Westminster.

Gaston, Lloyd. 1987. *Paul and the Torah*. Vancouver: University of British Columbia Press.

Gaventa, Beverly Roberts. 1986a. *From Darkness to Light: Aspects of Conversion in the New Testament*. Philadelphia: Fortress.

1986b. "Galatians 1 and 2: Autobiography as Paradigm." *NovT* 28: 309–26.

Gennep, Arnold van. 1960. *The Rites of Passage*. Translated by Solon Kimball. London: Routledge and Kegan Paul.

Georgi, Dieter. 1986. *The Opponents of Paul in Second Corinthians*. Translated by H. Attridge et al. Philadelphia: Fortress.

Gihilus, Ingvild Saelid. 1984. "Gnosticism: A Study in Liminal Symbolism." *Numen* 31: 106–28.

Gloer, W. Hulitt. 1996. *An Exegetical and Theological Study of Paul's Understanding of New Creation and Reconciliation in 2 Cor. 5:14–21*. Lewiston, Queenston, and Lampeter: Mellen Biblical Press.

Goppelt, Leonhard. 1968. *Christologie und Ethik: Aufsätze zum Neuen Testament.* Göttingen: Vandenhoeck & Ruprecht.

———. 1982. *The Theology of the New Testament,* vol. II: *The Variety and Unity of the Apostolic Witness to Christ.* Translated by John Alsup. Edited by Jürgen Roloff. Grand Rapids: Eerdmans.

Goulder, Michael. 1994. "2 Cor. 6.14–7.1 as an Integral Part of 2 Corinthians." *NovT* 36: 47–57.

Gowan, Donald E. 1986. *Eschatology in the Old Testament.* Philadelphia: Fortress.

Grainger, Roger. 1988. *The Message of the Rite: The Significance of Christian Rites of Passage.* Cambridge: Lutterworth Press.

Greunwald, I. 1979. "Jewish Apocalyptic Literature." In *ANRW* 19.1, 89–118.

Gundry, R. H. 1976. *Soma in Biblical Theology.* SNTSMS 29. Cambridge: Cambridge University Press.

Gunkel, Hermann. 1979. *The Influence of the Holy Spirit.* Translated by R. A. Harrisville and P. A. Quanbeck II. Philadelphia: Fortress.

Güttgemanns, E. 1966. *Der leidende Apostel und sein Herr.* Göttingen: Vandenhoeck & Ruprecht.

Hafemann, Scott J. 1990. *Suffering and Ministry in the Spirit: Paul's Defense of His Ministry in II Corinthians 2.14–3.3.* Eerdmans: Grand Rapids.

———. 1995. *Paul, Moses, and the History of Israel: The Letter/Spirit Contrast and the Argument from Scripture in 2 Corinthians 3.* WUNT 81. Tübingen: J. C. B. Mohr.

Hagner, Donald A. 1993. "Paul and Judaism. The Jewish Matrix of Early Christianity: Issues in the Current Debate." *Bulletin for Biblical Research* 3: 111–30.

Hahn, Ferdinand. 1973. "Siehe, jetzt ist der Tag des Heils: Neuschöpfung und Versöhnung nach 2 Kor 5.14–6.2." *EvT* 33: 244–53.

Hall, Robert G. 1991. *Revealed Histories: Techniques for Ancient Jewish and Christian Historiography.* JSPSup 6. Sheffield: JSOT.

Hals, Ronald M. 1989. *Ezekiel.* Grand Rapids: Eerdmans.

Hamilton, Malcolm B. 1995. *The Sociology of Religion: Theoretical and Comparative Perspectives.* London and New York: Routledge.

Hamilton, Neil Q. 1957. *The Holy Spirit and Eschatology in Paul.* SJTOP 6. Edinburgh: Oliver & Boyd.

Hansen, G. W. 1989. *Abraham in Galatians: Epistolary and Rhetorical Contexts.* JSNTSup 29. Sheffield: Sheffield Academic Press.

———. 1993. "Galatians, Letter to the." In *Dictionary of Paul and His Letters,* 323–34. Edited by G. W. Hawthorne et al. Downers Grove, IL and Leicester: InterVarsity Press.

Hanson, Paul D. 1975. *The Dawn of Apocalyptic.* Philadelphia: Fortress.

Harnack, Adolf von. 1918. "Die Terminologie der Wiedergeburt und verwandter Erlebnisse in der ältesten Kirche." In *Texte und Untersuchungen zur Geschichte der altchristlichen Literatur* 42.3: 97–143.

Harnisch, Wolfgang. 1987. "Einübung der neuen Seins: Paulinische Paränese am Beispiel des Galaterbriefs." *ZThK* 84: 279–96.

Harris, Murray J. 1976. *2 Corinthians.* In *The Expositor's Bible Commentary,* vol. X. Grand Rapids: Zondervan.

Harrison, Everett F. 1976. *Romans.* In *The Expositor's Bible Commentary,* vol. X. Grand Rapids: Zondervan.

Harrison, R. K. 1973. *Jeremiah and Lamentations*. Downers Grove, IL: Inter-Varsity Press.

Harvey, Graham. 1996. *The True Israel: The Use of the Names Jew, Hebrew, and Israel in Ancient Jewish and Early Christian Literature*. AGAJU 35. Leiden: E. J. Brill.

Hay, David M. 1969. "Paul's Indifference to Authority." *JBL* 88: 36–44.

Hays, Richard B. 1983. *The Faith of Jesus Christ: An Investigation of the Narrative Substructure of Galatians 3:1–4:11*. SBLDS 56. Chico, CA: Scholars.

1989. *Echoes of Scripture in the Letters of Paul*. New Haven and New York: Yale University Press.

Heinrici, C. F. G. 1887. *Der zweite Brief an die Korinther*. Göttingen: Vandenhoeck & Ruprecht.

Heiny, S. B. 1987. "2 Corinthians 2.14–4.6: The Motive for Metaphor." In *SBL 1987 Seminar Papers*, 1–22. Atlanta: Scholars.

Heitsch, Ernst. 1995. "Glossen zum Galaterbrief." *ZNW* 86: 173–88.

Helander, Eila. 1986. "On the Rituals of Transitional Societies." In *Transition Rites: Cosmic, Social and Individual Order*, 117–29. Edited by Ugo Bianchi. Rome: "L'Erma" di Bretschneider.

Hengel, Martin. 1967. "Der Kreuzestod Jesu Christi als Gottes soveräne Erlösungstat. Exegese über 2 Korinther 5.11–21." In *Theologie und Kirche. Reichenau-Gespräch*, by M. Hengel, F. Lang, and P. Stuhlmacher, 60–89. Stuttgart: Evangelische Landessynode in Württemberg.

1991. *The Pre-Christian Paul*. Translated by John Bowden. London: SCM Press; Philadelphia: Trinity Press International.

Héring, Jean. 1962. *The First Epistle of Saint Paul to the Corinthians*. London: Epworth.

1967. *The Second Epistle of Saint Paul to the Corinthians*. London: Epworth.

Heschel, Abraham J. 1962. *The Prophets*. New York and Evanston: Harper & Row.

Hickling, C. J. A. 1974/75. "The Sequence of Thought in 2 Corinthians Chapter 3." *NTS* 21: 380–95.

Hoens, D. J. 1965. "Initiation in Later Hinduism according to Tantric Texts." In *Initiation*, 71–80. Edited by C. J. Bleeker. Supplements to *Numen*, SHR 10. Leiden: E. J. Brill.

Hofius, Otfried. 1989. "Erwägungen zur Gestalt und Herkunft des paulinischen Versöhnungsgedankens." In *Paulusstudien*. WUNT 51. Tübingen: J. C. B. Mohr.

Holder, John. 1994. *The Intertestamental Period*. London: SPCK.

Holladay, William L. 1986–89. *Jeremiah 1–2*. Hermeneia. Philadelphia: Fortress.

Holm, Nils G. 1986. "Glossolalia as a Transition Rite." In *Transition Rites: Cosmic, Social and Individual Order*, 143–51. Edited by Ugo Bianchi. Rome: "L'Erma" di Bretschneider.

Holtz, T. 1968. "Christliche Interpolationen in 'Joseph und Aseneth.'" *NTS* 14: 36–58.

Holtzmann, H. J. 1911. *Lehrbuch der neutestamentlichen Theologie*. Vol. II. Second edition. Tübingen: J. C. B. Mohr.

Hong, In-Gyu. 1993. *The Law in Galatians*. JSNTSup 81. Sheffield: Sheffield Academic Press.

Hooker, Morna. 1990. *From Adam to Christ: Essays on Paul.* Cambridge: Cambridge University Press.

Hoover, Herbert Joel. 1979. *The Concept of New Creation in the Letters of Paul.* Ann Arbor: UMI Dissertation Services.

Horbury, William. 1992. "Jewish Christian Relations in the Epistle to Barnabas and Justin Martyr." In *Jews and Christians: The Parting of the Ways AD 70–135*, 315–45. WUNT 66. Tübingen: J. C. B. Mohr.

Houseman, Michael. 1993. "The Interactive Basis of Ritual Effectiveness in a Male Initiation Rite." In *Cognitive Aspects of Religious Symbolism*, 207–24. Edited by Pascal Boyer. Cambridge: Cambridge University Press.

Howard, George. 1990. *Paul: Crisis in Galatia. A Study in Early Christian Theology.* Second edition. SNTSMS 85. Cambridge: Cambridge University Press.

Hoyle, R. B. 1927. *The Holy Spirit in St. Paul.* London: Hodder & Stoughton.

Hubbard, Moyer. 1997. "Honey for Aseneth: Interpreting a Religious Symbol." *JSP* 16: 97–110.

1998. "Was Paul Out of His Mind? Re-reading 2 Cor 5.13." *JSNT* 70: 39–64.

Hübner, Hans. 1984. *The Law in Paul's Thought.* Translated by J. C. G. Grieg. Edinburgh: T. & T. Clark.

1990. *Biblische Theologie des Neuen Testaments*, vol. I. Göttingen: Vandenhoeck & Ruprecht.

Hughes, P. E. 1962. *Paul's Second Epistle to the Corinthians.* NICNT. Grand Rapids: Eerdmans.

Inowlocki, Sabrina. 1999. Review of *When Aseneth Met Joseph: A Late Antique Tale of the Biblical Patriarch and His Egyptian Wife, Reconsidered*, by Ross Shephard Kraemer. *JJS* 50.2: 334–35.

Isaacs, Marie. 1976. *The Concept of Spirit: A Study in Hellenistic Judaism and Its Bearing on the New Testament.* Heythrop Monographs 1. London: Heythrop College.

Jaubert, A. 1965. "The Calendar of *Jubilees*." In *The Date of the Last Supper*, 15–30. Staten Island, NY: Alba House.

Jeremias, J. 1952. "The Last Supper." *ExpT* 64: 91–92.

Jewett, Robert. 1971. *Paul's Anthropological Terms: A Study of Their Use in Conflict Settings.* Leiden: E. J. Brill.

Jones, C. P. 1978. *The Roman World of Dio Chrysostom.* Cambridge, MA: Harvard University Press.

Jonge, M. de. 1975. *Studies on the Testaments of the Twelve Patriarchs.* Leiden: E. J. Brill.

Jowett, B. 1859. *The Epistles of St. Paul to the Thessalonians, Galatians, Romans.* London.

Kamlah, E. 1954. "Buchstabe und Geist." *EvT* 14: 276–82.

Kampen, John. 1988. *The Hasideans and the Origen of Pharisaism: A Study in 1 and 2 Maccabees.* SBLSCS 24. Atlanta: Scholars.

Käsemann, Ernst. 1942. "Die Legitimität des Apostels." *ZNW* 41: 3–71.

1964. *Essays on New Testament Themes.* Translated by W. J. Montague. London: SCM Press.

1969. *New Testament Questions of Today.* Translated by W. J. Montague. London: SCM Press.

1971. "The Spirit and the Letter." In *Pauline Perspectives.* London: SCM Press, 133–66.

1980. *Commentary on Romans.* Translated by Geoffrey W. Bromiley. London: SCM Press.

Kee, H. C. 1983. "The Socio-Cultural Setting of Joseph and Aseneth." *NTS* 29: 394–413.

Kennedy, George. 1963. *The Art of Persuasion in Greece.* London: Routledge and Kegan Paul.

1972. *The Art of Rhetoric in the Roman World.* Princeton: Princeton University Press.

1980. *Classical Rhetoric and Its Christian and Secular Tradition from Ancient to Modern Times.* Chapel Hill: University of North Carolina Press.

1983. *Greek Rhetoric under Christian Emperors.* Princeton: Princeton University Press.

1984. *New Testament Interpretation through Rhetorical Criticism.* Chapel Hill: University of North Carolina Press.

1994. *A New History of Classical Rhetoric.* Princeton: Princeton University Press.

Kennedy, H. A. A. 1913. *St. Paul and the Mystery Religions.* London: Hodder & Stoughton.

Kent, John Harvey. 1966. *Corinth: Results of Excavations Conducted by the American School of Classical Studies at Athens,* vol. VIII, part 3: *The Inscriptions: 1926–50.* Princeton, NJ: ASCSA.

Kertelge, Karl. 1967. *Rechtfertigung bei Paulus: Studien zur Struktur und zum Bedeutungsgehalt des paulinischen Rechtfertigungsbegriffs.* Münster: Aschendorff.

Kieffer, L. 1982. *Foi et justification à Antioche. Interprétation d'un conflit (Gal 2. 14–21).* LD 111. Paris: Cerf.

Kiesow, Klaus. 1979. *Exodustexte im Jesajabuch: Literarkritische und motivgeschichtliche Analysen.* OBO 24. Göttingen: Vandenhoeck & Ruprecht.

Kim, Seyoon. 1984. *The Origin of Paul's Gospel.* Second edition. WUNT 2.4. Tübingen: J. C. B. Mohr.

Kimball, Solon T. 1960. Introduction to *Rites of Passage* by Arnold van Gennep. London: Routledge and Kegan Paul.

1968. "Gennep, Arnold Van." In *The International Encyclopedia of the Social Sciences,* 113–14. Edited by David L. Sills. Macmillan and the Free Press.

King, J. P. 1977. "Death, Burial and Baptism in Rom 6.1–14." Unpublished doctoral dissertation, Emory University, Georgia.

Kittel, Gerhard. 1964. "δοκέω." In *TDNT* II, 232–33.

Klaiber, Walter. 1982. *Rechtfertigung und Gemeinde: Eine Untersuchung zum paulinischen Kirchenverständnis.* FRLANT 127. Göttingen: Vandenhoeck & Ruprecht.

Klauck, H.-J. 1987. "Erleuchtung und Verkündigung. Auslegungsskizze 2 Cor 4.1–6." In *Paolo. Ministro del Nuovo Testamento (2 Co 2.14–4.6),* 267–97. Edited by L. de Lorenzi. Benedictina 9: Rome.

Klein, G. 1964. "Individualgeschichte und Weltgeschichte bei Paulus – Eine Interpretation ihres Verhältnisses im Galaterbrief." *EvTh* 24: 126–65.

Kleinknecht, Hermann. 1968. "πνεῦμα." In *TDNT* VI, 332–59.

Knibb, Michael A. 1987. *The Qumran Community.* Cambridge: Cambridge University Press.

Koch, D. A. 1986. *Die Schrift als Zeuge des Evangeliums: Untersuchungen zur Verwendung und zum Verständnis der Schrift bei Paulus.* BHT 69. Tübingen: J. C. B. Mohr.

Koch, Klaus. 1972. *The Rediscovery of Apocalyptic.* London: SCM Press.

1980. *The Prophets.* Vol. II. London: SCM Press.

Koenig, John Thomas. 1971. "The Motif of Transformation in the Pauline Epistles: A History-of-Religions/Exegetical Study." Unpublished doctoral dissertation, Union Theological Seminary, New York.

Körtner, Ulrich H. J. 1995. *The End of the World: A Theological Interpretation.* Louisville: Westminster John Knox.

Kraemer, Ross Shephard. 1998. *When Aseneth Met Joseph: A Late Antique Tale of the Biblical Patriarch and His Egyptian Wife, Reconsidered.* New York and Oxford: Oxford University Press.

Kraft, Robert. 1965. *Barnabas and the Didache.* New York: Nelson.

Kraus, Hans-Joachim. 1964. "Schöpfung und Weltvollendung." *EvT* 24: 462–85.

Kraus, Wolfgang. 1996. *Das Volk Gottes: Zur Grundlegung der Ekklesiologie bei Paulus.* WUNT 85. Tübingen: J. C. B. Mohr.

Kreitzer, Larry. 1993a. "Adam and Christ." In *Dictionary of Paul and His Letters*, 9–15. Edited by Gerald F. Hawthorne et al. Downers Grove, IL and Leicester: InterVarsity Press.

1993b. "Body." In *Dictionary of Paul and His Letters*, 71–82. Edited by Gerald F. Hawthorne et al. Downers Grove, IL and Leicester: InterVarsity Press.

Kugel, James. 1994. "Levi's Elevation to the Priesthood in Second Temple Writings." *HTR* 86: 1–64.

Kuhn, H. W. 1966. *Enderwartung und gegenwärtiges Heil: Untersuchungen zu den Gemeindeliedern von Qumran mit einem Anhang über Eschatologie und Gegenwart in der Verkündigung Jesu.* SUNT 4. Göttingen: Vandenhoeck & Ruprecht.

Kümmel, W. G. 1949. Notes in Lietzmann, *An die Korinther I–II.* HNT 9. Tübingen: J. C. B. Mohr.

1973. "'Individual Geschichte' und 'Weltgeschichte' in Gal. 2.15–21." In *Christ and the Spirit in the New Testament: Essays in Honour of C. F. D. Moule*, 157–73. Edited by B. Lindars, S. S. Smalley, and C. F. D. Moule. Cambridge: Cambridge University Press.

1975. *Introduction to the New Testament.* London: SCM Press.

Kuss, Otto. 1957–59. *Der Römerbrief.* Vols. I and II. Regensburg: Friedrich Pustet.

La Fontaine, L. S. 1985. *Initiation: Ritual Drama and Secret Knowledge across the World.* New York: Penguin.

Lagrange, M.-J. 1926. *Saint Paul: Epître aux Galates.* Third edition. EtBib. Paris: Gabalda.

1950. *Saint Paul: Epître aux Romains.* Fourth edition. EtBib. Paris: Gabalda.

Lake, Kirsopp. 1976. *Apostolic Fathers.* Vol. I. Loeb Classical Library. Cambridge, MA: Harvard University Press.

Lambrecht, J. 1977/78. "The Line of Thought in Gal. 2. 14b–21." *NTS* 24: 484–95.

1994a. "Once Again Gal 2. 17–18 and 3.21." In *Pauline Studies*, 205–9. Leuven: Leuven University Press.

1994b. "Transgressor by Nullifying God's Grace: A Study of Gal. 2.18–21." In *Pauline Studies*, 211–30. Leuven: Leuven University Press.

1994c. "The Structure and Line of Thought in 2 Corinthians 2.14–4.6." In *Studies on 2 Corinthians*, by R. Bieringer and J. Lambrecht, 257–94. Leuven: Leuven University Press.

1994d. "Transformation in 2 Corinthians 3.18." In *Studies on 2 Corinthians*, by R. Bieringer and J. Lambrecht, 295–307. Leuven: Leuven University Press.

1994e. "The Nekrosis of Jesus: Ministry and Suffering in 2 Corinthians 4.7–15." In *Studies on 2 Corinthians*, by R. Bieringer and J. Lambrecht, 309–33. Leuven: Leuven University Press.

1994f. "Reconcile yourselves . . .': A Reading of 2 Corinthians 5.11–21". In *Studies on 2 Corinthians*, by R. Bieringer and J. Lambrecht, 363–412. Leuven: Leuven University Press.

Lang, F. 1986. *Die Briefe an die Korinther.* NDT 7. Göttingen: Vandenhoeck & Ruprecht.

Lang, F. G. 1973. *2 Korinther 5.1–10 in der neueren Forschung.* BGBE 10. Tübingen: J. C. B. Mohr.

Lausberg, H. 1960. *Handbuch der literarischen Rhetoric.* 2 vols. Munich: Max Huebner.

Leach, Edmund R. 1968. "Ritual." In *The International Encyclopedia of the Social Sciences*, 520–26. Edited by David L. Sills. Macmillan and the Free Press.

Leaney, A. R. C. 1984. *The Jewish and Christian World 200 BC to AD 200.* Cambridge: Cambridge University Press.

Leenhardt, Franz J. 1961. *The Epistle to the Romans.* London: Lutterworth.

Levinson, Jon R. 1988. *Portraits of Adam in Early Judaism: From Sirach to 2 Baruch.* JSPSup 1. Sheffield: Sheffield Academic Press.

Liebers, Rheinhold. 1989. *Das Gesetz als Evangelium: Untersuchungen zur Gesetzkritik des Paulus.* AThANT 75. Zurich: Theologischer.

Lietzmann, Hans. 1949. *An die Korinther I–II.* HNT 9. Tübingen: J. C. B. Mohr. 1971. *An die Galater.* Fourth edition. HNT 10. Tübingen: J. C. B. Mohr.

Lightfoot, J. B. 1890. *Saint Paul's Epistle to the Galatians: A Revised Text with Introduction, Notes, and Dissertations.* London: Macmillan and Co.

Lincoln, Andrew T. 1981. *Paradise Now and Not Yet: Studies in the Role of the Heavenly Dimension in Paul's Thought with Special Reference to His Eschatology.* SNTSMS 43. Cambridge: Cambridge University Press. 1990. *Ephesians.* WBC 42. Dallas: Word.

Lincoln, Bruce. 1981. *Emerging from Chrysalis: Studies in Women's Initiation Rites.* Cambridge and London: Harvard University Press.

Litfin, D. 1994. *St Paul's Theology of Proclamation: 1 Corinthians 1–4 and Greco-Roman Rhetoric.* SNTSMS 79. Cambridge: Cambridge University Press.

Little, J. A. 1984. "Paul's Use of Analogy: A Structural Approach." *CBQ* 46: 82–90.

Longenecker, Richard. 1990. *Galatians.* WBC 41. Dallas: Word.

Lüdemann, Gerd. 1984. *Paul, Apostle to the Gentiles: Studies in Chronology.* Philadelphia: Fortress.

Lührmann, Dieter. 1978. *Der Brief an die Galater.* ZBK 7. Zurich: Theologischer.

Lull, David John. 1980. *The Spirit in Galatia: Paul's Interpretation of Pneuma as Divine Power.* SBLDS 49. Chico: Scholars.

Luz, Ulrich. 1967. "Der alte und der neue Bund bei Paulus und im Hebräerbrief." *EvT* 27: 318–36.

Lyons, George. 1985. *Pauline Autobiography: Toward a New Understanding.* SBLSDS 73. Atlanta: Scholars.

Mach, Michel. 1992. *Entwicklungsstudien des jüdischen Engelglaubens in vorrabbinischer Zeit.* TSAJ 34. Tübingen: J. C. B. Mohr.

Malherbe, Abraham J. 1986. *Moral Exhortation: A Greco-Roman Sourcebook.* Philadelphia: Westminster.

Mansoor, Menahem. 1961. *The Thanksgiving Hymns.* Leiden: E. J. Brill.

Mare, W. Harold. 1976. *1 Corinthians.* In *The Expositor's Bible Commentary,* vol. X. Grand Rapids: Zondervan.

Markschies, Christoph. 1994. "Die platonische Metapher vom 'inneren Menschen': eine Brücke zwischen antiker Philosophie und altchristlicher Theologie." *ZKG* 105.1: 1–17.

Marshall, P. 1987. *Enmity in Corinth: Social Conventions in Paul's Relations with the Corinthians.* WUNT 2.23. Tübingen: J. C. B. Mohr.

Martin, François. 1911. "Le livre des Jubilés." *RB* 8: 321–44; 502–33.

Martin, Ralph P. 1986. *2 Corinthians.* WBC 40. Waco: Word Publishing.

Martyn, J. L. 1967. "Epistemology at the Turn of the Ages: 2 Corinthians 5.16." In *Christian History and Interpretation,* 269–87. Edited by W. R. Farmer et. al. Cambridge: Cambridge University Press.

1985. "Apocalyptic Antinomies in Paul's Letter to the Galatians." *NTS* 31: 410–25.

1997. *Galatians.* AB 33A. New York: Doubleday.

Matlock, R. Barry. 1996. *Unveiling the Apocalyptic Paul: Paul's Interpreters and the Rhetoric of Criticism.* JSNTSup 127. Sheffield: Sheffield Academic Press.

McEleney, N. 1973–74. "Conversion, Circumcision, and the Law." *NTS* 20: 319–41.

McKane, William. 1986–96. *Jeremiah I–II.* ICC. Edinburgh: T. & T. Clark.

McKenzie, J. L. 1968. *Second Isaiah.* AB 20. New York: Doubleday.

Mead, Richard T. 1989. "Exegesis of 2 Corinthians 5.14–21." In *Interpreting 2 Corinthians 5.14–21,* 143–62. Edited by J. P. Lewis. Lewiston, NY and Queenston: Edwin Mellen.

Mell, Ulrich. 1989. *Neue Schöpfung: Eine traditionsgeschichtliche und exegetische Studie zu einem soteriologischen Grundsatz paulinischer Theologie.* BZNW 56. Berlin and New York: Walter de Gruyter.

Mendelson, E. M. 1965. "Initiation and the Paradox of Power: A Sociological Approach." In *Initiation,* 214–21. Edited by C. J. Bleeker. Supplements to *Numen,* SHR 10. Leiden: E. J. Brill.

Menzies, Robert P. 1991. *The Development of Early Christian Pneumatology with Special Reference to Luke–Acts.* JSNTSup 54. Sheffield: JSOT Press.

Meyer, R. 1938. "Levitische Emanzipationsbestrebungen in nachexilischer Zeit." *OLZ* 41: 722–28.

Michel, Otto. 1954. "'Erkennen dem Fleisch nach' (2 Kor 5.16)." *EvT* 14: 22–29.

1955. *Der Brief an die Römer.* MeyerK 4. Göttingen: Vandenhoeck & Ruprecht.

Milik, J. T. 1976. *The Books of Enoch: Aramaic Fragments of Qumran Cave 4.* Oxford: Clarendon Press.

Minear, Paul Sevier. 1979. "The Crucified World: The Enigma of Galatians 6.14." In *Theologia Crucis – Signum Crucis,* 395–407. Edited by C. Andresen and G. Klein. Tübingen: J. C. B. Mohr.

Moltmann, Jürgen. 1992. *The Spirit of Life: A Universal Affirmation.* Translated by Margaret Kohl. Minneapolis: Fortress.

Moo, Douglas. 1987. "Paul and the Law in the Last Ten Years." *SJT* 40: 287–307.

1991. *Romans 1–8.* WEC. Chicago: Moody.

Moores, John D. 1995. *Wrestling with Rationality in Paul: Romans 1–8 in a New Perspective.* SNTSMS 82. Cambridge: Cambridge University Press.

Morgan, Robert. 1995. *Romans.* Sheffield: Sheffield Academic Press.

Morris, Brian. 1987. *Anthropological Studies of Religion: An Introductory Text.* Cambridge: Cambridge University Press.

Morris, Leon. 1988. *The Epistle to the Romans.* Grand Rapids: Eerdmans.

Moule, C. F. D. 1959. *An Idiom Book of New Testament Greek.* Cambridge: Cambridge University Press.

1965–66. "St Paul and Dualism: The Pauline Conception of Resurrection." *NTS* 12: 106–23.

1970. "Death 'to Sin,' 'to Law,' and 'to the World': A Note on Certain Datives.' In *Mélanges bibliques en hommage au R. P. Béda Rigaux*, 376–76. Edited by A.-L. Descamps and A. de Halleux. Gembloux: Duculot.

Moulton, James Hope and George Milligan. 1930. *The Vocabulary of the Greek Testament Illustrated from the Papyri and other Non-Literary Sources.* Grand Rapids: Eerdmans.

Muilenburg, James. 1956. "The Book of Isaiah, Chapters 40–66." In *The Interpreter's Bible*, vol. V, 381–773. Nashville: Abingdon.

Müller, Karlheinz. 1978. "Apokalyptik/Apokalypsen III." In *TRE* 3, 202–51. Berlin and New York: Walter de Gruyter.

Münchow, Christoph. 1981. *Ethik und Eschatologie: Ein Beitrag zum Verständnis der frühjüdischen Apokalyptik mit einem Ausblick des Neue Testaments.* Göttingen: Vandenhoeck & Ruprecht.

Munck, Johannes. 1959. *Paul and the Salvation of Mankind.* London: SCM Press.

Murphy-O'Connor, Jerome. 1983. *St. Paul's Corinth. Texts and Archaeology.* Wilmington: Michael Glazier.

1984. "The Corinth that Saint Paul Saw." *Biblical Archaeologist* 47: 147–59.

1991a. *The Theology of the Second Letter to the Corinthians.* Cambridge: Cambridge University Press.

1991b. "Pauline Studies." *RB* 98: 145–51.

Murray, John. 1959. *The Epistle to the Romans.* NIGNT. Eerdmans: Grand Rapids.

Mussies, G. 1972. *Dio Chrysostom and the New Testament.* Leiden: E. J. Brill.

Mussner, Franz. 1974. *Der Galaterbrief.* HTKNT 9. Freiburg, Basel, and Vienna: Herder.

Neugebauer, Fritz. 1961. *In Christus.* Göttingen: Vandenhoeck & Ruprecht.

Newman, C. C. 1992. *Paul's Glory-Christology. Tradition and Rhetoric.* NovTSup 69. Leiden: E. J. Brill.

Newsome, James D. Jr. 1984. *The Hebrew Prophets.* Atlanta: John Knox.

Nicholson, E. W. 1970. *Preaching to the Exiles: A Study of the Prose Tradition in the Book of Jeremiah.* Oxford: Basil Blackwell.

Nickelsburg, George W. E. 1972. *Resurrection, Immortality, and Eternal Life in Intertestamental Judaism.* Cambridge, MA: Harvard University Press.

1981. *Jewish Literature between the Bible and the Mishnah: A Historical and Literary Introduction.* Philadelphia: Fortress.

1984a. "Stories of Biblical and Early Post-Biblical Times." In *Jewish Writings of the Second Temple Period*, 33–87. Edited by M. E. Stone. Assen: Van Gorcum; Philadelphia: Fortress.

1984b. "The Bible Rewritten and Expanded." In *Jewish Writings of the Second Temple Period*, 89–156. Edited by M. E. Stone. Assen: Van Gorcum; Philadelphia: Fortress.

1991. *Jewish Literature between the Bible and the Mishnah*. Philadelphia: Fortress.

Nolland, J. 1981. "Uncircumcised Proselytes?" *JSJ* 12: 173–94.

North, C. R. 1957. "The 'Former Things' and the 'New Things' in Deutero-Isaiah." In *Studies in Old Testament Prophecy*, 111–26. Edited by H. H. Rowley. Edinburgh: T. & T. Clark.

North, Helen. 1948. "The Concept of Sophrosune in Greek Literary Criticism." *Classical Philology* 43: 1–17.

Nygren, Anders. 1952. *Commentary on Romans*. London: SCM Press.

O'Brien, Peter Thomas. 1977. *Introductory Thanksgivings in the Letters of Paul*. NovTSup 49. Leiden: E. J. Brill.

1992. "Justification in Paul and Some Crucial Issues of the Last Two Decades." In *Right with God: Justification by Faith in the Bible and the World*. Edited by D. A. Carson. Carlisle: Paternoster.

Oepke, Albrecht. 1964a. *Der Brief des Paulus an die Galater*. ThKNT 9. Berlin: Evangelische.

1964b. "ἔκστασις." In *TDNT* II, 449–60.

Paget, James Carleton. 1994. *The Epistle of Barnabas: Outlook and Background*. WUNT 2.64. Tübingen: J. C. B. Mohr.

Paige, Terence P. 1993. "Holy Spirit." In *Dictionary of Paul and His Letters*, 404–13. Edited by Gerald F. Hawthorne et al. Downers Grove, IL and Leicester: InterVarsity Press.

Pate, Marvin C. 1991. *Adam Christology as the Exegetical and Theological Substructure of 2 Corinthians 4.7–5.21*. Lanham and New York: University Press of America.

Patte, Daniel. 1987. "A Structural Exegesis of 2 Corinthians 2.14–7.4 with Special Attention on 2.14–3.6 and 6.11–7.4." In *SBL 1987 Seminar Papers*, 23–49. Atlanta: Scholars.

Pentikäinen, Juha Y. 1986. "Transition Rites." In *Transition Rites: Cosmic, Social and Individual Order*, 1–27. Edited by Ugo Bianchi. Rome: "L'Erma" di Bretschneider.

Perriman, A. C. 1989. "Paul and the Parousia: 1 Corinthians 15.50–57 and 2 Corinthians 5.1–5." *NTS* 35: 512–21.

Petzke, G. 1990. "κτίζω." In *Exegetical Dictionary of the New Testament*, 325–26. Edited by Horst Balz and Gerhard Schneider. Grand Rapids: Eerdmans.

Pfleiderer, Otto. 1877. *Paulinism: A Contribution to the History of Primitive Christian Theology*, vol. I: *Paul's Doctrine*. Edinburgh: Williams and Norgate.

Philonenko, M. 1965. "Initiation et mystère dans Joseph et Asenéth." In *Initiation*, 147–53. Edited by C. J. Bleeker. Leiden: E. J. Brill.

1968. *Joseph et Aséneth: Introduction, texte critique, traduction et notes*. SPB 13. Leiden: E. J. Brill.

Plümacher, E. 1992. "στοιχεῖον." In *EWNT* III, 664–66. Second edition. Edited by Horst Balz and Gerhard Schneider. Stuttgart, Berlin, and Cologne: W. Kohlhammer.

Plummer, A. 1915. *A Critical and Exegetical Commentary on the Second Epistle of St. Paul to the Corinthians*. Edinburgh: T. & T. Clark.

Polk, Timothy. 1984. *The Prophetic Persona: Jeremiah and the Language of Self.* JSOTSup 32. Sheffield: JSOT Press.

Pomeroy, Arthur J. 1999. *Arius Didymus: The Epitome of Stoic Ethics*. Texts and Translations 44. Atlanta: Society of Biblical Literature.

Porter, Stanley E. 1993. "Peace, Reconciliation." In *Dictionary of Paul and His Letters*, 695–99. Edited by Gerald F. Hawthorne et al. Downers Grove, IL and Leicester: InterVarsity Press.

Potter, H. D. 1986. "The New Covenant in Jeremiah 31:31–34." *VT* 33: 345–57.

Preuss, Horst Dietrich. 1992. *Old Testament Theology.* Vol II. Edinburgh: T. & T. Clark.

Provence, T. E. 1982. " 'Who is Sufficient for These Things?' An Exegesis of 2 Corinthians 2.15–3.18." *NovT* 24: 54–81.

Prümm. K. 1967. *Diakonia Pneumatos*, vol. I: *Theologische Auslegung des zweiten Korintherbriefs*. Rome, Freiburg, and Vienna: Herder.

Rad, Gerhard von. 1958. "Das theologische Problem des alttestamentlichen Schöpfungsglauben." In *Gesammelte Studien zum Alten Testament*, 136–47. Munich: Chr. Kaiser.

    1965. *Old Testament Theology*. Vol. II. Edinburgh and London: Oliver & Boyd.

Rebell, Walter. 1992. *Christologie und Existenz bei Paulus: Eine Auslegung von 2. Kor 5.14–21*. Stuttgart: Calwer.

Reid, D. G. 1993. "Elements/Elemental Spirits of the World." In *Dictionary of Paul and His Letters*, 229–33. Edited by Gerald F. Hawthorne et al. Downers Grove, IL and Leicester: InterVarsity Press.

Reitzenstein, R. 1910. *Die Hellenistischen Mysterienreligionen. Ihre Grundgedanken und Wirkungen*. Leipzig and Berlin: Teubner.

Renwick, David A. 1991. *Paul, the Temple, and the Presence of God*. BJS 224. Atlanta: Scholars.

Reumann, J. 1973. *Creation and New Creation: The Past, Present, and Future of God's Creative Activity.* Minneapolis: Augsburg.

Rey, Bernard. 1966. *Créés dans le Christ Jesus: La création nouvelle selon saint Paul*. LD 42. Cerf: Paris.

Richard, E. 1981. "Polemics, Old Testament, and Theology: A Study of 2 Cor. 3.1–4.6." *RB* 88: 340–67.

Ringren, Helmer. 1963. *The Faith of Qumran: The Theology of the Dead Sea Scrolls*. Philadelphia: Fortress.

Rissi, Mathias. 1969. *Studien zum zweiten Korintherbrief: Der alte Bund–Der Prediger–Der Tod*. AThANT 56. Zurich: Zwingli.

Rist, M. 1962. "Apocalypticism." In *IBD*, vol. I, 157–61. New York and Nashville: Abingdon.

Robertson, A. T. 1934. *A Grammar of the Greek New Testament in the Light of Historical Research.* Nashville: Broadman.

Robertson, Archibald and Alfred Plummer. 1914. *A Critical and Exegetical Commentary on the First Epistle of St Paul to the Corinthians*. Second edition. ICC. Edinburgh: T. & T. Clark.

Robinson, John A. T. 1952. *The Body: A Study in Pauline Theology.* SBT 5. London: SCM Press.

Roetzel, Calvin. 1999. *Paul: The Man and the Myth.* Philadelphia: Fortress.

Rohde, Joachim. 1989. *Der Brief des Paulus an die Galater.* ThKNT 9. Berlin: Evangelische.

Rowland, Christopher. 1982. *The Open Heaven: A Study of Apocalyptic in Judaism and Early Christianity.* London: SPCK.

1985. *Christian Origins: From Messianic Movement to Christian Religion.* Minneapolis: Augsburg.

Rowley, H. H. 1947. *The Relevance of Apocalyptic.* London: SCM Press.

Rusam, D. 1992. "Neue Belege zu dem *stoicheia tou kosmou* (Gal 4,3.9; Kol 2,8.20)." *ZNW* 83: 119–25.

Rusche, H. 1987. "Zum 'jeremianischen' Hintergrund der Korintherbriefe." *BZ* 31: 116–19.

Russell, D. A. 1983. *Greek Declamation.* Cambridge: Cambridge University Press.

Russell, D. M. 1996. *The "New Heavens and New Earth": Hope for the Creation in Jewish Apocalyptic and the New Testament.* SBAL 1. Philadelphia: Visionary Press.

Russell, D. S. 1964. *The Method and Message of Jewish Apocalyptic.* Philadelphia: Westminster.

1967. *The Jews from Alexander to the Mishnah.* Oxford: Oxford University Press.

1987. *The Old Testament Pseudepigrapha: Patriarchs and Prophets in Early Judaism.* Philadelphia: Fortress.

1992. *Divine Disclosure: An Introduction to Jewish Apocalyptic.* London: SCM Press.

Sanday, W. and A. C. Headlam. 1914. *The Epistle to the Romans.* Fifth edition. ICC. Edinburgh: T. & T. Clark.

Sanders, E. P. 1976. "The Covenant as a Soteriological Category and the Nature of Salvation in Palestinian and Hellenistic Judaism." In *Jews Greeks and Christians: Religious Cultures in Late Antiquity: Essays in Honour of William David Davies,* 11–44 Edited by W. D. Davies and R. Hamerton-Kelly. Leiden: E. J. Brill.

1977. *Paul and Palestinian Judaism.* Minneapolis: Fortress.

1983. *Paul, the Law, and the Jewish People.* Minneapolis: Fortress.

1989. "The Genre of Palestinian Jewish Apocalypses." In *Apocalypticism in the Mediterranean World and the Near East: Proceedings of the International Colloquium on Apocalypticism, Uppsala, August 12–17, 1979,* 447–59. Second edition. Edited by David Hellholm. Leiden: E. J. Brill.

1992. *Judaism: Belief and Practice 63 BCE–66 CE.* London: SCM Press; Philadelphia: Trinity International Press.

Sandnes, K. O. 1991. *Paul – One of the Prophets? A Contribution to the Apostle's Self-Understanding.* WUNT 2.43. Tübingen: J. C. B. Mohr.

Sänger, Dieter. 1979. "Bekehrung und Exodus: Zum jüdischen Traditionshintergrund von 'Joseph und Aseneth.'" *JSJ* 10: 11–36.

1980. *Antikes Judentum und die Mysterien: Religionsgeschichtliche Untersuchungen zu Joseph und Aseneth.* WUNT 2.5. Tübingen: J. C. B. Mohr.

Savage, Timothy B. 1996. *Power through Weakness: Paul's Understanding of the Christian Ministry in 2 Corinthians*. SNTSMS 86. Cambridge: Cambridge University Press.

Schlatter, Adolf. 1922. *Die Theologie der Apostel*. Second edition. Stuttgart: Calwer.

——— 1934. *Paulus der Bote Jesu*. Stuttgart: Calwer.

——— 1935. *Gottes Gerechtigkeit: Ein Kommentar zum Römerbrief*. Fourth edition. Stuttgart: Calwer.

Schlier, Heinrich W. 1949. *Der Brief an die Galater*. Tenth edition. KEK 7. Göttingen: Vandenhoeck & Ruprecht.

——— 1977. *Der Römerbrief: Kommentar*. HTKNT 6. Freiburg: Herder.

Schmidt, H. W. 1963. *Der Brief des Paulus an die Römer*. THNT 6. Berlin: Evangelische Verlagsanstalt.

Schmidt, Werner H. 1979. *Introduction to the Old Testament*. London: SCM Press.

——— 1984. "Geist/Heiliger Geist/Geistgaben." In *TRE* 12, 170–73. Berlin and New York: Walter de Gruyter.

Schmithals, W. 1971. *Gnosticism in Corinth: An Investigation of the Letters to the Corinthians*. Translated by J. E. Steely. Nashville: Abingdon.

——— 1972. *Paul and the Gnostics*. Translated by J. E. Steely. Nashville: Abingdon.

Schnackenburg, Rudolf. 1982. *Der Brief an die Epheser*. Zurich: Benziger; Neukirchen-Vluyn: Neukirchener.

Schneider, B. 1953. "The Meaning of St. Paul's Antithesis 'The Letter and the Spirit.'" *CBQ* 15: 163–207.

Schneider, Gerhard. 1959. "KAINH KTISIS: Die Idee der Neuschöpfung beim Apostel Paulus und ihr religionsgeschichtlicher Hintergrund." Unpublished doctoral dissertation, Universität Trier, Trier.

——— 1983. "παλαιός." In *EWNT* III, 15–18. Stuttgart: W. Kohlhammer.

——— 1992. "'Neuschöpfung' in Christus: Zur Auslegung einer biblischen Leitidee." In *Jesusüberlieferung und Christologie*, 357–71. Leiden: E. J. Brill.

Schoefield, J. N. 1969. *Law, Prophets, and Writings: The Religion of the Books of the Old Testament*. London: SPCK.

Schrage, W. 1991. *Der erste Briefe an die Korinther*, vol. I. Zurich and Braunschweig: Neukirchener.

Schreiner, J. 1974. "Jeremiah 9.22–23 als Hintergrund des paulinischen 'Sich-Rühmens.'" In *Neues Testament und Kirche*, 530–42. Edited by Joachim Gnilka. Freiburg, Basel, and Vienna: Herder.

Schreiner, T. 1993a. *The Law and Its Fulfillment: A Pauline Theology of Law*. Grand Rapids: Baker.

——— 1993b. "Circumcision." In *Dictionary of Paul and His Letters*, 137–39. Edited by Gerald F. Hawthorne et al. Downers Grove, IL and Leicester InterVarsity Press.

Schrenk, G. 1949. "Was bedeutet 'Israel Gottes'?" *Judaica* 5: 81–94.

——— 1950. "Der Segenswunsch nach der Kampfepistel." *Judaica* 6: 170–90.

Schubert, P. 1939. *Form and Function of the Pauline Thanksgivings*. BZNW 32. Berlin: Töpelmann.

Schürer, Emil. 1973–86. *The History of the Jewish People in the Age of Jesus Christ (175 B.C.–A.D. 135)*. 4 vols. Revised and edited by Geza Vermes, Fergus Millar, and Martin Goodman. Edinburgh: T. & T. Clark.

Schütz, John Howard. 1975. *Paul and the Anatomy of Apostolic Authority.* SNTSMS 26. Cambridge: Cambridge University Press.

Schwantes, Heinz. 1963. *Schöpfung der Endzeit. Ein Beitrag zum Verständnis der Auferweckung bei Paulus.* AzTh 1.12. Stuttgart: Calwer.

Schwarz, Eberhard. 1982. *Identität durch Abgrenzung: Abgrenzungsprozesse in Israel im 2. vorchristlichen Jahrhundert und ihre traditionsgeschichtlichen Voraussetzungen. Zugleich ein Beitrag zur Erforschung des Jubiläenbuches.* Europaische Hochschulschriften 162. Frankfurt: Peter Lang.

Schweitzer, Albert. 1931. *The Mysticism of Paul the Apostle.* Translated by William Montgomery. London: A. & C. Black.

Schweizer, Eduard. 1967–68. "Dying and Rising with Christ." *NTS* 14: 1–14.

——— 1988. "Slaves of the Elements and Worshipers of Angels: Gal 4.3, 9 and Col 2.8, 18, 20." *JBL* 107: 455–68.

Schweizer, Eduard et al. 1960. *Spirit of God.* London: A. & C. Black.

Scott, James M. 1992. *Adoptions as Sons of God. An Exegetical Investigation into the Background of* 'ΥΙΟΘΕΣΙΑ *in the Pauline Corpus.* WUNT 48. Tübingen: J. C. B. Mohr.

Scroggs, Robin. 1966. *The Last Adam: A Study in Pauline Anthropology.* Oxford: Basil Blackwell.

Segal, Alan F. 1990. *Paul the Convert. The Apostolate and Apostasy of Saul the Pharisee.* New Haven: Yale University Press.

Sekki, Arthur Everett. 1989. *The Meaning of Ruach at Qumran.* SBLDS 110. Atlanta: Scholars.

Siber, P. 1971. *Mit Christus Leben: Eine Studie zur paulinischen Auferstehungshoffnung.* AThANT 61. Zurich: TVZ.

Sieffert, F. 1899. *Der Brief an die Galater.* KEK 7. Göttingen: Vandenhoeck & Ruprecht.

Sjöberg, Erik. 1950. "Wiedergeburt und Neuschöpfung im palästinischen Judentum." *ST* 4: 44–85.

Skinner, J. 1922. *Prophecy and Religion.* Cambridge: Cambridge University Press.

Smit, J. 1989. "The Letter of Paul to the Galatians: A Deliberative Speech." *NTS* 35: 1–26.

Soggin, Alberto. 1989. *Introduction to the Old Testament.* Third edition. London: SCM Press.

Southwell, Peter. 1982. *Prophecy.* London: Hodder & Stoughton.

Souza, Ivo du C. 1977. "The New Covenant in the Second Letter to the Corinthians: A Theologico-Exegetical Investigation of 2 Cor 3.1–4.6 and 5.14–21." Unpublished doctoral dissertation. Pontifical Gregorian University, Rome.

Sparks, H. F. D. (ed.). 1984. *The Apocryphal Old Testament.* Oxford: Clarendon Press.

Staab, Karl. 1933. *Pauluskommentare aus der Griechen Kirche.* Münster: Aschendorffschen.

Stalker, D.M.G. 1968. *Ezekiel: Introduction and Commentary.* London: SCM Press.

Stanley, David Michael. 1961. *Christ's Resurrection in Pauline Soteriology.* AnBib. 13. Rome: Pontifical Biblical Institute.

Stockhausen, Carol Stern. 1989. *Moses' Veil and the Glory of the New Covenant.* AnBib 116. Rome: Pontifical Biblical Institute.

Stone, M. E. 1971. "Apocryphal Notes and Readings." *Israel Oriental Studies* 1: 123–31.

1984. "Apocalyptic Literature." In *Jewish Writings of the Second Temple Period: Apocrypha, Pseudepigrapha, Qumran Sectarian Writings, Philo, Josephus*, 383–441. Edited by M. E. Stone. Assen: Van Gorcum; Philadelphia: Fortress.

1991. "Lists of Revealed Things in the Apocalyptic Literature." In *Selected Studies in the Pseudepigrapha and Apocrypha*, 379–418. STVP 9. Leiden: E. J. Brill.

Strachan, R. H. 1935. *The Second Epistle of Paul to the Corinthians*. London: Hodder & Stoughton.

Strack, Hermann L. and Paul Billerbeck. 1924–26. *Kommentar zum Neuen Testament aus Talmud und Midrasch*. Vols. II–III. Munich: Becksche.

Stronstadt, Roger. 1984. *The Charismatic Theology of St. Luke*. Peabody, MA: Hendrickson.

Strugnell, J. and D. Dimant. 1988. "4Q Ezekiel." *RevQ* 13: 45–58.

Stuhlmacher, Peter. 1967. "Erwägungen zum ontologischen Charakter der καινὴ κτίσις bei Paulus." *EvT* 27: 1–35.

1994. *Paul's Letter to the Romans: A Commentary*. Translated by Scott J. Hafemann. Louisville, KY: Westminster/John Knox Press.

Stuhlmueller, Carroll. 1970. *Creative Redemption in Deutero-Isaiah*. AB 43. Rome: Biblical Institute.

Sumney, Jerry L. 1990. *Identifying Paul's Opponents: The Question of Method in 2 Corinthians*. JSNTSup 40. Sheffield: JSOT Press.

Syren, Roger. 1994. "Ishmael and Esau in the Book of *Jubilees* and the Targum Pseudo Jonathan." In *The Aramaic Bible: Targums in their Historical Context*, 310–15. Edited by D. R. G. Beatlie and M. J. McNamara. JSOTSup 166. Sheffield: JSOT.

Talbert, Charles H. 1989. *Reading Corinthians: A Literary and Theological Commentary on 1 and 2 Corinthians*. New York: Crossroad.

Tannehill, Robert C. 1967. *Dying and Rising with Christ: A Study in Pauline Theology*. BZNW 32. Berlin: Alfred Töpelmann.

Taylor, Louis J. 1958. *The New Creation: A Study of the Pauline Doctrines of Creation, Innocence, Sin, and Redemption*. New York: Pageant.

Testuz, Michel. 1960. *Les ideés religieuses du livre des Jubilés*. Geneva and Paris: Librairie E. Droz and Librairie Minard.

Theissen, Gerd. 1987. *Psychological Aspects of Pauline Theology*. Edinburgh: T. & T. Clark.

1992. *Social Reality and the Early Christians*. Translated by Margret Kohl. Edinburgh: T. & T. Clark.

Thielmann, Frank. 1989. *From Plight to Solution: A Jewish Framework for Understanding Paul's View of the Law in Galatians and Romans*. NovTSup 61. Leiden: E. J. Brill.

Thompson, Alden Loyd. 1977. *Responsibility for Evil in the Theodicy of IV Ezra*. SBLDiss 29. Missoula, MT: Scholars.

Thompson, J. A. 1980. *The Book of Jeremiah*. NICOT. Grand Rapids: Eerdmans.

Thrall, Margaret E. 1982. "A Second Thanksgiving Period in 2 Corinthians." *JSNT* 16: 101–24.

1987. "Conversion to the Lord: The Interpretation of Exodus 34 in 2 Cor 3. 14b–18." In *Paolo. Ministro del Nuovo Testamento (2 Co 2.14–4.6)*, 197–232. Edited by L. de Lorenzi. Benedictina 9: Rome.

1994. *A Critical and Exegetical Commentary on the Second Epistle to the Corinthians*. ICC. Edinburgh: T. & T. Clark.

Tigchelaar, Eibert J. C. 1996. *Prophets of Old and the Day of the Lord: Zechariah, the Book of Watchers, and Apocalyptic*. OTS 35. Leiden: E. J. Brill.

Turner, Terrance. 1977. "Transformation, Hierarchy and Transcendence: A Reaffirmation of Van Gennep's Model of the Structure of Rites de Passage." In *Secular Ritual*, 53–70. Edited by Sally F. Moore and Barbara G. Meyerhoff. Assen and Amsterdam: Van Gorcum.

Turner, Victor. 1967. *The Forest of Symbols*. Ithaca and London: Cornell University Press.

1968. "Myth and Ritual." In *The International Encyclopedia of the Social Sciences*, 576–82. Edited by David L. Sills. Macmillan and the Free Press.

1969. *The Ritual Process*. London: Routledge and Kegan Paul.

1977. "Variations on a Theme of Liminality." In *Secular Ritual*, 36–52. Edited by Sally F. Moore and Barbara G. Meyerhoff. Assen and Amsterdam: Van Gorcum.

Unnik, W. C. van. 1973a. "Reisepläne und Amen-Sagen: Zusammenhang und Gedankenfolge in 2 Korinther 1.15–24." In *Spars Collecta: The Collected Essays of W. C. van Unnik*, part I, 144–59. NovTSup 29. Leiden: E. J. Brill.

1973b. "'With Unveiled Face': An Exegesis of 2 Corinthians 3.12–18. In *Sparsa Collecta. The Collected Essays of W. C. van Unnik*, part I, 194–210. NovTSup 29. Leiden: E. J. Brill.

VanderKam, James C. 1977. *Textual and Historical Studies in the Book of Jubilees*. HSS 14. Missoula: Scholars.

1978. "Enoch Traditions in Jubilees and Other Second-Century Sources." In *Seminar Papers of the Society of Biblical Literature*, 96–125. Missoula: Scholars.

1981. "The Putative Author of Jubilees." *JSS* 26.2: 209–17.

1989. *The Book of Jubilees*. CChr 511. Louvain: Peters.

1993. "Biblical Interpretation in 1 Enoch and Jubilees." In *The Pseudepigrapha and Early Biblical Interpretation*, 96–125. Edited by James Charlesworth and Craig A. Evans. Sheffield: JSOT Press.

1994. *The Dead Sea Scrolls Today*. Grand Rapids: Eerdmans.

Vanhoye, A. 1986. "Personnalité de Paul et exégèse paulienne." In *L'apôtre Paul. Personnalité, style et conception du ministère*, 3–15. Edited by A. Vanhoye. Leuven: Leuven University Press.

Vermes, Geza. 1993. *The Religion of Jesus the Jew*. London: SCM Press.

Vielhauer, Philip. 1976. "Gesetzesdienst und Stoicheiadienst im Galaterbrief." In *Rechtfertigung*, 543–55. Edited by J. Friederich, W. Pöhlmann, and P. Stuhlmacher. Tübingen: J. C. B. Mohr.

Vollenwieder, Samuel. 1989. *Freiheit als neue Schöpfung: Eine Untersuchung zur Eleutheria bei Paulus und seiner Umwelt*. FRLANT 147. Göttingen: Vandenhoeck & Reprecht.

Volz, Paul. 1932. *Jesaia II*. KAT 9. Leipzig: Werner Scholl.

1934. *Die Eschatologie der jüdischen Gemeinde im neutestamentlicher Zeitalter*. Tübingen: J. C. B. Mohr.

Vos, J. S. 1973. *Traditionsgeschichtliche Untersuchungen zur paulinischen Pneumatologie.* Assen: Van Gorcum.

Wachholder, Ben Zion. 1992. "Ezekiel and Ezekielism as Progenitors of Essenism." In *The Dead Sea Scrolls: Forty Years of Research,* 186–96. Edited by Devorah Dimant and Griel Rappaport. Leiden: E. J. Brill.

Watson, Francis. 1986. *Paul, Judaism, and the Gentiles: A Sociological Approach.* SNTSMS 56. Cambridge: Cambridge University Press.

Watts, John D. W. 1985. *Isaiah 1–33.* WBC 24. Waco: Word.

1987. *Isaiah 34–66.* WBC 25. Waco: Word.

Webb, R. L. 1990. " 'Apocalyptic': Observations on a Slippery Term." *JNES* 49: 115–26.

Webb, William J. 1993. *Returning Home: New Covenant and Second Exodus as the Context for 2 Corinthians 6.14–7.1.* JSNTSup 80. Sheffield: JSOT Press.

Wedderburn, A. J. M. 1987. *Baptism and Resurrection: Studies in Pauline Theology against Its Graeco-Roman Background.* Tübingen: J. C. B. Mohr.

Weder, Hans. 1981. *Das Kreuz Jesu bei Paulus: Ein Versuch über den Geschichtsbezug des christlichen Glaubens nachzudenken.* FRLANT 125. Göttingen: Vandenhoeck & Ruprecht.

Weima, Jeffrey A. D. 1993. "Gal 6. 11–18: A Hermeneutical Key to the Galatian Letter." *CTJ* 28: 90–107.

1994. *Neglected Endings: The Significance of the Pauline Letter Closings.* JSNTSup 101. Sheffield: Sheffield Academic Press.

Weinfield, M. 1976. "Jeremiah and the Spiritual Metamorphosis of Israel." *ZAW* 88: 17–56.

Weippert, Helga. 1979. "Das Wort vom Neuen Bund in Jeremia 31:31–34." *VT* 29: 336–51.

Weiss, Bernhard. 1882. *Biblical Theology of the New Testament.* Vol. I. Edinburgh: T. & T. Clark.

Wendland, Heinz-Dietrich. 1952. "Das Wirken des Heiligen Geistes in den Gläubigen nach Paulus." *TLZ* 8: 457–70.

1964. *Die Briefe and die Korinther.* Göttingen: Vandenhoeck & Ruprecht.

West, S. 1974. " 'Joseph and Aseneth': A Neglected Greek Romance." *CQ* 24: 70–81.

Westermann, Claus. 1969. *Isaiah 40–66: A Commentary.* Old Testament Library. Philadelphia: Westminster.

Whybray, R. N. 1975. *Isaiah 40–66.* New Century Bible. Greenwood, SC: Attic.

Wilckens, Ulrich. 1980. *Der Brief an die Römer.* EKK 6.2. Neukirchen-Vluyn: Neukirchener; Einsiedeln: Benziger.

Williams, S. K. 1987. "Justification and the Spirit." *JSNT* 29: 91–100.

1988. " 'Promise' in Galatians: A Reading of Paul's Reading of Scripture." *JBL* 107: 709–20.

1989. "The Hearing of Faith: ΑΚΟΗ ΠΙΣΤΕѠΕ in Galatians 3." *NTS* 35: 82–93.

Wills, Lawrence M. 1995. *The Jewish Novel in the Ancient World.* Ithaca, NY: Cornell University Press.

Windisch, Hans. 1920. *Der Barnabasbrief.* HNT. Tübingen: J. C. B. Mohr.

1924. *Der zweite Korintherbrief.* KEK 69. Göttingen: Vandenhoeck & Ruprecht.

Wintermute, O. S. 1985. "Jubilees: A New Translation and Introduction." In *The Old Testament Pseudepigrapha*, vol. II: 35–142. Edited by J. H. Charlesworth. Garden City, NY: Doubleday.

Witherington III, Ben. 1995. *Conflict and Community in Corinth: A Socio-Rhetorical Commentary on 1 and 2 Corinthians*. Grand Rapids: Eerdmans.

1998. *Grace in Galatia: A Commentary on St. Paul's Letter to the Galatians*. Grand Rapids: Eerdmans.

Wolff, Christian. 1976. *Jeremiah im Frühjudentum und Urchristentum*. TU 118. Leipzig: Hinrich.

1989a. *Der zweite Brief des Paulus an die Korinther.* ThHKNT 8. Berlin: Evangelische.

1989b. "True Apostolic Knowledge of Christ: Exegetical Reflections on 2 Corinthians 5.14ff." In *Paul and Jesus: Collected Essays*, 81–98. Edited by A. J. M. Wedderburn. JSNTSup 37. Sheffield.

Wolter, Michel. 1978. *Rechtfertigung und zukünftiges Heil: Untersuchungen zu Röm 5.1–11*. BZNW 43. Berlin and New York: Walter de Gruyter.

Wright, N. T. 1991. *The Climax of the Covenant*. Edinburgh: T. & T. Clark.

Young, F. and David F. Ford. 1987. *Meaning and Truth in 2 Corinthians*. London: SCM Press.

Zahn, Theodor. 1910. *Der Brief des Paulus an die Galater.* HKNT 9. Leipzig: Deichert.

Zeitlin, Solomon. 1939/40. "The Book of Jubilees: Its Character and Significance." *JQR* 30: 1–32.

Zerwick, SJ, Maximilian. 1963. *Biblical Greek Illustrated by Examples*. Rome: Scripta Pontificii Instituti Biblici.

Ziesler, John. 1989. *Paul's Letter to the Romans*. London: SCM Press; Philadelphia: Trinity International Press.

Zimmerli, Walther. 1978. *Old Testament Theology in Outline*. Edinburgh: T. & T. Clark.

1979–83. *Ezekiel*. 2 vols. Philadelphia: Fortress.

INDEX OF PASSAGES CITED

INDEX OF MODERN AUTHORS

Index of modern authors

289

Feinberg, Charles L., 220
Feldman, Louis H., 56
Findeis, Hans-Jürgen, 138, 139, 148, 152, 158, 165, 171, 172, 174, 175, 176, 177, 179, 183
Finsterbusch, Karin, 211, 213
Fischer, Ulrich, 58
Fitzmyer, Joseph A., 93, 95, 97, 100, 102, 105, 107, 111, 125, 155, 156, 158
Foerster, W., 196, 197, 202
Forbes, C., 147
Ford, David F., 133, 134, 136, 137, 138, 139, 183
Frankemölle, Hubert., 93, 94, 95, 96, 97, 99, 100
Freese, J. H., 166, 167
Friederich, Gerhard, 167, 222
Fung, R. Y. K., 188, 205, 222, 224
Furnish, Victor Paul, 4, 6, 7, 11, 111, 133, 136, 137, 138, 140, 142, 144, 145, 152, 156, 158, 162, 164, 168, 170, 171, 172, 173, 174, 175, 176, 177, 178, 179, 180, 181, 185

Gale, H. M., 104, 105
Gaston, Lloyd, 123, 126
Gaventa, Beverly Roberts, 123, 191, 192, 193, 194, 195, 198, 216, 229
Gennep, Arnold Van, 69, 79, 80, 81, 82, 83, 84, 85, 86
Georgi, Dieter, 140
Gihilus, Ingvild Saelid, 80
Gloer, W. Hulitt, 7
Goodman, Martin, 55, 56
Goppelt, Leonhard, 111, 169
Goulder, Michael, 133
Gowan, Donald E., 18, 20, 21, 23, 44, 115
Grainger, Roger, 80
Greunwald, I., 35
Gundry, R. H., 98, 99
Gunkel, Hermann, 2, 113, 120
Güttgemanns, E., 140, 162

Hafemann, Scott J., 111, 134, 135, 140, 142, 151, 156, 158
Hagner, Donald A., 188
Hahn, Ferdinand, 169, 172
Hall, Robert G., 29, 36
Hals, Ronald M., 23
Hamilton, Malcolm B., 80, 81, 83, 84, 86
Hamilton, Neil Q., 113, 116, 120, 138
Hansen, G. W., 123, 132, 188, 190, 192, 194, 195, 198, 203, 229
Hanson, Paul D., 16, 32, 33, 35

Harnack, Adolf von, 3, 67, 89, 180, 234, 235
Harnisch, Wolfgang, 191, 215, 216
Harris, Murray J., 163
Harrison, Everett F., 95, 99, 100, 105, 110
Harrison, R. K., 220
Harvey, Graham, 228
Hay, David M., 195, 196, 197, 198
Hays, Richard B., 150, 151, 156, 160, 199, 200, 203
Headlam, A. C., 93, 96, 99, 105, 110
Heinrici, C. F. G., 145, 156, 162, 174
Heiny, S. B., 148, 152
Heitsch, Ernst, 196
Helander, Eila., 80
Hengel, Martin, 27, 158, 176
Héring, Jean, 136, 137, 143, 156, 162, 171, 181
Heschel, Abraham J., 20
Hickling, C. J. A., 134, 151, 152
Hoens, D. J., 83
Hofius, Otfried, 169, 170, 181
Holder, John, 26, 27
Holladay, William L., 18, 21
Holm, Nils G., 80
Holtz, T., 56, 71
Holtzmann, H. J., 2, 3, 104, 241
Hong, In-Gyu, 191, 203, 205, 213, 215, 222
Hooker, Morna, 158, 185, 186
Hoover, Herbert Joel, 4, 11
Horbury, William, 66
Houseman, Michael, 80, 81, 82, 83, 84, 85, 86
Howard, George, 193, 205, 213
Hoyle, R. B., 113, 120, 121
Hubbard, Moyer, 142, 161
Hübner, Hans, 111, 206, 221
Hughes, P. E., 162, 163, 168, 172, 174, 176, 180, 185

Inowlocki, Sabrina, 56
Isaacs, Marie, 113, 115, 120, 138

Jaubert, A., 34
Jeremias, J., 71
Jewett, Robert, 98, 105, 110, 175, 208, 213
Jones, C. P., 144
Jong, M. de, 44, 115
Jowett, B., 232

Kamlah, E., 111
Kampen, John, 27